Cromwell's War Machine
The New Model Army, 1645–1660

Oliver Cromwell (1599–1658). He had no military experience before the English Civil War began, but he was a charismatic leader and one of the best cavalry commanders to serve on either side. He was second in command of the New Model Army when it was first formed, but though Sir Thomas Fairfax was the commander of the New Model Army (until 1650), Cromwell was seen as representing its heart and soul.

Cromwell's War Machine
The New Model Army, 1645–1660

Keith Roberts

Pen & Sword
MILITARY

For my father, Tony Roberts

First published in Great Britain in 2005 by
Pen & Sword Military
an imprint of
Pen & Sword Books Ltd
47 Church Street
Barnsley
South Yorkshire
S70 2AS

Reprinted in paperback in 2009
Copyright © Keith Roberts 2009

ISBN 978 1 84415 898 0

Typeset in 11/13pt Plantin by Mac Style, Beverley, E. Yorkshire
Printed and bound in England by CPI UK

Pen & Sword Books Ltd incorporates the Imprints of Pen & Sword Aviation,
Pen & Sword Maritime, Pen & Sword Military, Wharncliffe Local History, Pen
& Sword Select, Pen and Sword Military Classics and Leo Cooper.

For a complete list of Pen & Sword titles, please contact
Pen & Sword Books Limited
47 Church Street, Barnsley, South Yorkshire, S70 2AS, England
E-mail: enquiries@pen-and-sword.co.uk
Website: www.pen-and-sword.co.uk

Contents

Preface

The New Model Army was one of the toughest and most successful armies ever raised in England. It was created during the English Civil War and was formed out of existing Parliament armies as the means to break a stalemate and end the war by victory on the battlefield. In its first campaign it succeeded beyond all expectations, crushing the main Royalist army so completely at the battle of Naseby on 14 June 1645 that the Royalist cause never recovered.

The following chapters set out the military context of the time, in mainland Europe as well as Britain, the campaigns of the New Model Army and the experiences of its soldiers from recruitment through training to skirmish and battle, and their everyday life in camp or garrison.

As a fighting army, the New Model Army followed a highly aggressive strategic and tactical style of warfare. Its generals and junior officers modelled their approach on the campaigns of the great Swedish commander King Gustavus Adolphus during the Thirty Years War (1618–48) in Germany, seeking battlefield solutions to campaigns rather than relying on long-drawn-out siege warfare. The accounts which many of them had read in the newsbook the *Swedish Intelligencer*, printed during 1632 and 1633, were slanted favourably towards Gustavus Adolphus's Swedish/German army, but its underlying doctrine of being ready, willing and able to fight was reliably described. Oliver Cromwell's comment in 1648, on taking the decision to march towards a numerically superior opponent, 'it was thought that to engage the enemy to fight was our business' demonstrates this attitude. However, although aggressive, the strategy it followed was always a measured approach. The New Model Army commanders made use of English naval superiority to transport heavy siege artillery and supplies by water, and made careful use of printed propaganda pamphlets offering the local population where it campaigned, whether in England, Scotland or Ireland, fair treatment for any not in arms against it and payment in ready money for local supplies.

The composition of the New Model Army was unusual for its day because it included a broad cross-section of society. In most parts of Europe, military service as a private soldier was seen as something to be avoided, but the origins of the New Model Army lay in the outbreak of the English Civil War, and the first armies of both sides had been formed largely of volunteers. Although diluted by conscription from the second year of the English Civil War, this sense of fighting for a cause they believed in remained a strong factor amongst Parliamentary armies, particularly amongst the cavalry, and was transferred to the New Model Army. This sense of purpose made it less amenable to the Parliament's attempt to disband it without its arrears of pay after the New Model Army had won the First Civil War, and the broader social origins of its soldiers and NCOs provided literate, argumentative soldiers with easy links to friends in civilian political movements, such as the loose association called the Levellers. Lack of pay and a burning sense of injustice brought this army to mutiny, and mutiny brought the army's leaders into power.

The proud boast of the New Model Army pamphleteers who sought to influence opinion in London in 1647, that 'Noe other Army could doe the Business' – that the New Model Army had been victorious where other armies could achieve only a stalemate – proved to be literally true in the later campaigns of the New Model Army in England, Scotland, Ireland and Europe.

Terminology

I have referred to this army as the New Model Army throughout the book. Strictly speaking the term New Model Army or 'The Model' was used when it was first raised and, sometimes, for those regiments in the English army in Ireland reorganized by Michael Jones. After the mutiny Sir Thomas Fairfax became commander of all English forces, and it became usual for its officers to refer to 'the English Army' or simply 'the Army'. However, neither of these terms is particularly distinctive, as there were English armies on both sides during the Civil War. So I have retained the term 'New Model Army' throughout.

Dates

Dates in this period can be confusing for two reasons. Firstly, there are two different calendars in use, one the Julian or 'Old Style' calendar, and the other the Gregorian or 'New Style' calendar. The latter was introduced by Pope Gregory XIII in 1581 and its impact was to advance the date by ten days, but not all countries adopted it immediately. So, for example, the battle of Lützen during the Thirty Years War was fought in November 1632. For those in the Catholic Imperial German Army the date was 16 November, as they used the Gregorian or New Style calendar, while for those on the other side in the Protestant Swedish/German army the battle was fought on 6 November, as they still used the Julian or Old Style calendar. The second area of confusion is that in the Old Style calendar the new year begins on 25 March, not 1 January.

At this period in history, England still used the Julian calendar and I have retained the dates as they would appear in contemporary documents, with the exception that I have taken the year to begin on 1 January, not 25 March. For dates of the wars in mainland Europe I have used the Gregorian calendar because most modern writers do so, and to convert the dates back to the Julian calendar would create confusion for anyone reading any work on mainland European history.

Money
The currency used in England was pounds (£), shillings (s) and pence (d). Twelve pence make 1 shilling, and 20 shillings (240 pence) make £1.

Note also that a groat is fourpence, and so a half-groat is twopence; a crown is 5 shillings, so half a crown is 2 shillings and sixpence; a double crown is 10 shillings; an 'Angel' or 'Unite' is a coin worth £1; and a Triple Unite is a coin worth £3.

Keith Roberts
January 2005

Acknowledgements

I would like to thank my friends for their support in helping me with my research over the years, particularly those who formed part of the (sometimes heated) discussion and research group which grew up around Dave Ryan's Partizan Press lectures. This is a large group but I owe particular thanks to John Barratt, Richard Brzezinski, Ivor Carr, Dave Cox, Neal Gray, Bob and Zoe Groves, Hawk Norton, Mike Osborne, Les Prince, Stuart Reid, Dave Ryan, Dave Snowden, John Sutton, John Tincey and Neil Wright. Thanks also to Derek Stone for his artwork for the campaign and battle plans. Illustrations are from the author's collection unless otherwise credited.

Chapter One

Background to Civil War, 1637–1642

Introduction

Charles I succeeded to the thrones of England (England and Wales), Scotland and Ireland in 1625. These were three separate kingdoms, not a unified state, and he ruled through different political structures in each kingdom. There were underlying political problems in all three but this was by no means unusual for the time, and other European states faced similar problems during the late sixteenth and early seventeenth centuries. In Europe this was a period of international and religious war, as well as internal unrest. Although there was no single cause for this general instability, there were three common themes which affected European states.

Firstly, religious disputes between Protestant and Catholic had become increasingly interlinked with local provincial rebellion and international warfare in the Low Countries, France and the various states of the German Empire. The same pressures could be seen in Charles's three kingdoms where religious divisions between Protestant and Catholic were one of the key factors which determined allegiance to one side or the other. Religion was not an absolute factor and alliances were formed between factions in civil war, or between states in international war, which were based on expediency or realpolitik rather than religion. However, once invoked, religious differences could escalate beyond any political control causing any dispute to become polarized, and its adherents to become ever more bitterly and brutally opposed to one another.

Secondly, there was a desire by central governments throughout Europe to rationalize their administration over the various components – kingdoms, provinces, duchies, free cities – over which they ruled. For a centralizing government, local custom and historic forms of local government were seen, then as now, as an inconvenience. But this perspective was not shared by the people whose lives were affected, and most felt allegiance to their locality, their nationality or their religion rather than some distant central government. For the Spanish Empire, whose administration was centred on the kingdom of Castile, this can be seen in several provincial rebellions – the Dutch Revolt in the Low Countries (1567–1648) and, closer to home, uprisings in Aragon in 1591 and Catalonia and

Vera effigies CAROLI I. REGIS ANGLIÆ
SCOTIÆ, FRANCIÆ, ET HIBERNIÆ.
DEFENSORIS FIDEI. *etc.*
Tacit: Hist. Lib. I. Alii diutius imperium tenuerunt;
Nemo tam fortiter reliquit:

Charles I (1600–1649). King of England, Scotland and Ireland. By the outbreak of the English Civil War in 1642, Scotland had already rebelled successfully and there was an uprising in Ireland.

Portugal in 1640. The rebellions in Catalonia and Portugal were not connected directly, but the Catalan rebellion certainly demonstrated to the Portuguese that military opposition to the Castilian government was possible. In the event the Catalan rebellion was unsuccessful but Portugal recovered its independence.

Thirdly, this period saw rapid inflation, with the actual value of traditional sources of revenue declining while the expenses of government and the display of royal power were increasing. Above all the costs of waging war, or simply stockpiling the military equipment necessary to prepare for it, were escalating as modern war required ever larger numbers of soldiers. The cost of war was the key element as governments could usually manage the day-to-day costs of administration, and while low-level increases in taxation, as with the imposition of 'ship money' in England, caused some unrest, this proved to be manageable. But warfare had a huge and, above all, an immediate cost and this was often the catalyst which brought festering discontent to a head. No one likes to pay taxes.

The same three themes can be seen in England, Scotland and Ireland. In England, there was rising discontent during Charles I's reign over the unpleasant personal experience, as well as the cost, of billeting unpaid soldiers together with the imposition of forced loans to pay for a series of expensive military failures. The English were generally in sympathy with wars against the Spanish and intervention in France in support of French Protestants; it was the failure of these campaigns which made their cost and the government which mismanaged them so unpopular. Charles's decision to follow a series of short-lived parliaments with a period of personal rule between 1629 and 1640 did little to restore confidence in his government. Nor did his marriage to a Catholic French princess, Henrietta Maria, do much in terms of endearing him to an English popular opinion which had distrusted Catholics since the failed invasion attempt of the Spanish Armada in 1588 and the 'Gunpowder Plot' to blow up King and Parliament in 1605. The reforms of Archbishop William

Laud, which many English Puritans saw as becoming far too close to Catholic practice, also made the government unpopular during the 1630s. However, although these factors made Charles unpopular and created an underlying sense that the country was not being ruled in the best interests of its people, there was no easy channel through which opposition could be directed and co-ordinated. Although his policies gave rise to discontent, in the absence of regular parliaments there was no effective national opposition to his rule.

The First Bishops' War (1639)

The catalyst which created conditions whereby unrest could be turned into outright rebellion came in Scotland rather than England. In 1637 Charles I and his adviser Archbishop William Laud sought to impose a new version of the English prayer book on the Protestant Presbyterian church. Political dissatisfaction and violent popular unrest combined to break royal power in Scotland, and opposition was formalized by the drawing up of a National Covenant binding its signatories to support one another and their Presbyterian faith. The Scottish opposition probably expected this stance to form the basis of negotiation, but instead Charles I sought a solution to his Scottish problem by military means, using troops from his other two kingdoms, England and Ireland. In doing so he began the first of the wars which ultimately involved all three of his kingdoms. This was known as the First Bishops' War as it was seen as an attempt to impose bishops on the Scottish Presbyterian system.

England was the most powerful of the three kingdoms in terms of its potential to provide greater numbers of men, money and military supplies than the other two. The main problems facing Charles I were that he lacked experienced soldiers to form the core of a newly raised army, as well as the money to pay for them and their supplies, and that the war itself was not popular with his English subjects. In the absence of a standing army, King Charles sought to form an army by enforcing the feudal obligations of his nobility and gentry to provide cavalry, by calling out contingents of the Trained Bands (Militia) and by levying conscripts to provide his infantry. In theory the Trained Band soldiers would provide a nucleus of infantry drilled to handle their weapons and deploy in the tactical formations of the day. But in practice many Trained Band soldiers made use of the clause in the King's orders which allowed them to supply substitutes to go in their place. The general atmosphere of despondency in the English camp after this was expressed by Edmund Verney when he wrote:

> our army is very weake, and our supplyes comes slowly to uss, neyther are thos men we have well orderd. The small pox is much in our army; there is a hundred sick of it in one regiment. If the Scotts petition as they ought to doe, I believe they will easily bee heard, but I doubt the roagse [rogues] will be insolent, and knowing our weakness will demand more then in reason or honner the king can graunt, and then wee shall have a filthy business of it. The poorest scabb in Scotland will tell us to our faces

that t[w]o parts of Ingland are on theyr sides, and trewly they behave themselves as if all Ingland were soe.[1]

The Scottish army was probably weaker than Edmund Verney and other Englishmen thought, and in these circumstances both sides were willing to agree a truce termed the 'Pacification of Berwick'.

The Second Bishops' War (1640)

The treaty signed at Berwick provided a breathing space rather than a solution for either side, and King Charles lost little time in preparing a new army for

Thomas Wentworth, Earl of Strafford (1593–1641). A powerful and ruthless administrator, he was lieutenant governor, then governor, of Ireland. Commander of the English army during the Second Bishops' War. Impeached for the careless comment that the army raised in Ireland could be used in England, and executed.

another campaign the following year, the Second Bishops' War. This time he sought to raise funds and national support for his war by summoning Parliament, his first for eleven years. However, the hopes of the King's advisers that Parliament would be compliant were unfounded, as it set out a long list of grievances for redress before it would vote funds for the King. In response Charles dismissed the Parliament, which became known as the Short Parliament as it had only sat between 13 April and 5 May 1640.

English strategy for 1640 envisaged a three-pronged attack on Scotland with a main army on the border, an amphibious landing on the east coast of Scotland and an attack from Ireland using newly levied Catholic Irish troops. Before either of the flanking movements could be made the Scots took the initiative on 20 August and crossed the border into England. This time the Scots sought a decisive action to win their war at a stroke. On 28 August they attacked and overwhelmed an English detachment at the battle of Newburn, and the demoralized English army retreated south, abandoning the city of Newcastle to the Scots. With his army disintegrating and the Scots occupying the north of England, King Charles had no option but to come to an agreement with the Scots, the Treaty of Ripon, for an immediate cessation of hostilities, with further negotiations to be held in London. As a further humiliation the English had to pay the costs of the Scottish army in England at the rate of £850 a day. Charles had now lost control of Scotland and was obliged to summon a new parliament in England to obtain the money that the Scots demanded.

Disarming Catholics. Suspicion of the King's intentions during 1641 led to heightened concerns over the reliability of English Catholics. An 'Order was made by both Houses for disarming all the Papists in England'.

The Irish Revolt

The implications of the successful rebellion in Scotland were not lost on the Catholic Irish. Already under pressure from the plantation of English and Scottish Protestant settlers in the north and concerned over the possible enforcement of restrictions on the practice of their faith, Catholics in Ireland were experiencing widespread unrest. England appeared weak and divided politically, and the English garrison in Ireland was small and scattered. There were just thirty-nine companies of infantry and fourteen troops of horse in the garrison,[2] a total of around 2,300 infantry and 1,000 cavalry.

This force was outnumbered by a stronger body of Catholic soldiers in Ireland. One of Charles I's more disastrous decisions during the Bishops' Wars had been the acceptance of a suggestion by the Earl of Strafford to raise an army of 8,000 infantry and 1,000 cavalry from amongst the Catholic Irish for service against the Scots. While there was some logic in using Catholic soldiers against Scottish Presbyterians, these regiments represented a serious danger to the English government in Ireland. When the Scots' success at the battle of Newburn brought King Charles's campaign to an abrupt end, the soldiers refused to disband without settlement of their arrears of pay. This army now represented an obvious problem, as the Venetian ambassador to London reported:

> the 10,000 [*sic*] foot and 1,000 horse, assembled these last months by His Majesty's order to be sent to Scotland, now refuse to disband, after the need for them has passed, as they wish first to hear what satisfaction their delegates will bring back from the King. So it is to be feared that if they do not promptly grant some satisfaction to that people, a fresh fire will break out in Ireland also, no less difficult to quench than the others (i.e. in Scotland).[3]

The King's reasons for retaining this army in being, apart from the genuine difficulty of finding the £10,000 necessary to pay its arrears, remain unclear. It represented a clear threat to the security of English rule in Ireland as it outnumbered the small and scattered English garrison. Perhaps more importantly from Charles I's perspective at that point, the Catholic Irish army could be used as part of the bargaining in negotiations with the Scots – who remained concerned that it might still be used against them for a landing in western Scotland – and, possibly, with the English Parliament. There were also ongoing negotiations with Spanish representatives willing to pay generously to have the whole Catholic Irish army shipped overseas for service with the Spanish army. Whatever the reason for the delay, few soldiers had been shipped to Spain by the time the Irish rebellion broke out, and the addition of thousands of trained men represented a real advantage to the newly raised rebel armies.

The Irish rebellion began on the night of 22/23 October 1641. An attempt to take control of Dublin, the seat of English government and the location of the main arsenal in Ireland, failed. But elsewhere the rebellion took hold across

Ireland with the Catholic Irish driving out or massacring English and Scottish Protestant settlers. The numbers killed were exaggerated, and the numbers grew in the telling, but the underlying reality was the murder of settlers and their families. This bloody beginning set a pattern of atrocity and reprisal which then continued throughout the campaigns in Ireland. Without siege artillery the new Irish armies could not break into Dublin and other fortified strong points, and the English and Scottish settlers looked to their home countries for support.

As Parliament and King were unable to agree over the appointment of the officers who would command an English army for service in Ireland, a compromise solution was agreed whereby a Scottish army would be sent, paid for by England. The Scots were willing to do this partly because Protestant Scottish settlers were being killed or driven from their settlements in Ulster, but also because English strategy during the Bishops' Wars had shown that Scotland was vulnerable to attack from northern Ireland. Geographically, there was only a short sea crossing between the coast of the Irish province of Ulster and the western lowlands of Scotland or the highlands.

The threat to the Scottish lowlands was invasion by regular soldiers, but the threat to the highlands was intervention in clan warfare. The dominant clan in the highlands was the Protestant Clan Campbell whose head, Archibald Campbell, Earl of Argyll, was a leading figure in the Scottish Covenanting government in Edinburgh. The Campbells had successfully crushed their opponents the MacDonalds in the Scottish highlands, but the Irish branch of the clan, led by the Earl of Antrim, was a strong presence in Ulster. The Earl of Antrim had made unsuccessful attempts to obtain English support for an invasion of the highlands, essentially an attack on the Campbells, as part of Charles I's strategy for the Second Bishops' War. For the Scottish government in Edinburgh the presence of a Scottish army in Ulster would reduce the risk of invasion from Ireland, and for the Earl of Argyll and the Campbells it offered an opportunity to crush clan enemies. This was also a chance to use circumstance to keep a substantial Scottish army under arms, paid for by England, which could easily be withdrawn by sea back to Scotland. The impact of the Scottish army in Ireland was restricted by the strategic aims of the Scottish government and, while it was useful in securing Ulster – the gateway for any invasion of Scotland from Ireland – it proved unwilling to march far outside it.

The Civil War in England, 1642–1644
The Civil War Begins: 1642
There is no single or simple reason why opposition to the King and his ministers moved from protest to armed revolt in 1642. Generations of historians have debated this, often interpreting political events from the perspective of the politics of their own day, whether eighteenth, nineteenth or twentieth century. The net effect of this is that any analysis of the causes of the Civil War becomes confused in the debate of its supporters and opponents.

However, in the end the one undeniable fact is that the English Civil War did take place. There was probably no single cause and it is likely that popular discontent over a range of different political and religious issues was successfully managed by political leaders, such as the MP John Pym, to the point at which trust in the King and his government collapsed. As a simple example, whatever the actual reasons King Charles may have had to maintain Catholic Irish regiments in Ireland, his decision could be set against a general background of popular suspicion to provide an opportunity for opposition propagandists to portray the King as a religious and political threat to his English Protestant subjects.

The King and his advisers may have been unlucky or incompetent, but their opponents were certainly able propagandists, quick to make use of any incident. John Pym was able to use the King's bungled attempt to seize the head of the Scottish Covenanting government in Edinburgh as an excuse to persuade Parliament to call upon the Trained Bands to provide guards at

John Pym (c.1584–1643). A Member of the House of Commons, he was a consistent opponent of court policies and ministers, and prominent in the impeachment of the Earl of Strafford. Pym became the unofficial leader of the Parliamentary opposition during the Long Parliament, and was one of the five members Charles I failed to arrest in the House of Commons.

Westminster. Whether necessary or not, this was a highly visible step to take, and one which inevitably added to the highly charged atmosphere in the City of London and the city of Westminster. The discovery of an 'army plot' amongst officers of the garrison of Portsmouth provided another opportunity, and Parliament's response was to pass the 'Grand Remonstrance' which, amongst other requirements, set out its suspicions of the King's ministers and requested that he did not appoint anyone to any senior military or civil post without Parliamentary approval.

The King's next move played into the hands of his opponents when he went to Parliament with a body of soldiers intending to arrest the five leading members of the Parliamentary opposition. Warned of his intention beforehand, the five MPs had left the Commons by the time Charles arrived. A successful coup might have crushed Parliamentary opposition, but a bungled attempt served only to make heroes of the five MPs the King had tried to arrest. Royalist control over the City of London collapsed and Queen Henrietta Maria took ship from Dover to buy arms and armour in the

Colonell Lunsford assaulting the Londoners at Westminster Hall, with a great rout of ruffinly Cavaleires

Sir Thomas Lunsford assaulting Londoners. On 27 December 1641, Colonel Sir Thomas Lunsford and other Royalist officers drew their swords on London citizens protesting outside Westminster. He was a hot-headed officer and an archetypal rake-hell cavalier; it was said that he 'feared neither man nor God' and had 'given himself over to all lewdness and dissoluteness'. His action that day was a propaganda gift to the Parliamentary opposition to Charles I.

Netherlands, the main centre of the international arms trade at the time, while the King went north to York.

1642: The First Campaign

King Charles reached the city of York on 19 March 1642, hoping to raise forces amongst his supporters in the north of England and, above all, to gain control of the nearby city of Hull. The value of the latter was that 'the great magazine of arms and ammunition which was left upon the disbanding of the army [from the Bishops' Wars] remained still at Hull, and was a nobler proportion than remained in the Tower of London or all other his Majesty's stores'.[4] King Charles badly needed the equipment in Hull to equip his army, but the importance of this arsenal was equally obvious to his opponents in the Parliament, and 'as soon as it was known that his majesty meant to reside in York, it was easily suspected that he had an eye upon the magazine'.[5] On 29 April the King arrived before Hull with a small escort of 'two or three hundred of his servants and gentlemen on the country [i.e. Yorkshire]', but the governor, Sir John Hotham, 'plainly denied to suffer his majesty to come into the town. Whereupon the King caused him immediately to be proclaimed a traitor, which the other received with some expressions of undutifulness and contempt'.[6]

HIS
MAIESTIES

PROCLAMATION
AND DECLARATION

To all His loving Subjects, occasioned
by a Falſe and Scandalous Imputation
laid upon his MAIESTY, of an Intention of
Raiſing or Leavying war againſt His Parliament: and of having raiſed Force
to that end.

Publiſhed at His Court at YORK, the
16. day of Iune, 1642.

With His Majeſties Declaration and Profeſſion, diſavowing any Preparations or Intentions in him, to leavy Warre
againſt His Parliament.

And the Declaration and Profeſſion of the
Lords, and others, of His Majeſties moſt Honourable Privy-Counſell, now at *York*, diſavowing any apparence of the ſame.

Reprinted by His MAIESTIES Command.

OXFORD,

Printed by LEONARD LICHFIELD,
Printer to the Vniverſity. 1642.

*Royalist propaganda. The English Civil War was fought over popular opinion as well as battlefields,
and both sides published a stream of pamphlets setting out the justice of their cause and failings of their
opponents.*

The loss of Hull was a serious blow to the King's cause, and the ease with which the arms could be shipped back to London underlined the strategic importance of the Royal Navy. After a series of failed intrigues by supporters of the King, the Earl of Warwick, as newly appointed admiral, moved swiftly to gain control of the navy in July 1642, and 'immediately summoned all the captains to attend him in council', where he 'communicated the ordinance, letters, and votes from the two Houses' to the captains and, with two exceptions, they 'obliged themselves to obey the Earl of Warwick in the service of the Parliament'. After this the Parliament was 'fully and entirely possessed of the whole royal navy and militia by sea' and the King was 'without one ship of his own in his three kingdoms at his devotion'.[7] With control of the fleet, Parliament could supply and support any coastal city that declared for it, and make the shipment of European arms or mercenaries to support the Royalist cause a much more dangerous and difficult process.

Both sides, the King at York and the Parliament in London, set about recruiting soldiers. Each side concentrated its efforts on raising a single army to oppose the other, and both moved towards the Midlands. The King marched south from York and formally raised his standard at Nottingham. The Parliament's general, the Earl of Essex, moved north, leaving London on 9 September to join his army and set up his headquarters at Northampton. The Earl of Essex's operating instructions from the Parliament were to:

> march with such Forces as you think fit, towards the Army raised in his Majesties Name against the Parliament and Kingdom. And you shall use your utmost Endeavours, by Battel or other wise, to rescue his Majesty's Person, and the Persons of the Prince and the Duke of York, out of the hands of those desperate persons who are now about them.[8]

The reference to rescuing 'his Majesty's person' maintained the fiction that the Parliament was opposed to the King's 'evil councilors' rather than the King himself, but the order to fight if necessary was clear enough.

The King's army had been weak when the standard was raised at Nottingham, so much so that Sir Jacob Astley advised the King that 'he could not give any assurance against his majesty's being taken out of his bed if the rebels should make a brisk attempt to that purpose',[9] and now marched west through Derby and Stafford to Shrewsbury in order to link up with recruits from north Wales and Lancashire. The King's army reached the town on 20 September and 'within twenty days after his coming to Shrewsbury he [Charles] resolved to march in despite of the enemy even towards London, his foot by this time consisting of about 6000 and his horse of 2000, his train [artillery and artillery train] in very good order', a far cry from the low despised condition the King was in Nottingham after the setting up of his standard.[10] The Earl of Essex's army was the stronger of the two, with all available troops being ordered to the front by a Parliamentary ordinance of 23 September requiring all regiments of infantry recruited to a strength of 400, and all troops of cavalry of 40 or more 'shall within Forty eight hours after publication hereof

March towards the place where they shall understand the Lord General to be'.[11]

With both armies in close proximity, their manoeuvrings were bound to bring them into contact before long. As the King's army marched to threaten the Parliament garrison at Banbury, and the Earl of Essex marched to support his garrison, both sides met at the battle of Edgehill. The battle itself was indecisive. The Earl of Essex's army stood upon the defensive, and waiting at the stand to receive a charge proved too much for the nerves of the newly raised Parliamentary cavalrymen. The charges of the Royalist cavalry swept away both wings of the Parliamentary cavalry and, seeing their cavalry routed, five regiments of the Parliament infantry fled as well. This should have led to a decisive defeat for the Parliamentary army, but two factors prevented it. Firstly, the Royalist cavalry, although trained in cavalry tactics, were as inexperienced as their Parliamentary opponents. Instead of rallying or using their second-line supports to attack the Parliament infantry in the flanks, they, 'seeing none of the enemy's horse left, thought there was nothing more to be done but to pursue those that fled, and could not be contained by their commanders, but with spurs and loose reins followed the chase' of the fleeing Parliamentary cavalry.[12] Secondly, the Earl of Essex had set out a thoroughly professional deployment including that of a few of his best cavalry troops behind his infantry. As the remaining Parliamentary infantry stood and fought, these few Parliamentary cavalry were now the only cavalrymen on the field, and the truth of the contemporary view that 'the Foote being overlayd with an Enemies Horse, having no Horse at hand, to charge and second them, might easily be routed and overthrown' became apparent.[13] This did not require many cavalrymen as it was considered that 'a small squadron of cavalry, acting promptly, can wreak great havoc amongst large infantry battle lines'.[14] The combination of Parliamentary infantry and their cavalry support beat off the Royalist infantry attack and forced them to retreat to Edgehill. By this time, the scattered Royalist cavalry were returning to the battlefield and, although they were too disorganized to mount a counter-attack, there were enough of them to force the Parliamentary army to decide not to push their luck as 'it was not held fit we should Advance upon them'.

The Parliamentary army fell back on its base at Warwick and then, concerned over the effect news of the battle might have on popular opinion in London, Essex retired through Daventry and St Albans back to London, where he received a hero's welcome on 7 November. The Royalist army marched to Banbury and then on through Oxford, which it reached on 29 October, towards London. On 12 November, Prince Rupert attacked the Parliament troops, two infantry regiments and a troop of cavalry, stationed at Brentford on the outskirts of London, in order to open the way for an approach on London. Although it was a successful military operation in itself, rumours of the harsh treatment of Parliamentary prisoners, most of whom would have been Londoners as both infantry regiments had been raised there, increased the fears of London citizens. Their fear was that the Royalist army might sack

THE ROYALIST AND PARLIAMENT ARMIES AT THE BATTLE OF EDGEHILL - 22 OCTOBER 1642

ROYALIST BATTLE PLAN FOR THE BATTLE OF EDGEHILL

FOOT

A· Sir Nicholas Byron's Brigade: King's Lifeguard, Lord General's Regiment and Sir John Beaumont's Regiment.

B· Richard Fielding's Brigade: Richard Fielding's Regiment, Sir Thomas Lunsford's Regiment, Richard Bolle's Regiment, Sir Edward Fitton's Regiment and Sir Edward Stradling's Regiment.

C· Charles Gerard's Brigade: Charles Gerard's Regiment, Sir Lewis Dyve's Regiment and Sir Ralph Dutton's Regiment.

D· John Belasyse's Brigade: John Belasyse's Regiment, Thomas Blagge's Regiment and Sir William Pennyman's Regiment.

E· Henry Wentworth's Brigade: Sir Gilbert Gerard's Regiment, Sir Thomas Salusbury's Regiment and Lord Molineux's Regiment.

HORSE

RIGHT WING

F· King's Lifeguard
G· Prince of Wales' Regiment
H· Prince Rupert's Regiment
I· Prince Maurice's Regiment
K· Sir John Byron's Regiment

LEFT WING

L· Lord Wilmot's Regiment
M· Lord Grandison's Regiment
N· Earl of Carnarvon's Regiment
O· Lord Digby's Regiment
P· Sir Thomas Aston's Regiment

RESERVE

Q· Gentlemen Pensioners and William Legge's 'Firelocks'.

·STRENGTH·
Foot : 10,000.   Horse : 2500 to 2800.   Dragoons : 800 to 1000.   Artillery : 20 pieces.

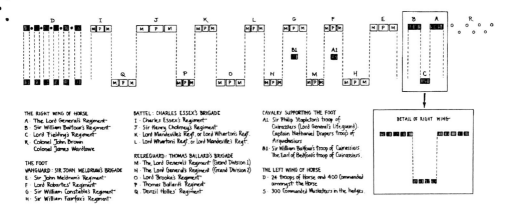

SIR BERNARD DE GOMME'S PLAN

A RECONSTRUCTION OF THE BATTLE PLAN FOR THE
EARL OF ESSEX'S ARMY AT THE BATTLE OF EDGEHILL
BASED ON CONTEMPORARY ACCOUNTS
AND CONTEMPORARY PRACTISE

DETAIL OF RIGHT WING

THE RIGHT WING OF HORSE
A· The Lord General's Regiment
B· Sir William Balfour's Regiment
C· Lord Fielding's Regiment
R· Colonel John Brown
    Colonel James Wardlawe

THE FOOT
VANGUARD : SIR JOHN MELDRUM'S BRIGADE
E· Sir John Meldrum's Regiment
F· Lord Robartes' Regiment
G· Sir William Constable's Regiment
H· Sir William Fairfax's Regiment

BATTEL : CHARLES ESSEX'S BRIGADE
I· Charles Essex's Regiment
J· Sir Henry Cholmley's Regiment
K· Lord Mandeville's Regt. or Lord Wharton's Regt.
L· Lord Wharton's Regt. or Lord Mandeville's Regt.

REEREGUARD : THOMAS BALLARD'S BRIGADE
M· The Lord General's Regiment (Grand Division 1)
N· The Lord General's Regiment (Grand Division 2)
O· Lord Brooke's Regiment
P· Thomas Ballard's Regiment
Q· Denzil Holles' Regiment

CAVALRY SUPPORTING THE FOOT
A1· Sir Philip Stapleton's troop of Cuirassiers (Lord General's Lifeguard). Captain Nathanael Drapers troop of Arquebusiers.
B1· Sir William Balfour's troop of Cuirassiers. The Earl of Bedford's troop of Cuirassiers.

THE LEFT WING OF HORSE
D· 24 troops of Horse and 400 Commanded amongst the Horse.
S· 300 Commanded Musketeers in the hedges.

STRENGTH
Foot : 9000 to 10000.   Horse : 2000 to 2300.   Dragoons : 700.   Artillery : 16 field-pieces.

Battle formations at the battle of Edgehill. The deployment of the Royalist army is known from a surviving plan amongst the papers of Sir Bernard de Gomme, an officer on the staff of Prince Rupert. The Parliamentary army's plan is a reconstruction from written sources. Note the 'Swedish Brigade' formation of the Royalist infantry.

London in the same way that several German cities had been sacked or, as at Magdeburg in Germany in 1632, burnt to the ground amidst the rape and slaughter of most of the inhabitants.

It was with these concerns in their minds that the City Militia, the Trained Bands of London, marched out at full strength of some 8,000 infantry to join with the Earl of Essex's army to deploy and face the advance of the King's army at Turnham Green. The London-trained Bands were led by the Sergeant Major General of the City of London, the experienced and highly respected veteran Philip Skippon, whose encouraging words were recorded by the MP Bulstrode Whitelock: 'Come my Boys, my brave Boys, let us pray heartily and fight heartily, I will run the same fortunes and hazards with you, remember the Cause is for God; and for the defence of your selves, your wives, and children: Come my honest brave Boys, pray heartily and fight heartily, and God will bless us'. Whitelocke went on to say that 'Thus he [Skippon] went all along the Souldiers, talking to them, sometimes to one Company, and sometimes to another; and the Souldiers seemed to be more taken with it, then with a sett formal, Oration.'[15] With the addition of 8,000 Trained Band soldiers, Bulstrode Whitelocke estimated that the Earl of Essex now had a 'whole Army of Horse and Foot' which consisted of 'above 24,000 Men'. The Parliament soldiers were in good spirits as the Earl of Essex, always popular with his men, 'rode from Regiment to Regiment encouraging of them; and when he had spoken to them, the Souldiers would throw up their Caps, and shout, crying, Hey for old Robin'.[16] The King had taken a chance, hoping to overawe opposition amongst the citizens and force a surrender, but his army was running short of ammunition, some Royalist officers claiming later that they 'had not Bullet enough to have maintained fight for a quarter of an hour',[17] and seeing the Parliamentary army and London Trained Bands in such numbers and apparently with such good morale, the Royalist army retired from London back to Oxford, making it the main Royalist base for the rest of the First English Civil War.

1643

The first campaign of the English Civil Wars and the bloody battle of Edgehill had shown that both sides were now committed to all-out warfare, not simply negotiation from a position of strength. The stalemate at Turnham Green had also shown that the war would not be ended in a single battle or campaign, and both sides now sought to dominate territory, and the resources that represented in terms of recruits, money and military supplies, to control the ports through which military supplies and soldiers could be imported and to control key fortified strong points along the communication routes linking the new armies and their territories together. The leading supporters of both King and Parliament had initially concentrated their resources in the field armies of either side, but now men of local influence returned to their home counties in an effort to establish control for their own side.

Some supporters of both sides had already established control over towns and cities, but there was also a strong feeling amongst people in the counties that they would prefer to have nothing at all to do with the war, and several groups attempted to set up neutrality pacts either as a local truce or an agreement to defend the county against either side. None of these survived, as neither the Royalists nor the Parliament could afford to let parts of the country opt out of the war. However, this desire for self-defence did create popular support for the formation of Parliament Associations of several counties, the Midlands Association, the Western Association, the Southern Association, the Northern Association and, the most successful of all, the Eastern Association. Some of the new armies raised for the King or the Parliament had a brief existence, but others, particularly in the north and the west, soon had a significant impact on the war. Initially, both sides still saw the local armies as subsidiary to their main field army and its campaigns, but as the war continued both discovered that many local soldiers, both officers and men, were prepared to fight in local armies but were unwilling to join the main field army while any substantial enemy garrison remained in their territory as a threat to their homes. This was a particular problem for the Royalists, as Parliament's control of the navy enabled it to bring supplies and re-enforcements to any besieged port. Apart from the main campaigns, which now involved several major field armies rather than just one on each side, local commanders with smaller resources and numbers of soldiers kept the war going in an endless series of raids and counter-raids, and few parts of England were untouched.

The Earl of Essex began his campaign early in 1643 with an attack on the Royalist garrison at Reading on 15 April, the significance being that the single largest Royalist store of gunpowder was held at Reading and the capture of this ammunition plus the sizeable garrison would seriously weaken the main Royalist field army. In the event, the approach of a Royalist relief force persuaded the Earl to let the Royalist garrison surrender on terms which allowed them to march to Oxford, but he kept the gunpowder. However, this promising start to his campaign was brought to an abrupt halt because an outbreak of typhus destroyed his army. In the north the Royalist commander the Earl of Newcastle, assisted by the veteran James King, had raised troops with the intention of securing Newcastle upon Tyne as a port to receive a major arms shipment which Queen Henrietta Maria had purchased in the Netherlands. The Queen's arms shipment was pursued by Parliamentary ships and was unable to reach the River Tyne, but its stores were landed at Bridlington on 22 February. The Earl of Newcastle's army then escorted the Queen and her military supplies to York, and then sent the arms south to Oxford in two convoys; the Queen accompanied the second, which reached Newark on 16 June, and, after a short stay, arrived at Oxford on 14 July.

Once the Queen had landed, the Earl of Newcastle had the options of whether to

> march with ye Queen & so joyne wth ye King, or else with ye army to stay and only give order for some regiments to wait upon her majesty. If he

march'd up, his army would give a gallant addition to ye King's, but yn he left ye country in my Ld Fairfax his power, & it might be he should have him in ye rear of him.

In the event, the Earl of Newcastle held a council of war with his leading officers and decided to send 'some forces only with ye Queen, & try ye mastery with my Ld Fairfax',[18] a decision which may have been influenced by some of his supporters being unwilling to abandon the north to the local Parliamentary army commanded by the Fairfaxes, Lord Ferdinando Fairfax and his son Sir Thomas Fairfax. Once the Queen's convoy and its escort had started south, the Earl of Newcastle marched against the Fairfaxes' headquarters at Bradford and decisively defeated their army at Adwalton Moor on 30 June 1643. This victory gave Newcastle control over most of the north of England as the Fairfaxes were forced to retreat to the port of Hull. In the west the war was also going badly for the Parliament as its commander there was decisively defeated at the battle of Roundway Down on 13 July 1643, and the Royalists followed this up by besieging and taking the key port-city of Bristol on 26 July.

The overall Royalist strategy for 1643 certainly included the intention to concentrate attention once more on London, the focal point and power base of the Parliament cause. However, in practical terms, the local interests of the officers in the Western and Northern armies made them reluctant to march away from their own territory unless the local Parliamentary forces there had been neutralized, and, unfortunately for them, the Parliament could supply Plymouth in the west and Hull in the north by sea. This did not prevent the Royalists from bringing propaganda pressure to bear on London with the threat of an advance on several fronts, and encouraging support of the political group in London urging peace at almost any price. In these circumstances, when the King's main 'Oxford army' marched to besiege the city of Gloucester, it was evident that the fall of one more loyal city without any effort to relieve it

ROBERTUS FREYHERR ZU ESSEX DES PARLAMENTS in England General.

Robert Devereux, Earl of Essex (1591–1646). Commander of the Parliament's army at the outbreak of the English Civil War. This is a European engraving from Theatrum Europaeum, an indication that the Civil War in England was closely observed in Europe.

might lead to a collapse of confidence in the Parliament's ability to continue the war. The mood in the Royalist camp was confident as it considered the Parliament 'had no army, nor by all intelligence, was like to form any soon enough to be able to relieve it [Gloucester]; and if they had an army, that it were much better for his majesty to force them to that distance from London, and to fight there, where he could be supplied with whatsoever he wanted, could choose his own ground, where his brave body of horse would be able to defeat any Army they could raise'.[19]

However, appeals by the Earl of Essex and Parliament persuaded the London authorities to agree to send a brigade of London Militia to form part of a Parliamentary army to relieve the siege of Gloucester, and this gave the Earl of Essex enough men to contest the field with the Royalist army. The Earl of Essex, who was, despite his detractors, a competent strategist, deceived the Royalists by appearing to march on Oxford – a common tactic in siege warfare being to counter a siege of one of your own towns by besieging one of your enemy's – and then marching in a loop north of Oxford and down to Gloucester. The Royalist cavalry, without infantry support, were unable to stop the Parliamentary army on its march, and the King was unwilling to move his infantry away from Gloucester as that would have broken the siege anyway. As the Earl of Essex's army approached Gloucester, the Royalist army withdrew, allowing the Earl to resupply the city with provisions and ammunition. For his

Plots in London. A Royalist plot to 'betray the Cittie' led by the MP Sir Edmund Waller was discovered in May 1643. Two of his closest associates, Nathaniel Tomkins (Waller's brother-in-law) and Richard Challoner, were executed on 5 July 1643. Waller himself escaped the death sentence, because his fellow MPs did not like the idea of this sort of precedent.

return march, the Earl made a feint north as if he intended to retrace his approach route north of Oxford, but then quickly took the route south of Oxford. The Parliament soldiers marched quickly, and both they and the pursuing Royalists left exhausted soldiers along their line of march, but at Newbury the Royalists out-marched the Parliament troops and reached the city first, blocking the road to London.

The Earl of Essex had little option except to fight, but he did so with a show of confidence that encouraged his men, and he had the advantage that the northern sector of the battlefield was broken up with hedgerows, where cavalrymen were of little use. The Royalists' best strategy would have been to have waited where they were, preventing the Parliamentary army, now short of rations, from foraging, and falling on the rear or flanks of the army as it sought to continue its march. However, as the Parliamentary army offered battle, a series of skirmishes escalated into a full-scale engagement on the type of terrain that did not favour the Royalist cavalry, and after a day's hard but indecisive fighting the Royalist army had almost run out of ammunition. The following morning the Earl's army resumed its march, and the Royalists, too low on ammunition to continue fighting, could not oppose it.

After the battle, the Royalists shadowed the remainder of the Parliamentary army's march home and reoccupied Reading, but the mood in the Royalist camp was now far less confident, particularly because the London Militia regiments had fought so effectively. In a strategic sense the willingness of the London Militia regiments to go on campaign alongside the Parliamentary army meant substantial infantry re-enforcements for the Parliament field armies, but also made London practically impregnable to the Royalists. The Parliament victory at the battle of Winceby on 11 October 1643 by a combination of troops from the Eastern Association forces under the Earl of Manchester and Oliver Cromwell and from the Northern Association under Sir Thomas Fairfax can only have added to the general Royalist gloom.

Both sides had also sought assistance from outside England during 1643. The Parliament was negotiating with the Scots, who feared that a victory for King Charles would mean that his next action would be a third Bishops' War against them, but this time with a veteran English army. The King was negotiating with the Catholic Irish Confederation on the basis that a ceasefire in Ireland would allow him to withdraw the weak, but veteran, English regiments then in Ireland and use them as re-enforcements for the Royalist armies in England. The King also hoped that he might obtain Catholic Irish re-enforcements, a much more politically dangerous option given the widespread suspicion in England of Catholics in general and Irish Catholics in particular.

The first approach by the Parliament to the Scots was made on 27 June 1643, and this was formalized into a 'Solemn League and Covenant' on 25 September. A final treaty was signed on 29 November by which the Scots undertook to support the Parliament cause with a field army of 18,000 infantry, 2,000 cavalry, 1,000 dragoons and a train of artillery. The King's negotiations with the Irish were concluded with the agreement of a ceasefire, or cessation, on 15 September 1643. The first re-enforcements from Ireland were transported from Leinster to north Wales in November 1643 to join Lord Byron's army, while another contingent from Munster landed in Bristol to join Lord Hopton's new 'Western Army'.

1644

As his council considered its position during the winter of 1643/1644, 'The King was not all this while without a due sense of the dangers that threatened him in the growth and improvement of the power and strength of the enemy, and how impossible it would be for him without some more extraordinary assistance to resist that torrent which he foresaw by the next spring would be ready to overwhelm him.' Since 'it was not in his [the King's] power to compose the distractions of England, or to prevent those in Scotland' the King's attention turned to the possibility of using 'any expedients which might allay the distempers in Ireland; that so, having one of his kingdoms in peace, he might apply the power of that towards the procuring of it in his other dominions'.[20] This meant going beyond a cessation to free English soldiers serving in Ireland and expanding his agreement with the Irish Confederation in order to provide Catholic Irish re-enforcements to fight for the Royalist cause in England.

Two Royalist generals, Sir Ralph Hopton and John, Lord Byron, whose armies received the first re-enforcements from Ireland, were intended to change the strategic balance after the stalemate of 1643. In the west, the intention was that a new army under Hopton would be drawn 'into the field' and 'so point forward as farr as he could go towards London'.[21] But, unfortunately for Hopton, his opponent Sir William Waller caught his army dispersed in winter quarters and overran the Royalist brigade at Alton on 13 December 1643, and followed this up by taking Arundel on 6 January 1644. After a series of manoeuvres in the spring of 1644 the two generals and their armies met, and Sir Ralph Hopton was decisively defeated at the battle of Cheriton on 29 March 1644. From the Royalist perspective the outcome of this battle provided a 'very doleful entering into the year 1644, and broke all measures, and altered the whole scheme of the King's counsels: for whereas he had hoped to have entered the field early, and to have acted an offensive part, he now discerned he was wholly to be upon the defensive'.[22]

Affairs were also going badly for the King in the north. The intention had been to use the combination of veteran English regiments from Ireland and local troops in Cheshire to create a new army under John, Lord Byron. This new army was successful initially and was able to force the local Parliamentary forces based in Cheshire to retreat into Nantwich, where Lord Byron's army besieged them, but the besieging Royalist army was surprised and defeated on 25 January 1644 by a relieving army commanded by Sir Thomas Fairfax. Prince Rupert was sent to replace Lord Byron and continue with the objective of creating a second Royalist army in the north, consisting of the veteran regiments he brought with him, regiments from Ireland – survivors of Byron's

Sir William Waller (1598–1668). Commander of
the Parliament's forces in the west, Waller was a
bold and competent general noted for the care with
which he made use of any advantages in the terrain
over which he fought and for his night attacks on
Royalist quarters. This is an engraving from
Theatrum Europaeum.

defeat at Nantwich and further re-
enforcements – and the recruits his
reputation attracted.

With this new army Rupert
marched to relieve Newark, which
had been besieged on 29 February by
a force of Eastern Association and
local Parliamentary troops under Sir
John Meldrum. Newark, where the
Great North Road crosses the River
Trent, was a centre where several
roads converged and a key strategic
strong point on the supply route
between the Royalist capital at
Oxford and their territory in the
north of England. Its loss would be a
serious blow to the Royalist cause.
Prince Rupert made a night march
on the Parliament position in the
early morning of 21 March, and at
around 9 o'clock, although his
infantry and part of his cavalry were
still on the march, he drew up the
cavalry troops with him and
mounted a successful attack on the
Parliamentary cavalry. Sir John
Meldrum's Parliamentary army was now surrounded and trapped in its base
with only two days' provisions, and it surrendered on terms which allowed it
to march away after giving up its weapons. From Prince Rupert's perspective
this was a victory which proved the potential rewards of swift and decisive
action.

On the northern border, the Scottish army crossed into England on 19
January 1644, and although numbers were probably not in the strength set out
in the treaty there were enough to change the balance of power in the north of
England. The Marquess (he was made such on 27 October 1643) of Newcastle
marched north to oppose the Scots. In his absence the Fairfaxes, Lord
Ferdinando and his son Sir Thomas, won a victory at Selby on 11 April 1644
over the small Royalist army which Newcastle had left behind under the
governor of York, Colonel John Belasyse. With his base at York threatened by
the Fairfaxes, Newcastle had no alternative but to retreat with the Scots in close
pursuit. He reached York on 16 April, and the city was besieged by the
combined forces of the Scots and the Fairfaxes on 21 April. Newcastle sent
away his cavalry on 22 April, before the siege lines were completed, and
appealed for help from King Charles. The Royalist position became more
desperate as the main body of the Army of the Eastern Association, led by the

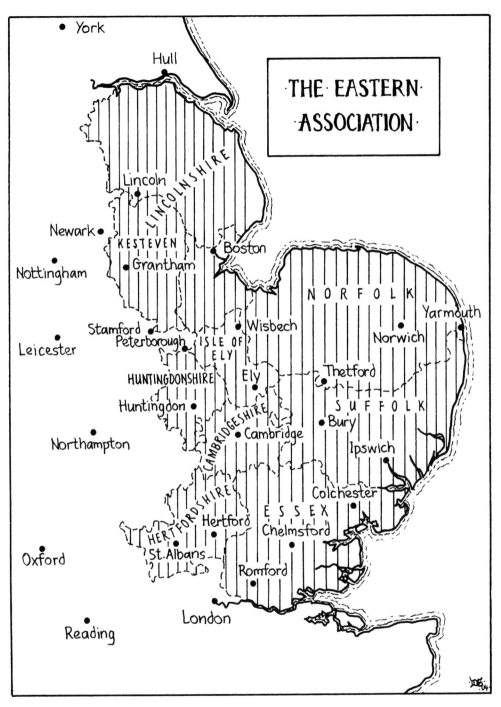

Counties of the Eastern Association. This plan shows the strategic location of the counties which formed the Eastern Association, which bordered upon Hull, the stronghold of the Northern Association, to the north; London to the south; and the Royalist strongholds of Newark in the centre and Oxford to the south.

Earl of Manchester and his Lieutenant General of the Horse, Oliver Cromwell, marched to join the siege, arriving on 3 June. Prince Rupert, conscious of the need to relieve York, marched first to bring Lancashire under his control, taking Stockport on 25 May, Bolton on 27 April and Liverpool on 11 June. The small army which Prince Rupert had led out of his base at Shrewsbury had now been re-enforced by local Royalist troops from Lancashire and Derbyshire, and was joined by Newcastle's cavalry and a few of his infantry to give a total of around 14,000 men, half cavalry and half infantry.

In the south, the Parliament armies were in the ascendant after the defeat of Sir Ralph Hopton's army at Cheriton on 29 March. The combined armies of the Earl of Essex and Sir William Waller gave them a numerical advantage, but the comment of Sir Edward Walker, secretary of war to Charles I, that the two Parliamentary generals 'perfectly hated each other' was entirely accurate, and this undermined their ability to co-operate with one another. They still represented a serious threat, however, and, following Cheriton, the Royalists withdrew the garrisons of Reading on 18 May and Abingdon on 25 May in order to re-re-enforce their 'Oxford Army'. In these circumstances Charles I, after some discussion amongst his leading counsellors, sent orders on 14 June to Prince Rupert which the latter took as his instructions not only to relieve the siege of York, but also to commit both his own and the Marquess of Newcastle's armies to battle against the combined Parliamentary and Scottish armies.

On learning that Prince Rupert's army was on the march, the Parliament and Scottish commanders abandoned the siege of York and concentrated their forces with the objective of preventing the combination of the two Royalist armies, Prince Rupert's marching army and the Marquess of Newcastle's

infantry in the York garrison. The Parliament and Scottish armies took up a position blocking the main approach to York from the west, as they knew Prince Rupert's army was at Knaresborough. But, Rupert outmanoeuvred them by keeping their attention with a strong body of cavalry, while his main army moved north and then looped back to York to complete his junction

William Cavendish, Marquess of Newcastle (1592–1676). A general with no professional military experience, he was appointed commander of the Royalist army in the north because of his local and court connections, and the funds he would use to raise and equip an army. He relied for professional advice on the Scottish officer James King.

with the Marquess of Newcastle's army. Prince Rupert's manoeuvring had successfully relieved the siege of York.

Prince Rupert then gave orders to the Marquess of Newcastle, on the strength of his written orders from the King, to combine both armies on Marston Moor outside York and offer battle to the joint Parliamentary and Scottish armies. The question remains, then, as to why Rupert chose to fight against superior numbers. His written instructions from King Charles were not a model of clarity, but they did offer him the discretion to fight if he chose, and he was, above all, an adherent of King Gustavus Adolphus's aggressive Swedish school of warfare, believing that a single decisive battle could alter the course of a war. He would have been encouraged in believing in his tactical preference by his recent success at Newark and, perhaps, may also have been jealous of the recent success of the young French Prince de Condé, then aged only twenty-two, over the Spanish army of Flanders: he had chosen to fight – and had won – at the battle of Rocroi in 1643 when he could have forced the retreat of the Spanish army by manoeuvre. Whatever his reasons, Rupert ordered a concentration of his and the Earl of Newcastle's armies and deployed for battle on 2 July 1644. His intention was to concentrate the Royalist forces quickly, deploy them in battle formation and then fall upon his opponents before they were fully prepared, a tactic which had served him well at Newark and which would have given him the initiative, making him the driving force on the battlefield. But his hopes of doing so were dashed because the Marquess of Newcastle's infantry had dispersed to plunder the besiegers' camps and could not be brought to join the Royalist forces on Marston Moor until the afternoon. By this time the Parliament and Scottish armies had ample time to organize their armies and prepare for a formal battle, with the advantage of superior numbers.

Marston Moor was a hard-fought battle but numbers were against the Royalists, as the combined Parliamentary and Scottish armies numbered approximately 8,000 cavalry and some 12,500 infantry, while the combined Royalist armies probably numbered around 6,500 cavalry and 11,000 infantry. The evidence that the result of this battle was not a foregone conclusion can be seen in the fact that of the three commanders opposed to Prince Rupert, two – Ferdinando, Lord Fairfax, commander of the Northern Association, and Alexander Leslie, commander of the Scottish army – fled the field believing they had been defeated. The superior discipline of the Eastern Association cavalry on the left wing of the combined Parliamentary and Scottish army proved to be a decisive factor in the Royalist defeat.

The north of England was now lost to the Royalist cause but an unexpected turn of events in the south provided a counterbalance, as the Royalists defeated the army of Sir William Waller at the battle of Cropredy Bridge on 29 June and then forced the surrender of the Earl of Essex's infantry at Lostwithiel in Cornwall on 2 September, after his cavalry had managed to cut their way out and flee early in the morning of 31 August. Relations between the Earl of Essex and Sir William Waller worsened after Lostwithiel as the former believed that Sir William had not made any serious effort to come to his relief.

In September the position in England was balanced, as in the north the Royalists had lost the battle of Marston Moor, but the two main Parliamentary field armies in the south had been defeated. However, the Parliament's position was still stronger as, although weakened, both its southern armies were still operational and could be re-enforced with fresh brigades of Militia infantry from London. In addition the Army of the Eastern Association marched south to join a combined Parliamentary force. On 22 October the Royalist army set up its headquarters at Newbury and the combined Parliamentary armies converged on its position. The Earl of Essex had become ill and retired to Reading, leaving overall command to the Earl of Manchester. The Parliamentary commanders held a council of war on the evening of 26 October to decide what tactical approach to adopt for the second battle of Newbury, and came to the bold decision to split their forces and attack the Royalist position from both front and rear. They hoped to achieve this by having one part of the army under Sir William Waller make a night march to attack the rear of the Royalist army, while the remainder attacked frontally. Perhaps unsurprisingly, it proved impossible for the Parliament armies to co-ordinate their attacks, and after fierce but inconclusive fighting the King's army retreated that night, leaving its guns, baggage and wounded at Donnington Castle, outside Newbury.

The Parliament armies in overwhelming numbers had brought the King's main army in the south to battle but had failed to destroy it. Worse was to come as King Charles, now re-enforced with troops under Prince Rupert and contingents from Wales and the garrison around Oxford, returned to Donnington Castle to recover his artillery and ammunition. On 9 November the Royalist army deployed outside the castle as it recovered its artillery, but the opposing Parliamentary commanders were unable to reach a decision to oppose it and let the Royalist army march away without any significant opposition. With his army's morale improved following their successes in the south, 'the King's position was now much better than in the beginning of the summer he had reason to expect [since] he had absolutely broken and defeated two armies of the Parliament, and returned into his winter quarters with triumph, and rather with an increase than a diminution of his forces'.[23]

From the Parliament's perspective, the year ended with its cause in the ascendant as the two Royalist armies in the north – the Earl of Newcastle's and Prince Rupert's – had been overwhelmed at Marston Moor, and, though its Scottish allies showed little inclination to march further south, the simple presence of the large Scottish army supporting the Parliamentary Army of the Northern Association would hinder any Royalist resurgence. The Parliament armies' problem remained that quarrels amongst its generals prevented the armies in the south from co-operating successfully to defeat the main Royalist army, the King's Oxford Army. Of the three generals, the Earl of Essex was ill and his reputation had been damaged at Lostwithiel, and Sir William Waller was in no better position following his defeat at Cropredy Bridge.

The last of the three, the Earl of Manchester, was now accused by his Lieutenant General of the Horse, Oliver Cromwell, who set out on 25 November in a long report reported to the House of Commons that:

the Earl of Manchester was most in fault for most of those miscarriages and the ill consequences of them. And because I had a great deal of reason to think that his Lordship's miscarriage in these particulars was neither through accidents (which could not be helped) nor through his improvidence only, but through his backwardness to all action, and had some reason to conceive that that backwardness was not (merely) from dullness or indisposedness to engagement, but (withal) from some principle of unwillingness in his Lordship to have this war prosecuted unto a full victory, and a design to have it ended by accommodation (and that) on some such terms to which it might be disadvantageous to bring the King too low.[24]

Chapter Two

The European Background: War, Politics and the Military Revolution

Introduction

The English Civil Wars were not fought in isolation from contemporary events in Europe: the organization and tactics of the armies that fought in England and the political or religious ideals of the men who fought in them were influenced by European wars and their political and, for many people, very personal consequences. The objective of this section is to provide something of that contemporary perspective, to see world events and their impact on England as Englishmen saw it, referred to it, and sought to avoid its disasters and be inspired by its successes.

Englishmen and women, particularly those who were citizens of major trading centres and regularly received news from abroad, were well aware of the threat posed by marauding armies. The examples of the sack of several towns and cities in the Low Countries during the Dutch revolt or, more recently, in Germany during the Thirty Years War were in the minds of London citizens when they marched out to oppose King Charles and his army at Turnham Green, outside London. For these men, it was the threat to their homes and their families, and the very real examples of past European events, which led them to march out in strength and support the Parliamentary cause. Many officers who served in the New Model Army, such as Oliver Cromwell or Sir Thomas Fairfax, took a more positive inspiration from accounts of what they saw as a disciplined and godly Swedish army and deliberately sought to emulate it. They and their supporters were influenced by the popular accounts of the *Swedish Intelligencer* which described the Swedish involvement in the Thirty Years War, so much so that the brief panegyric of Sir Thomas Fairfax in his chaplain's account, *Anglia Rediviva*, is a conscious imitation of the admiring summary of the character of Gustavus Adolphus in the *Swedish Intelligencer*.

In purely military terms, all armies fighting in the English Civil Wars were influenced by the development of strategy and tactics during the late sixteenth and early seventeenth centuries. Most English officers with any professional experience had served in the Dutch army, and the English Militia had been

Sack of Antwerp. Mutineers of the Spanish Army of Flanders sacked Antwerp on 4 November 1576, an event which horrified the citizens of all major cities.

trained using English translations of Dutch manuals. However, the Dutch army with its concentration on siege warfare no longer represented the latest model in modern warfare, being overtaken by the more fast-moving strategic style introduced during the Thirty Years War by Gustavus Adolphus. This new style was focused on victory on the battlefield rather than siege warfare, a far riskier strategy which offered the opportunity to win or lose a campaign or perhaps even the war itself in a single battle. The generals on both sides considered their campaign strategies in the light of these two opposing models, with commanders such as the Royalist Prince Rupert or the Parliamentary commanders Sir Thomas Fairfax and Oliver Cromwell having strong preferences for seeking solutions through decisive battles.

Most Englishmen saw European conflict in the Low Countries and in Germany as both political and as an extension of religious warfare between Catholic and Protestant. In England suspicions of Catholic Habsburg powers had, justifiably, run deep since the failed invasion attempt of the Spanish Armada in 1588. English soldiers had fought against the Spanish army in the Low Countries in support of the Dutch revolt and, closer to home, against the Spanish expeditionary force in Ireland which had been forced to surrender at Kinsale in 1602. The 'Gunpowder Plot' by English Catholics to blow up King and Parliament in 1605 had served only to harden attitudes. The general suspicion of Catholics that these conditions fostered continued after an official peace between England and Spain, and entire regiments of English soldiers continued to fight against the Spanish, serving as mercenaries in the Dutch army. The impression of religious conflict in Europe was increased during the early years of the Thirty Years War, as English volunteers fought in the Rhine Palatinate against Spanish Habsburg troops seeking to secure their military corridor from Italy to the Low Countries. During its early stages, the war in Germany was seen by Englishmen, and by those directly experiencing it in Germany, as setting Catholic against Protestant. The success of the Catholic League and Imperial armies seemed to present a threat to all Protestants until they were checked by the armies of the Swedish King. This general background created the underlying popular impression of a Catholic threat to England. As a result, the Catholic uprising in Ireland in 1641 was seen as creating a vulnerable frontier, and the English Catholics that King Charles commissioned as officers in his armies were distrusted, even by many Royalists.

The Spanish Army

The Spanish army was the leading army of the later sixteenth century, feared for its competence in a wide range of military theatres on land and sea. It fought in the Americas, in the Mediterranean against the Ottoman (Turkish) Empire and North African corsairs, in Italy against the French and their Swiss mercenaries and Italian allies, in the Netherlands against Protestant rebels and in France in support of the Catholic League. The Spanish Army of Flanders was also famous as the first modern army to perfect systematic mutiny as a means of obtaining its arrears of pay and to make mutiny an established part of

Spanish Infantry. Arquebusiers of the Spanish Army of Flanders, the leading European army of the late sixteenth century.

military life. The later mutiny of the New Model Army has to be considered in this European context, where it had become an accepted method for ordinary soldiers to press for the money they were owed.

Although it was a Spanish army in the sense that it was the army of the King of Spain, it was always a multinational force consisting of different national contingents, Spanish, Italian, German, Walloon (Belgian), Burgundian and, after 1587, Irish. Mercenaries or exiles who served in the Spanish army were able to transfer their expertise to other armies when they returned home. For example, two of the leading Irish commanders during the Irish Revolt against English rule (1641–53), Owen Roe O'Neill and Thomas Preston, had both served as colonels in the Spanish Army of Flanders. The Germans and Irish, and some Englishmen, serving in this army were not subjects of the Spanish crown, but most were Catholic. There was always a sense in this army that its soldiers fought in defence of Catholicism against the external threat of the expanding power of the Muslim Ottoman Empire and the internal threat of Protestant heretics. Many, perhaps most, of the soldiers who served in this army did so for pay, but the sense that in doing so they also supported their Catholic faith created the feeling that they fought for a higher cause than just money or international politics. This was particularly true for soldiers

Siege warfare in the Low Countries. A typical view of siege lines in front of a fortified city. The defensive fortifications developed in Italy were enhanced and extensively used in the wars in the Low Countries.

Sub Philippo Secundo, Gubernante Don Ludovico de Requefens.

obfidione gravi cingebat mœnia LEIDÆ
BALDÆUS, merita eft bello quæ Graja Saaunthos,

(Pefte, fame .obfefsis Cerealia munera deerant,
Non tamen ipfe Deus magnis his abfuit aufis.

recruited in Spain itself, where the crusading ideal remained strong following the completion of the *Reconquista*, the Christian recovery of Spain from the Moors, and Christian heretics were seen as traitors weakening the unity of the Christian world.

The tactical style of this army was flexible and it was experienced both on the battlefield and in siege warfare. Although sieges came to dominate warfare in Italy and in the Low Countries, Spanish and Italian military theorists never lost sight of the need to have an army which could fight effectively on the battlefield. The key to its success lay in the professionalism the Spanish Army achieved through continuous service and the advantages this brought in terms of veteran cadres of officers, non-commissioned officers and soldiers, and a centre for developing military theory and practice. Of all the Spanish forces, the most famous and most competent was the Spanish Army of Flanders, and it was this army that most Englishmen came into contact with. At a time when armies were usually raised for particular campaigns and then disbanded, the continuous service of the Spanish army created an experienced veteran army with solid and evolving tactical expertise in battle, skirmish or siege warfare.

The Dutch Army

The Spanish Army in Flanders was seen by English officers as the leading army of its day, described in the correspondence of the English general the Earl of Leicester as 'the best soldyers at this day in Christendom', but ultimately it proved unable to crush rebellion in the Netherlands. English soldiers served in the Dutch army as allies and as mercenaries, and their experience was influential in English perspectives on the theory and practice of war, on the conventions of siege warfare and on the defence of the Protestant religion from the Catholic Spanish and German empires. To appreciate this contemporary English perspective, it is necessary to consider something of the background.

From a military perspective, there were two main reasons for the failure of the Spanish in the Netherlands. Firstly, although the Spanish Empire of Philip II was the leading military power of its day, there was still a limit to its resources, and it faced too many different threats in too many different theatres of war to be able to concentrate its resources in any one place for long. Secondly, the military reforms of the Dutch leader, Prince Maurice of Orange, created a well-disciplined Dutch army whose tactical style was different from, and more flexible than, the Spanish. The new Dutch army proved at the battle of Nieuwpoort (30 June 1600) that it was a credible opponent, able to oppose and defeat the Spanish army in battle.

The origin of this new Dutch army lay in the rebellion of the Netherlands against the rule of Philip II, King of Spain. The seventeen provinces of the Netherlands had a history of local independence and attachment to their local rights and privileges long before dynastic inheritance brought them under the control of Philip II. Religious dissent brought another dimension to an already volatile background of opposition to new taxation and anger over attempts to weaken the provincial government. The result was opposition to Spanish rule by both Catholic and Protestant, including the formation of alliances with Protestant leaders in Germany and amongst the Huguenots (French Protestants) in France.

In response, the Spanish determined to send veteran soldiers from their garrisons in Italy under the Duke of Alva to restore order and to arrange a state visit by Philip II, with the objective of settling disputes and re-establishing relations with the population – a strategy which was intended to show that Philip II was prepared to listen to his subjects' concerns, but that he would do so from a position of strength. In the event, the threat of Alva's army caused many of those who had opposed the Spanish government to waver, and the Spanish governor, Margaret of Parma, was able to regain control using her own local troops. However, the Spanish were concerned that this might only be a temporary solution for the Netherlands, and its example was already causing unrest in other areas of the Spanish Empire, particularly in Italy. The pro-Spanish Cardinal Granvelle, then in Rome, wrote in June 1566 that 'All Italy says clearly that if the insurrection of Flanders continues, Milan and Naples will follow'.[1] The Duke of Alva pressed for a military solution, and made the valid point that if Philip II was to visit the Netherlands it was essential to have firm control in the interest of maintaining the King's personal safety. This could only be done with a strong force of Spanish and Italian troops, as the loyalty of local soldiers was suspect. By chance, this was also a convenient time to spare veteran troops from the garrison in Italy because the Ottoman Sultan, Suleiman the Magnificent, had died in 1566 and it was thought that his successor would be occupied for the next couple of years in consolidating his authority.

The Duke of Alva's army arrived in the Netherlands in 1567 and quickly made itself unpopular in the cities where its units were billeted. In 1569 the strategic problems of the Spanish Empire caught up with Alva's army as the Spanish faced problems in Spain itself, with a revolt of Muslim *moriscoes* against efforts to convert them to Christianity, as well as renewed warfare in the Mediterranean against the Ottoman Empire. While the Spanish were faced with expenses in other theatres of war, funds could not be spared for the Netherlands, and Alva was forced to raise taxation to pay his army. Opposition to increased taxation, as well as to Alva's religious policies, created a fertile ground for a new rebellion in 1572, and Alva determined to put an end to all opposition by terror, essentially by making horrific examples of those who opposed him. During 1572 he sacked three towns, Mechelen, Zutphen and Naarden, the worst case being Naarden, a town on the Zuider Zee, where the whole population was massacred after the town surrendered on terms. In his report to King Philip, Alva wrote that 'not a mother's son escaped'. This was an understatement; the Welsh professional soldier Walter Morgan wrote in his account of the campaigns of 1572–74 that the citizens 'repented full sore' after opening the city gates as 'the soldiours entryd the toune and putt all the inhabitants thereof men women and chilldern too the sword sackinge the same of such spooylles [spoils] as they thoughte for themselves most convenient'.[2] The following year, 1573, Alva reneged on the terms offered to the town of Haarlem and, after its surrender, massacred the garrison and executed some of the leading citizens.

Alva's strategy did work in the short term in crushing the will to resist in several other rebellious towns, but its fatal flaw was that it was all stick and no carrot. His basic approach can be judged from his comment to his successor as governor, Don Luis de Requesens, in December 1573: 'These troubles must be ended by force of arms without any use of pardon, mildness, negotiations or talks until everything has been flattened. That will be the right time for negotiation.' But the whole point of the accepted conventions of siege warfare was that a besieging commander's word could be trusted and the garrison and townspeople had a way out, rather than having to fight to the bitter end; Alva had shown that the word of a Spanish commander could not be relied upon. The net effect of this was that once committed to resistance there was no point in surrendering on terms to a Spanish army as it would not keep to any terms offered: better then to hold out to the last as this offered at least a hope of survival. The slaughter at Haarlem proved to be a turning point, and no more towns surrendered to the Spanish without determined resistance. As Cardinal Granvelle wrote from Naples: 'the Duke of Alva now complains that other areas have not surrendered spontaneously, but he should remember that there are soldiers defending the [other] towns who, fearing the same treatment as the garrison of Haarlem, will fight on until they die of hunger'.[3]

The remaining two rebel provinces, Holland and Zealand, were in more easily defended terrain, described by an English writer as 'the great bog of Europe. There is not such another Marsh in the World'. Apart from the purely technical military difficulties this represented for siege warfare, Spanish and Italian soldiers used to a warmer climate found the siege lines in this territory a thoroughly cold, wet and generally miserable place to be. While these provinces held out, the Spanish army mutinied for lack of pay, the first of a series of similar mutinies that would periodically cripple the Spanish war effort in the Netherlands. Apart from its impact on their general's strategy, the behaviour of mutinous soldiers created serious problems with the civilian population in Spanish-held territory. 'If they had loved us as sons before', the governor Don Luis de Requesens wrote in 1574, 'the Spanish mutinies would be enough to make us loathed.' When the mutineers stormed and then brutally sacked Antwerp, the major commercial centre in the Netherlands, in 1576 they killed 8,000 people and destroyed 1,000 homes in the process. The sack of Antwerp was seen, and publicized in print and engravings, as a major atrocity by all who opposed or feared the Spanish Empire, and as a warning of what Spanish soldiers were capable of. It made a considerable impact in England when the horrors of the sack became known.

The new governor appointed in 1578, Alexander Farnese, Prince of Parma, made more progress using a mixture of diplomacy and war. However, after the Dutch leader, William of Orange, was assassinated in 1584, neighbouring powers grew more concerned at the threat that a Spanish victory might create, and in 1585 Elizabeth I, Queen of England, sent English troops to Netherlands under the command of her favourite Robert Dudley, Earl of Leicester. Leicester's position was discredited when unpaid English and Irish garrisons sold Deventer and an important fort near Zutphen to the Spanish, but English troops continued to be an important part of the Dutch army. Parma's progress was brought to a standstill first by preparations to support the invasion of England by the Spanish Armada and then by the need to deploy troops from the Spanish army of Flanders in the civil war in France between the Catholic League and supporters of the Protestant Huguenot claimant to the throne, Henri of Navarre. Over the same period further mutinies continued to paralyse Spanish strategy under Parma and his successors. While the Spanish army was committed elsewhere the Dutch army made progress in recovering lost territory, and in 1609 the two sides agreed a twelve-year truce – the Truce of Antwerp. The Netherlands was effectively split between a Catholic south, controlled by the Spanish army and its local Catholic supporters, and a Protestant north, governed by an independent States General with the Prince of Orange as its military commander. Neither side trusted the other sufficiently to fully disband its armies, and they continued their war by proxy, by providing military support to their allies.

The expiry of the truce and the resumption of war with Spain coincided with the opening stages of the Thirty Years War in Germany. After the death of Prince Maurice in 1625, command passed to his half-brother Prince Frederick Henry. A much more aggressive commander, the latter followed a strategy of recovering territory to the south and made steady progress, taking 's-Hertogenbosch in 1629 and Maastricht in 1632. In 1634 the Spanish position in Flanders was improved by the arrival of a new Spanish army which had fought its way up through Germany and been part of the joint Imperial/Spanish army which had defeated the Swedes and their allies at Nordlingen (6 September 1634), but this advantage was brief. In 1635 the French became formally involved in the Thirty Years War and committed armies to the war in Germany itself and, in alliance with the Dutch, against the Spanish Army of Flanders. A war of sieges, with the Dutch retaking Breda in 1637, continued until 1643 when a Spanish/Imperial army besieged the French border fort at Rocroi. Under a different commander, the French would probably have been content to break the siege by manoeuvre and small actions but their new commander, Louis, Prince de Condé, was far more aggressive. The young Condé, then only 22, took the risky decision to offer battle and was victorious at the decisive battle of Rocroi (19 May 1643). The most serious outcome of the battle was the loss of irreplaceable Spanish veterans, the old tercios of the Spanish Army of Flanders. After Rocroi, the Spanish were ready to end the war and the Dutch were becoming concerned that a strong France could be worse than a weakened Spain. A peace treaty was finally agreed at Munster on January 1648. The war between the French and the Dutch continued until the Peace of the Pyrenees was signed in November 1659.

The battle of Nieuwpoort, 2 July 1600. Prince Maurice of Orange's famous victory over the Spanish Army of Flanders. It was seen by contemporaries as evidence that his military reforms and innovative tactics were effective. Note that the Dutch are shown in three lines of small battalions while the Spanish have fewer, more massive, tercios.

In conclusion, circumstances had weakened the ability of the Army of Flanders to campaign successfully against the Dutch: these included the diversion of major elements from war in the Netherlands to support the Catholic cause through the attempted invasion of Protestant England; intervention in the French civil war; and the lack of money which had led to army mutinies. However, if the Dutch had been unable to field an effective army to oppose the Spanish this would only have delayed an inevitable defeat. Experienced soldiers could defend a town, but to compete with the Spanish it would ultimately be necessary to be able to fight them on the battlefield on equal terms. The contemporary logic was expressed in 1629 by an Englishman, John Bingham, who had served in the Dutch army as 'indeed our actions in Warre are onely now a dayes and sieges [and] oppugnations of Cities; Battailes wee heare not of, save onely of a few in France, and that of Newport in the Low-Countries. But this manner will not last alwayes, nor is there any Conquest to be made without Battailes.'[4] Essentially, the point was that without the ability to fight a battle on equal terms, in any campaign the Dutch would lose the initiative to the Spanish. The achievement of Prince Maurice of Nassau's military reforms, admired and copied in England and elsewhere in Protestant Europe, was his creation of an army to rival the Spanish on the battlefield.

Prince Maurice's Reforms: A Military Revolution

Prince Maurice was not the sole author of the military changes which he introduced to reform the Dutch army during the 1590s, but as the military leader of the rebel Dutch provinces he had the authority to turn developing military theory into practice. Educated at the University of Leiden, Prince Maurice cut short his studies at the age of seventeen and joined the army after his father, Prince William, was assassinated in 1584. Although his formal education was curtailed, Maurice had an enquiring mind, as his correspondence and the inventory of his personal library demonstrate, so much so that one of the leading scientists of the day, Simon Stevin, wrote of him that 'he encompassed so many kinds of learning that even without his other achievements he would have been a famous man'.[5]

An interest in the potential advantages of models, civil or military, drawn from the classical past was a general trend of the Renaissance, and was not unique to the Low Countries. Throughout the sixteenth century there had been increased interest in the military potential offered by the Roman art of war described in translations of surviving Roman military books, particularly Flavius Vegetius' *De re militari* and Sextus Julius Frontinus' *Strategemata*, as well as Roman histories such those by Julius Caesar, Livy or Polybius. Other writers such as Niccolò Machiavelli had taken this a step further by linking classical example with their own ideas on contemporary warfare and politics, his *Libra della arte della guerra* (Florence, 1521) being the most famous example.

However, while the available military books provided a tantalizing impression of what could be achieved by a disciplined army and could be

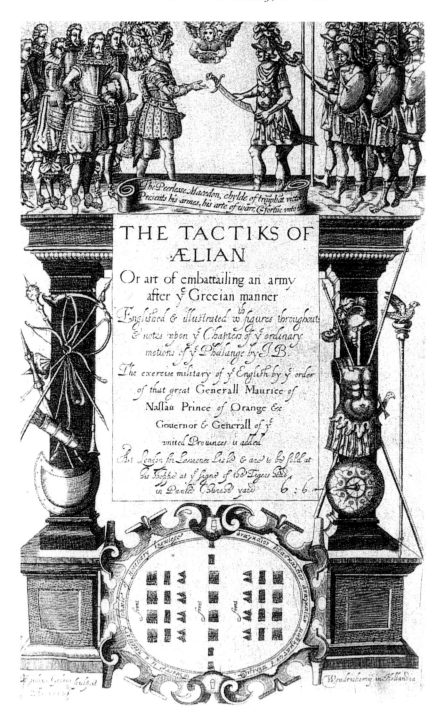

Frontispiece of The Tactiks of Aelian (London, 1616) by John Bingham, an English officer who had served in the Dutch Army. The engraving shows Alexander the Great handing over his sword, and by implication his military pre-eminence, to the Dutch Stadtholder, Prince Maurice.

Sub Philippo II, Gubern. Archid. Alberto,& Principe Mauritio.

Interea lectas ex omni gente cohortes   *MAVRITIVS legit peditumq, equitumq, cohortes ,*
228   *TVRNHOVTI locat ALBERTVS, queis territat Vrbes ,   Atq, hostem insequitur fugientem, armisq, lacessit.*

The battle of Turnhout, 24 January 1597. A victory achieved by the use of combined arms, 'shot' and cavalry.

copied in areas such as the layout of military camps, they did not include detailed explanations on how Roman military formations actually worked – in the sense of exactly how they were drawn up and manoeuvred, and what orders were given. Translations of two less well known books, Claudius Aelianus' *Tactica* and Byzantine Emperor Leo VI's *Tactica*, which drew upon it, provided the missing information. Aelianus' work provided the detailed information necessary to recreate a sequential training system and classical unit drill, as John Bingham, an English professional soldier in Dutch service, commented in the preface to his book *The Tactiks of Aelian* in 1616:

> Howbeit the practice of Aelians precepts hath long lien wrapped up in darknes, & buried (as it were) in the ruines of time, until it was revived, & restored to light not long since in the united Provinces of the low-Countries, which Countries at this day are the Schoole of war, whither the most Martial spirits in Europe resort to lay downe the Apprenticeship of their service in Armes, and it was revived by the direction of that Heroicall Prince Maurice of Nassau.[6]

Dutch infantry at Nieuwpoort. This illustration shows the linear formation of the Dutch battalions.

Aelianus' work actually describes the Greek and Macedonian rather than the Roman practice, but the key was to have a working description of the sequence of training, which led to an understanding of the unit drills and the ability to use them.

Both Aelianus' and Leo's books were in circulation at the time of Prince Maurice's reforms, but their introduction to modern warfare required the combination of classical scholarship and practical interpretation. Prince Maurice and his cousins William Louis van Nassau and Johan van Nassau-Siegen, together with their advisers, provided that combination. Circumstances also provided the ideal environment for the introduction of new military theories and practical training in the early 1590s, because a large part of the Spanish army of Flanders was occupied campaigning in France. This relieved the pressure on the Dutch army and gave Prince Maurice breathing space to introduce his reforms and train his solders. The Dutch also had the advantage that another key figure, Johan van Oldenbarnevelt, advocate of Holland, the wealthiest of the rebellious provinces, placed their finances on a sound base and was able to provide the money necessary for soldiers' pay. Without regular pay it would have been difficult, perhaps impossible, to introduce reforms which required far more effort and continuous training than previously. In this period it was difficult to persuade unpaid soldiers to obey any order, let alone introduce a rigorous training regime. The attraction to the officers whose enthusiastic involvement would be necessary to train their soldiers and make the reforms work was partly intellectual. An argument based on the idea of learning from the classical past was attractive to officers who were, or wished to be seen as, educated gentlemen, at least provided that the reforms could be demonstrated as workable.

The Thirty Years War

The Thirty Years War in Germany began in 1618 with a rebellion in Bohemia against Habsburg rule and the offer of the crown to Frederick, Count Palatine, a Protestant German ruler. One reason why this caused so much immediate concern was that the position of emperor of Germany was elective, but with only seven princes and archbishops able to cast a vote, one of these being the Elector Palatine and another the King of Bohemia. In 1618 there were three Catholic electors (the archbishops of Mainz, Cologne and Trier) and three Protestant (the Duke of Saxony and the Margrave of Brandenburg, who were both Lutherans, and the Count Palatine, who was a Calvinist). The seventh elector was the King of Bohemia, since 1617 Ferdinand, the heir of the current emperor. The emperor had influence rather than direct authority over the mass of political units within the German Empire (known as the Holy Roman Empire), consisting of kingdoms, duchies, counties, independent cities and many more small states, but it was not a position the Habsburgs were willing to give up. From their perspective the acceptance of the crown of Bohemia by Frederick, Count Palatine, represented a religious, political and dynastic threat. The Habsburg King of Spain would support his German relatives for all three reasons, and the Habsburgs could also rely on support from the German

Catholic League, headed by Maximilian of Bavaria. On the other hand, a closer Spanish/German Habsburg alliance was likely to mean stronger Habsburg power in Germany, and this was seen as a threat by other states – the Protestant Dutch and Denmark, and Catholic France – and both Protestant and Catholic rulers in Germany who valued their independence within a weak empire.

With so many potential participants, including several states which changed sides or chose to remain neutral at particular times and the more exotic involvement of Bethlen Gabor, Prince of Transylvania, this was not a straightforward series of campaigns. Essentially it can be broken down into broad phases. In the first phase the initial rebellion in Bohemia sparked off war in Bohemia and in Germany, where it was centred on the territory of the Elector Palatine. The rebellion in Bohemia was crushed by Catholic League and Imperial troops under Jean, Count Tilly, at the battle of White Mountain (8 November 1620) outside Prague. The Spanish Army of Flanders invaded the Palatinate under Ambrosio Spinola and had overcome the last resistance in 1624. In the second phase Christian IV, King of Denmark, entered the war in 1625 as the Protestant champion, and was supported by those Protestant leaders who now felt that they had little to lose in continuing to fight. For this phase the Emperor's own army had been reformed into an effective force through the efforts of the mercenary general Albrecht von Wallenstein. The Danish and their allies were defeated in a series of battles, notably Wallenstein's victory at Dessau (25 April 1626) and Count Tilly's Catholic League victory at Lutter (26 August 1626). Christian IV was driven out of mainland Denmark and onto its offshore islands. However, as the Imperial army was unable to take the islands themselves and as the expense of maintaining it was becoming difficult, the Emperor finally made peace on reasonable terms with Christian IV in 1629.

The Emperor Ferdinand failed to reach a general peace as French diplomacy and subsidies now encouraged Gustavus Adolphus, King of Sweden, to intervene in the third phase of the war, while political manoeuvring by Ferdinand's ally Maximilian of Bavaria led to the weakening of the Imperial army through the dismissal of its general, Wallenstein. The third phase commenced as Gustavus Adolphus landed his army in Germany in 1630, but his campaign was initially cautious as the local support he had hoped for did not materialize. While he negotiated for support with Protestant leaders, one of his few declared allies, the Protestant city of Magdeburg, was besieged by the Imperial and Catholic League armies under Count Tilly. Magdeburg fell to assault on 20 May 1631, and the city was sacked and then burnt to the ground with most of the population, over 20,000 men, women and children, massacred or dying in the fire. Sacking a town that resisted was commonplace at this time, but the scale of the slaughter at Magdeburg was exceptional, and newspapers, pamphlets and broadsheets illustrated with horrific details of the sack circulated throughout Europe.

As Tilly's army approached Saxony, its ruler, John George, made common cause with Sweden, joining his inexperienced Saxon army with Gustavus Adolphus's troops. The opposing armies met at the battle of Breitenfeld

Gustavus Adolphus, King of Sweden. The 'Lion of the North', he followed a very different strategic model to the Dutch leader, Prince Maurice, seeing victory in battle rather than siege warfare as the key to successful campaigning. Greatly admired by officers of the New Model Army both as a successful general and as a Protestant champion.

on 17 September 1631. Tilly's deployment was overconfident, and he deployed his army without a reserve because he believed that his veteran troops would sweep away his opponents. It was a fatal error, as although he was correct in his assessment of the Saxons, who fled, he had seriously underestimated both the experience of the Swedish army and the versatility of its tactical formations. The excesses of Tilly's army and its decisive defeat caused a major shift of power within Germany as wavering Protestant princes now joined with King Gustavus Adolphus.

In response, the Emperor recalled his mercenary general Wallenstein, and both sides recruited heavily for a new campaign the following year. After an abortive attack on Wallenstein's camp at Alte Feste (3–4 September 1632), Gustavus Adolphus outmanoeuvred Wallenstein by attacking the Imperial army at Lützen (16 November 1632), near Leipzig in Saxony, as it was dispersing into winter quarters. Wallenstein's Imperial army was defeated there, abandoning most of its artillery on the battlefield, but it was not broken.[7] From a strategic perspective, the Swedish suffered the greatest loss as their commander, King Gustavus Adolphus, was killed in the battle, and he was irreplaceable. The 'Lion of the North' had been more than the military commander of the Swedish and their allied German armies: he had been their inspiration and the cornerstone of an alliance of Protestant princes.

The Swedish maintained their German alliances until the main Swedish army was defeated at the battle of Nordlingen in 1634 by a combined Spanish and Imperial army. After this, most Protestant German princes abandoned the Swedish cause as quickly as they had joined it after the Swedish victory at Breitenfeld. Most German princes made peace with the empire at the Peace of Prague in 1635, but the Thirty Years War continued as the French became formally involved and committed armies to the war in Germany itself and, in alliance with the Dutch, against the Spanish Army of Flanders. The war in

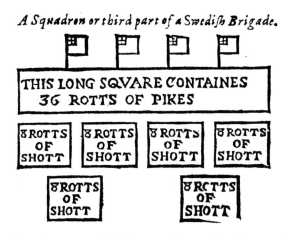

A Squadron or third part of a Swedish Brigade.

THIS LONG SQVARE CONTAINES
36 ROTTS OF PIKES

8 ROTTS OF SHOTT   8 ROTTS OF SHOTT   8 ROTTS OF SHOTT   8 ROTTS OF SHOTT

8 ROTTS OF SHOTT   8 RCTTS OF SHOTT

Swedish squadron. The squadron was a battlefield formation intended to provide a unit of 504 men. In numbers it was the equivalent of a Dutch battalion but its deployment and tactical use were different. The bottom two blocks of musketeers could be detached for service elsewhere, often in support of the cavalry wings.

Germany continued but had now become a political conflict, as the French pursued their ongoing national opposition to the Habsburgs, the Swedes sought to consolidate their gains in northern Europe, and both hired mercenary soldiers whose allegiance was only to their paymaster. This attitude is exemplified by the comment of the Scottish professional soldier Sir James Turner that he 'had swallowed, without chewing, in Germanie, a very dangerous maxime, which militarie men there too much follow, which was, that soe we serve our master honestlie, it is no matter which master we serve'.[8] By the late 1640s the war was going badly for the Imperial cause, culminating in a crushing defeat at Jankow (6 March 1645) by Field Marshal Lennart Torstensson. Swedish war aims were now to consolidate their territorial gains in north Germany through a formal treaty, and the French, after the outbreak of another civil war – the War of the Fronde – in 1648, were willing to reduce their requirements to an extent that the Emperor could accept. The Peace of Munster was agreed on 24 October 1648, ending the Thirty Years War.

The Art of War in England
Introduction
Continuous service by English troops in the later years of Queen Elizabeth's reign saw the creation of veteran English units fighting in Ireland and in France, and of veteran English mercenary companies in Dutch service. Initially, English troops would have been trained in the Spanish style of warfare, and this model would have been used by both regular soldiers and militia preparing to resist the invasion force carried by the Spanish Armada in 1588. During the 1590s English soldiers in Dutch service, and probably the English companies fighting in France, were trained in the new Dutch style introduced by Prince Maurice of Nassau, but those serving in Ireland may have retained the older Spanish model. The training of militia soldiers became confused during the 1590s and the style adopted – Spanish or Dutch – depended on the preference of the local deputy-lieutenants of the counties and the past military experience of their muster masters (county training officers). An indication of the problem can be seen in the correspondence of William

Waad, who wrote in 1596: 'I think, if you shall but ask the opinion of three captains how horsemen ought to charge, and how they should receive a charge, and so likewise of footmen in their retraicts, the three captains will be therein of two opinions at the least.'[9]

The war with Spain drew to a close with the failure of a Spanish expedition to Ireland and the defeat of the main native Irish force under Hugh O'Neill, Earl of Tyrone, at the battle of Kinsale (3 January 1602). James I, who succeeded Queen Elizabeth in 1603, saw himself as a peaceful monarch, and the war was formally ended with the Peace of London in 1604. Thereafter, English mercenary regiments continued in Dutch service, but in England itself there was no longer any requirement for a standing army, and the only regular soldiers were in small garrisons in England and Ireland. From this point English military theory and practice is influenced by three main factors: firstly, the English soldiers who remained in professional service in the Dutch army; secondly, the main body of the English Trained Bands (Militia); and thirdly, the exceptional London Trained Bands and the London voluntary companies.

The English Regiments in Dutch Service

The provisions of the Peace of London in 1604 meant that James I would not authorize any formal levies in England for soldiers to serve in the Dutch army. However, Spanish efforts to persuade James I to recall English officers and men already in Dutch service were unsuccessful, and there was nothing in the treaty to prevent Englishmen from serving in the Dutch army if they chose to do so. Continuity of service created an English military community in the Dutch United Provinces and offered opportunities for those Englishmen who wanted to pursue a military career. It also provided many English gentlemen with a means of rounding out their education by serving 'swallowlike, for a summer or only for a siege'[10] as gentlemen volunteers, known as 'voluntaries',[11] in convivial company with the English regiments.

For many English professional officers, service in the Dutch army was the beginning of a military career and, as promotion was slow, they would then go on to serve in other armies or return to England to serve the King whenever he raised armies himself. In theory, the Dutch might also be persuaded to release cadres of veteran soldiers as well as officers, but this rarely worked in practice as veteran soldiers were valuable and the Dutch were reluctant to lose them. The net effect of this was that although Charles I could obtain the services of officers trained through service in the Dutch army – either on temporary leave of absence or by resigning their commissions in Dutch service to obtain higher rank in the English army – he could not obtain the cadres of experienced non-commissioned officers and soldiers which would be needed to form effective new regiments quickly. Professional officers could do their best, and they did, but they needed time for training, pay for their men, adequate arms, equipment and sufficient food supplies, and, usually, none of these were forthcoming. Professional officers also suffered from court influence in the granting of some commissions to gentlemen with no military experience, as Sir Robert Cecil commented on the officers commissioned for the expedition to Cadiz: 'for the Captaines that I found heere, and that your Lo[rdship] hath againe recommended, I could take exceptions, bycause I know manie of them have not beene soldiers'.[12]

As the political situation between England and Scotland worsened, professional English soldiers with this background of service in the Dutch army and earlier English expeditions saw potential opportunities in England. However, although some professional officers found positions in the regiments serving in the Bishops' Wars, most English officers were amateurs. The English armies were distinctly unimpressive during the Bishops' Wars, but their amateur officers did obtain some military experience as well as the benefit of serving alongside professional officers, experience which would prove useful in the wars in Ireland and the English Civil War. However, these professional soldiers were the minority and most officers serving in the Civil War had little or no military experience outside of militia training when the Civil War began.

Overall more professional officers served in the Royalist army or in Ireland than in the Parliamentary army. The comment by Sir Thomas Fairfax's chaplain, Joshua Sprigge, after the battle of Naseby is exaggerated but does mark a genuine distinction between the officer corps of the two armies:

> in this the enemy had much the odds of us, that they had on their side not so few as fifteen hundred Officers, that were old souldiers, of great experience through long experience in forraign parts; when on the other hand, we had not ten Officers that could pretend to any such thing, as the experience of a souldier, save what this war had given them, being for the most part such, whose Religion, Valour and present Reason was their best Conduct.[13]

The Trained Bands (Militia)

The English Militia were known as Trained Bands, a term dating from Queen Elizabeth's reorganization of the English Militia as a precaution against war with Spain. The intention was to replace the general responsibility of free men to serve in defence of the country with smaller contingents, armed with the latest European weapons (pike, arquebus and musket) and trained to use them. They were composed of citizens with some stake in their society on the basis that they would be able to afford to purchase their own arms and would not use them to cause civil disturbance. In this sense the expense of buying military equipment was essentially a form of taxation, and training to use it was time-consuming, neither of which was popular. For these reasons the Trained Bands could be kept in a state which even approached competence only with constant effort by central government. Otherwise the temptation was for Trained Band soldiers to buy military equipment as cheaply as possible and to treat their training days as a form of local festival.[14]

Renewed government attention improved the level of military equipment of the Trained Bands and provided a standard set of training instructions, but ultimately only the community itself could build on this framework to provide an effective military force, and there was little enthusiasm for it. The position was not helped by the fact that the officers of the Trained Bands were men of local influence, nobility and gentry in the provinces and the merchant elite in cities or towns, and these men rarely had any practical military experience. On the eve of the Bishops' Wars the results were clearly not impressive, as noted by the military writer Robert Ward in his book *Anima'dversions of Warre* (London, 1639), in discussing the importance of military training: 'I would to God that notice may be taken hereof, and that greater care might be had of our Trainings than is; that they might no longer be used as matters of disport, and things of no moment.'[15] Most of the Trained Bands were not well trained and did not want to be, but there was an exception, the London Trained Bands, which was to have a major impact on the outcome of the Civil War.

The Society of the Artillery Garden and the London Trained Bands

The position in London was different, partly because the court and government being in Westminster meant the state of its Trained Bands was highly visible, but mostly because of the activity of a voluntary military group, the Society of the Artillery Garden. The society had existed in one form or another since at least the time of Henry VIII, and 'Captains from the Artillery Garden' had provided officers for the London Trained Bands during the Armada crisis of 1588. It was effectively a form of military guild which drew its members from amongst the wealthier citizens and was not unique amongst the leading European cities of the time, the most significant example being the Dutch Schuttersgilden.[16]

The society was revitalized in 1610 and became very popular amongst London citizens, partly because it coincided with a general interest in the new patterns of training introduced in the Dutch army of Prince Maurice of Nassau. The Dutch drill was uniform, and as well as its military application could be used for visually impressive displays of arms drill and unit

William Barriffe. A member of the Society of the Artillery Garden and an officer in the London Trained Bands before the English Civil War, he was the author of the most widely read English military manuals of the time. He was appointed sergeant major and later lieutenant colonel of John Hampden's regiment, serving on the Edgehill campaign (1642) and at the siege of Reading (1643), but died of sickness in July 1643.

evolutions. The society itself also developed a strong social side with its meetings and feasts, and membership clearly offered some degree of social prominence and the display of wealth in expensively decorated arms.

The example of the Society of the Artillery Garden led to the formation of other voluntary companies around London, the Military Company in Westminster and the Martial Yard in the Borough of Southwark, and in the provinces.[17] The role of the voluntary companies as a part of the English Militia system was also transferred to the Americas, where the 'Military Company of Boston' was authorized by the governor and Council of Boston in 1638.[18] By the 1620s the voluntary companies were becoming centres for military experiment and tuition for the national Trained Bands. The military company of Norwich was well regarded by the deputy lieutenants of Norfolk, who recommended in 1633 that potential Trained Band officers should be sent to Norwich for training by its lieutenant.[19]

The greatest impact of the voluntary companies was felt in London, where they provided officers for the London

Phillip Skippon Efqr Majoi Generall of the Army etc

Philip Skippon (d.1660). A professional soldier who had served in the English regiments in Dutch service, Skippon took up the position of 'Captain-Leader' or training officer to the Society of the Artillery Garden. The Society provided the officers for the London Trained Bands, and this established a strong and durable connection when Skippon went on to command the London Militia as sergeant major general of the City of London in 1642.

Trained Band companies. The members of the Society of the Artillery Garden were trained by professional officers, captain-leaders, paid for by the society. The most famous of these was the veteran professional soldier Philip Skippon, who was appointed captain-leader of the society in 1639 and sergeant major general of the London Trained Bands in 1642. The result of professional tuition and the citizens' own enthusiasm made the London Trained Bands an effective military force which was to be influential at two key events during the English Civil War, as well as performing the broader strategic function of providing a large self-sustaining garrison for the principle Parliament base, the City of London. In 1642 it marched out at its full strength of some 8,000 men under Skippon to join with the Earl of Essex's army to face the King's army at Turnham Green, and in 1643 the Earl of Essex's army would have been too weak to march to the relief of the city of Gloucester without the support of a brigade of London Militia, Trained Bands and Auxiliaries.

Training by professional officers made the men of the London Militia effective on the battlefield as they were practised in military evolutions and musketry, but they heartily disliked the discomforts of campaigning and regarded themselves as an allied force rather than one absolutely under the control of the general in whose army they fought. This did not cause too much trouble when they served with the Earl of Essex's army, as their former commander, Skippon, was Essex's sergeant major general, but the regiments serving under Sir William Waller were often mutinous. Their contribution was to preserve the Parliamentary cause in the early stages of the English Civil War, but their dislike of campaigning for any length of time meant their support would not be enough to win the war.

Chapter Three
Recruitment, Uniform, Arms and Equipment

Recruitment

Before the Civil Wars, soldiers could be raised in England by enlisting volunteers or by levying conscripts. An officer wishing to recruit volunteers would have permission to do so from the Crown, and the typical approach was to have drummers beat a tune through a town to attract attention and lead the curious to a tavern, where the recruiting officer would extol the attractions of a military life over a liberal amount of beer. Those volunteering had their names entered on a list – *en liste*, hence the term enlisted.

Recruitment. This is the first of a series of military engravings Les Miseres et les Mal-Heurs de la Guerre as it represents the beginning of a soldier's military life.

Levied soldiers were raised by allocating set numbers to each county. It was then the responsibility of the lord lieutenant to arrange for instructions to be passed further down the chain of local administration – through the justices of the peace to the constables of the hundreds or the churchwardens in the parishes – to levy the men. The county then had the responsibility to clothe and billet the levies and pay for them to be conducted to the muster point. Levies were extremely unpopular as the casualty rate from campaigning and, especially, disease meant that few men returned home after military service overseas. This had an impact on the whole community, the men themselves, their families, those who relied on their skills or those who employed them. The whole system was also quite remarkably corrupt as the local officials responsible for selecting the men often used the levy as an opportunity to pay off local scores or to make money by accepting bribes to release one man and select another in his place. The Trained Bands were exempt from the levies and fulfilling this Militia duty was always more popular when the country was at war.

At the outbreak of the Civil War both sides were cautious of popular opinion and raised troops from volunteers rather than conscription. As levies were so unpopular and many people were now uncertain which authority, King or Parliament, was legitimate, neither side felt it could enforce conscription. The actual nature of voluntary enlistment varied throughout the country, and in the more rural parts of England and Wales, where the influence of the local landowner was dominant, many men followed the habits of civilian life and volunteered because they were told to do so.[1] Others enlisted for pay, but many were genuine volunteers who joined the armies from a sense of loyalty to one side or the other, probably hoping that a show of force would be all that was required to lead to some compromise arrangement.

By 1643, the second year of the First Civil War, the two sides were able to exercise stronger influence over the areas of the country that they controlled and, as it was increasingly difficult to find sufficient volunteers, both sides now resorted to levying men by conscription to find recruits for their armies. Conscription was as unpopular during the war as it had been before it. This was particularly the case with infantry, as it was still possible for a charismatic cavalry commander such as Oliver Cromwell or Prince Rupert to raise volunteers. The levy was accompanied by the same level of bribery and general corruption seen before the Civil War, and many levied soldiers made strenuous efforts to desert before they reached the army or as soon as possible after they joined it. After the First Civil War large numbers of former soldiers, from both Parliamentary and Royalist armies, were disbanded. Many of them had become used to a military life and the New Model Army was able to obtain many of its recruits from voluntary enlistment, some of them former Royalists. Levies for the New Model Army were still required until 1651 when a final levy of 10,000 men was made to re-enforce the army in Ireland. Thereafter the New Model Army was able to rely on volunteers to fill its ranks.

Uniform, Field Words and Field Signs

The New Model infantry were famous as the first English army where all the regiments wore red coats. A report in the contemporary newsbook *Perfect Passages* for 7 May 1645, describing the New Model infantry marching out of Windsor on 1 May, recorded that 'the men are Redcoats all, the whole army only are distinguished by several facings of their coats'.[2] The facings at this time were the lining of the soldier's coat which would be visible where the coat sleeves were turned back to form a cuff. Surviving contracts for the manufacture of uniforms for the New Model Army and contemporary accounts describing New Model infantry show that it continued to be issued with red uniforms throughout its existence. By the 1650s the term 'red-coat' had been generally adopted by New Model Army soldiers to describe themselves, an example being Major General Sir Thomas Morgan's robust comment to the French Marshal Turenne, when commanding New Model soldiers serving with the French against the Spanish army, that 'it was an usual custome of the red-coats when they saw the enemy to rejoice'.[3] James II, then Duke of York, who was serving with the Spanish army, recorded in his memoirs that at the battle of the Dunes (14 June 1658) he recognized the New Model infantry as they began to deploy 'whom I easily knew by their redcoats'.[4] New Model dragoons would also have worn red coats, as they were mounted infantry, but cavalrymen were not issued with uniform coats.

Prior to this infantry were provided with uniform coats by the county where they were levied, the colonel who raised the regiment or the military administration, Parliamentary or Royalist, which provided uniforms from a centrally organized supply. The original objective in issuing a man with a coat was not to create a uniform appearance in the army or even the regiment but, as many soldiers were poorly clothed when they were first recruited, simply to provide him with the clothing he would need if he was to survive on campaign. This inevitably led to a number of different-coloured coats being worn by the same army, with popular colours being worn by both sides. Coats from a single supplier would often be the same colour, and a regiment might present a uniform appearance when first raised, but the coats of the next batch of recruits or new coats issued to veteran soldiers might not be the same colour, so after its first year of service a regiment would present a motley appearance. Red and blue had been popular colours for soldiers' coats since Elizabethan days and were popular with both sides during the Civil War. Other colours were green, yellow, tawny-orange, white, grey and, for the regiment of Fulke Greville, Lord Brooke, in the Parliamentary army, purple. An indication of the mixture of colours in the Royalist army can be seen in the report of a rendezvous of its soldiers at Banbury in October 1643 prior to setting out on a raid on Parliamentary territory. This Royalist contingent comprised 22 troops of horse and 700 'commanded' infantry,[5] described as '700 Foote, choice men, ten or more from every company in and about Oxford, they were 300 Red-coats, and 200 Blue, and 200 mixed coloured coats'.[6] Against this diverse background, the New Model Army's uniform appearance in red coats would have made an impact on observers.

The answer to the question of how anyone could tell one side from the other on the battlefield in these circumstances is that, once battle commenced, no one could with certainty. After the initial advance the battle lines of the two armies could become confused as some regiments defeated their immediate opponents and others retreated, and overall would lie the smoke from musketry and artillery. The contemporary answer to this practical problem was for each army to wear a common field sign for that day on its hats and helmets and to have a particular field cry, again only for that particular day. The Earl of Orrery commented in his *Treatise of the Art of War* (London, 1677) that field signs were usually 'a green branch [i.e. a sprig of leaves], a piece of Fern, or a handful of Grass or a piece of white paper'. Examples of field signs are the sprig of leaves (gorse and broom) worn by the Parliament soldiers of the Earl of Essex's army at the first battle of Newbury, and the white cloth or piece of paper worn by the allied Parliamentary and Scottish armies at the battle of Marston Moor the following year. Alternatively the field sign could be the absence of something commonly worn, so the Royalists at Marston Moor had as their field sign the absence of any sashes or ribbons, while the field sign for the New Model Army at Dunbar was that they would 'have no white about them'.

The Earl of Orrery explained the requirement for a field word as well as a field sign:

> because such Field Marks, wherever you place them, are not still visible on all sides of the Head or Body of everyone who wears them, the Field Word is also given: For it often happens that in a Battel, the Field Mark is by accident lost by many out of their Helmets, or Hats, and that if they had not the Field Word, they might be kill'd by those of their own Party who knew them not personally.[7]

Examples of Parliamentary field words are 'Religion' at the first battle of Newbury and at Newark, 'God with us' at Marston Moor, 'Jesus Blesse us' at Cheriton, 'Victory without quarter' at Cropredy Bridge, 'God our strength' at Naseby and 'The Lord of Hosts' at the battle of Dunbar. Examples of Royalist field words are 'Queen Mary' (the name being commonly used to refer to Queen Henrietta Maria) at the first battle of Newbury, 'King and Queen' at Newark, 'God and the King' at Marston Moor, 'Hand and sword' at Cropredy Bridge and 'Queen Mary' again at Naseby. The field word of the Scots at Dunbar was 'The Covenant'. During a siege the storming parties attacking the breach in a wall would also use field words and field signs; 'God with us' was particularly popular with the New Model Army and was used by it at Dartmouth in 1646 and Dundee in 1651, probably because of the men's admiration for the great Protestant champion Gustavus Adolphus, as 'Gott mit uns' had been the field word for his Swedish/German army at both of his famous victories at Breitenfeld (1631) and Lützen (1632).

An impression of the uniform issue for infantry immediately before the Civil Wars can be seen in the standard set in September 1642 for soldiers serving in Ulster. This consisted of a cap, canvas doublet, cassock (coat), breeches, two pairs of stockings, two pairs of shoes and two shirts at a cost of 42 shillings and sixpence for the whole.[8] The item whose supply caused most concern was the shoes, as without these the soldiers 'are neither able to march nor do any service at all'. Another necessary item of equipment was the soldier's knapsack or snapsack, essentially a tube-like sack slung over one shoulder and tied at the chest which contained a soldier's possessions on campaign. At the beginning of the Civil War neither side had the resources to equip its soldiers to this optimum level, and Parliamentary infantry in 1642 were issued with only coats, shirts, shoes, caps (probably knitted 'Monmouth' caps) and snapsacks, so would have to serve in the breeches they were wearing when they joined the army.[9] The Royalist army in Oxford received a more complete issue in 1643 as the merchant Thomas Bushell undertook to provide suits (which meant a coat and breeches, usually from the same colour of cloth), stockings, shoes and mounteroes (a peaked cloth montero cap), 'some all in red, some all in blue'. The terms 'cassock' and 'coat' may originally have had distinct meanings, but by the time of the Civil Wars both were used to refer to the soldier's coat. In theory, new uniforms were issued once a year but there were often delays.

The most complete set of records for uniforms, arms and equipment issued to the New Model Army are the surviving contracts for the period April 1645 to March 1646 which are preserved in the collection of the Museum of London.[10] Most workshops in the City of London and elsewhere were quite small, consisting of the merchant, his family and apprentices, and the practice of the day was for a merchant to contract for a set quantity of uniforms or arms and then subcontract the work to other merchants in London and other cities. Some degree of uniformity was imposed by the practice used in England and elsewhere in western Europe of requiring the items produced to conform to a standard pattern, and this was achieved by having an example or 'patterne' which was retained by the Ordnance Office and compared with the goods delivered. With several different suppliers involved in making up the contract there was inevitably some variation against the 'patterne' but this would be accepted as long as the difference was not significant. A contract dated 14 February 1645 illustrates this practice, as it includes the proviso:

> that although it is impossible for any person to undertake to make ye sayd provisions exactly suitable for goodness to any patterne for yt many wil be better and some may be a little worse yet it is ye resolution of ye said Contractor and he does hereby promis that as neere as he can none of ye said provisions of Coates, Breeches and Stockins shall be worse than ye patternes presented to ye sid honorable Comttee [Committee for the Army] and that ye said Comttee or such as they shall appoint to view & supervise ye said provisions shall have power to refuse any of them against which there is inst. exceptions.[11]

Of course, a little money changing hands at this point would ease acceptance of minor imperfections.

The contract with 'Richard Downes Citizen of London' provides a complete description of the specification for coat, breeches and stockings:

> The coates to be of a Red Colour and of Suffolke, Coventry or Gloucester-shire Cloth and to be made Three quarters and a naile [29¼ inches] long faced with bayse or Cotton with tapestrings according to a pattern delivered into ye said Committee. The Breeches to be of Gray or some other good Coloure & made of Reading Cloth or other Cloth in length Three quarters one eighth [31½ inches] well lined and Trimmed suitable to ye patternes presented, the said Cloth both of ye Coates and of ye Breeches to be first shrunke in Cold Water. The stockins to be of good Welsh Cotton.[12]

The cost was set at 17s for a suit of coat and breeches and 13½d for a pair of stockings. A separate contract with Richard Downes for 4,000 sets of coats and breeches specified that 'ye tape to bee white, blew, greene and yellow', and another contract at the same time with Edward Harrice and Arthur Dew was for a further 100 sets with orange ribbon. The reference may indicate tapes used in the production of the coat itself and so provide an indication of the colour of the different linings to the coats as well. It is also possible that this reference meant that the coats were actually fastened with tapes or ribbons instead of buttons, but this is unclear and there is no known contemporary illustration of New Model infantry with their coats fastened in this way. A later contract agreed with the same supplier, Richard Downes, in October 1649 for coats and breeches for the army in Ireland at 17s a suit specified that the coats were to be made of 'Coventry or Gloucester cloth of Venice colour, red shrunk in cold water' and the breeches were to be 'grey or other good colours of Reading or other good cloth'. The measurements for the coats were the same as before but the breeches were to be of two sizes, 12,000 to be three-quarters and a half, but the remaining 4,000 were to be three-quarters and a nail.[13] The breeches were to 'well lined and with hooks and buttons'.

For shirts the New Model accounts record contracts with 'Henry Pettite for 4000 shirts' at 2s 6d a shirt, and with Christopher Nicholson for 3,000 shirts of 'good lockram' at 2s 10d a shirt. There are a number of contracts for shoes, a typical example being that with:

> Jenkin Ellis of Katheren Tower for 4,500 payre of shooes of good neate leather wth good soles of the severall sizes of Tennes, Eleavens, Twelves and thirteenes of each size a like number all of them to be punched & each payre tacked together & marked on the soles wth the severall markes hereafter mentioned at 11s 111d [2 shillings and 3 pence] a payre to be brought into the Tower of London to be viewed wthin one moneth nowe next following ffor wch it is contracted he shalbe payd when he bringe them in ffor pformance whereof he hath sett his hand.[14]

The sizing system used for shoes at this time was based on a rising scale of a quarter of an inch starting with 8 and a half inches, and the sizes 10, 11, 12 and 13 correspond to the modern British shoe sizes between 8 and 10;[15] 'neate' or 'neats' leather meant leather made from an ox or a cow. There are also contracts for that other essential item the snapsack, a typical example being the contract with 'Raph fferbanke in Cheapside for 3000 Snapsacks large and of good leather at 8s a dozen'.[16]

Dragoons would have been issued with the same coats and other clothing as the infantry, and probably wore shoes rather than cavalry boots, as their main service was on foot. Cavalrymen were not issued with uniform clothing and were only occasionally issued with clothing of any kind. The reason may simply be that as cavalrymen were better paid and generally better off financially it was thought that they would be able to provide their own clothing. The only exception to this was the scarves or sashes worn by cavalry troopers to indicate their allegiance to one side or the other. In 1642 Parliamentary cavalry troopers were issued with orange sashes at a cost of 10s. Orange was the colour of their commanding general, the Earl of Essex. There is no direct evidence to indicate what colour sashes would have been worn in the New Model Army, but they were probably blue while it was commanded by Sir Thomas Fairfax. Royalist cavalry troopers wore red sashes. The sash fulfilled an important function because the equipment of cavalry troopers was so similar: the recommendation for the re-equipment of Parliamentary cavalry troopers after their retreat at Lostwithiel in 1644 indicates 'that new scarffs may be allowed to ye troopers in regard of ye great inconvenience we find it upon service we cannot know one another from the enemy'.[17]

Commissioned officers on both sides wore their own clothing with the addition of military paraphernalia such as a buff coat, armour and weapons, together with a sash to show their allegiance. There is a reference by the contemporary Jersey diarist Jean Chevalier that an ensign of one of the New Model Army regiments in 1651 'preached in the town church, though he was not an ordained pastor. He went into the pulpit in his red coat wearing his sword, but took his sword off when he preached'.[18] So it is possible that junior officers, at least, in the New Model Army wore red coats as well as their men. 'Inferior officers', the non-commissioned officers such as sergeants or corporals, may have received uniform coats, but sergeants at least were allowed some leeway and may have worn their own clothes and sashes. Nehemiah Wharton, a sergeant in the Earl of Essex's army, wrote to his master in the City of London in September 1642, thanking him for the present of 'my mistresses scarfe and Mr. Molloyne's hatband' and mentioning that he had 'had this day made for me a soldier's sute for winter, edged with gold and silver lace'.[19] Another indication is the comment by Sir Samuel Luke in a letter dated 11 April 1645 that 'by Maj. Gen Skippon's persuasions all sergeants and corporals which were formerly employed are willing to serve as common soldiers and took both pay, coats and shirts according to the Parliamentary allowance'.[20]

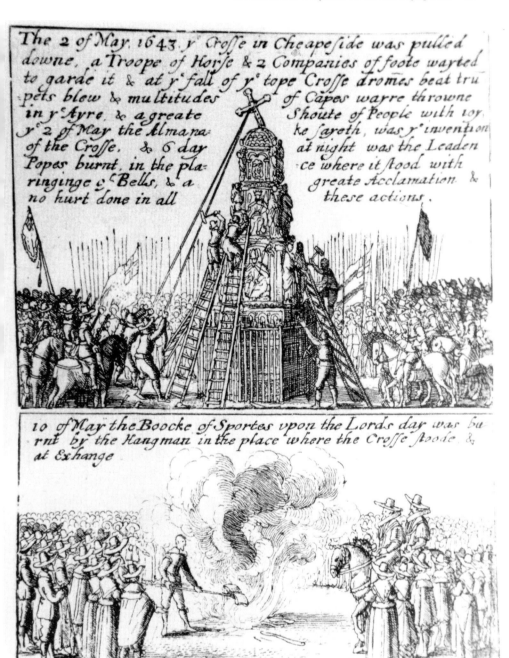

The 2 of May. 1643. y Croſſe in Cheapeſide was pulled downe, a Troope of Horſe & 2 Companies of foote wayted to garde it & at y fall of y tope Croſſe dromes beat tru pets blew & multitudes of Capes warre throwne in y Ayre, & a greate Shoute of People with io y 2 of May the Almana ke ſareth, was y invention of the Croſſe, & 6 day at night was the Leaden Popes burnt, in the pla ce where it ſtood with ringinge y Bells, & a greate Acclamation. & no hurt done in all theſe actions.

10 of May the Boocke of Sportes vpon the Lords day was bu rnt by the Hangman in the place where the Croſſe ſtode & at Exhange

Cavalry at Cheapside Cross. A contemporary engraving of the destruction of the cross at Cheapside on 2 May 1643. As this shows a particular event, these figures were probably drawn from life. Note the cavalrymen wear back and breast armour over their buff coats, have pistols in their saddle holsters and carry carbines. They wear broad-brimmed hats instead of helmets. The pikes carried by the infantry are also drawn to the correct scale, and they also wear broad-brimmed hats.

The colour of the sash worn by officers and cavalry troopers indicated either the state or the particular commander in whose army they served. Red sashes were commonly worn by officers in Spanish service, and the Imperialist general Albrecht von Wallenstein ordered his officers to wear red sashes as a distinguishing feature in May 1632. Officers in Dutch service wore orange sashes, the colour of their commander, Prince Maurice of Orange. At the outbreak of the English Civil War, Royalist officers wore red sashes while their opponents in the Parliamentary army wore orange sashes, the family colour of their commander, the Earl of Essex. Royalist officers continued to wear red sashes throughout the Civil War but Parliamentary officers may well have worn different colour sashes if they served in an army whose general held an independent commission – that is if their general was not, or did not regard himself to be, directly under the command of the Earl of Essex. Officers in the New Model Army in 1645 would have worn the blue of their general, Sir Thomas Fairfax. Correspondence relating to a dispute between Sir John Gell and the major in his cavalry regiment, Thomas Sanders, provides a unique indication of this practice. The dispute caused friction within the regiment, with some troops supporting the Colonel and others supporting the Major. Major Sanders hoped to persuade Sir Thomas Fairfax to take the cavalry regiment into the New Model Army and appoint him colonel, and wrote in a letter to his friend Captain Nathaniel Barton, 'my soldiers wear his Excellency's colours and for that are called rogues and threatened to pull them out of their hats – Gell's soldiers wear his colours and brave it to our faces'.[21]

Musicians, drummers in an infantry or dragoon company or trumpeters in a troop of horse, would wear a more elaborate uniform. There are no direct sources for the Civil War describing drummers' coats, but Elizabethan references and contemporary paintings of Dutch militia companies show that it was customary then, as now, for the colonel or the captain to have his drummers more elaborately dressed than the ordinary soldier, usually by the addition of silver lace to the coat and feathers in the drummers' hats. There is more evidence that cavalry trumpeters could have quite elaborate costumes from contemporary Dutch paintings, where a trumpeter delivering a message was a popular subject, and invoices from the English Civil War showing the cost. For example, Colonel Edmund Hervey of the City of London horse paid out the quite considerable sum of £7 10s 8d for 'clothing, boots, spurs and hat for a trumpeter', and a more detailed invoice for trumpeters in General William Brereton's troop showed the following:[22]

2 yds of silver parchment at ½d per yd
5 yds of fustian at 10d
1½ doz coat buttons at 10d each
7 skeans of silk at 6d each
1 yd cullered buckram ¼d
6 yds of tape
1 doz trussers 9d
4¼ [yds] of 12d ribbon.

Arms and Equipment

The manufacture of weapons and armour was a skilled job, particularly for the firing mechanisms used for muskets, carbines and pistols. Prior to the Bishops' Wars there had been a limited demand in England to meet the requirements of the Trained Bands and orders from the Ordnance Office, but not enough to establish an English arms industry capable of supplying entire armies. As the main English market for arms was based in London, most arms manufacturers were in the south-east, and this territory was under control of the Parliament. This in itself gave the Parliament a significant advantage, which was increased still further as access to the sophisticated financial centre of London made large-scale purchases abroad much easier to arrange and to pay for, while control of the English navy made arms imports from abroad more dangerous for its opponents, whether English Royalists, Scots or Irish.

At the outbreak of the Civil War the Parliament also had the advantage of control over England's existing arsenals of weapons at the Tower of London, Greenwich and Hull (arms which had been stored there during the Bishops' Wars had not yet been returned to London), together with military equipment from the London city guilds. In some parts of the country both sides also made use of equipment taken from the local Trained Bands. The Royalists set up their own ordnance office in Oxford to store, repair and manufacture arms and armour, and established another major centre at Bristol. But although this increased the supply of arms available to them, they remained heavily reliant on imported arms.

To some extent this would have caused some distinction in the arms and equipment used by the main Royalist army and its Parliamentary opponents, particularly as the English arms industry supplying the Parliament had expanded to meet (and make a profit from) the increased demand. A particular visual distinction would have been the use of English-made three-barred cavalry helmets by many Parliamentary cavalry troopers, compared to the single-barred Dutch *zischagge* helmet imported by Royalists. Another would have been the difference in pistol firing mechanisms, with many imported pistols using the wheel-lock mechanism while English-produced weapons used a form of flintlock. On a more practical level, contracts for locally produced weapons could specify the bore of the barrel, but Royalists desperate for arms were often supplied with sub-standard, often second-hand, arms by unscrupulous Dutch or French arms dealers. The Royalist captain John Strachan was clearly writing from a full heart after his dealings with the suppliers of a delivery:

> we have viewed their powder which is nothing else but old cannon powder that hath lyen in some magazine these 4, or 5 yeares it will never doe good service tyll it bee refined, and the muskets, there are about 1000 of them, I am assured they are of 3, or 4 score sundry bores, some pistol bores, some carabine bores, some little fowling peeces, and all the old trash that could bee rapt together; I must say that the pistols are good, and the

swords are reasonable (but to come to the price) shall I eat Queen Maries [Henrietta Maria's] bread and see a company of cheating marchants to deceive openly (hang mee, draw mee, quarter mee, or beggar mee let it be what it will I will speak the trueth).[23]

The difficulty with several different bores was in supplying ammunition, as it was far easier if all the muskets in an army used the same size of musket ball. The Scots faced similar difficulties with supply as their local arms industry, based in Edinburgh, was on too small a scale to provide the arms they required, and they were obliged to import arms. The position in Ireland was worse as the local Irish arms industry was smaller than the Scottish.

Cavalry

Before the outbreak of the English Civil War, the dominant military theory in England was based on the Dutch model. The leading English cavalry manual of the day was John Cruso's *Militarie Instructions for the Cavall'rie* (Cambridge, 1632) and this was, as its author stated, 'collected out of divers forrain authors, ancient and modern, and rectified and supplied, according to the present practice of the Low Country Warres'. John Cruso was a translator of European military books and an amateur military writer, not a professional soldier, but he was well read in the leading European military texts of the day, including Giorgio Basta's *Il governo della cavalleria leggiera* (Venetia, 1612), Ludovico Melzo's *Regole militari sopra il governo e servitio particolare della cavalleria* (Anversa, 1611) and the writings of the prolific military author Johann Jacobi von Walhausen; Cruso's work is actually a very useful manual with chapters on most of the practical aspects of cavalry service. Cruso records in his introduction that his text was reviewed by an officer then in Dutch service who 'during the short discontinuance from his regiment, while it lay in winter garrison, hath been courteously pleased to go through it, correcting what here and there was amisse'.

John Cruso's book was written for the education of Militia cavalry officers in England, and he commented in his introduction that 'the defects of our trained bands of horse, will argue the work neither unecessarie nor unseasonable', a polite way of saying that the current state of English Militia cavalry in 1632 was appallingly bad. This was the manual which would be most commonly used by the amateur officers on both sides of the English Civil War and, in common with many pre-war military books, it was reprinted during the Civil War, in 1644. Its main weakness, however, was that the tactical use of cavalry changed significantly during the 1630s, with increasing use of lighter armed cavalry to replace cuirassiers as the main battle cavalry in west European warfare, and greater emphasis on the use of the sword rather than the pistol.

Cruso divided cavalry into four types, plus the mounted infantry called dragoons (these will be covered under a separate heading later in this chapter, and the descriptions in this section relate only to cavalrymen). Cruso's four types were (1) lancers, (2) cuirassiers, (3) arquebusiers and (4) carbines, the first two being heavily armoured battlefield cavalry and the latter two more lightly armoured and intended, in the Dutch army, for a supporting role on the battlefield.

Cruso included heavy cavalry lancers in his manual for the sake of completeness but by 1632 only an occasional general's lifeguard would be equipped in this way in western Europe, and the author himself comments that 'the use of the lance be now left off in the Low-countreys', giving three reasons: 'first by reason of their horses, which must be very good, and exceeding well-exercised: secondly, by reason their pay was abated through scarcity of money: thirdly, and principally, because of the scarcitie of such as were practised and excercised to use the lance, it being a thing of much labour and industry to learn'.

The second cavalry type, the cuirassier, was also a heavy cavalryman and was armoured from head to knee, with the lower leg protected by leather cavalry boots. This was the main battle cavalryman of the Dutch army and in those European armies during the Thirty Years War who could afford the cost of equipping them. The Dutch, with their concentration on siege warfare and manoeuvre, had a relatively small cavalry component in their armies and they could afford expensive equipment. At the battle of Nieuwpoort in 1600, Prince Maurice's Dutch army had consisted of around 10,000 infantry but only some 1,300 cavalry. But the wars in Germany, particularly after Gustavus Adolphus became involved in 1630, were fought over far greater distances with larger armies and with a much higher ratio of cavalry to infantry. By the later stages of the Thirty Years War there were often equal numbers of infantry and cavalry in Swedish and Imperial armies, and sometimes more cavalry than infantry. For example, at the second battle of Breitenfeld in 1642, the Swedish army had approximately equal numbers of cavalry and infantry at 10,000 of each, and the opposing Imperial army has been estimated at around 10,000 infantry and 16,000 cavalry. In combat, cuirassiers retained an advantage over more lightly armed cavalry and they remained the most effective battlefield cavalry of the day. However, warfare over long distances made the weight of full cuirassier armour a burden which exhausted both cavalrymen and their horses, and the greater cost of cuirassier equipment, and horses strong enough to carry it, meant cuirassiers were more expensive than lighter armed cavalry, as well as being of less overall use on campaign.

The full cuirassier equipment described by Cruso consisted of:

> a close casque or head-piece, gorget, breast, pistol proof (as all the cuirasse in every piece of it) and calliver proof (by addition of the placate) the back, pouldrons, vanbraces, 2 gauntlets, tasses, culets or guard de rein, all fitting to his bodie: A good sword (which was to be very stiffe, cutting and sharp-pointed) with girdle and hangers, so fastened to his cuirasse that he might readily draw it: a buff coat with long skirts to wear between his armour and his clothes.

Cuirassier. Charles I in cuirassier armour from the frontispiece of Robert Ward's Anima'dversions of Warre, which he dedicated to his King.

A cuirassier should also have 'two cases with good firelocks, pistols hanging at his saddle, having the barrel of 18 inches long and the bore of 20 bullets to the pound (or 24 rowling in)', and 'his saddle and bit must be strong, and made after the best manner ... he is to have his bridle made with a chain to prevent cutting'. The Parliament officer John Vernon, whose book *The Young Horseman, or, The Honest Plain-dealing Cavalier* was published in London in 1644, repeated this list of equipment and added the requirement for 'a good poleaxe', a more effective weapon than a sword for combat with another armoured cavalryman as it can be used either to punch through armour or to break the bones of the man wearing it. Both John Cruso and John Vernon recommend a horse of 'fifteen hands high' for a cuirassier.

In England the nominal Trained Bands requirement of several counties included cuirassiers, and the summons by King Charles required a number of gentlemen to serve in the First Bishops' War 'as a cuirassier in russett armes [armour], with gilded studds or nayles, and befittingly horsed'. However, the county Trained Bands were notoriously poorly equipped, so it is debatable just how much complete cuirassier armour there was in England, and many of the gentlemen summoned by the King are more likely to have served in lighter arquebusier armour. Sir Edmund Verney certainly did, writing that he was 'resolved to use nothing but back, brest and gauntlet [bridle gauntlet worn on the left forearm]; if I had a pott for the Hedd that were Pistoll proofe it maye bee I would use it if it were light'.[24] Apart from the cost and inconvenience of wearing heavy cuirassier armour, another factor was simply the difficulty in obtaining it quickly: an indication of the comparative time to manufacture cuirassier armour can be seen in the response of the City of London Armourers company on 19 November 1638 that they could manufacture each month 'either 800 footmen's armours, 80 cuirassiers or 400 arquebusiers'.[25]

During the Civil Wars some individual cavalry officers wore cuirassier armour, but the only formed units of cuirassiers served with the army of Parliament. These were three lifeguard troops of the Earl of Essex, commander of the Parliamentary army; the Earl of Bedford, General of the Horse; and Sir William Balfour, Lieutenant General of the Horse – the only full cuirassier regiment to fight in the Civil War was Sir Arthur Haselrig's 'Lobsters'. The superior equipment of these troopers did have an impact in the early stages of the Civil War. The three lifeguard troops played an important role in the drawn battle of Edgehill in 1642, and the Royalist Earl of Clarendon wrote of Haselrig's regiment that:

> [they] were so prodigiously armed that they were called by the other side the regiment of lobsters, because of their bright iron shells with which they were covered, being perfect cuirassiers; and were the first seen so armed on either side, and the first that made any impression upon the King's horse, who, being unarmed, were not able to bear a shock with them; besides that they were secure from hurts of the sword, which were almost the only weapons the other [Royalist cavalry] were furnished with.[26]

Haselrig's Lobsters were routed when Sir William Waller's Parliamentary army was defeated at the battle of Roundway Down on 13 July 1643; the regiment was recruited back to strength but, having lost most of its cuirassier equipment, it was reformed as an arquebusier regiment. By the end of 1643 the only cuirassier unit still in service was the Earl of Essex's lifeguard. It was recorded as cuirassiers at a muster on 30 February 1644,[27] but it is not clear at what point this last unit was also converted to arquebusiers. The use of cuirassiers was still considered by professional soldiers because of their value as battlefield cavalry, and General George Monk, writing his *Observations upon Military & Political Affairs* around 1645/1647 while a prisoner in the Tower, commented: 'I have omitted to speak any thing of the armour of a good Cuirassier, because there are not many Countries that do afford Horse fit for the Service of Cuirassiers: but where Horses are to be had fit for that Service, there a General ought to have two thousand of them in his army.' However, this was not adopted in practice and no new cuirassier units were formed during the Civil Wars.

King Charles I and his Secretary of War, Sir Edward Walker. This engraving of the famous painting was printed with the 1705 edition of Walker's Historical Discourses. It shows that the usual campaigning dress for the King, and presumably his senior officers, was the arquebusier equipment of back and breast plates worn over a buff coat, rather than cuirassier armour.

The third and fourth cavalry types listed by John Cruso were described as 'Harquebusier' and 'Carabine', the distinction between the two being, in theory, the amount of defensive armour worn and the bore of the firearm carried. Both terms relate to the cavalryman's firearm carried by the trooper, and their use as a classification is an indication of the fire support role for which these cavalrymen had originally been raised. Although the terms Cruso used in 1632 were certainly technically correct, and cavalrymen in the county Trained Bands are listed distinctly under the separate descriptions of 'Harquebusiers' and 'Carabines' before the Civil War, this distinction had become meaningless by 1642. The terms were still used during the Civil War: for example, the Earl of Essex's guards included a troop of fifty 'Carbines', and musters of the Earl of Essex's cavalry often list the troopers as 'harquebusiers', but by this time the terms 'harquebusier' or arquebusier and 'carabine' or carbine were used to describe the same type of cavalrymen, and the more general term 'Horse' was usual.

According to John Vernon, writing in 1644, the equipment for the

> Harquebusiers and Carbines is chiefly offensive, his defensive Arms, are only an open Caske or Head-peece, a back and brest with a buff coat under his armes [armour]; his offensive Armes are a good Harquebusse, or a Carbine hanging on his right side in a belt by a sweble [swivel], a flask and Carthareg case, spanner, and to [two] good firelock pistols in houlsters. At his saddle a good stiffe sword sharp pointed, and a good poll-axe in his hand, a good tall horse of fifteen handfuls high, strong and nimble, with false reines to your bridle made of an Iron Chain.

General George Monk set out his recommendations for the standard as 'A Head-piece with three small iron bars to defend the Face, Back, and Breast; all three Pistol-proof: a Gauntlet for his left hand or a good long Buff Glove. A Girdle of double Buff about eight inches broad, which is to be worn under the skirts of his Doublet, and is to be hooked unto his Doublet.'

John Vernon's description was the optimum, and George Monk's 'buff girdle' referred to a particular invention of his own intended to provide a light and cheap defence for the thighs. Monk's description of the cavalry helmet as 'a Head-piece with three small iron bars to defend the Face' is particularly interesting, as it refers to the three-barred cavalry helmet which was manufactured in England and sometimes described as an English helmet, to distinguish it from the single-barred zischagge style imported from the Netherlands. Although some troops are recorded as having been equipped to John Vernon's standard, many were not. Looking back on the Civil Wars, the military writer J.B., whose manual *Some Brief Instructions for the Exercising of the Horse-Troopes*[28] was published in 1661, wrote of 'many Troopes and Regiments, only with Sword and Pistol armed', and as late as 1644 a Royalist cavalryman could pass muster according to the Oxford *Articles of War* published that year if he was armed only with a sword.

The mass of surviving contemporary accounts and records provide evidence of wide variations in cavalry equipment throughout the Civil Wars, with some soldiers wearing old-fashioned armour modified for modern war, and others using civilian 'pocket-pistols' as they had nothing else; some having no defence except a buff leather coat, and others with neither buff coat nor armour. Practical commanders tended to make the best arrangements they could, putting the best armed men in the front rank. The main marching armies, both Parliamentary and Royalist, were better equipped than those serving in smaller local wars, as the main armies were preferred when it came to issuing equipment. Scottish cavalry wore helmets but few would have had any other armour; they did have a particular preference for firearms, some being observed in 1639 'with five shot, with a carbine in his hand, two pistols by his sides [possibly shoved in his boots] and other two by his saddle'.[29] A proportion of Scottish cavalry was equipped with lances both in England and in Ireland. These were light lances, not the heavy lances used by the heavily armed lancer described by John Cruso; the military writer J.B. referred to 'some few that the Duke of Hamilton had when he invaded England in 1648, but their lances were but half-pikes [meaning they were shorter and lighter than the lance of the heavy cavalry lancer], and their Defensive Armes very mean'. All the Scottish cavalry levied in 1650 were to be equipped as lancers. In Ireland the Confederate cavalry experienced difficulties in obtaining cavalry armour and found themselves at a disadvantage as a result. In response to the Earl of Castlehaven's rousing speech asking his troopers 'what would you give to come to a day's work with the enemy', his men answered that 'they would be glad of it, if their doublets and skins could be made proof against the lances of the Scots'. Faced with this less than enthusiastic response, Castlehaven then took steps to find enough armour to equip the two front ranks of his cavalry.

By the time the New Model Army was formed in 1645, the Parliament had managed to solve most of its arms supply problems and most New Model cavalry troopers were probably equipped with an English three-barred helmet, back and breast armour worn over a buff coat, sword with a baldric to hang it from, two short barrelled pistols (with barrels of 14 or 15 inches) with 'English lock' flintlock mechanisms, a powder flask and a metal cartridge box containing paper cartridges (the lead balls were carried separately). The extent to which New Model cavalry troopers carried carbines remains unclear. Surviving contracts for the New Model Army include carbines, but not very many. This may be because the New Model cavalry had been recruited almost entirely from veteran cavalry troopers who would still have had most of their equipment while the infantry regiments had to be brought up to strength with newly conscripted men, or it may be an indication that only a few troopers in any troop were issued with carbines.

Additional equipment which may have been used by individual troopers was an iron bridle gauntlet worn on the left hand and forearm, to protect against cuts from opposing cavalrymen, and a poleaxe, a weapon like a hammer with a spike on one side of the head and a small axe or a hammer head on the other.

Another weapon which may have been issued to a small number of cavalrymen in a troop was the blunderbuss, essentially a short barrelled gun 'of a great bore, wherein they may put several Pistol or Carabine-Balls, or small slugs of Iron'. Sir James Turner believed 'the word is corrupted, for I guess it is a German term, and should be Donnerbuchs, and that is, Thundering Guns; Donner signifying Thunder, and Buchs a Gun'.[30] The Leveller mutineer William Thompson may have been killed with a weapon of this type, as the contemporary account recorded that 'Major Butler's corporal had Colonel Reynolds his carbine, which being charged with 7 bullets gave Thompson his death's wound'.[31] Although the blunderbuss was carried by only a minority of cavalry troopers, possibly, as the Earl of Orrery recommended, for use by a few men in the front rank,[32] there is evidence that New Model Army cavalry troopers used them, as 265 were repaired for the Board of Ordnance in 1654.[33]

The cost of cavalry equipment varied according to the supply and the urgency of demand. The accounts of Captain Lionel Copley, an officer in the Earl of Essex's regiment, show that he raised seventy-two troopers in 1642 and equipped each man with armour consisting of helmet, back and breast at a cost of 24s a set, a pair of pistols at 30s, and saddle and tack at 20s. The horses cost between £10 and £12, and he also issued twenty of his seventy-two troops with carbines at 25s each.[34] Arms contracts for the New Model Army show that in 1645 the cost of cavalry equipment was armour consisting of 'backs, breasts and potts [helmets]' at 20s a set, pistols with holsters were purchased for 26s a pair and for 20s 4d a pair, saddles and tack at 16s or 16s 6d and carbines at 12s 9d, plus a further 8d for the belts to hang them from.

Many cavalry troopers, probably most in the New Model Army, wore their armour over buff coats, and the association of these coats and cavalry troopers was strong enough for the term 'Buffe-Coate'[35] to be used in the record of the meeting of the mutinous army at Putney in October 1647 to refer to an unnamed cavalry trooper putting the case for his fellow soldiers. However, entries relating to the issue of buff coats are as rare as the issue of clothing to cavalrymen and its possible that this was an item troopers would buy privately. An officer's buff coat was expensive, but surviving accounts show that an ordinary trooper's buff coat cost between 30 and 40s: Joseph Vaughn, a leather seller, provided fifty-three buff coats at 38s each for a troop of Parliamentary cavalry in 1642, and Lieutenant Colonel Thorpe receiving three buff coats for 30s each.[36]

There are occasional references to light horse in English military books and Trained Band records in the years before the English Civil Wars, but these refer to arquebusiers or carbines, and the term is used to draw the distinction that they were lighter armed cavalry than cuirassiers. There were units of true light cavalrymen serving in the Imperialist and Swedish armies – Croatians, Hungarians and the Polish Lisowski Cossacks with the Imperialists, and Finnish 'Hakkapelites' or 'Hackapels' with the Swedes. Although these were useful soldiers for scouting, raiding, marauding and particularly, as the Imperialist General Raimondo Montecuccoli wrote, 'for pursuing the foe when he is in flight rather than for the act of routing him', they were raised from particular national groups accustomed to light cavalry raiding and warfare. Montecuccoli commented that the 'Hungarians, Croats, and other kinds of persons much employed in the Imperial army' were well suited to this role because of the 'natural lightness and rapidity of the horses used by these nationalities, the character of their saddles, bridles and clothing'.[37] In England, neither the King nor the Parliament was in a position to hire mercenary soldiers from this far away. This was probably just as well, as these light cavalrymen had a terrible but well-deserved reputation for brutality, the term 'Hackapell' used to describe Finnish cavalry being derived from their war cry 'hakkaa paalle', meaning 'hack them down'. The hardbitten Scottish professional soldier Sir James Turner recalled in his memoirs his shock as a young soldier when 'after this battell, I saw a great many killd in cold blood by the Finns, who professe to give no quarter'.[38]

The closest similar type of cavalryman to fight in the English Civil Wars was the Scottish 'Moss-trooper' or 'Mosser'. These were marauders who fought against Cromwell's army in Scotland in 1650 and 1651, and whose activities included both military raids and more generalized highway robbery. Oliver Cromwell was incensed by the Moss-troopers' raids in which 'divers of the army under my command are not only spoiled and robbed, but also sometimes barbarously and inhumanely butchered and slain, by a sort of outlaws and robbers, not under the discipline of any army', and warned those that sheltered them that 'wheresover any under my command shall be hereafter robbed or spoiled by such parties, I will require life for life'.[39] The 'Moss-troopers' were suppressed by taking control of the fortified houses which sheltered them, Cromwell's summons to the Lord Borthwick, governor of Borthwick Castle, requiring the surrender of the castle, including the chilling reminder: 'You have harboured such parties in your house as have basely and inhumanely murdered our men; if you necessitate me to bend my cannon against you, you may expect what I doubt you will not be pleased with.'[40] Borthwick Castle surrendered shortly afterwards. Scottish Moss-troopers were marauders, not battlefield cavalry, although 200 fought as part of the Scottish army at Inverkeithing in July 1651 under their most noted commander, 'Captain Augustin the great Mosse Trooper'.[41]

Infantry
Regiments of infantry were composed of two distinct types of infantrymen throughout most of the seventeenth century, one type armed as pikemen and the other as 'shot', the latter being armed with various types of musket or arquebus. The reason for the distinction was that infantrymen armed with muskets or arquebuses had no effective defence against cavalry. The solution to this problem would ultimately be the invention of the bayonet which effectively allowed a musketeer to turn his musket into a pike to hold off cavalry, but this French invention was adopted by English infantry only after the Restoration of King Charles II. Until the introduction of the bayonet, the

only way infantry could defend themselves against cavalry was the pike, essentially a staff 15 to 18 feet long tipped with a spear point.

The pike was considered to be the more honourable weapon than the arquebus or musket because, as Richard Elton commented in his manual *The Compleat Body of the Art Military*, 'it is so in respect of its antiquity; for their hath been the use of the Pike and the Spear, many hundred years before there was any knowledge of the Musket'.[42] It was also more the sort of weapon that a gentleman could rather use, rather than serving as a powder-stained musketeer. Although this attitude was in decline during the Civil Wars it was still current, and the officers who marched in the Earl of Essex's funeral procession in 1646 chose to do so amongst the ranks of pikemen.

The optimum equipment for a pikeman was a pike, armour consisting of a helmet, back and breast, tassets (thigh defences) and gorget (a collar to defend the throat), and a sword hung from a shoulder-belt or from 'hangers' attached to a waist-belt. The heavy defensive armour had been necessary when the main infantry combat had been hand to hand, described in contemporary accounts as the 'push of pike'. It was certainly true that, when fighting hand to hand, the protection offered by armour gave a real advantage over unarmoured opponents both in terms of practical defence from wounds and in terms of morale, as Sir James Turner indicated with his comment that armour 'encourages those who wear it'. There were two disadvantages. Firstly, armour was no defence against musketry, and recent tests by the Landeszeughaus at Graz in Austria have verified the contemporary comment that musket balls would go straight through armour at 100 yards.[43] Secondly, armour was heavy and it had been common for soldiers to discard the tassets even in Queen Elizabeth's time. While the weight of armour was inconvenient in the Low Countries where war consisted of sieges, it was seen by many officers during the Thirty Years War as a real hindrance as their campaigning was then over far greater distances and armies were often required to move more quickly. Even Sir James Turner reluctantly admitted a common argument amongst some professional officers: 'the long and continuated marches of our Modern Armies, not only for many days, but for many weeks and months, both in the extream heat of Summer, and rainy and tempestuous weather of winter, require that the Souldiers should be eased of the weight and trouble of their Defensive Arms, that with less toyl they may endure and undergo those marches'. However, he went on to say that it was still possible for armoured men to march these distances: if their officers took care to ensure that 'our Souldiers from the time of their first Levy were habituated to wear at their Exercises and Drillings constantly their Armour, and accustom'd twice a week to march a good many miles in Arms ... they would find it then an easie matter to march everie day in Armour, for custom is another nature.'[44]

English infantry had a consistent reputation in Europe as reliable fighting soldiers, good men to storm a breach or defend one, or to fight on the battlefield. The Dutch highly prized their English mercenary regiments and the French were impressed by the aggressive qualities of the New Model Army

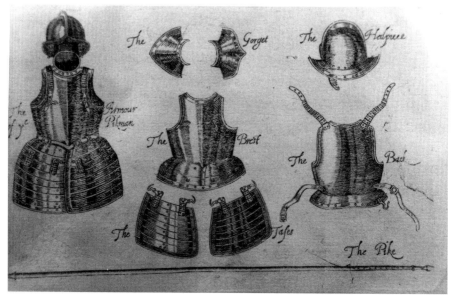

Pikeman's armour. The armour and equipment of a pikeman from John Bingham's The Tactiks of Aelian (London, 1616). Armour was issued to at least some of the infantry in the Parliamentary army of the Earl of Essex, but there is no record of the issue of infantry armour to the New Model Army.

who served alongside them against the Spanish, the French Marshal Turenne commenting that they were 'men of brave resolution and courage'. The net effect of this was that although infantry firepower was becoming increasingly important on the battlefield, English infantry were often aggressive enough to keep advancing under fire until they could fight hand to hand at 'push of pike'. In these circumstances armour was still useful as, although it provided no protection against musket fire, it did provide an advantage in hand to hand fighting against unarmoured infantry. General George Monk writing circa 1645/1646 recommended that pikemen should be armed with 'an Head-piece with Back and Breast' together with his own invention 'a Buff Girdle of double Buff eight inches broad, the which is to be worn under the Skirts of his Doublet instead of Taces [tassets]'. General Monk's practical solution was to retain armour but reduce the amount worn, as his suggestion meant doing without the gorget and tassets.[45]

The extent to which infantry armour was actually used during the Civil Wars remains unclear. In 1642 the military theory used by both Parliamentary and Royalist commanders would have assumed the use of armour for pikemen as many, probably most, officers with a professional background had served in the Dutch army. Orders placed in the Netherlands and France in 1642 on behalf of the Parliament for pikemen's equipment were consistent with this approach, as they specified 6,000 pikes and 6,000 'corslets',[46] and surviving accounts record the issue of armour to at least some of the Earl of Essex's infantry. For the Royalist army, the Earl of Clarendon famously commented in 1642 that 'in the whole army there was not one pikeman had a corslet' (back and breast armour), but he also recorded that the King's army had been compelled 'to borrow the arms from the traine-bands', and this would have included the infantry armour that Trained Band soldiers had to own and show for inspection at musters. So Clarendon's comment is likely to have been an exaggeration meant as a partial excuse for the defeat of the King's infantry at the battle of Edgehill. There is no record of any armour being issued to the English infantry regiments sent to Ireland in 1642. Scottish pikemen were not issued with armour, and it is unlikely that the poorly equipped Irish Confederate infantry were able to make much use of it.

In the New Model Army there was a ratio of one pikeman to two musketeers, but there are no entries in the army's accounts for 1645/1646 for the purchase of new infantry armour. This does not necessarily mean that none was worn by New Model infantry. Veteran soldiers may have continued to wear the armour they had received in the armies which preceded the New Model, and there may have been sufficient already in storage. As noted above, professional officers such as George Monk still saw armour as a necessary part of a pikeman's equipment and would make use of it when they could, possibly only for the first one or two ranks of a battalion. William Lockhart, commanding New Model infantry serving as allies to the French, wrote to John Thurloe on 9 July 1658 to ask 'if his highness [Oliver Cromwell] could spare 12 [or] 1500 corslets for our pikemen, I would accustome them to wear them, when they mount their guards, and at all other reviews: a stand of 500 pickes well armed, with headpiece and corslett, will be a very terrible thing to be seen in these countries'.[47] William Lockhart clearly had similar views to those expressed by Sir James Turner, and Lockhart did receive at least 500 corslets from the armoury in the Tower of London.[48]

The main weapon of a pikeman, the pike itself, consisted of a staff made of ash which was 15 to 18 feet long with a steel head. Beneath the head were two steel strips known as 'langets', about 2 feet long, which were intended to prevent the heads being broken off by pressure in the melee of opposing pikemen or hacked off by attacking cavalrymen. The Earl of Orrery, who had served extensively in Ireland, commented in his military manual that 'I remember we once carried a Fort by storm, because the Enemies Pikes had not those Plates [langets], whereby the Heads of them were cut off'.[49] Military theorists or commanders recommended different lengths for pikes, varying between 15 and 18 feet long, with the proviso that all the pikes in an army were to be the same length. In practice, the length could also vary because, as Sir James warned, 'if Officers be not careful to prevent it, many base soldiers will cut some off the length of that, as I have oft seen it done'. This was certainly the case amongst English pikemen in Ireland, as one of their officers recorded that some of his soldiers would 'cut off a foot, and some two of their pikes, which is a damned thing to be suffered'. The New Model Army accounts for 1645/1646 and later are consistent in showing orders for pikes 16 feet long.

The other weapon carried by all infantrymen was a cheap sword, and George Monk recommended that each infantryman ought to be issued with a 'little

Hatchet for the cutting of Wood for Firing, and Wood for Hutting'.[50] Monk had a low opinion of army-issue swords and recommended the issue of a 'Tuck', a stabbing rather than a cutting sword, on the basis that otherwise 'half the Swords that you have in your Army amongst your common men, will upon the first March be broken with cutting of Boughs'.[51] The cost of a full set of infantry armour was around £1 2s for a helmet, back, breast, tassets and gorget. In the New Model Army accounts, the cost of a pike varied between 3s 10d and 4s 2d, a typical contract being that 'with Elizabeth Thacker widow for five hundred long pikes at ffower shillings two pence p pike ready money to be delivered into the Tower for the use of Sir Thomas ffairfax Army'.[52] Swords and belts cost between 4s 6d and 5s a set.

Musketeers made up two-thirds of an infantry company and most were armed with matchlock muskets. A useful description of the full equipment expected for a musketeer before the Civil War was set out in instructions for the Trained Bands in 1638. This specified 'The Musketier must be armed with a good Musket, (the barrel of 4 foot long, the bore of 12 bullets to the pound rowling in) a [musket] rest, Bandelier, Head-piece, a good Sword, Girdle and Hangers'.[53] The musketeer would also carry a couple of yards of the match-cord used to fire the musket. The bandoleer was a leather belt from which twelve wooden containers were suspended, each container holding sufficient gunpowder for a single shot, together with a priming flask with the finer grade powder used to prime the musket. The number of containers usually corresponded to the size of the musket balls used for a particular gun, so the bandoleer for a musket with a standard bore taking twelve bullets to the pound of lead would have twelve powder containers, but the bandoleer for a lighter 'bastard musket' using smaller musket balls of sixteen bullets to the pound would have sixteen powder containers. The reference 'rowling in' meant that the balls would literally roll down the barrel and would not stick on the way, an important consideration as musket barrels quickly became fouled with powder residue, and if the ball had been a tight fit in a clean barrel it would be much harder to load after the first few shots in battle. The 'Girdle and Hangers' referred to a sword belt worn around the waist and the straps from which a scabbard was hung from the belt. Although not mentioned in these instructions, a musketeer should also carry cleaning tools with a screw thread to attach them to the ram rod for his musket – at the opposite end to the rammer used to ram home powder and ball. The tools were a brush for cleaning powder residue out of the barrel and a screw (shaped like a corkscrew) used for withdrawing the lead musket ball and its paper wadding or 'tampking'[54] if the musket misfired. Very few musketeers would have worn a helmet during the Civil Wars, and there is no indication that any New Model Army musketeers ever did so.

A wide variety of firearms was in use during the war, varying from the latest patterns to some commandeered from county Trained Band arsenals or donated personally by supporters of either side, which must have been antiques. The officer inspecting the arms of the Lincolnshire Trained Bands in

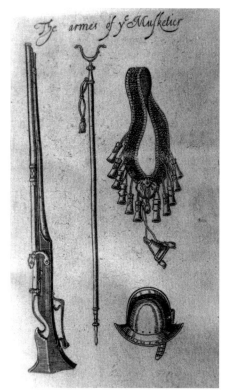

Musketeer equipment from John Bingham's The Tactiks of Aelian (London, 1616). This equipment was being superseded during the late 1630s with the issue of a lighter pattern musket which could be fired without a musket rest. In the 1640s few musketeers would have had helmets. The bandoleers of wooden powder charges remained in use. Bullets were kept separately in the pouch and the small powder flask contained priming powder.

February 1639 reported that he had 'defected' several musketeers (found their arms unacceptable) 'by reason of the weight and length, some weighing 18 or 20 lbs (pounds), for no man is able to do service with them',[55] and there are references during the Civil War to very heavy weapons which are likely to be the same pattern. These were probably the sixteenth-century Spanish type of musket which fired balls of eight to the pound of lead, weighed about 20 pounds and had to be fired from a musket rest. The Lincolnshire examples may have dated from the time of the defence of England against the Spanish Armada in 1588.

A lighter musket was introduced as standard in the Dutch army in 1599 which had a 4 foot barrel and fired musket balls at twelve to the pound, but was still heavy enough to require a musket rest. This was the English standard from the beginning of the seventeenth century to the outbreak of the Civil War, and orders placed by the Parliament in France and Holland in 1642 would have been for this type of weapon, as they specified both musket and musket rests. The weight of these weapons led to the production of lighter muskets, as even the Dutch pattern musket required a strong man to use them. A lighter 'bastard' musket firing sixteen bullets to the pound was introduced, and during the 1630s a streamlined musket was produced which was lighter than the Dutch pattern but still with a barrel 4 feet long and a bore of twelve bullets to the pound: both of these lighter muskets could be fired without the need for a musket rest. Most armies fighting in the Civil Wars made use of whatever equipment they could obtain, with the leading field armies of both sides receiving the most modern arms. The New Model Army accounts for 1645/1646 include orders for a small number of 'bastard muskets' and the ammunition required for them, but the majority are for the lighter full musket pattern with a bore of twelve bullets to the pound of lead but which did not need a musket rest.

Lighter pattern musket. An example of the type of musket used by the New Model Army. This type does not require a musket rest.

The cost of a musket in the New Model accounts varied from 10s to 11s 6d. The bandoleers cost between 14 and 20d each, a typical contract specifying 'the boxes of wood with whole bottoms to be turned within and not boared the heads to be of wood & to be layd in oyle vizt three tymes over & to be coloured blue with blewe and white strings [to attach them to the bandoleer belt] of strong thread twist & wth good belts at xxd [20 pence] a peece'.[56] Musketeers carried the same type of swords as pikemen. Both musketeers and pikemen carried a knapsack or snapsack, and those issued for the New Model Army were to be 'large and of good leather at 8s a dozen'.

The other type of musket in use at this time had a flintlock mechanism, and was usually referred to as a 'firelock' or 'snaphanse'. This was carried by the specialist infantry companies which guarded the train of artillery, on the entirely reasonable grounds that the smouldering match-cord required to fire a matchlock musket and stores of gunpowder do not go together well. Richard Elton summarized this perspective with his comment that these soldiers should 'be Fire-locks, or to have Snap-hances, for the avoiding of the danger which might happen by the Cole [smouldering ends] of the Match'.[57] These companies had no pikemen and consisted entirely of musketeers. The flintlock was seen to have other advantages at this time as it was a better weapon for sentinels and had advantages for service in wet weather or night attacks. The advantage for sentinels was firstly that the light from smouldering match-cord would give away their position and secondly that guards armed with matchlock muskets used up substantial amounts of match-cord every night. One solution to this, used in the city of Stafford during the Civil War, was to issue a limited number of flintlock muskets to each company for them to use when on guard duty, giving as the reason that 'for want of muskets with Firelocks upon the guards in this garrison there hath beene much Match spent'.[58] The Stafford Committee issued '5 firelock muskets' for every 'twenty soldiers they have in there severall companies'. Several companies of firelocks served in Ireland and the New Model accounts for 1645/1646 record orders for 8,050 matchlock muskets and 3,300 'snaphanse' muskets, suggesting that some may have been issued to each infantry company. At the battle of the Dunes, the English infantry included a body of 400 firelocks 'commanded' or drawn out of the infantry regiments. A 'snaphanse' musket for the New Model Army cost 14s 4d.

Dragoons

Dragoons were mounted infantry, specifically mounted musketeers. The practice of mounting infantry armed with arquebuses probably originates with the French Huguenot armies of the late sixteenth century, particularly under Henri of Navarre, but the term 'dragoons' comes from the use of this type of soldier in the Dutch army of Prince Maurice of Nassau. Sir James Turner suggested that 'we may suppose they may borrow their name from Dragon, because a Musketeer on Horse-back, with his burning Match riding at a gallop, as many times he doth, may something resemble that Beast, which Naturalists call a Fiery Dragon'.[59] However, the origin of the word is Dutch and is more pragmatic, as the Dutch word 'tragons' is used to describe mounted infantry. In Prince Maurice's army mounted infantry are described in contemporary Dutch correspondence as 'trachonz oder musqutirer zu pferdt'[60] ('pferdt' meaning horse, i.e., mounted musketeers) or 'tragons'. The English professional soldier Henry Hexham's English/Dutch dictionary shows that the Dutch word 'tragen' translates as 'carry', which suggests that the word 'tragon' was originally used to describe 'carried men', infantrymen carried by any method.

There was some confusion in England and elsewhere during the 1620s and 1630s as to how a dragoon regiment or company should be armed, because one of the leading military theorists and military writers of the day, Johann Jacobi von Walhausen, had recommended that an entire regiment, musketeers and pikemen, should be mounted as dragoons. This was widely copied in English military books, and there is one example during the Civil War of a provincial officer arming his company of dragoons in this way, but Walhausen was describing his personal invention rather than the actual practice of the day. In practice dragoons were mounted musketeers. George Monk described the equipment of a dragoon as:

> A Musquet, or a good Snapance to a Musquet; the which I hold much better for Dragoon-Service, being upon occasion they may be able to make some use of their Snaphances on Horseback, and upon any service in the night they may go undiscovered. He must also have a belt to hang

his Musquet in, with a pair of Bandeliers, and a good long Tuck [sword] with a Belt. And all your Dragoons ought to have Swine-feathers.[61]

In addition a dragoon 'ought to have a good ordinary Horse, Saddle, Snaffle, Rains, Stirrups, and Stirrup-Leathers, an Halter, and two Girts'.[62] The reason for a issuing a dragoon with a flintlock rather than a matchlock firearm was partly the advantages it offered in wet weather or night attacks, but also that burning match-cord and horses are not a happy combination. A dragoon musket usually had a shorter barrel than an infantry musket but fired the same weight of bullet, twelve bullets to the pound of lead. Dragoon horses were of lower quality, and cheaper, than a cavalry trooper's horse. In the New Model Army accounts, dragoon muskets or 'snaphaunce Dragoones' cost 12s 4d, and dragoon saddles cost 7s 6d for 'saddles with furniture'.

Artillery and Baggage Trains

The artillery and baggage trains of an army were separate. The artillery train was the responsibility of the general of the ordnance and the baggage train was the responsibility of the wagon-master general.

The artillery train carried 'all manner of provisions both for Artilerie, Munision and all sortes of Armes, both offensive and defensive'. This included supplies of ammunition for cannon, infantrymen and cavalrymen, as well as the wide range of spare parts for equipment, replacement weapons, specialist

Artillery and Baggage Train. A European illustration of an army's supply train.

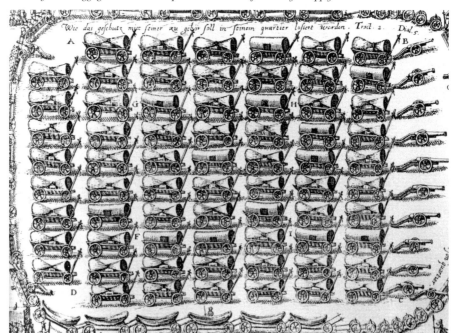

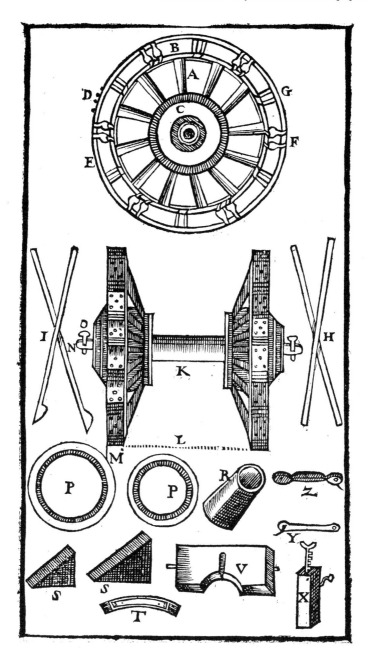

Artillery. The gun carriage. A=spokes; B=Felloes; C=The nave; D=Nails; E=The plates for shoing or tire of the wheels; F=The barres over the felloes to strengthen them; G=The stirrups; H=Leavers or handspikes; I=Crow leavers; K=The axletree; L=The distance between the wheels; M=The rut of the wheels; N=The end of the axletree; O=The lintspin; P=The great and small hoops; R=The bosse of iron for the nave; S=The great and little coins; T=The dowledge of the wheel; V=The sight rule, to be placed upon the base-ring; X=An handscrue; Y=A bar, to be placed over the felloes; Z=A stirrop.

military tools and equipment which any army required. A list of equipment to be held on store, and which would also be required for transport with a marching army, included:

> Quintalls of Cannon-powder and other powder, and Oxe hides to cover and defend the same; Shot of Iron, Leade, and Stone in great quantitie and for all manner of Peeces, Match in great abundance, Iron shovels, Mattocks, Pickaxes, Axes, Hatchets, Hookes, Planks, Boards, Maunds, Baskets, Nailes for Tyers, and all other purposes, Sawes, Sledges, Iron Barres, Crowes, Augers, Engines for all purposes, Chargers, Ladles, Rammers, Spunges, Chaines, Cart-clouts, Weights, all sortes of Smiths tooles, Horse-shoos and Nailes, Cordage, Coffers, Candles, Lanthorns, Ceare-cloathes, Soape, Tarre, soft Grease, Scalling ladders beside a world of other things which are needlesse to recite and yet depend upon the Ordnance.[63]

A good artillery train would also include specialist vehicles such as a smith's wagon, and as George Monk wrote, 'It is very fit a General of the Ordnance should have belonging to his Train some certain number of Boats, or Punts with Carriages to carry them on, for to make a Bridge over unpassable Rivers.'[64] The Earl of Essex had a bridging train when his army was first raised, and used it to make a feint over the River Severn as his army marched back to London after its successful relief of the city of Gloucester in 1643.[65] There are several other examples of the use of boats to make temporary bridges – the Scottish army made at least two temporary bridges over the River Ouse during its siege of York in 1644, and the New Model Army constructed two outside Worcester, but it is not clear in these cases whether these bridges were made using specialist army pontoons or commandeered river boats, or a combination of the two. The Royalist commander Prince Rupert also made use of the 'leather boats' described by Robert Ward as being invented by the Dutch, 'whereby some suddaine and unexpected exploit may be done before the Enemy is aware of it',[66] as there is an entry in the Royalist ordnance papers requiring the governor of Shrewsbury to provide '12 Large Leather Boates, such as the Prince had last yeare'.[67] The Royalist army did make efforts to make use of specialist wagons, as an entry in the ordnance papers for January 1645 indicated. This recorded the requirement for the governors of Exeter, Bristol, Worcester and Bridgewater 'to cause covered wagons to bee made' for the 'Traine of Artillery'.[68]

George Monk also recommended that 'the Waggons that carry your Powder, ought to be planked with thin planks on the sides, and over the top. Then you may have locks set on them, and keep them locked; by which means a Rogue will not be able easily to fire your Powder upon a March'.[69] This was also a sensible precaution against simple carelessness and one which the Royalist General Sir Ralph Hopton must have wished he had paid more attention to. After the battle of Lansdown (5 June 1643), Hopton was 'viewing the prisoners

Bridging train. Several of the armies fighting on both sides during the English Civil War made use of these.

taken, some of which, were carried upon a cart wherein was our ammunition; and (as I heard) had match [i.e. lengths of the smouldering match-cord used to fire a musket] to light their tobacco'. As a result the

> ammunition was blown up, and the prisoners in the cart with it; together with the Lord Hopton, Major Sheldon and Cornet Washnage, who was near the cart on horseback, and several others; it made a very great noise, and darkened the air for a time, and the hurt men made lamentable screeches. As soon as the air was clear, I went to see what the matter as; there I found his Lordship miserably burnt, his horse singed like parched leather.[70]

This was simple carelessness, as contemporary officers were well aware of the danger of bringing smouldering match-cord and gunpowder together. For this reason the specialist infantry companies which had responsibility to guard the artillery train were armed with flintlock muskets and not matchlocks. In part this accident was the result of the ad hoc nature of the artillery train of Sir Ralph Hopton's army.

The baggage train consisted of a variety of vehicles used to carry the army's provisions, together with the regimental baggage and the carts of 'Victuallers, Vianders and Sutlers'. Although European armies did use purpose-built supply wagons, the demand for transport always outstripped the supply, and all types of vehicle were commandeered for moving army supplies. Regimental and other baggage was even more diverse. Francis Markham, commenting on his experience in the Dutch army, referred to the use of 'Horses, Mules, Garrons, Waggons, Carts, Sleads and other implements whatsoever, to carry & convey all the needful Baggage either of Meate, Drinke or Aparrell which any way dependeth upon the Armie'.[71] Wagons and, particularly, carts were often impressed from local farmers, and there were frequent complaints that these were not then returned to their owners.

The New Model Army accounts provide some detail of supplies for both the artillery train and the baggage train. For example, 'Thomas Scinner of Southwarke & John Pitchford of the same' contracted to supply '30 horse harness according to the former Contractes to be brought to the Tower of London as aforesaid & then alsoe Contracted for 22 greate harness at 14s a harness of the wch these must be two thillers harness the body traces 12 pounde weight'.[72] Another entry specifies an order for 400 horse harness at 12s each, with 'every fifth harness to be a thill horse harness'. The reference to the 'thill' provides an indication as to the way some of the horse teams were harnessed. The thills are the two shafts of a cart or wagon or the limber used to pull a cannon, to which the rear horse of a team was harnessed. The remainder of the team, usually four to make a team of five, could be harnessed in front either in single file or in pairs. With a different design of wagon, the team of horses was harnessed in pairs to a central wagon pole, and this type seems to have been more common for military wagons and cannon limbers in European armies. This form of harness was probably used for heavier loads or to pull the heavier field artillery pieces. There are four references to specific contracts for military wagons in the New Model Army accounts, twenty-two 'close wagons' at £13 each (including six for Sir Thomas Fairfax and two for Sergeant-major General Skippon) and eleven 'open wagons' at £12 each.[73]

Chapter Four
Training Methods and Training Manuals

Introduction

The soldiers of any army have always required some training in handling the weapons they use as individuals, and the tactical formations in which they are grouped on the battlefield. As armies become larger and the number of men committed to the battlefield increases, more precise training is necessary as the key success factors become the extent to which soldiers can co-operate in units both offensively and defensively, and the ability of those units to support one another on the battlefield. Essentially, the more complex the tactical formations become, the more training is necessary if they are to work effectively.

The training sequence described below was introduced by the Dutch leader Prince Maurice of Nassau, and was then widely copied by other European armies. Its objective was to train soldiers to be able to fight in formation in a major battle, as the ability to do so was the cornerstone of all military theory and practice at the time. The logic was that for an army to be effective it had to be able to contest a battlefield with its opponents, even if its commander preferred siege warfare and manoeuvre to the risk of battle. Soldiers trained in this way could still use the same principles in smaller actions and simply reproduced them on a smaller scale, so a commander with a small army would still seek to have a number of units, battalions or squadrons in his deployment because that gave him more flexibility. He would simply reduce the number of soldiers in each battalion or squadron.

The weakness of this as a training system was that while it produced soldiers trained to operate on the flat ground which provided enough space for a commander to draw out his men in their battle lines, it did not teach soldiers how to operate in broken or wooded ground, or anything about the tricks needed to survive on campaign, such as foraging for food or building hutments if the army had no tents. This difference between trained soldiers and veteran soldiers is the basis of the comment by one of the Spanish commanders, the Duke of Alva, in the Low Countries: 'one cannot fight any "actions" with other troops – unless it comes to a pitched battle where entire formations are engaged'.[1] The impact of the London Trained Bands provides a good example for the English Civil War as they and their officers had been well trained by professional officers and they were competent in battlefield deployment and tactics, but they were wholly inexperienced when it came to the hardships of campaign or less straightforward actions of warfare.[2] For this the only teacher was experience, and this is one reason why a small army of veteran soldiers was expected to be able to defeat a larger but less experienced force: veteran soldiers survived longer on campaign, were far more versatile and could react quickly when their commanders saw any opportunity.

Training

The leading army of the sixteenth century, the Spanish Army of Flanders, was a well-trained veteran army with an established and evolving military theory. On the battlefield its infantry were formed into a small number of large fighting units. Its opponents, the Dutch army under Prince Maurice of Nassau, were deployed in more complex formations using a larger number of small units deployed in two or three lines. The Dutch military theory, which was copied widely after its success at the battle of Nieuwpoort in 1600, was more flexible but more complex, and required more effort in training the soldiers. The English copied Dutch military theory from the beginning of the seventeenth century and by the 1640s all west European armies had been influenced by the Dutch style and were trained according to the learning curve described below.

The Scottish professional soldier Sir James Turner described this sequence in his military manual *Pallas Armata*, writing that:

> Another part of the Military exercise consists in teaching the Soldiers both of Horse and Foot to fight orderly and readily with an Enemy, and this is that which properly we call Training and Drilling. It consists of two parts, the first is to teach them to handle their offensive Arms (whatsoever they be) handsomely, readily and dexterously, and this is ordinarily called the Postures. The second is to make them, when they are in a Body, to cast themselves in such a figure or order as shall be commanded them, and this is commonly called the Motions and Evolutions.[3]

Overall, it is easier to see this training process as a learning curve with five key points: (1) arms training or weapon handling; (2) recognizing the drum beats or military 'calls' used for basic instructions, such as a call to arms or the order to advance; (3) basic training in ranks and files; (4) unit drill by a battalion of infantry or a troop of horse; and (5) practice sessions in full army deployment of foot, horse and artillery. The most successful armies of the day – such as the Dutch under Prince Maurice and his successors, and the Swedish/German army of King Gustavus Adolphus – rigorously followed this complete training sequence, including full army deployments in the battle formations favoured by their commanders. There were, certainly, armies which were nothing like as well trained as this, but then, they weren't as successful either.

The Learning Curve
The First Stage: Arms Training

Although the principle is the same, there are differences in training infantry and cavalry, and the two will be described separately. There is a difference in the way that they will use their weapons, as infantrymen are intended to use their weapons to fight as a unit, while cavalrymen will also need to be able to use pistol and sword when fighting hand-to-hand in the melee. Apart from this, of course, when training a cavalryman it is necessary to train both the man and his horse.

At the beginning of the seventeenth century, infantrymen were either pikemen or 'shot', the latter consisting of soldiers armed with arquebuses, calivers or the heavier muskets. The English followed the example of the Dutch army and had withdrawn the arquebus and caliver from service by the early 1620s, leaving an infantry unit armed as either pikemen or musketeers. Although also armed with swords, the main weapons of these soldiers in combat were their pikes or muskets. A 16 foot pike is, of course, quite useless as an individual weapon, and the value of firepower with inaccurate smooth-bore firearms lies in firing by volleys, not in individual shots.

The different weapons, pike and musket, offered different problems in terms of training. For the pikeman these principally concerned the difficulties of using a weapon of such length in the close-packed ranks of an infantry battalion, where the advantages of each man making the same move at the same time are obvious. The musketeer had to manage a matchlock musket, lighted match-cord and, for earlier models of musket, a musket rest as well. In each

case repetitive training in a series of movements or 'postures' was the only way to achieve effectiveness in a unit of soldiers.

The detailed sequence of these 'postures' for pike, musket and the lighter firearm the caliver was set out pictorially by the engraver Jacob de Gheyn on the instructions of Johann of Nassau and published as *The Exercise of Armes* in 1607. This was a superior piece of engraving in itself, and was widely imitated by other authors and publishers. The

Sieur de Lostelnau, French musketeer, 1647. From the Sieur de Lostelnau's Le Mareschal de bataille. Note that this musketeer still uses a musket-rest although he is using a much lighter musket. His uniform is the latest French fashion of the day, but was not copied by the New Model Army.

series of illustrations is very precise in illustrating the movements necessary to follow the orders, and this has led some modern writers to assume that the process of firing a musket was very slow, but this is a misunderstanding, and the detail is simply a guide for initial repetitive training. Once trained, musketeers received only three orders for firing – make ready, present and give fire – and experienced soldiers would be able to load and fire twice in a minute. This was specifically understood at the time and was clearly stated within the original text to de Gheyn's manual, which specifies: 'But above all it is to be well considered that which seemes here to require a leasurly and slow proceeding in the apprehension (by reason of the smaleness of the sculpture which could not conveniently be other wise formed) that (I say) must the industrious learner with a diligent practice strive to bringe to a nimble and quicke readiness of action.' The objective of this stage of training was to reach a stage where armed men became more of a danger to their enemies than their friends, as the text to Jacob de Gheyn's manual also indicated that the process was intended to ensure 'in the best fashion and with the most care and providence that he make it appear that it is to offend the enemy without hurting or annoying himself or his fellowe',[4] which must be the eternal hope of training officers throughout the ages.

The first stage of training for a cavalryman required both the rider and the horse to be trained, this being on the simple premise that 'an Officer shall finde it a thing impossible to exercise a troope of horses, unless they be first prepared for that Service'.[5] In this first stage the horse was trained to obey its rider's commands by his voice, legs, whip or spurs, and was taught the basic

movements by riding around a training ground called the 'ring'. By regularly riding the horse around the same course, each horse would be trained in the same way, and should then be able to obey the same instructions from its riders as other horses in the troop, including taking approximately the same number of paces over a given distance of ground.

The horse would also be trained to be familiar with the noise, sounds and images of the battlefield. To accustom a horse to be able to endure:

Jacob de Gheyn, pikeman. The first illustrated drill manual was engraved by him in 1607. This illustration is from the second edition (1608). The large number of illustrations are for use as a training aid.

Gunshot, Drumme, or clattering of armour; or any hideous noyse whatsoever; let your horse goe hard by another horse, or rather betwixt two other horses, that are accustomed to the like noyse, and are not afrayd, and as you ride together cause three or foure Pistols to be discharged, first a good distance off, then neerer hand, according as your horse beginneth to abide them, during which time forget not to make much of him.[6]

In order to accustom horses to bodies of infantry the rider was to 'cause halfe a dozen footemen or more to stand in his way, making a great shouting and noyse, threatening him with their loude voices, against whom you must incourage him to goe forwards', and then have 'the footemen retreate, fayning to runne away'.[7] Without this level of exposure horses would bolt when they first heard gunfire. Many of the men who joined the cavalry during the English Civil War already knew how to ride a horse, but they still needed training if they were to ride with other cavalrymen in a troop. Weapons training was in the use of sword, pistol and carbine from the saddle, but this did not require the same absolute precision as infantry 'postures'.

The Second Stage: Drum Beats and Trumpet Calls
Recruits were taught to recognize a series of tunes or calls, drumbeats for infantry and trumpet calls for cavalry, which acted as signals both in camp and in battle. As William Barriffe wrote: 'our Souldiers being sufficiently instructed in the Postures of such Arms as they carry (or are appointed to use) the next thing they are to learn is the knowledge of the several beats of the Drum'.[8]

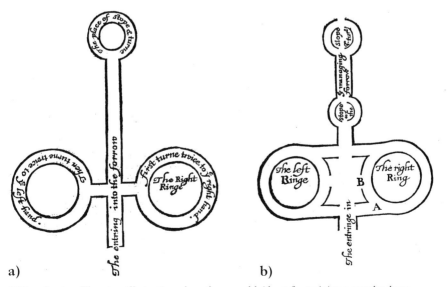

a) b)

Riding the ring. These two illustrations show the ground laid out for training a cavalry horse.

William Barriffe gave the following as the drum beat used for the infantry:

- the call, by which 'you must understand to prepare to hear present Proclamation, or else to repaire to your Ensigne'
- the troop, by which the soldier was to 'understand to shoulder your Musket, to advance your Pike, to close your Ranks and Files to their Order, and to troop along with (or follow) your Officer to the place of Rendezvous, or elsewhere'
- the march, by which 'you are to understand to take your open order in rank, to shoulder both Musket and Pikes, and to direct your March either quicker or slower, according to the beat of the Drum'
- the preparative, which meant the soldier was to 'close to your due distance, for skirmish both in rank and file, and to make ready, that so you may execute upon the first command'
- the 'Battail or Charge', by which the soldier was to 'understand the continuation or pressing forward in order of battaile without lagging behind, rather boldly stepping forward in the place of him that falls dead or wounded before thee'
- the retreat, which signalled 'an orderly retiring backward, either for relief, for advantage of ground, or for some other political end, as to draw the enemy into some ambushment, or such like'.

The most complete description for the cavalry is given by Robert Ward,[9] who set out the following as trumpet calls for the cavalry.

- *Butta Sella*, 'the warning to clappe on the saddles'
- *Moute e Cavallo*, 'the warning for the souldiers to mount upon horse backe'
- *Tucquet*, 'the warning for a March'
- *Carga, Carga*, the 'command for to charge the Enemy'
- *Ala Standardo*, 'a command for to retreate to the Colours'
- *Auquet*, the 'command for the souldiers to repaire to their Watch or Guards, or for the discharging of the Watch or Guards'.

Although they used English names for the drumbeats, the English tended to use foreign orders for the cavalry. These could also be expressed in a bastardized form of French, and John Vernon, whose manual was printed in 1644, referred to the trumpet calls of *Boutezselle* and *Chevall*.

In addition life in camp was punctuated by particular calls in the morning and evening by the beating of *Revallie* and *Taptoo*. Sir James Turner, who spent much of his life in camps and garrisons, recalled that the 'word *Zapzu* or *Taptoo* is High and Low Dutch and signifies, no more drink is to be tapp'd or sold; and is not, as some fancy, to advertise the Guards to place their Night Sentinels but to acquaint Sutlers to serve no more drink, and Souldiers to go home', and that 'it should be beat constantly at one hour Summer and Winter, and ten o'clock at night is a proper time for it'.[10] The morning beat,

Revallie, on the other hand, 'cannot be done at one constant hour (as the *Taptoo*) for in Winter it may be eight, and in Summer three or four in the morning'.

The Third Stage: Basic Training in Ranks and Files (the Five Vowels)

For infantry, this stage was to draw the soldiers together into groups of either musketeers or pikemen for training under the supervision of their sergeants in the basic orders for unit drill. The soldiers would first be formed into files, and then the files would be joined to form the basic subdivision of an infantry company. A 'file', as the name suggests, was 'a sequence of men, standing one behind another',[11] and could be ten, eight or six men deep. The Dutch army used a depth of ten men, and some provincial infantry may still have used this depth at the beginning of the English Civil War. By the 1630s the English were beginning to reduce this to eight: William Barriffe's training manual for the Trained Band officers used eight-man files, and the Earl of Strafford 'in his Instructions for the better Discipline of his Army, order'd every Captain of Foot to draw up his Company eight deep'.[12] However, this was not universal, and both government instructions for the Trained Bands printed in 1638 and Robert Ward's printed in 1639 retained the Dutch depth of ten men. However, Gustavus Adolphus, influenced by the debate in Protestant north Germany at the time, reduced the depth to six for his armies, and his battlefield success led others to copy his example.

At the outbreak of the English Civil War the London Militia and at least part of the Earl of Essex's Parliamentary army were still using a depth of eight, but the Royalist army was strongly influenced by Prince Rupert's admiration for Gustavus Adolphus and used a depth of six men. By 1643 both Royalist and Parliamentary armies were drawn up six deep. Richard Elton, in the second edition of his manual *The Compleat Body of the Art Military*, by which time he was a lieutenant colonel in the New Model Army, described 'Our companies, consisting of one hundred men, two parts being muskettiers and a third Pikes, the depth of our Files being always six deep in the Armies of England, Scotland and Ireland'.[13] The files were combined to form blocks composed of either four, five or six files. In England these blocks were usually called 'divisions' or 'squadrons'. In the Swedish army these blocks were called 'corporalships', and each was composed of either three files or 'rots' of pikemen, or four files of musketeers. A Swedish company had six corporals, where a Dutch or English company had only three, an indication of the greater flexibility the Swedish required at all levels of their battle formations.

The objective of this stage of training was to teach the soldiers the basic orders they would need to understand if they were to follow those given for unit drill in battalions. Barriffe wrote that this stage was the means

> whereby to fit and enable them [the soldiers] to the quicke, true, and
> orderly performance of all formes and figures of Battaile, as may best suit

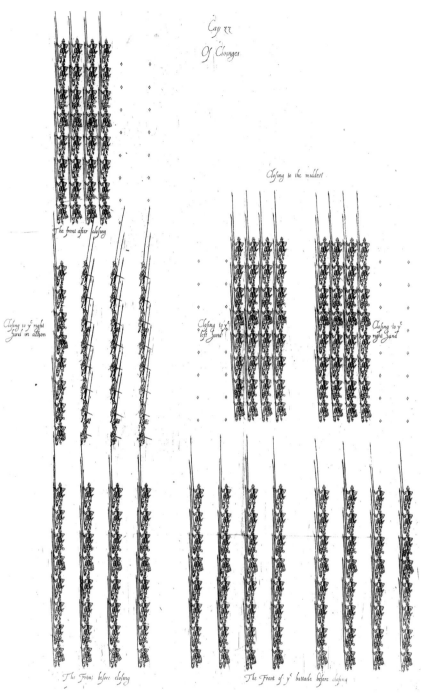

Infantry drill from John Bingham's The Tactiks of Aelian (London, 1616). This shows a division of pikemen changing the distance between files. The three pictures show the pikemen as they stand initially at the bottom; three files facing to their right; then closing the distance to the final order seen at the top.

with the time, number, place, and discretion of the Commander. And may rightly be divided into the these five generall heads (viz.) Distance, Facings, Doublings, Counter-marches and Wheelings, which have (not unaptly) been compared to the five Vowels; for as without one or more of the Vowels, no word can be spelled, so without one or more of these, neither form nor action can be performed.[14]

'Distance' referred to the space between files and files, and between ranks and ranks. For infantry this included the space on which a soldier stood, and there were two key distances, 'Order' and 'Open Order', but the complete sequence, as given by Richard Elton[15] was:

Closest Order	Half a foot (six inches)
Close Order	One foot and a half
Order	Three foot
Open Order	Six foot
Double Distance	Twelve foot
Twice Double Distance	Twenty four foot.

'Facing' was an order to face to the right, to the left or to face about (the equivalent of the modern order to about face). 'Doubling' was to double the number of men *in* a file or a rank, not to double the number *of* files or ranks. There were three countermarches, all derived from classical models, and of all the five vowels Barriffe considered that 'Counter-marches might be best spared of all Motions, as being the least beneficial to this our Modern Discipline'. The fifth and last vowel was 'wheelings', and this was essentially the wheeling of a body of infantry, with the stationary point being either the centre of the body or a point at either end of it, depending on the order given.

Cavalry training at this stage was essentially similar, with John Vernon describing the distance 'betweene Horse and Horse, which is to be six foote at their open order, and three foot at their close order, the distance being taken from the head and tail of the Horses; in the File and the like distance in rank'.[16] There was a difference in the way the frontage required for infantry or cavalry was calculated: this was set out by John Cruso in his manual *Militarie Instructions for the Cavall'rie*, where he wrote, 'here we must observe a difference between the manner of taking the distance of the Cavallrie, and that of the Infanterie: for in the foot, the distance is taken to from the center of the souldiers bodie, which here cannot be so understood, but onely of the space of ground between horse and horse'.[17] As Vernon wrote, after describing how 'Distance' should be calculated, the 'Motions for the Cavalrie are of foure kinds, Facings, Doublings, Countermarchings, and Wheelings',[18] essentially the same as for the infantry. By 1644, when his manual was printed, cavalry would march in files of six but would always fight three deep.

The Fourth Stage: Unit Drill by Battalion of Infantry or Squadron of Cavalry

The basic battlefield unit for infantry was the battalion. This was strictly a battlefield unit and, in this period, was not a formal subdivision of a regiment. It was formed to create units of the strength their general required for his battle lines: he might require a strong regiment to be divided to make two or even three battalions, or he might combine several weak regiments to make a single battalion. The infantry company was not a fighting unit but an administrative one, and it would take several companies, at least, to form a fighting battalion. There would be some continuity as the battalion would be formed of 'divisions' drawn from each company, and men from the same company would serve alongside one another in the same 'division'. Each Dutch battalion was about 500 men strong: Henry Hexham, an English professional soldier who served in the Dutch army, wrote in his manual *The Principles of the Art Militarie; Practised in the Warres of the United Netherlands* that a battalion in the Dutch service was 'accounted to be 500 pikes and Musketteires, that is 25 files of Pikes, and 25 files of Musketeires, or more or lesse of the one or the other as they fall out'. This was also the basis of the model used by the Swedish army, as each of the 'squadrons', four in 1630 but three thereafter, making up a Swedish brigade consisted of 504 men plus officers.[19] The Imperialist German army tended to prefer larger numbers than this for its battlefield units, and at least one New Model Army officer, Colonel Thomas Rainsborough, preferred to draw up his whole regiment in one large body.[20] This said, the battalion system was flexible and could operate successfully on the battlefield with numbers of around 250 to 300 men plus officers, and these numbers were commonly found for an operational unit in small actions during the English Civil War.[21]

Unit drill for an infantry battalion was based on the deployment of a unit which consisted of a centre of pikemen with wings of musketeers on each side. The centre of pikemen was static but there were several variations in the tactics which could be used by the musketeers. While there were drills for the firing by individual files or ranks of musketeers in order to 'amuse' (amaze or puzzle) or keep an enemy's attention, the main objective of these firing systems was to keep up as fast a rate of fire as possible once the enemy reached the optimum killing range of a musket, about 100 to 120 yards. Musket shot will carry and is lethal at longer distances, but this range was seen by contemporaries as the optimum.

There were several different drills for firing by rank, of which the two most commonly types used in the Dutch service were 'firings by two ranks' and firing by 'introduction'. The first of these did not involve firing two ranks together. Instead, the first two ranks of each 'division' of musketeers in the battalion would be advanced ten paces forward, and the first rank would fire while the second 'made ready' (prepared to fire). Once the first rank had fired, its musketeers would face to the right or left (depending on which side of the battalion their 'division' stood) and retire down the intervals between 'divisions' to reload. As soon as the second rank had presented its muskets ready to fire the next two ranks started to march forward ten paces to take their places. An alternative of the same drill was to follow the same process but without advancing any musketeers ten paces in front of the battalion. Fire by introduction was described as a 'passing thorow or between', because after the first musketeer in the file had fired, the others passed him to step forward and fire in turn. This was usually done in 'one of these two wayes. The first, when the Motion is begun by the second rank from the Front. The other, when it is begun by the Bringers-up [the rear rank of the file].' In each case it was necessary to increase the distance between files from 'order' to 'open order' so that there was space for the next rank to pass through, and this increased the unit frontage as well as making the battalion less manoeuvrable.

Different officers had different opinions on which was the best system. The most widely used in Dutch service was the first, but both were practised. An opinion on the second, 'introduction', was given by one officer who wrote, 'I will not dispute how usefull it is; but sure I am, it is over-ballanced with danger'.[22] The Westminster Trained Bands were probably using some form of firing by introduction when making an attack at the siege of Basing House on 12 November 1643, when the sequence got out of the control of their officers and sergeants, and

> whether the fault were in their chiefe Leader, at that present either throgh want of courag or discretion I know not, but their Front fired before it was possible they could doe any execution, and for want of intervals to turn away speedily the second and third wranks, fired upon them, and so consequently the Reare fired upon their owne Front, and slew or wounded many of their owne men.[23]

The Swedish army preferred to use fewer but more powerful volleys and achieved this by two methods. They used the Dutch drill of firing rank by rank but also introduced a variation whereby they fired two ranks together in one volley, and their second method was to fire by 'salvee' either by firing the front three ranks (of six) and then the next three immediately afterwards, or by bringing forward the rear three ranks alongside the front three and having every available fire in one massive volley. Both types were used in the Swedish army, with fire by 'salvee' being 'ordinarie in Battell, before an enemy joyne, or against Horsemen'.[24] Sir James Turner, who had fought in the Thirty Years War, recorded that when this was practised 'by three ranks together' the stance adopted by the musketeers was 'the first kneeling, the second stooping, and the third standing'. He also considered that 'firing by three ranks at a time, should not be practised, but when either the business seems to be desperate, or that the Bodies are so near, that the Pikemen are almost come to push of Pike, and then no other use can be made of the Musquet but of the Butt-end of it'. Turner also considered than if firing by three ranks was to be used than it was preferable to use the second version in which every musketeer in the battalion would fire in one single 'salvee', on the basis that 'thereby you pour as much

```
                                              * * * * *   * * * * *
                                              MMMMM     MMMMM
                                                 M             M
                                                 M             M
  MMMMM   MMMMM                                  M             M
  MMMMM   MMMMM                                  M             M
  MMMMM   MMMMM                                  M             M
  MMMMM   MMMMM
  MMMMM   MMMMM                               * * * * *   * * * * *
  MMMMM   MMMMM                               * * * * *   * * * * *
  MMMMM   MMMMM                               MMMMM     MMMMM
  MMMMM   MMMMM                               MMMMM     MMMMM
  MMMMM   MMMMM                               MMMMM     MMMMM
  MMMMM   MMMMM                               MMMMM     MMMMM
                                              MMMMM     MMMMM
                                              MMMMM     MMMMM
                                              MMMMM     MMMMM
                                              MMMMM     MMMMM
```

Firing rank by rank. Two of the divisions into which any body of musketeers would be divided. In this case each division consists of five files on ten men. The first shows the formation as it stands and the second shows the practice of sending out two ranks in advance. The first rank has just fired and is retiring down the interval between divisions. When it reaches the rear of its division it will reload.

lead in your enemies bosom at one time as you do the other way at two several times, and thereby do them more mischief'.[25] The Royalist army certainly followed this pattern at Naseby, where the account by the Royalist Sir Edward Walker recorded that 'The Foot on either side hardly saw each other until they were within Carabine Shot, and so only made one Volley; ours falling in with Sword and butt end of the Musquet did notable Execution, so much as I saw their Colours fall, and their Foot in great Disorder.'[26]

At the beginning of the English Civil War most English officers were familiar with the Dutch military system and would have trained their men to follow it. But the more innovative professional officers, even those whose only European service was in the Dutch army, were well aware of the Swedish 'salvee' system and would have included it in their training exercises. An example of this is George Monk, an officer whose experience had been in Dutch and English armies, but whose manual *Observations upon Military & Political Affairs* refers to firing systems based on both the Dutch and the Swedish practice. Monk, who wrote his book while imprisoned in the Tower of London following his capture at the battle of Nantwich (20 January 1644), described unit deployments which included instructions for 'two ranks of Musqueteers to give fire at one time',[27] and an alternative method of firing when formed up three deep whereby the first two ranks fired, one kneeling and the other standing; the seconds then knelt also and the third stepped forward and fired.[28] The Royalist army was more likely to be influenced by the Swedish 'salvee' styles of firing in the early stages, and it was certainly suited to Prince Rupert's aggressive tactical style, but Parliamentary infantry were using it by 1644. The practice of the New Model Army is described by Richard Elton in the second and third editions of his book *The Compleat Body of the Art Military*, by which time he was an officer in the New Model Army: 'We usually fire in the Front sometimes in two ranks standing, the rest passing through by turns; then standing after they have gained the ground before their Leaders, do fire', and 'other times three ranks fire together; the first kneels down, the second stoops, the third stands upright'.[29]

The use of cavalry troops was more flexible. While troops could be used as independent units for small actions, they would be combined for a battle into 'squadrons' composed of several troops. As with the infantry battalion, the squadron was not a permanent formation, and the general's main interest was in the size of his units. There was some debate amongst cavalry officers at this time as to whether the most effective use of cavalry was in large squadrons or in a larger number of small squadrons, and the general of the army would decide which option would be used. The Dutch practice, which most English officers would have been more familiar with, was to deploy several squadrons of seventy to eighty troopers alongside one another in groups of three or four using a depth of five. According to the Imperialist General Raimondo Montecuccoli, Swedish cavalry were usually deployed to fight three deep in squadrons of 200 to 300 strong, while cavalry in the Imperial army were deployed in squadrons of about the same size but four or five deep. At the outbreak of the English Civil War, the main Royalist army followed the Swedish practice and deployed three deep, while their Parliamentary opponents retained the pre-war practice and deployed six deep until late 1643 or early 1644. By 1644 the cavalry in the main armies of both sides deployed

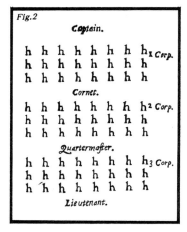

Cavalry training. Fig. 1 shows a troop of cavalry marching as they would 'through a Town or highway'. They are marching six deep and are divided into three squadrons. Fig. 2 shows the same three squadrons as they march, three deep, for 'exercise' or combat. From this formation they would deploy to fight with all three squadrons, in a single line, one beside the other.

their cavalry three deep, although it is possible that some provincial forces still retained the older Dutch style beyond this date. Most of the New Model Army cavalry was deployed at the battle of Naseby in squadrons of three troops, giving a strength of about 300 troopers and officers.

The Fifth Stage: Practice in Army Deployment, the 'Formes of Battle'
The fifth and final stage of training was full arm deployment, and the leading commanders of the day, such as Prince Maurice of Nassau and Gustavus Adolphus, certainly used this. Prince Maurice took particular care over this form of practice both at formal parades or reviews and while his army was on the march. The best documented example in English is his campaign in 1610 in Julich: his army was fully deployed on several occasions during the march there and, following the successful conclusion of the campaign, was deployed in battle formation as a demonstration. This was an essential stage in army training for soldiers, regimental officers and senior offices, as their general's tactical ideas could only be used effectively if his soldiers were able to carry them out. With a veteran army of experienced officers and men, a general could be more flexible in his approach as he could be confident that his officers could be relied upon to interpret more general instructions according to the nature of the ground and the quality of the opponent in front of them.

The bridge between the battalions of infantry and squadrons of cavalry formed in the second stage and the full army deployment of the fifth is the brigade. This was not a permanent formation and was usually formed as either an infantry brigade or a cavalry brigade, with the senior colonel, by the date of his commission, as the brigade commander. Senior officers down to, at least, brigade commander would receive a copy of their general's battle plan – which would show the place of their respective commands within the overall deployment – and the technical responsibility of seeing the units were in the right position would be the responsibility of the 'Major of the Brigade'. The term brigade was also used more loosely to refer to any group of units, which could include both cavalry and infantry in the same brigade, under a subordinate commander.

Training Manuals
Several armies produced training manuals, either manuscript or in print, prior to the army reforms of Prince Maurice of Nassau, and the English would have used training models based on Spanish practice as they made preparations to resist the Spanish Armada. However, Maurice's reforms had far more uniform requirements for his battle formations, and uniformity required much more detailed training manuals. The Dutch army was multinational and included English, Scottish, French and German national regiments as well as Dutch soldiers, so its operational training manuals had to be produced in a variety of languages. One effect of this was to make the adoption of Maurice's military reforms outside the Low Countries much easier, as the key texts already existed in other languages. The earliest versions in England were circulated as

Richard Elton. An officer with a similar background to William Barriffe, Elton was a member of the Military Company in Westminster and was sergeant major in the White Auxiliaries of the City of London. After the First Civil War he joined the New Model Army, becoming a lieutenant colonel. His manual The Compleat Body of the Art Military was published while he served in the militia and is in the same style as William Barriffe's but expanded to include regimental formations.

manuscript copies of the Dutch, and at least one of the most influential was known by the name of its author but never printed. Printed versions of the Dutch practice followed both as a commercial venture and in 1623 in the form of the government manual *Instructions for Musters and Armes and the Use Thereof*, and these were fairly straightforward.

While government efforts to revitalize the Trained Bands met with indifferent success, the voluntary companies in London and elsewhere created a great deal of enthusiasm for military training and displays based on military exercises. This created a market for military books in itself, and any of the booksellers and printers involved in these books were members of the leading voluntary company, the Society of the Artillery Garden. This had a particular effect on the contents of the most popular military books, as their audience was interested in a book which included the basics of military training but which could also be used as a basis for the more elaborate deployments they used purely for display. For this reason books such as William Barriffe's *Militarie Discipline, or, The Young Artilleryman* and Richard Elton's *The Compleat Body of the Art Military* are useful guides to the basics of contemporary practice,[30] as it was necessary to learn the same basics for actual army practice as well as Militia displays, but they also include formations which would never be used on a battlefield. Ironically, Richard Elton made precisely this point in the addendum to the second and third editions of his book. When Elton's book was first published he was essentially a Militia officer, a member of the voluntary Military Company of Westminster and a sergeant major of the White Auxiliaries of the City of London, but by the time a second edition was issued in 1659 he was a lieutenant colonel in the New Model Army. In his addendum to this edition Elton gave more practical advice and wrote: 'My advice is that on their days of publick Meeting, they would have chiefly before their eyes the main Grounds and Principles in the Art of War, which (through permission) I am perswaded, would cause greater appearances, and make their Ground to flourish more than ever.' He went on to say that 'because the Ambition of some doth strive to aime at higher things in their thoughts then what is practiced abroad, I have thought good to set down the plain way of exercising a Company, as usually it is practiced in the Army'.[31] This brief addendum, consisting of four pages, is the most useful record which survives of the practice of the New Model Army in its training.

Chapter Five

Pay, Rations and Free Quarter

Introduction

These three subjects, pay, rations and free-quartering, were inescapably connected in the minds of professional officers of this period. Sir James Turner, who gives the most complete description of them in his book *Pallas Armata*, includes all three in the same chapter and sets out the connections between them. The starting point is simply that war was the most expensive activity a seventeenth-century ruler, whether emperor, king or prince, could undertake. 'At first view', wrote Turner:

> it would seem strange, why Princes pay their Souldiery very well and duly in the time of Peace, when they have little or nothing to do with them, and very ill and very seldome in the time of War, when they have most to do with them. But the reason is soon found, they need greater numbers in time of War than Peace, and many are not paid with so little money as a few are.[1]

Large armies were hugely expensive and incurred the cost not only of paying, equipping and feeding the soldiers, but also of the artillery train, the purchase of arms and ammunition, and both specialist supplies and those simpler everyday essentials, such as horseshoes, which were constantly required. The cost of an army's train was famously described by the Earl of Clarendon in his *History of the Rebellion*,[2] writing that the train of artillery was 'a spunge that can never be filled or satisfied'. The net effect was that there was never enough money to pay the soldiers the wages promised by the recruiting sergeants. As Turner commented, 'being that most men who follow the Wars over all the World, receive wages, they justly deserve the name of Mercenaries; but if you will consider how their wages are paid, I suppose, you will rather think them Voluntaries, at least very generous, for doing the greater part of their service for nothing'.[3]

However, if a commander could not pay his men he must, at least, make efforts to feed them, or some will desert and the others will be too weakened or mutinous to be effective. His objective was, after all, to keep his army in the

Soldiers and brigands. An engraving by Jacques Callot from the series Les Bohemiens showing soldiers in company with wandering beggars – a popular perspective that unpaid soldiers were as bad as brigands, just more numerous and better armed.

field, and to do this he must feed men and horses – both cavalry horses and those required for the artillery and baggage trains. If a commander lacked the money or the credit to purchase and transport supplies in bulk, then his only option was to feed his men by quartering them on the surrounding countryside, and paying for this not by cash but by issuing 'tickets' in lieu of payment. These would be redeemed at a later date on presentation to the army treasurer. This practice, widely practised in Europe, was known as 'free Quarter which Princes and their Generals are many times forc'd for want of money to grant where they can Quarter their Armies in Towns and Villages, and this proves oft the destruction of a Country'.[4] The quartering was not free in the sense that no payment would be made, but was so called because no immediate payment was necessary. This was a vicious practice, easily and frequently subject to abuse, but it did work in the sense that it provided a means for a commander to keep his army operational.

In theory, regulations governed the requirements which soldiers could make of a householder, but in practice armed men could ignore the regulations. In European armies, as Sir James Turner commented, when 'any of their Generals be enabled to quarter his Army in a plentiful Countrey, and there it is, where the common Souldiers may put themselves in Clothes, the Officers in good equippage, and the Colonels make themselves rich'.[5] In practice, free quarter was used, in the English Civil Wars as well as in Europe, as an excuse for general plundering from the population of anything the soldier felt that he required.

Pay

Military opinion in the seventeenth century considered 'it may easily be discerned, that the best Means that can be used to cause the Souldiers to observe good Orders and Discipline, is to give them their promised pay in some competent measure, and due time'.[6] The same perspective can be found expressed by diplomats: for example, the English diplomat Dudley Carleton, writing from The Hague in March 1622 to his friend John Chamberlain in England, commented that the army being assembled by Count Ernst von Mansfeld and Duke Christian of Brunswick would have a large number of men, 'but how they can be well paid or disciplined without pay, I must confess I see not'.[7] But the problem remained that few governments could find the money to pay their soldiers in full, and the officers themselves often reduced the amount that was received by various forms of corruption. This was not a new problem in the seventeenth century, and English soldiers serving Queen Elizabeth in the 1590s had a very similar experience. Their solution, on some occasions at least, was to refuse to march out on a new campaign without receiving at least part of their arrears of pay.

Commanders in the English Civil War faced similar problems, and it was general practice to encourage unpaid soldiers to march out on some special service by providing them with, at least, some cash in hand out of their arrears. The Earl of Essex, before his army marched on its great expedition in August 1643 to relieve the siege of Gloucester, provided his soldiers with 'one fortnights' pay at Colebrook (being much in arere) they were content to march against all those difficulties and expose themselves in that long expedition, not only against the sword of an enemy too strong in probability for their encounter, but to another enemy too strong for mankind to resist, famine'.[8] A later example can be seen from a letter by Sir Samuel Luke, governor of Newport Pagnell for the Parliament, when he wrote in May 1645, 'having received orders from the Committee of both Kingdoms for sending 300 foot towards Oxford, you know it will be impossible to get them forward without money and clearing their arrears'.[9]

While the war was in progress, governments had an incentive to provide some pay and make promises for the balance, but once the war was over their main interest was to disband their armies as cheaply as possible. This was the practice in the wars in Europe where Princes 'give their Officers a little satisfaction-money (for so it was called) in lieu of all their Arrears, when they disbanded them'.[10] The Parliament chose to follow the example of European practice when it sought to disband its armies without paying sufficient attention to its soldiers' demands for their arrears of pay.

There were some local variations in the pay of both officers and soldiers, as some local commanders sometimes offered better rates, but the table (pp. 98–99) sets out the pay scales of the main Parliamentary armies during the

Daily rates of pay

	Pounds	Shillings	Pence
Infantry			
Staff			
Colonel (as colonel)	1	10	
Colonel (as captain of his own company)		15	
Lieutenant colonel (as lieutenant colonel)		15	
Lieutenant colonel (as captain of his own company)		15	
Sergeant major (as sergeant major)		9	
Sergeant major (as captain of his own company)		15	
Preacher		8	
Quartermaster		5	
Provost marshal		5	
Chirurgeon (surgeon)		4	
Wagon-master (or carriage master)		3	
Chirurgeon's mate		2	6
Drum major		1	6
Company			
Captain		15	
Lieutenant		4	
Ensign		3	
Sergeant		1	6
Corporal		1	
Gentleman at arms, or gentleman of the arms (this officer was often paid at 1s not 1s 6d)		1	6
Drummer		1	
Clerk		1	
Private soldier			8
Cavalry (including officers' allowances for extra horses)			
Staff			
Colonel (as colonel)	1	10	
Colonel (as captain of his troop)	1	4	
Colonel (for 6 horses at 2s 6d each)		15	
Sergeant major (as sergeant major)	1	2	
Sergeant major (as captain of his troop)	1	4	
Sergeant major (for 6 horses at 2s 6d each)		15	
Preacher		8	
Provost marshal		5	
Chirurgeon		4	
Troop			
Captain	1	4	
Captain (for 6 horses at 2s 6d each)		15	
Lieutenant		8	
Lieutenant (for 4 horses at 2s 6d each)		10	
Cornet		6	
Cornet (for 3 horses at 2s 6d each)		7	6
Quartermaster		4	
Quartermaster (for 2 horses at 2s 6d each)		5	
Corporal		3	
Trumpeter		3	

	Pounds	Shillings	Pence
Sadler		2	6
Trooper		2	6
Farrier		2	6
Dragoons (including officers' allowances for extra horses)			
Staff			
Colonel (as Colonel)	1	10	
Colonel (as captain of his company)		15	
Colonel (for 5 horses at 1s each)		5	
Sergeant major (as sergeant major)		9	
Sergeant major (as captain of his company)		15	
Sergeant major (for 5 horses at 1s each)		5	
Provost marshal		5	
Preacher		4	
Chirurgeon		4	
Chirurgeon's mate		2	6
Company			
Captain		15	
Captain (for 5 horses at 1s each		5	
Lieutenant		4	
Lieutenant (for 3 horses at 1s each)		3	
Cornet		3	
Cornet (for 2 horses at 1s each)		2	
Sergeant		1	6
Sergeant (for one horse at 1s)		1	
Corporal		1	
Corporal (for one horse at 1s)		1	
Drummer		1	
Drummer (for one horse at 1s)		1	
Farrier		1	
Dragoon		1	6

Civil War. For the private soldier this did not mean that he would ever see the full amount, because deductions were made for his clothes, shoes, arms, food and lodging, with the largest deduction being for food and lodging. In 1641 the lords justices in Dublin assessed that infantry soldiers paid 4s 8d a week (the standard rate) were only receiving 1s after deductions.[11] This is consistent with European practice, as the example given by Francis Markham, an English officer serving in the Dutch army in the 1620s, was that if each infantryman received 3s a week, then 'shall the victual-master allow him victuals at the rate of foure pence by the day and a penny for drinke, which amounts to two shillings and eleaven pence the weeke'.[12] Cavalry troopers and Dragoons would either provide their own horses or have to pay for the horses issued to them. When first raised, the New Model Army continued the practice of earlier Parliamentary armies in withholding part of their officers' pay. Officers who were paid between 5 and 10s a day had a third of their pay withheld, and those receiving over 10s a day had half of it withheld.[13]

An infantryman's pay. The daily pay of an infantry soldier was 8d; the coins shown here are a sixpence and half-groat (2d). But he would not receive it in full as deductions were made for his food and clothing, and his pay was usually in arrears. By permission of Dolphin Coins and Medals, Leighton Buzzard

The three senior officers of an infantry regiment, colonel, lieutenant colonel and sergeant major, drew their pay for their rank, plus captain's pay as commander of their own company. The same principle was followed in cavalry and dragoon regiments. Another infantry rank which was known at the time, but was not used in the New Model Army, was the 'lanspassadoe' or lancepesade. The only references during the Civil Wars are found in two regiments of the Army of the Eastern Association where this officer was paid 10d a day.[14]

There were some fluctuations in the pay scales of the New Model Army. The most significant of these affected the pay of the captain and the private soldier. By 1648 the captain's pay had been reduced to 8s, affecting the total pay for all company commanders. More importantly, the soldier's pay was temporarily increased in May 1649[15] because of a general rise in the cost of bread, to add a penny to the pay of a soldier in garrison and two pennies to a soldier in the field. In July 1655 the pay was reduced by a penny, so soldiers were back to 8d a day in garrison and 9d in the field.

As with the infantry there were some fluctuations in the pay of cavalry. The pay of cavalry troopers was reduced in 1655 by 3d to 2s 3d a day. The pay of officers was particularly affected by a reduction in their allowances for extra horses. J.B., who provides the most complete list of pay scales in *Some Brief Instructions for the Exercising of the Horse-Troopes*, referred to this change with separate notes. For a cavalry captain – whose pay plus horse allowances was originally £1 19s – J.B. noted 'the captain's pay reduced since to 27 s and no horses mustered: lately to 14 s and his Horses for service mustered'.[16]

Dragoon officers had the same basic rate as infantry officers plus a horse allowance, while the dragoon's pay was for himself and his horse. The inferior quality of a dragoon's horse, when compared to that of a cavalryman, can be see in the amount of the daily horse allowance, 1s for a dragoon officer's horse, while it is 2s 6d for a cavalry officer. Dragoon officers' pay fluctuated in line with that of infantry officers, and the pay of a dragoon was first increased to 2s a day and then in July 1655 was reduced to 1s 8d.

Apart from his pay, a soldier had other potential sources of money. While in garrison, a soldier might do some civilian work when he was not on duty. From a more military perspective, he might receive special payments for extra duty or acts of particular bravery. Examples of special payments are to be found in Joshua Sprigge's account of the siege of Sherborne Castle by the New Model

Army, where 'very freely did the souldiers work in the Mines and Galleries, and making of Batteries, every man being rewarded twelve pence a day a piece for the day, and as much for the night, for the service was hot and hazardous'.[17] At the same siege the artillery were running short of cannon balls, and daring soldiers 'fetch off the Bullets [i.e. cannon balls] (that we had shot) from under the enemies Walls, and had six pence a piece for every Bullet they so brought off'. The men carrying the ladders when storming a city would also receive an additional reward, for example at Bristol in September 1645 there were to be '20 Ladders to each place, two men to carry each Ladder, and to have 5 s a piece; two Serjeants that attended the service of the ladder, to have 20 s. a man; each musqutire that followed the ladder, to carry a fagot, a Serjeant to command them, and to have the same reward'.[18] Before the storm began, Sir Thomas Fairfax provided encouragement to the whole army when he made 'good his promise to reward them for the service at Bridgewater, orderd them immediately to receive 6 s. a man, which by the care of the Commissioners of Parliament, was forthwith paid unto them'.

There were opportunities for greater rewards from the possessions of prisoners taken in battle or siege warfare, and from plundering – or receiving a payment in lieu of plunder of towns or cities. It was generally accepted that the possessions of prisoners and casualties on the battlefield were 'lawful plunder'. This was acknowledged by both sides: one New Model captain captured at the failed assault of Castle Cornet in March 1651 was given leave to return to Guernsey to recuperate, and on reaching his quarters in the town he 'divested himself of his buff coat and the clothes he had worn at the assault and sent them to the soldiers in the Castle, saying that they were their booty and belonged to them'.[19] But the main source of income from plunder came from the sack of a town or city, where the soldier could seize what he could when the fighting was over. At the sack of the English Catholic stronghold of Basing House 'one soldier had 120 pieces of gold for his share, others plate, others jewels'. At the sack of Dundee in September 1651, General George Monk's soldiers 'had gotten above two hundred thousand pound stirling, partly of ready gold, silver and silver work, jewels, rings, merchandise and merchant wares and other precious things belonging to the town of Edinburgh, by and beside all that belonged to the town and other people of the country, who had sent in their goods for safety to that town'.[20] The soldiers would form a

Commonwealth coinage. Two examples of the coins issued by the Commonwealth – without the King's head, these show the cross of St George on one side and the cross of St George and the harp of Ireland on the other. By permission of Dolphin Coins and Medals, Leighton Buzzard

market for anything that was not readily negotiable in order to sell the household items they had seized. Small wonder, then, that when the garrison of a town or city surrendered on terms, the civilian inhabitants were prepared to pay a bounty to the soldiers in lieu of plunder. In March 1650, as the governor and garrison of Kilkenny in Ireland sought terms, Oliver Cromwell advised the mayor of the town that he would be able to save the town from pillage if 'the inhabitants shall give them a reasonable Gratuity in money, in lieu of the pillages'.[21] This was agreed and included in the formal surrender terms as article 5, 'that the city of Kilkenny shall pay £2000 as a gratuity to his Excellency's army; whereof £1000 to be paid on the 30th of this month, and the other on the first day of May next following, to such as shall be by his Excellency thereunto appointed'.[22]

Victuals

The most complete description of a soldier's rations was given by Sir James Turner, and it provides a useful starting point for this subject. Drawing the connection between pay and provisions, he wrote, 'Since money is generally scarce in the Wars, in so much that Soldiers cannot receive their Wages duly, let us see what allowance of Meat and Drink (ordinarily called Proviant) Princes allow their Soldiery.' He described the soldier's ordinary rations:

> There are few Princes who have not their particular establishment for their Proviant both in Field and Garrison, as well as for Money; the order whereof commonly is this, they allow so much Bread, Flesh, Wine or Beer to every Trooper and Foot Soldier, which ordinarily is alike to both; then they allow to the Officers according to their dignities and charges, double, triple and quadruple portions; as to an Ensign four times more than to a common Soldier, a Colonel commonly having twelve portions allow'd him. The Ordinary allowance of a Soldier in the field, is daily two pound of bread, one pound of Flesh, or, in lieu of it, one pound of Cheese, one pottle of Wine, or in lieu of it, two pottles of Beer. It is enough, crys the Soldiers, we desire no more, and it is enough in conscience. But this allowance will not last very long, they must be contented to march sometimes one whole week, and scarce get two pound of Bread all the while, and their Officers as little as they, who if they have no provisions of their own carried about with them, must be satisfied with Commis-bread, and cold water as well as the common Soldier, unless they have money to buy better entertainment from Sutlers.[23]

There was a distinction between the types of food which were suitable for storage in garrison or carriage with an army, and the types which might be readily available from the surrounding countryside when a soldier was in a military camp or a quiet garrison.

The professional soldier Francis Markham, who had served in the Dutch army, wrote that the Victuall-Master ought to accommodate his victuals unto the place in which they are spent; as if it be in Garison or setled Campe, then hee shall spend those victuals that are worst for carriage and most troublesome for the Souldiers to dresse, as Butter, Bread, Fish or the like, except his plenty be great, and then he may let them have two daies flesh as either Beefe or Bacon, for Sundaies and Thursdaies: two daies Butter as on Monday and Tuesday, one day Cheese as Wensday; and two dayes Fish as Friday and Satterday.[24]

The butter and meat would be in addition to bread.

Markham went on to comment that 'if it be in Marching or Journeying, then he shall give them the victuals which is most easie for carriage, and the longest lasting, as Bisket, Beefe ready boyld, cheese, or the like'. There is no precise description of how 'Biskit' was made, but a clear distinction was made between 'Biskit', as a ration which could be stored, and bread; most probably it was something like the naval 'hard tack' of the eighteenth and early nineteenth centuries as it was expected to last in storage for a year.[25] The same practice as that described by Markham was followed by the New Model Army, where biscuit and cheese comprised the basic field rations, so much so that 'bread and cheese' or 'biscuit and cheese' became army slang for provisions. The amount of a soldier's rations in Scotland was described in an entry in General George Monk's order book on 15 January 1657, where he referred to the rations 'for 9 companies, accompting 80 men (officers and soldiers) to each companie, allowing each man 2 lb [pounds] of bread and a quarter of a pound of cheese per diem'.[26] In addition to this they should receive a daily ration of beer, although they often had to make do with water when on campaign.

The amount of rations provided varied. The Royalist garrison at Oxford was issuing 'bread and Cheese according to the usuall proporcon of one pound in bread and half a pound in Cheese to each man' in June 1644;[27] on campaign, provisions were often far short of this, and both Royalist and Parliamentary soldiers had little food before Edgehill, the first battle of the Civil Wars. Some Royalist infantry had 'scarce eaten bread in eight and forty hours before' the battle, while Edmund Ludlow, then serving in the Earl of Essex's cavalry lifeguard, wrote in his memoirs that on the evening of the battle 'no man nor horse got any meat [food] that night, and I had touched none since the Saturday before'. Ludlow did receive supplies the following day when 'the country brought in some provisions; but when I got meat I could scarce eat it, my jaws for want of use having almost lost their natural faculty'.[28]

Rations in garrison would be more varied when the town or city wasn't under threat, but preserved food was relied on during a siege. Sir James Turner commented that 'Garrisons, and fortified places' should be

sufficiently provided with such Meats and Drinks as are most fit to preserve; these are Corn, Grain, and Meat of several kinds, Stock-fish, Herrings, and all other Salted-fishes, Salted and Hung-fleshes, especially

Beef and Bacon, Cheese, Butter, Almonds, Chesnuts, and Hazel-nuts, Wine, Beer, Malt, Honey, Vinegar, Oyl, Tobaco, Wood and Coal for Firing, and as many living Oxen, Cows, Sheep, and Swine, Hens and Turkies as can be conveniently fed; for which purpose as also for Horses, he is to provide Straw, Hay and Oats.[29]

The Earl of Orrery added some useful additional comments, writing that

Biskit, Butter, Cheese and Oatmeal, if carefully look'd unto, would be better relish'd, and keep longer than most Flesh or Fish salted, and are commonly in Sieges better liked by the Soldiery; for they carry their Bread, Butter and Cheese with them to their Guards, those being dress'd to their hands without their labour to cook it, or to get fire to do it; and make them less thirsty by much, than powdered or dryed Flesh or Fish. The Oatmeal also boiled in their Quarters, is a great refreshment to them, and very grateful whether they be sick or well.[30]

Grain could be stored for baking bread during a siege, but the Earl of Orrery also warned of the importance of careful storage and the necessity of regular inspection as 'the Wheat in them [the magazines] must be laid thin, and often turn'd, else it will heat, and be loathed by the Soldiery, who when on most danger, (as in time of a Siege) ought not to have their Staff of Life nauseous unto them'.

The published record of supplies[31] captured when Winchester surrendered in October 1645 provide a useful indication of the provisions stored in a garrison:

7 Peeces of Ordnance
17 Barrels of Powder
2000 Weight of Musquet bullet
800 Weight of Match
38 Hogsheads of Beef and Pork
15000 Weight of Cheese
800 Pound of Butter
140 Quarters of Wheat and Meale
3 Hogsheads of French Wine
10 Quarters of Salt
20 Bushel of Oatmeale
70 Dozen of Candles
30 Load of Wood
40 Quarters of Charcoale
30 Bushels of Seacoale
14 Sheep
4 Quarters of Fresh Beef
7000 Weight of Biskets
112 hogsheads of strong beer.

These were the rations in the early stages of a siege, but after several months the soldiers' rations from the garrison magazine would begin to run low and the citizens would be in an even worse position. Before long the garrison would be eating its horses: a contemporary account of the siege of Chester recorded that by January 1646 'the Citizens were more sensible of their desparate condition than the Commanders, resolved to feede no longer upon lyes, which had brought them a long time to feed on horseflesh'.[32] A Royalist describing the conditions in 1648 in Colchester, besieged by the New Model Army, provided a more evocative account: horseflesh had

> grown so delicious a food amongst the soldiers that we could scarcely secure our horses in the stables, for every morning one stable or other was robbed, and our horses knocked on the head and sold in the shambles by the pound; nor was there in a short time a dog left, for it was customary for each soldier to reserve half his ammunition loaf, and in a morning walk the streets, and if he discovered a dog to drop a piece of bread, and so decoy him on till within his reach and then with the butt end of his musket knock his brains out, and march away with him to his quarters. I have known six shillings given for the side of a dog, and yet but a small one neither.[33]

When the garrison of Beeston Castle marched out on terms in November 1645 'they were brought so low that they had eaten their catts'.[34]

An impression of the overall cost of provisions was given by Colonel Edward Popham in July 1649, with the calculation that:

> There is not a place in England that you can victual in under £1.5s a man a month, which for 6,000 men for two months amounts to £15,000, for though some things be cheaper in one place than another yet other things are dearer; if beef be cheap, pork pease and fish are dearer, and so in other provisions, that there is little difference in victualling in any place unless we could buy in all places those things which are best cheap in every place, which we have not time to do.[35]

Records of the New Model Army's campaigns in Scotland provide several references to the cost of individual items. For example, entries in General George Monk's order book for 18 September 1654 record the cost of cheese as 4d a pound and biscuit as 15s a bag, although the weight of bread in a bag is not specified. The records of Colonel Thomas Fitch, governor of Inverness, show he had set prices in the town in 1654 for the sale of various provisions to his soldiers. In this record a good slaughtering cow could be bought for £1 6s 8d, a sheep for 4s 6d, a 'veale' for 3s, a hen for 5d, a goose for 1s 2d, a pound of bacon for 4d, a pound of pork for 2d, a pound of salmon for 1d, bread weighing 9 ounces for 1d and brown bread weighing 13½ ounces for 1d.[36] By this time the army was moving more towards regular payment of the soldiers and, when not in the field, encouraged them to buy their own rations rather than rely on the army quartermaster.

Free Quarter

The third part of these three connected aspects of military life was the practice of free quarter, where

> Princes and their Generals are many times forc'd for want of money to grant where they can Quarter their Armies in Towns and Villages; and this proves oft the destruction of a Country: for though no exorbitancy be committed, and that every man both Officer and Souldier demand no other entertainment than what is allowed by the Prince or State where they serve; yet when an Army cannot be Quarter'd but close and neare together, to prevent Infalls, Anslachts and Surprisal of an Enemy, it is an easie matter to imagine what a heavy burthen these places bear, whom in poor mens houses, six seven, eight, it may be fourteen or fifteen soldiers are lodged, for in such cases it is ordinary to quarter two thousand Foot, or a thousand Horse in a little Town, where perhaps there are not above three or four hundred houses. And withal it is very hard to get Souldiers and Horsemen kept within the limits of their Duty within these Quarters, after they have endured hunger, thirst and other hardships in the field.[37]

The English diplomat Dudley Carleton could write casually in 1622 of the difficulty of provisioning one of the Protestant German armies 'unless, as they hold here, la guerre nourrit la guerre; they being masters of the field can feed and maintain themselves upon the enemy's countries, which will make a hot summer of the next in Germany'.[38] But it is one thing to write laconically of the difficulties which German states might suffer, and entirely another when free quartering was practised at home in England.

The allowances for food that soldiers would make of their hosts' food have been discussed above, but the impact on their unwilling hosts also included the hay, straw and oats required for cavalry, artillery, baggage and officers. The 'service which every host is bound to furnish either in Town or Country' also included 'a Bed, Lodging, Table, and Table-linnen, Fire, Salt and Vinegar'. But it was easy, and commonplace, for armed men to extort more than the set allowance. In his memoirs Sir James Turner illustrated this general perspective with the recollection that while a mercenary officer in the European wars he received little pay, but soon 'learnd so much cunning, and became so vigilant to lay hold on opportunities, that I wanted for nothing, horses, clothes, meate, nor moneys, and made so much good use of what I had learned, that the whole time I serv'd in Germanie, I suffer'd no such miserie as I had done the first yeare and a halfe that I came to it'.[39]

Sir Thomas Fairfax, commander of the New Model Army, and Oliver Cromwell after him made every effort to reduce reliance on free quarter because it alienated the local population. The New Model soldiers themselves, perhaps feeling a stronger connection with the general population than the mercenary soldiers they despised, objected to the practice of free quarter because:

nothing is so difficult and grievous to us as to consider how the poor Soldier (for his mere Subsistence) is compelled to grind the Face of the Poor, to take a Livelihood from them who are fitter to receive Alms, to undo Families, threaten the Ruin of the whole, and all Propriety, and to be an abhorring to himself (which some ingenuous of them acknowledge) and this for want of that constant Supply and Pay, whereby they might cheerfully, and with Content to the People, discharge their Quarters, and so ease both the Country and their own Minds of an intolerable Burthen.[40]

Chapter Six

Regiments, Roles and Responsibilities

Introduction

During the English Civil War, the basic organization of the regiments (whether cavalry, infantry or dragoons) and the general command structure was based on the model used by the Dutch army. This presented some problems in terms of the command structure, as the war in the Low Countries typically saw one main field army opposed to another, and this meant that the Dutch command structure was based on the general officers required for a single army. This was workable during the first year of the English Civil War when each side, Royalist and Parliament, concentrated its forces in a single field army. However, once it became apparent that the war would not be ended in a single campaign, each side raised additional regional armies to continue the war in other parts of England and Wales. This created a situation similar to the campaigns of the Thirty Years War in Germany, where the greater number of states and soldiers under arms, and the greater geographic area over which the war was fought, led to the creation of several armies, each with its own command structure.

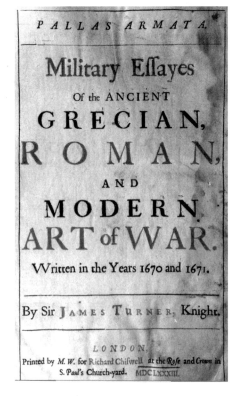

Frontispiece of Sir James Turner's Pallas Armata. Turner wrote this book between 1670 and 1671 looking back on his career as a mercenary in Europe during the Thirty Years War and at home in Scottish armies. Of all those writing military books printed in this period, he was the most widely experienced soldier.

PALLAS ARMATA

Military Essayes

Of the ANCIENT

GRECIAN,

ROMAN,

AND

MODERN

ART of WAR.

Written in the Years 1670 and 1671.

By Sir JAMES TURNER, Knight.

LONDON.

Printed by M. W. for Richard Chiswell at the Rose and Crown in S. Paul's Church-yard. MDCLXXXIII.

SIR THOMAS FAIRFAX *Knight*
General of the Forces raised by the Parliament
Published by Edward Jeffery 1808

Sir Thomas Fairfax (1612–1671). He had limited military experience before the English Civil War, serving briefly in the Dutch army. He made his reputation as the bold and competent cavalry commander of the Parliamentary Army of the Northern Association, and was the first lord general of the New Model Army.

This led to some interesting questions of precedence when several armies with their separate command structures were briefly combined for a major campaign, and the same was true in England after 1642. Sir James Turner commented on the easy proliferation of generals that 'no sooner is a Lieutenant or Major-General sent with a part of the Army on some exploit, which may require some considerable time' than they make up a 'compleat General staff'.[1] This problem also occurred during the English Civil War: the Royalist Earl of Clarendon recorded one example when the Marquess of Hertford brought both re-enforcements and a complete staff of general officers with him when he joined – as commander – Sir Ralph Hopton's Cornish army, commenting that 'how small soever the Marquis' party was in numbers, it was supplied with all the general officers of a Royal army, a general, lieutenant general, general of the horse, general of the ordnance, a major-general of horse, and another of foot'.[2] It was usual to find fewer general officers in the Parliament armies, and the New Model Army, when first raised, had the Lord General Sir Thomas Fairfax as army commander, with a lieutenant general to command the cavalry, a sergeant major general to command the infantry, a lieutenant general of the ordnance and a commissary general as second in command of the cavalry.

The sections below set out the roles and responsibilities of the various general officers as well as the regimental officers and the basic organization of cavalry, infantry and dragoon regiments.

General Officers

The Captain General or Generalissimo

By 1642 the general holding 'the supreme Command of Royal Armies, one or more'[3] was usually known in England as the captain general. In the Imperialist army this general officer was often known as the generalissimo, hence the flippant claim by Charles I's Queen, Henrietta Maria, that she was 'She Majesty Generalissima' of the force which accompanied her and the arms shipment she had brought from Holland on their march south to join the King.

This command was 'of the highest nature, the greatest honour, and deepest consequence that can be confer'd on any single person of what quality or degree soever, for he is intrusted not only with the lives of those that are in Arms under his Command, but with the defence of the whole Country, Towns, Forts, and Castles, with the honour, welfare, and standing of the Prince and State, and with the lives and properties of all their Subjects'. This was a heavy responsibility, as:

> the loss of his Army, or Armies by his negligence, inadvertency, rashness or cowardice, may occasion the loss of all these, or make them run a very great hazard by his indiscretion, much more by his treachery; he may in one moment of time lose the lives and liberties of many thousands, make numbers of women widows, children fatherless, and fathers childless, he may lose the honour and beauty of a whole Province, yea of a whole Kingdom, all which he was bound by his office and charge to preserve.[4]

The necessary qualities for such a commander were considered to be that:

> our General should be stout, not rash, resolute to lay hold on occasion, as knowing, she is bald behind; he should be very secret, and ready to hearken to advice and have judgement to discern, whether it be good or bad. Very young this General ought not to be, for he must not be a meer novitiate, (I speak still of Subjects;) very old he must not be, for age dries up the radical moisture, cools the blood, and weakens the body, and thereby makes a man unfit for these Actions, which require both present resolution, and present expedition: in short, if you have a General indued [imbued] with some knowledge in Military Affairs, with some prudence, with some liberality, and an unblemish'd reputation; he may pass for sufficient enough, though he be not all these qualities in the Superlative degree: for perfection is not to be look'd for in the depraved condition of mankind.[5]

A general was also expected to be brave, both as an encouragement to his men and because he 'may lose more to his Prince, by too much care to preserve his own person, than by freely hazarding it'. Not all the general officers who participated in the Civil Wars had this quality, and at Marston Moor, where three armies had combined to fight against the Royalists, two out of three generals commanding the allied armies fled the field believing the day was lost;[6] the Scottish commander, the Earl of Leven, 'fled furthest, for he did not draw bridle till he was at Wedderbie, four and twentie miles from the place of battell'.[7] Most, however, were made of sterner stuff, as a description of Sir Thomas Fairfax at the battle of Naseby shows:

> The General had his Helmet beat off, and riding in the field bare headed up and down from one part of his Army to another, to see how they stood, and what advantage might be gained, and coming up to his owne Life Guard commanded by Colonel Charles d'Oyley, he was told by him that he exposed himself to too much danger, and the whole Army thereby, riding bareheaded in the fields, and so many Bullets flying about him, and D'Oyley offered his General his Helmet, but he refused it, saying 'It is well enough, Charles'.[8]

Field Marshals, Generals and Lieutenant Generals

After the first year of the English Civil War, both sides raised separate armies to control or dispute control over different parts of England and Wales, sometimes commanded by a general with an independent commission and sometimes by a general whose commission made him, theoretically at least, subordinate to another.

The term 'field marshal' was used originally for the officer who marshalled the field, 'called in French, Marshal of the Camp', but the seniority of the term was extended during the Thirty Years War, where 'for the present in Germany,

Sweden and Denmark, those who command Armies Royal consisting of Cavalry, Infantry, and Artillery, are qualified by the Titles of Feltmarshals'.[9] The Royalist Sir Ralph Hopton was commissioned by Charles I as 'Field Marshall of the westerne Army' on 10 October 1643, the first of several commissions of the rank of field marshal issued for the Royalist army from Oxford during 1643 and 1644.[10] John, Lord Byron, was commissioned as field marshal of forces in Worcester, Salop, Chester and six Welsh counties in December 1643. The rank of general was more usual for the commander of an independent army, and that of major general was used for a subordinate commander with a separate command either over an army or a specific area; for example, Sir William Waller received a subordinate commission in February 1643 as major general in the west from the Parliamentary captain general, the Earl of Essex.[11]

An army commander could have both a general of horse and a general of foot serving under him, although 'Generals of the Foot are but rare'.[12] Both Royalist and Parliamentary armies had a general of the horse at the outbreak of the English Civil War, Prince Rupert being the Royalist general of the horse and the Earl of Bedford holding this position for the Parliament. However, it became the practice in Parliamentary armies, including the New Model Army, to dispense with the use of a general of horse and place the cavalry under the command of a lieutenant general of horse. Oliver Cromwell held this rank in both the Army of the Eastern Association and the New Model Army. J.B., writing after the Restoration of Charles II, noted that 'in the Parliaments Armies, there was no General of Horse allowed, but only a Lieutenant Generall, which was not a little charge saved to them'.[13] Since most military authors at this time agreed that the role of the lieutenant general was to act as deputy to the general, whether of cavalry or infantry, there was really no practical requirement to have both officers.

The commander of the cavalry, whether general or lieutenant general, was

> to see the Troops and Regiments of Horse kept at that strength that they are appointed to be of; and if by Battel, long marches, great fatigue, or other accidents of War, the numbers of men be diminisht, Horses lost, or made unserviceable, it is his duty when they come to Quarter, to see the Troops made strong, the Horses put in good case, and the Riders well cloth'd and arm'd. In Musters he is obliged to see that no Colonel or Rittmaster wrong the Muster-masters by making a show of borrow'd men, Horses or Arms, whereby the Prince may be cheated in his Purse, or disappointed in his service. He is to take care that the Cavalry be paid, and provided with Proviant and Fodderage, and good Quarter.[14]

Sir James Turner also recommended that a cavalry commander should 'also be a person who understands something of the Foot-service [infantry], in regard that when the greatest part of the Horse is sent in any Expedition, ordinarily some Foot are sent with them, and then it is the General of the Cavalries office to command both'. However, this degree of competence was clearly unusual, as Sir James Turner also wrote, 'But it is a pity that all General persons should not make it their study and their work to understand both the Foot and Horse-service, for I have seen considerable parties of Foot more harass'd and spoil'd in a short time under the command of an Officer of Horse, than if they had been routed by an enemy; so little discretion some have to know the difference between a man and a Horse.'[15]

Major Generals

The major general of the horse had the responsibility to marshal 'the Cavalry in Battel, having first advised about the matter with the General of the Horse, or in his absence with the Lieutenant-General'. He was also the officer to whom 'all complaints and differences between Officers and Horsemen, or among themselves' were first brought,

> which he should endeavour to compose in an amicable way, but if he cannot, he is to proceed by according to the Articles and Constitutions of War. He hath the inspection of all the Guards of Horse, and orders them, and keeps lists of Convoys and Parties, that the several Officers and Troopers may have their turns, in which the Major-General should show himself very impartial; for very few or none there be, who will not think themselves wrong'd in their reputation, if others be prefer'd to them, where either danger may probably be look'd for, or profit expected, unless it can be made clear to them that it is not their turn to go on that party, or with that Convoy.[16]

The rank 'major general of the horse' was used in Europe, but 'This Officer the English qualifie with the Title of Commissary General of the Horse'.[17] As there was no general of the horse in the New Model Army, the lieutenant general of the horse would usually command the cavalry deployed on the right-hand wing of an army, as the right was traditionally the most honourable position,[18] and the commissary general as second in command would lead the left wing. This was the deployment of the cavalry of the New Model Army at Naseby where the cavalry commander, Lieutenant General Oliver Cromwell, commanded the right-wing cavalry and his commissary general, Henry Ireton, commanded the left wing.

The sergeant major general or major general of foot was usually the commander of an army's infantry. As Sir James Turner commented, the post of general of the foot was rare:

> some Lieutenant-Generals of the Infantry I have likewise known, but these not in all Armies. But a Major-General of Foot is thought a necessary Commander in all Armies, though they be never so weak; when any of them is wanting, or out of the way, the oldest Colonel officiates for him. The English call him Serjeant-Major General of the Foot, and in some places he is order'd to be constantly President of the Council of War.[19]

Key	Area	Major Generals
1.	Cumberland, Northumberland and Westmorland	Charles Howard
2.	Durham and Yorkshire	Robert Lilburne
3.	Cheshire, Lancashire and Staffordshire	Charles Worsley and then Tobias Bridge
4.	Derbyshire, Leicestershire, Lincolnshire, Nottinghamshire and Warwickshire	Edward Whalley
5.	Bedfordshire, Huntingdonshire, Northamptonshire and Rutland	William Boteler
6.	Essex, Cambridgeshire, Isle of Ely, Norfolk and Suffolk	Hezekiah Haynes
7.	Buckinghamshire, Hertfordshire and Oxfordshire	George Fleetwood in Buckinghamshire, and and William Packer in Hertfordshire Oxfordshire.
8.	Herefordshire, Shropshire, Worcestershire and Wales	James Berry
9.	Middlesex, London and Westminster	Sir John Barkstead
10.	Kent and Surrey	Thomas Kelsey
11.	Berkshire, Hampshire and Sussex	William Goffe
12.	Cornwall, Devon, Dorset, Gloucestershire, Somerset and Wiltshire	John Desborough

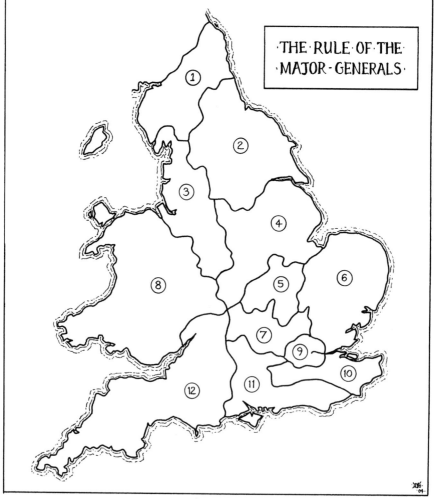

·THE·RULE·OF·THE·
·MAJOR-GENERALS·

The jurisdiction of the Cromwellian major generals.

The sergeant major general had to be a competent and experienced officer as he was responsible for deploying an army's infantry centre in the formation chosen by the army commander, a role which required extensive practical experience if it was to be done well. Wherever possible a general would seek to obtain the services of an experienced professional for this role. The first sergeant major general of the New Model Army was Philip Skippon, who had previously held that rank under the Earl of Essex and had background of 'foure and twentie years Militia in Denmark, Germanie and the Low Countries';[20] others with similar professional backgrounds were Andrew Potley, a veteran of the Swedish army who was sergeant major general of foot in Sir William Waller's Parliamentary army, and Jacob Astley, who held this position in the main Royalist army at Oxford.

The rank of sergeant major general was also used for a commander who led a complete army in another theatre of war as a subordinate to the captain general, or for an officer with responsibility over a group of associated counties. The latter use of the rank was used when Oliver Cromwell briefly divided England and Wales during 1655 and 1656 into military districts and appointed officers with the rank of major general to administer them. The rank could also be used for the commander of a separate infantry contingent: for example, the London Trained Band and Auxiliary regiments serving with the Earl of Essex's and Sir William Waller's armies did so as distinct brigades with their own major generals to command them.

The General or Master of the Ordnance
He who commanded in chief over the artillery

> is called by the English, General, or Master of the Ordnance; by the French, Grand Maistre del Artillerie, Great Master of the Artillery; by the Germans, General fetz Feugmeister, which is General Overseer and Master of the Munitions for the Field, a term very proper, as he hath not only the inspection of the Ordnance, but of the Munitions of War, such are the Guns, greater and lesser, all manner of Arms and Weapons, all Materials belonging to Smiths and Carpenters, Powder, Match, Bullets, Granado's for Pot-pieces, and to be cast by the hand, store of Instruments and Utensils for Artificers Shops, Bridges or Materials for them, Boats or Materials for them, to be made and join'd quickly, for passing unfordable waters, all kinds of Instruments for working in Fortification or Approaches, such as Spades, Mattocks, Pickaxes, and Shovels. In Scotland we call this great Officer, the General of the Artillery.[21]

The quality of this officer, with his many responsibilities, was described at length in contemporary manuals, but as one wrote,

> if you take his description from some notional writers, you would justly conclude, that there is no such man below the Moon. Indeed I shall tell you there are two qualifications absolutely necessary for him, these are to

be a good Mathematician, and to be something, if not right much, experimented in all the points of the Gunners Art, he must be of a good judgment, and a very ready dispatch. The rest of his parts and abilities (which some require in him alone) I think he may divide among those who are under his command and authority.[22]

On 'the day of Battail' it was the duty of this general officer 'to see that the Ordnance be well placed; for at such time his wisdom is most discern'd, keeping (with the assistance of his Lieutenant) the Train of Artillery together in good order. He must have a vigilant eye upon all accidents that may fall out, and make choice of such ground for their planting, as the General of the Army and he shall think most fit and convenient.' In planting or positioning his artillery the Master of the Ordnance 'by his wisdom and discretion may make choice of the best advantages, which might annoy an Enemy most, and give the least offence to his own men, either by dazzling them by the Sun, or by raising of the dust, observing the winde which drives the Smoak both of the Ordnance and Small-shot full upon them'.[23]

The Cavalry

By 1642 cavalry, both cuirassiers and arquebusiers, were formed into regiments with a headquarters and several troops, but there was no universal model governing the number of troops in a regiment or the number of cavalrymen in a troop. The formation of cavalry troops into regiments was relatively recent, and Sir James Turner, writing during 1670 and 1671, recorded that 'Seventy or eighty years ago there were no Regiments of Horse (properly so called) only Troops or Companies', but

> upon occasion of service, Troops were join'd together, and the command of some of them given for a time by the Prince or State to some person of great quality, whom they thought fit for that imployment. Sometimes three Troops were join'd together, sometimes five or six, yet they had not the name of a Regiment, nor had he who commanded that Body so composed, the title of Colonel. The Estates of the United Provinces [i.e. the Dutch] used this much, but now they levy Regiments.

Sir James Turner considered that the change had been brought about by the increase in the number of soldiers in service during Thirty Years War, commenting

> the furious Wars which began in Christendom in the year of our Lord 1618 (whereof in process of time we had a deep share at home) reversed many good old customs and constitutions, and with other things introduced Regiments of Horse, and not only so, but brought in such numbers of them that in many Armies there were near as many Regiments of Horse as of Foot.[24]

The composition of cavalry regiments varied. As Turner commented, in European Armies:

> you may see in that same Army a Regiment of six Companies, each of Seventy men, another of eight Troops, each of fifty horse, so little is an uniformity in equal numbers of Troops, or of Horsemen in every Troop regarded, or look'd after. I saw one Regiment in the Sweedish service (I may say one, for I saw not such another in any of their Armies) in which were according to Capitulation, twelve Troops, each of them consisting of one hundred Riders effectively, but four of the Regiments of that Army were not so strong, as that Regiment was alone.[25]

In the years before the English Civil War, the numbers of English cavalry in the county Trained Bands and the English garrison in Ireland were too small for there to be any advantage in forming them into regiments. At the outbreak of the Civil War, adherents of each side raised what men they could, and for cavalry this meant raising both regiments and independent troops of cavalry. *The List of the Armie Raised under the Command of His Excellency Robert Earle of Essex*, which was printed in London at the outbreak of the Civil War, lists infantry by regiment, but for the cavalry it records the names of six colonels and lists the cavalry under each of the seventy-five troop commanders – the sixty-seventh being Captain Oliver Cromwell. There were both compete regiments and independent troops in the Parliamentary army when it fought its first battle, at Edgehill. The composition of a cavalry troop in the Earl of Essex's army was '60 Horse, besides 2 Trumpeters, 3 Corporalls, a Sadler and a Farrier',[26] with the commissioned officers – troop commander, lieutenant, cornet and quartermaster – being listed by name for each troop. This number – sixty cavalry troopers to a troop – is the same as the specification for English cavalry troops for service in Ireland in 1642. The Royalist army, which drew upon the same military background as its Parliamentary opponents, followed a similar theory. The pamphlet *A True Description of the Discipline of War both of Horse and Foot used in his Majesties Army* stated 'Our horse Troops are to be Carbines, sixty men compleat besides officers'. As the Civil War continued, both sides made greater efforts to formalize their cavalry organization into regiments in their main field armies. The Parliament was more successful in this, but both sides still included independent troops in their main field armies, smaller local armies and garrisons.

Sixty troopers plus eleven officers (troop commander, lieutenant, cornet, quartermaster, three corporals, two trumpeters, farrier and saddler) was probably the preferred model for troops of arquebusiers or 'carbines' for both sides at the outbreak of the Civil War. The Royalist army also issued commissions for colonels to raise '500 Horse volunteers', but it is not clear what breakdown into numbers of troops or the number of troopers in each troop was intended. However, regardless of theoretical numbers, the practical difficulties of recruitment and losses on campaign meant that most cavalry troops always found it difficult to put this many troopers into the field. This was true from the beginning of the Civil War, and in September 1642 the

Parliament ordered newly mobilized 'Troops of Horse that consist of Forty or more' should march to join the Earl of Essex's army in the field.

This said, a charismatic colonel – such as Oliver Cromwell in the Parliament's army or the Royalist Prince Rupert – could still attract numbers of recruits. The establishment of troops of horse raised for the Parliament's Army of the Eastern Association was larger. Oliver Cromwell's own troop, when it first served in the Earl of Essex's army, was stronger than the usual establishment, as payment records for November 1642 show he had eighty troopers,[27] not sixty, and a pay warrant in December 1642 referred to Cromwell's 'troope of eightie harquebusiers'.[28] Eighty seems to have been Cromwell's preferred model when he first raised his regiment as, in his letter to the 'Young Men and Maids' of Norwich in August 1643, he recommended that the funds they had raised to equip an infantry company should be used instead for 'a troop of horse; which indeed will by God's blessing, far more advantage the Cause', and offered to provide eighty horses for the troopers if they would provide the pistols and saddles.[29]

In 1644 the theoretical cavalry establishments of both the Earl of Essex's army and the Army of the Eastern Association were reassessed. The cavalry in Essex's army was to consist of six regiments, with each regiment comprising six troops. The colonel's troop was to have 100 troopers plus officers, and the other five troops were to consist of 80 troopers plus officers.[30] The cavalry in the Army of the Eastern Association was to consist of 3,000 cavalry troopers in four regiments, two with ten troops in each and two with five troops in each, and probably with 100 troopers in each troop.[31] The troop establishment used in the Army of the Eastern Association was followed in the cavalry regiments of the New Model Army, although the number of troops in each regiment was standardized at six. The Royalist army was never able to successfully reorganize its regimental structure. The number of troopers in a New Model cavalry troop fluctuated in peacetime and was reduced to eighty troopers in each troop in 1648.

The troop establishment for cuirassiers was set for Parliamentary forces in 1642 at eighty cuirassier troopers plus twelve officers (the additional officer being a third trumpeter). However, as J.B., the author of the cavalry manual *Some Brief Instructions for the Exercising of the Horse-Troopes*, wrote shortly after the Restoration, 'some few troopes of Cuirassiers were in use at the first, but afterwards Reduced and the charge saved'.[32] Three troops of cuirassiers served in the Earl of Essex's army – two of them were lifeguard troops for Essex and his general of the horse, the Earl of Bedford, and were established at 100 cuirassier troopers plus officers, and only the third was established on the official model of 80 troopers plus officers. The only complete regiment of cuirassiers was Sir Arthur Haselrig's regiment of 'Lobsters'. By 1644 the only cuirassier unit in service was the Essex's lifeguard troop. Although this troop continued in service into the New Model Army as Sir Thomas Fairfax's lifeguard, the men were no longer equipped as cuirassiers, and there were no cuirassier troops in the New Model Army.

The officers of a regiment of cavalry were divided into staff officers and the officers and troopers of individual troops. Sir James Turner set out the contemporary definition of staff officers, stating that a regiment included officers 'whose charges belong equally' to all of its constituent companies (of infantry) or troops (of horse) and

> are called Officers of the Staff, in high Dutch the Etymology of the word I cannot give you; these are the Colonel, the Lieutenant-Colonel, and the Major, these three are called likewise Officers of the Field. Besides them there belongs to the Staff, a Preacher, A Chirurgeon, A Quarter-master, and a Provost-Marshal; these four are entertain'd in all Regiments, by all States and Princes who maintain armies, and some have also a Regiment-Scrivener, or Clerk, an Auditor, and Hangman.[33]

The officers of a regiment of arquebusiers were set by the Parliament in 1642.[34] The staff officers were:

colonel
lieutenant colonel
sergeant major
quartermaster
preacher
provost marshal
chirurgeon and two mates.

Although commonly found in Royalist cavalry regiments, a lieutenant colonel was included in Parliamentary establishments for only exceptionally large regiments.

The officers and men of the troop included:

captain (the colonel, lieutenant colonel or sergeant major was 'captain' of his own troops or a captain for the remaining troops in the regiment)
lieutenant (captain lieutenant in the colonel's troop)
cornet
quartermaster
corporals (three)
trumpeters (two)
saddler
farrier.

Although the number of cavalry troopers fluctuated, the number of officers (commissioned and non-commissioned) remained the same. In the seventeenth century the word 'officer' was used to describe a man holding a military position or 'office', and a distinction was made between commissioned officers – who held a signed commission from their general or their colonel – and non-commissioned officers.

Staff Officers

The Colonel

John Vernon's description of the roles and responsibilities of cavalry officers begins with 'the Colonell who is appointed Commander in Chief over his own Regiment, he ought to be a Souldier of extraordinarie experience & valour, as having comand of a little army, sometimes singled from the greater; on him dependeth the good successe of many brave designes & actions, therefore he must be well skilled in inbattailing of the Cavalrie'.[35] A colonel obviously should have these qualities, but in practice he was often appointed on the basis of his influence or position at court or the government of the day, or because his local influence would make recruitment easier, rather than because of his skill or experience. A typical colonel was often absent from the regiment either because he had other responsibilities as a general officer in the army or because he was involved in politics at Westminster. This changed with the creation of the New Model Army, as members of both houses of Parliament were prohibited from serving in the army, and by 1645 the officers who remained with the army had developed considerable practical military experience.

Richard Elton, in describing the responsibilities of an infantry colonel, set out the importance of any colonel, of cavalry or infantry. In

> all matters of Advice and Counsel, but more especially when any Strategem, Siege, or intended Battail is in agitation to be put in action, the Colonel ever as one of the primary Field-Officers is summoned to consult with the General, and with all freedom to deliver his opinion in all things that shall be there discussed, for the best advantage (as he shall conceive) for the designs in hand, how weighty and important soever, and to be ready to go upon any such service as shall be cast into his charge to be executed by the major part of the said Council, and to express his obedience to his General, although it be a service that correspond not with his own opinion at the first, but being cleared by the larger number to be more conducing to the good of the Design, courageously to undertake it, and faithfully to perform it.[36]

The Lieutenant Colonel

The lieutenant colonel was the second in command of the regiment, his rank meaning literally that he stood in the place of – *en lieu tenant* – the colonel when the latter was absent from the regiment. His main role was to act as the colonel's deputy and he had few specified duties apart from this. European cavalry regiments include this officer in their establishment and this rank is also found amongst Royalist cavalry regiments. However, most Parliamentary cavalry regiments did not include a lieutenant colonel and had the sergeant major as their second in command. There were exceptions where a Parliamentary cavalry regiment was unusually large, and the cavalry regiments in the Army of the Eastern Association of both the Earl of Manchester and his lieutenant general, Oliver Cromwell, had lieutenant colonels.[37] The double regiment raised for Oliver Cromwell's campaign in Ireland in 1649 also had a lieutenant colonel.

The Sergeant Major

While the colonel *ought* 'to be a Souldier of extra-ordinarie experience & valour', the sergeant major actually had to be a competent and experienced officer, as he was responsible for the everyday operation of the regiment, its training and its deployment in battle or skirmish. John Vernon considered that this officer should be

> most usually a man of the most practice in the Regiment, in marching he ought to be well acquainted with the ways that so he may with the best advantage encounter the Enemy, if it hapneth they met, if the Regiment marches in high ways, In the Enemies Countrie or where the people do most affect their Enemie: it is his dutie in all places or fields convenient, to cause all the Regiment to be drawn up into Battalia, which will both annuer the Soudiers to this kinde of Exercise, and cause them to be more Expert, and Readie at all times to Encounter there Enemies.

The sergeant major was 'likewise to take care that the Captaines doe not wrong their Souldiers, and that they keepe the Troops in good state and well armed, and that they themselves and their Officers do frequently Exercise and Discipline their Troops, and cause them to observe good order'.[38]

The Preacher or Chaplain

In European armies whether the preacher was

> Priest or Minister, whether Lutheran, Reformed, or Roman Catholiqu, his office is well enough known, there is much respect paid him, and the Laws of War provide sever punishments to those who offer any injury or offence to his person or charge. His duty is to have *Curam Animarum*, the care of Souls, and it is well if he meddle with no other business but makes that only his care.[39]

Both sides in the Civil War had regimental preachers on their establishment. The colonels appointed their regimental preacher and would choose a man who followed not only their side in the Civil War but also their personal religious persuasion, particularly Presbyterian or Independent. George Monk had a very clear view of the importance of the preacher's role: 'it is most necessary for a General in the first place to approve his Cause, and settle an opinion of right in the minds of his Officers and Souldiers: the which can be no way better done, than by the Chaplains of an Army'.[40]

Provost Marshal

The regiment's provost marshal had the power to apprehend any soldier whom he saw transgressing the Laws and Articles of War, from doing whereof no Officer may hinder him; but he hath not power to set any Prisoner at liberty, no not those whom himself hath imprison'd. He is Gaoler, and keeps those who are committed to him, either in Irons, or without Irons, for which he hath a Guard allow'd him. He is to present the Prisoners to the Court of War, and to desire that Justice may be done on them for the crimes they have committed, which he is obliged to specifie, and he is to be present at the execution of every sentence; and when a Soldier is to run the Gatloupe [gauntlet] he is to give him the first lash.[41]

The Chirurgeon or Surgeon

The chirurgeon 'must be skilful in curing all manner of wounds (so they be not mortal) for many brave Gentlemen get their bones broken with Bullets, which would not so frequently prove deadly to the Patients if they were attended on by good and experienced Artists'. This comment by Sir James Turner illustrated the unfortunate reality that a post as an army surgeon did not attract the most proficient medical officers. The hopeful comment that he 'should be a sober man, and ought to do his duty warily and carefully, since the lives of both Commanders and Soldiers are often in his hands' is also an indication that many chirurgeons did not possess these qualities. In October 1654 George Monk queried the appointment of one surgeon directly with his commander, Oliver Cromwell, on the reasonable basis that

he is one that was never bound prentice to the profession, and the surgeon-general looks upon him as unfit to take such an employ upon him ... I earnestly entreat your highness, that if possible I may have an able surgeon to the train, in regard I know not what occasion I may have to make use of him myself, and I conceive this person not fit to undertake it, as well for his want of skill as his former miscarriages.[42]

The chirurgeon 'besides his monthly pay' should 'have his Surgeon's Chest furnish't with all manner of Necessaries for curing Wounds of all kinds; and this Chest is to be furnisht at the Princes charge and all Wounds received in the Princes or States service, he is obliged to cure (if he can) without demanding any thing from the Patients, but all other got accidentally, or by quarreling and Duels, he is not obliged to cure but for payment.'[43] This was the practice in both the Royalist and Parliamentary armies, and it was usual for the chirurgeon to be assisted by two mates: these were to provide assistance to the chirurgeon but were unskilled in the sense that they were not apprentices. In June 1649 the cost of sixteen pairs of surgeon's chests for the New Model Army regiments concentrated for Oliver Cromwell's campaign in Ireland amounted to £345, and each chest was to be examined and certified correct by a physician before it was dispatched.[44]

Captain and lieutenant. Officers of the Trained Bands c.1635.

The Officers and Men of the Troop
The Captain
Like the colonel, there were high expectations of the captain, who should be 'a man of Wisdome and Policy, as being one of the Colonels counsel, and wel exercised in Arms that he may be the better able to Discipline his own Troop'. He was encouraged to 'diligently and punctually observe those orders which shall either be given or sent to him from his superiour Officers, and be at the place at the appointed houre with his Troop, and others under his command on all occasions'. He was also expected to be a 'good example to his Souldiers, hee must be careful to keepe his owne Troope full and compleat, he must endevour to know every one of his souldiers by their names, that he may distinctly name them upon all occasions of employment'.

However, much of the actual running of the troop usually fell to his lieutenant, upon whom 'all difficulties doe rest, because oftimes the Troops are given unto young Gentlemen which want experience'.[45] At the outbreak of the English Civil War many of those who raised troops of horse had little military experience. Just as the colonel relied upon the support of a professionally competent sergeant major, so too did an inexperienced captain rely on the professional expertise of his lieutenant and his quartermaster. By the time the New Model Army was raised, most captains of horse were experienced, veteran officers.

The Lieutenant
John Vernon considered that the lieutenant should be 'a man of known experience, nursed and well educated in Cavalrie, it properly belongs unto his care and office to exercise and discipline the Troope, in the Captains absence he commands the Troope, his name signifieth so much in the French Lieutenant, that is one who supplieth the place of another'. This officer 'must

be able to write and read, because hee must keep a List of the Troopers names, and likewise be able himselfe to read those Orders and Letters that shall be sent him from his Superiour Officers'. It was also the Lieutenant's responsibility to ensure that 'when the Troope lodgeth in a Village, he must cause the Billits assigned to be distributed before the Cornets lodging, so that in case of an Alarm, the Souldiers may know where to repaire to their Colours'.[46] It was the responsibility of the troop's quartermaster to obtain the details of billets (the houses where the troopers would be billeted) from the quartermaster general, but they would be distributed to the corporals of the troop in the presence of the lieutenant. The corporals would then allocate particular billets to the troopers. The formal distribution of billets at the lodging of the cornet was a necessary and practical activity, and not a formality, because cavalrymen were vulnerable when quartered in villages and needed to know exactly where to rally if attacked. If the troop quartered for more than one night in a village, the lieutenant was expected to 'visit the Souldiers Quarters, and to see what good Orders are kept by them, and to take notice of the Names of the Souldiers, and of their Landlords Names, and to keep a Register of them, that so upon Complaints of the Landlord, it may easily be discovered who are the Offenders, and punishment indicted according to the offence'.[47]

The senior lieutenant in the regiment was the lieutenant and de facto commander of the colonel's troop; this officer was known as the captain lieutenant in recognition that his responsibilities were broader than the other lieutenants'. He drew the same pay and allowances as the other lieutenants but was likely to be preferred to fill the next vacancy as captain in the regiment.

The Cornet

The cornet was the third commissioned officer in a troop, and had the particular responsibility of carrying the troop's flag, also called a cornet. It was seen as a terrible disgrace for a troop to have its flag taken from it in battle and, technically, it was not supposed to use a replacement until it had redeemed itself by taking a flag from the enemy. However, there is no evidence to suggest that this restriction was followed in practice during the English Civil War.

The Quartermaster

The quartermaster was another officer who ought to be

> a good Souldier, and well quallified, he being a Commission-Officer, and hath attained a good step of Preferment, and will not long rest there, especially if he be dilligent in the Duty of his Place, and of a good Behaviour, which he ought to have an especial Care of; For such Examples as the Officers are to the Souldiers, such commonly are the Souldiers; but its too often seen, that if the Officers be of a loose Deportment, the Souldiers are worse.

When the army marched in one body 'then he is to attend on the Quartermaster Generall for Orders, and a Ticket for the Troopes place of Quarter, if in Towns or Villages; If the Troop martch with a Brigade or Regiment, then he is to attend the Chief Officer that Commands, both for Orders and Quartering'.[48] He was to march

> before the Troop to provide quarter for them, he is to take two or more of the nimblest mounted Troopers along with him, and having provided quarter [i.e. found quarters for the troop], sends them back to direct the Troop to their quarters; there is likewise much fidelity required of them that are Quartermasters, by reason they distribute the word [the password to sentries] and the billits in the absence of the Cornet and superiour Officers.[49]

The Corporal

Corporals were also regarded as officers as they held an office or place within the hierarchy of the troop. But they did not have written commissions and so were not 'commission officers'. There were usually three corporals to each troop of cavalry, and each of them would be responsible for the day-to-day management of the troopers in one of the three squadrons into which most troops were divided.

It was 'requisite that they should have good experience in the Cavalry, being commonly sent forth with a party of horse to scout, and scoure the high wayes before the body, and to guard some passages of danger, and to assist the Lieutenant in placing the Sentinels where there particular squadrons are to perform that service'.[50] As noted above, the corporal would also be responsible for receiving details of the quarters allocated to troopers in his squadron and allocating specific quarters for the night to each man and his horse.

The Trumpeter

There were usually two trumpeters to a troop of cavalry, one of whom 'ought always to Quarter where the Cornet or Standard is lodged, because of the Orders that are brought to that place, that so he may be in a readiness to perform his Duty, by giving notice to the Troop, by Sounding of his Trumpet, according as the nature of the Command given him'.[51] Amongst his duties he 'must precisely at the time appointed him by his superiors, sound the Bouteszelle, that is clap on your saddles, the next is the Chevall, that is mount of horseback, the next sound of the Trumpet is the standard, that is repaire to your standard'. As part of their basic training the troopers were taught to 'know the severall sounds of the Trumpet, as when to saddle, when to mount, when to repaire to their standard; when to troop on, when to give the charge, when to retreat, when to attend the watch, and the like'.[52]

The other duty of a trumpeter, or a drummer from an infantry regiment, was to carry messages to an enemy garrison commander or to the commander of an opposing army, the theory being that a musician sounding his trumpet or beating his drum was giving obvious notice of his approach. While carrying a message he would be expected to 'observe if they can have so much liberty the enemies works [siegeworks or defences] and guards, and what they can further gather or espy in the enemies quarters, and so report it unto his commander in chiefe'.[53] Obviously both sides understood this, and it was common practice to blindfold the musician before he could see too much or deliberately try to mislead him about the morale of enemy soldiers or the state of their supplies. A general's lifeguard troop may also have had a trumpet major.[54]

The Kettledrummer

Sir James Turner, drawing upon his experience as a professional soldier in European wars, recorded that

> there is another Martial Instrument used with the Cavalry, which they call a Kettle-drum, there be two of them which hang upon the Horse before the Drummers Saddle, on both which he beats: They are not ordinary, Princes, Dukes and Earls, may have them with those Troops which ordinarily are called their Lifeguards, so may Generals and Lieutenant Generals, though they be not Noble-men.[55]

The Farrier and the Saddler

The value of these two specialists to a troop of cavalry was evident, and there is no contemporary comment on their duties other than they should be competent at their craft.

The Infantry

The infantry were formed into regiments with a headquarters and several companies but, as with the cavalry, there was no universal model governing the number of companies in a regiment or the number of soldiers in a company. Francis Markham, writing on the practice of the Dutch army in the early seventeenth century, commented:

> for the Regiment or full numbers of men which every Colonell should command, they are exceeding diverse and uncertaine, at no time holding any just rule or quantitie: for they sometimes containe five hundred men, sometimes a thousand, now fifteen hundred, then two thousand ... as I said in a former Epistle, I hold it best agreeing good discipline, that no regiment should exceed the number of one thousand.[56]

By the 1630s this was the generally held view in England and Scotland, expressed in *General Lessley's Direction and Order for the Exercising of Horse and Foot*, as he referred to there being 'ten Companies in a Regiment, consisting of a 1000 or 1200 men'.[57] The difference in the theoretical or optimum number was based on the number of men in the companies. A regiment of 1,000 men plus officers would have ten companies with 100 private or common soldiers in each company, an example of this model being the Scottish army sent to

Ireland in 1642.[58] A regiment of 1,200 soldiers plus officers was also organized in ten companies but with the three senior officers having stronger companies. This model worked on the basis that the colonel's company consisted of 200 soldiers, the lieutenant colonel's of 160 and the sergeant major's of 140, and each of seven captains commanded companies of 100 men. This model was followed as the optimum when the Earl of Essex's Parliamentary army was first formed,[59] but in 1644 the Earl of Essex's army was reformed with his own regiment to consist of 1,500 soldiers in thirteen companies plus officers, and other regiments to consist of 1,000 men in eight companies.[60] In each case the higher number of soldiers in the three staff officers' companies was retained. It is unclear which model the Royalist army used and, in practice, few colonels had anything approaching this number of men, and many found it difficult to raise the full number of companies. Sir Ralph Hopton, when lieutenant governor of Bristol, was left at first with 'sixe very weake Regiments of foote, in all not makeing above 1200 men' as his garrison.[61]

The New Model Army was formed using the Earl of Essex's original model of ten companies totalling 1,200 soldiers plus officers. The number of soldiers in a company fluctuated, following the usual contemporary practice of decreasing the number of private soldiers in a company when circumstances were peaceful, and increasing them for a new campaign. The objective of this practice was to maintain the officers, non-commissioned officers and a veteran cadre in being as it was far more effective to add recruits to a veteran regiment than raise a new one. The New Model infantry regiments were reorganized in 1648, with a reduction in numbers of private soldiers to eighty men in each of ten companies in a regiment, leaving the number of officers and non-commissioned officers unchanged. Once committed to a new campaign the number of soldiers was quickly increased by recruits, usually back to 100 soldiers for each company, but occasionally up to the original model of ten companies of 1,200 men plus officers. In August 1651 Lieutenant Colonel Cobbett was authorized to make up his regiment to 1,200 in ten companies.[62] By 1652 the establishment of an English infantry regiment in England and Scotland had returned to the original model of ten companies comprising 1,200 men plus officers.[63] However, numbers continued to fluctuate according to local conditions and, in Scotland, had reduced to around seventy men in a company by 1658, when General Monk issued instructions to 'entertaine ten men in each companie whereby the regiment may be recruited to the number of 800'.[64]

The infantrymen in the New Model Army were armed on a ratio of two musketeers to one pikemen, although this could alter where local conditions – such as in Ireland after the defeat of the main Irish armies – required a higher proportion of musketeers. Richard Elton specifically comments on this in his manual *The Compleat Body of the Art Military*, when he describes the 'plain way of exercising a Company, as usually it is practiced in the Army, our Companies consisting of one hundred men, two parts being Musketeer, and a third Pikes, the depth of our Files being always six deep in the Armies of England, Scotland and Ireland'.[65]

The staff officers of a regiment according to the establishment of October 1652 was as follows:[66]

colonel
lieutenant colonel
sergeant major
quartermaster
provost marshal
wagoner or carriage master
preacher
[chirurgeon plus two chirurgeon's mates]
gunsmith plus one gunsmith's mate
drum major

The establishment list omits the chirurgeon and his two mates, but this must be an error as these officers are found on all establishments throughout this period. The make-up of the regiment is shown in the table below.

Staff Officers
The role of most of the staff officers was essentially the same for the infantry as for the cavalry. There were five differences in the officers' positions:

- an infantry regiment always had a lieutenant colonel
- an infantry regiment had only one quartermaster for the whole regiment, and he was part of the headquarters staff, while in the cavalry there was one quartermaster for each troop
- an infantry regiment had a wagon-master on the regimental staff[67]
- the staff of an infantry regiment included an armourer
- an infantry regiment included a drum major in addition to the drummers in each company; this officer can be found listed with the staff or, sometimes, on the roll of the colonel's own company.

Regimental make-up

Colonel's company	Lieutenant colonel's company	Sergeant major's company	Each of the 7 captains' companies
Colonel (as captain)	Lieutenant colonel (as captain)	Sergeant major (as captain)	Captain
Lieutenant (captain lieutenant)	Lieutenant	Lieutenant	Lieutenant
Ensign	Ensign	Ensign	Ensign
4 sergeants	3 sergeants	3 sergeants	2 sergeants
4 corporals	3 corporals	3 corporals	3 corporals
2 drummers	2 drummers	2 drummers	2 drummers
Gentleman of the armes	Gentleman of the armes	Gentleman of the armes	Gentleman of the armes
200 soldiers	160 soldiers	140 soldiers	100 soldiers

The duties of two of the three field officers, the colonel and the lieutenant colonel, were similar to those described above for the cavalry. But those of the infantry sergeant major were more specific to the infantry role.

Sergeant Major

This officer had the technical responsibility to draw up the regiment in the formation for the march or battle, and he had to be an experienced officer if he was to do this successfully. Richard Elton described the responsibilities of this officer:

> his duty is every morning, and evening, or upon any other occasion, to attend upon the General, Martiall of the Field, or Serjeant-Major-General of the Army, to receive his Orders how, or in what manner, the Regiment shall march, whether in a single Battalion, or else in two, [or] to be joined with others. After which he gives order accordingly unto the Captains how to draw up their Companies & orders them accordingly. At which time of imbattelling or marching, he ought to be as near as the midst of the Regiment as he can, for the better regulating of them.

In order to carry out his duties in deploying the regiment the sergeant major had to be 'well verst in the severall drawing up of Regiments, with their various forms of Battail, that according to the condition of the place, ground, number of men and Orders received from the Major General, or Majors of the Brigades, he may not shew himself a Novice, or one that is to seek'.[68]

On the battlefield 'he is to be on horse-back, in regard he is the eyes, hands and feet thereof [of the regiment]: in time of battail he is to see every Officer to perform his charge, and Souldier his duty, forcing and compelling them forward, if in case they turn their backs'.[69] In the absence of the colonel or lieutenant colonel, the sergeant major was responsible for training and exercising the regiment, and in practice he would usually be the officer who did so. In summary, he 'ought to be well grounded in all Military Affaires, and to be both wise and valiant'.[70]

One of the sergeant majors in a brigade of infantry also fulfilled the role of 'major of the brigade'. This officer 'receives the Word [password] and other orders from the Major-General, and gives them to the Majors of the other Regiments of the Brigade, and they to their Colonels and Lieutenant-Colonels'. Sir James Turner recorded that 'This Major of the Brigade is ordinarily he who is Major of the oldest Regiment of that Brigade',[71] presumably on the basis that he would be the most experienced and best fitted for the job.

The Wagon-Master

The regimental wagon-master was responsible for the regiment's baggage and the sutlers, soldiers' wives and other followers who accompanied it. Turner considered that:

every Regiment, whether of horse or foot, should have a Waggon or a Baggage-master, and where the establishment of the Prince doth allow him no pay, the Colonel should order a sufficient Serjeant or Corporal to exercise that Office by turns, these are to see that every Officers Baggage from the highest to the lowest, march according to the Dignity and Precedency of him to whom it belongs, whether it be carried on Waggons, Carts or Horses. But these Regiment Baggage-Masters are not to suffer the Baggage of the Regiments to march, till they have received their Directions from the Waggon-Master General, when, and in what manner it shall be done.[72]

During the English Civil War, the staff of an infantry regiment formally included a wagon-master, but that of a cavalry regiment did not. Some cavalry regiments did include an officer with this title, but others presumably followed Turner's advice and gave this responsibility to one of the corporals.

The Drum Major

The drum major or drummer major had the responsibility

to receive from the Major of the Regiment at what hour he is to beat to the watch, when the Dian and when the Taptoo wherewith he is to acquaint the several Drummers of companies, and appoint them by turns for these Beatings. He is also to order them in what divisions each of them shall beat when the Regiment marcheth, and they are to obey all his directions punctually.[73]

The point of this last comment was that 'if all the Captains Drums should beat together, it would quickly tire them out; therefore for their ease, it is his place and duty to order them according to discretion to take their turnes to beat'.[74]

The Gunsmith

This officer is not usually listed on an infantry regiment's staff but he and an assistant do appear on the establishment of October 1652. George Monk sought the retention in 1657 of this position in each infantry regiment – and several other specialists in his army in Scotland – in a statement: 'Reasons for the continuance of the officers undernamed that were not in the former Establishment, but afterwards continued by particular order, being it was thought necessary to continue them'. He described the value of this position:

A Gunsmith to each regiment of foote is desired to bee continued, for truly they are very useful to the regiments in mending of their armes, besides where regiments have any companies that are in out garrisons where there are none to mend their armes, the Gunsmith[s] goe and mend them, and I thinke it will not be safe to have soe many armes as we shall have to bee mended should be in the hands of Scotchmen.[75]

Officers and Men of an Infantry Company

The roles and responsibilities of the captain, lieutenant and ensign were broadly similar to those of the captain, lieutenant and cornet in the cavalry. One important difference is that an infantry company was not a battlefield unit, while a cavalry troop could be. The companies of an infantry regiment were combined for battle to create one, two or possibly three battalions, or if the regiment was weak, it was combined with another weak regiment to form a single battalion. The net effect of this was that, in battle, the role of the company officers related to requirements of the battalion of which their soldiers formed a part. In a weak regiment there would be more officers than there would be active positions for them to fill on the battlefield. The non-commissioned officers had different roles in an infantry company from their counterparts in the cavalry.

Sergeants

Most infantry companies had two sergeants, although the colonel's company might have three or four and the lieutenant colonel's might, occasionally, have three. George Monk recommended the use of six sergeants to a company of 150 soldiers plus officers, although his suggestions were not taken up, and this followed his general opinion that a company needed more NCOs for practical operations than the English establishment allowed.

Richard Elton considered that 'he that is a Serjeant to a Company, ought to be well skill'd in the Postures, and all Military Motions, whereby in the first place he may endeavour to correct the errours of such who handle not the Arms in a handsome, or a serviceable way'. He carried a halberd as an

indication of his rank and 'perceiving any Souldier out of order, he may cast in his Halberd between their Ranks, to cause him to march even a brest with his right and left hand men'. In battle he was to see that 'the Muskettiers in time of skirmishing present all even a brest, with their Matches all cockt, giving fire all together in good Order; and to direct them to fall off and rally again in the Reer of their own divisions. His duty is likewise to fetch Ammunition, Powder, Match and all other Materials of the Companie.' In camp he was 'every perticuler evening to attend at the place of Parade, or at the Major's Lodging, to fetch the Word, and carry it to his

Sergeant. As indicated by the halberd, a sergeant of the Trained Bands c.1635.

Captain, Lieutenant, Ensigne and Corporals; and likewise as soon as he is come unto his Guard he must direct the Corporals where to set out the Perdues and Sentinels, and how to order his Watch'.[76]

Corporals

There were usually three corporals in an infantry company, although the colonel's company may have had four. The corporal was armed as the other infantrymen, typically one of the three as a pikeman and the other two as musketeers. While the sergeant may have supervised and observed the soldiers at arms training, it was the specific responsibility of the corporal to

> teach and instruct them in the use of the Pike, and Musket, and to have a Roll and List of his men in his division or squadron. And when a souldiers name is crossed out, he is to give notice unto his Serjeant; and when a new one shall supply his place, his care must be to instruct and enable him in the Postures of such armes as he shall bear. Being with his squadron upon his Guard, he is to provide them with wood, coal, candle and light.

The Corporal was also to 'take care of the baggage and money of such as are hurt or sick, and to be in his own carriage sober, wise and discreet, for the avoiding ill example unto others'.[77]

Drummers

There were usually two drummers in an infantry company who were to 'know how to beat all the several points of War'. The drummer's other duty in respect of carrying messages was the same as that described above for the trumpeter.

Gentleman of the Armes

This officer was not always found on the company strength. He was responsible for the weapons of the company, and it was his duty 'to see that the souldiers keep their armes neat and clean, and that they be well fixed; and if any thing be amiss or broken, he is to have them carried to the Armourers to be repaired'. He would also take responsibility for keeping the arms of any sick or dead soldiers in order to prevent them being lost or stolen, and he 'was likewise to mark and figure the armes of the Company, and to preserve and keep a List of what number of figure each Souldier shall bear upon his Arms. He is likewise to keep the powder, bullet and match, and to deliver it forth upon occasions to the Corporals.'[78]

Lanspassadoe

Although this non-commissioned officer was found in European armies, there is little record of his use during the English Civil War. This rank appears on the roll of two of the infantry regiments of the Eastern Association, Sergeant Major General Lawrence Crawford's regiment and Colonel Sir John Palgrave's regiment.[79] The lanspassadoe was, essentially, an assistant to the corporal. He is not found in the New Model Army.

The Clerk

Although he was not on the formal establishment of all companies, most would have a company clerk or scrivener who 'keeps the Rolls of the Company, receives the Pay and gives it out according to the directions of the Captain, to whose command he is only lyable, and to whom only he is accountable, and in his absence to the Lieutenant. He ought to have so much literature as to read and write fair, and to have some skill at Arithmetick'.[80] He was on 'every pay-day to deliver up a true bill, giving an account unto his Captain of all such moneys he hath either received or paid forth'.[81] A seventeenth-century army generated a surprising amount of paper work, and although the responsibilities of several officers required them to undertake it, much of it must actually have been done by the regimental clerk. Richard Elton commented that the clerk 'ought to be very just and honest', a comment which might indicate that a captain would be fortunate to find one that was.

Dragoons

As they marched with the cavalry, dragoons 'are subordinate to the General, Lieutenant General or Major-General of the Horse'. However, their main fighting role was as infantry, since dragoons were 'Musketeers mounted on Horses, appointed to march with Cavalry, in regard there are not only many occasions, wherein Foot can assist the Horse, but that seldome there is any occasion of service against an Enemy, but wherein it is both fit and necessary to joyn some Foot with the Horse'.[82] J.B., writing circa 1660/1661, considered they 'were invented for special Services, to assist the Cavalry as Infantry'.[83] They were very useful soldiers, versatile on campaign and effective for internal security. They had a bad, though probably well-deserved, reputation as plunderers.

Since they were, essentially, mounted infantry, dragoons were organized on the same lines as an infantry regiment. When it was first raised, the New Model Army included one complete dragoon regiment comprising ten companies of 100 dragoons each plus officers, but this was exceptional and was probably the only regiment raised at this strength during the Civil War. It was more usual for regiments to consist of five or six companies and quite common to find independent, unregimented companies. The Earl of Orrery recommended that each regiment of cavalry should consist of six troops of cavalry troopers and one company of dragoons, as he believed that 'Dragoons thus annexed to the Horse, are much better than they are, when Regimented entire, and by themselves'. He gave some substantial practical reasons for this on the basis that the cavalry commanders would be 'more careful of them, and will not needlessly harass them by extraordinary and unequal duty', and the

Horse Officers knowing all their Dragoons by name, and they knowing all the Horse Officers, they are the more likely to fight chearfully for them, or not to escape unpunished if they be remiss; for every one being known, none can escape by ignorance; the contrary to which is often experimented [experienced] in commanded Parties, when the Officers are unknown to the Soldiers, and the Soldiers to the Officers.[84]

Orrery left another practical reason until last, as he wrote that 'to omit many other particulars, some have observed that as the Dragoons are commonly the briskest, and daringst of the private Soldiers, so they are also the least sober; and 'tis likelier to wean them from that fault, when they are but a seventh part of the Regiments, then when they are an entire Regiment, and all Birds of one Feather'.[85]

The most complete list of the officers and men of a dragoon regiment is set out in J.B.'s *Some Brief Instructions for the Exercising of the Horse-Troopes*. This showed the following staff officers:

colonel
sergeant major
quartermaster
preacher
provost marshal
chirurgeon and two mates.

The second in command of the regiment of dragons in the New Model Army was the sergeant major, as shown in the list above. However, there is an example of a lieutenant colonel of dragoons, as John Lilburne was lieutenant colonel and de facto commander of the dragoons in the Earl of Manchester's regiment in the Army of the Eastern Association.

The officers and men of the company were given as:

captain (the colonel or sergeant major as 'captain' of his own troops or a
    captain for the remaining troops in the regiment)
lieutenant (captain lieutenant in the colonel's troop)
cornet
two sergeants
three corporals
two drummers
a farrier.

The non-commissioned officers of a dragoon regiment show its mixed status. It had the sergeants and drummers of an infantry company, but included a farrier. The corporal in a dragoon company held the rank and position of an infantry corporal, not that of a corporal in the cavalry. The junior commissioned officer carrying the company flag was called a cornet – the cavalry rank – not an ensign.

The Artillery Train

The artillery train included a wide range of specialists, together with one or more companies of 'firelocks' to provide guards. The most complete list is provided by J.B. and contains the following 'Officers, Artificers, and Attendants of the Trayne of Artillery, consisting of 26 Peeces':[86]

General of the Ordnance
Lieutenant General
Assistant
2 clerks
Surveyor or Controller
2 clerks
The Chief Engineer
A clerk
Six Engineers for ordering Trenches, Fortifications, and Approaches
6 clerks
Fifteen Guides or Conductors
A Pay–Master
2 clerks
Two Commissioners of Ordnance, Mattrosses and Amunition
2 clerks
20 Gentlemen of the Ordnance
A Commissary to distribute Victual
2 clerks attending him
A Purveyor General for Munition, and all necessaries for the Ordnance
2 Horses [horsemen] to assist him
A Waggon-master for the Artillery
2 Assistants
20 Conductors attending him
A Principal Conductor for the Artillery for draught Horses and Ammunition
A Commissary for the Trayne of Artillery for the draught horses
Quartermaster for the Trayne of Artillery
Master of the Miners
25 other Miners
3 Captains to 600 Pioneers
3 Lieutenants
3 Overseers of the Pioneers work
2 Petardiers or Fire-workers
To each of them [the Petardiers] 4 Attendants
One Master Gunner
3 Master Gunner's Mates
20 Gunners
30 Gunners [the 30 Gunners being on a lower rate of pay than the 20 above]
200 Labourers
A Provost Marshal of the Artillery

3 Under Jaylors
A Battery Master
A Bridge Master with 100 Matrosses to work about Rivers
An Assistant to him
100 Mattrosses
A Chaplain
An Ensign
A Drum
A Trumpeter
A Chirurgeon
2 Under Barber Chirurgeons
A Master Carpenter
2 Mates
A Master Black-Smith
2 Mates
6 Servants
A Master Wheelwright
2 Mates
8 Servants
600 Pioneers
3 Tent Keepers
9 Servants
An Armourer
4 Servants under him
A Basket-maker for Gabions, hurdles and Baskets
4 Servants
A Collor-maker
4 Servants
A Gun-Smith
2 Servants
A Ladle-maker
4 Servants
A Cooper
4 Servants
A Ropemaker
4 Servants

Chapter Seven
Strategy, Tactics and Siege Warfare

Campaign Strategy

In the early seventeenth century there were two contrasting campaign strategies which influenced English military theory and practice. One – the Dutch style – had evolved during the siege warfare which characterized the war in the Low Countries and the other, the Swedish style, had evolved during the warfare in Germany during the Thirty Years War. Both used garrisons and fortified strong points to maintain or contest control over territory, and the resources of recruits, money and military supplies which that control could bring, or to hold strategic strong points along military supply routes. The terrain over which these wars were fought influenced strategy, as the Dutch fought their war in a relatively small geographic area against a Spanish army which was, at first, superior to their own. This made the option of siege warfare more attractive than risking the outcome of the war on the open battlefield, and the Dutch became proficient in the use of defensive earthworks built according to the latest Italian theory on fortifications. The Thirty Years War in Germany was fought over a far greater area and one where cities and towns were not as heavily fortified as in the Low Countries. This said, the key difference was the intentions – the campaign strategy – of the commanders who followed one style or the other and led their armies accordingly. A commander who followed the Dutch military style pioneered by Prince Maurice of Nassau tended towards caution and, although he trained his army to fight in the open field, he would see battle as a last resort. But a commander who followed the example of the Swedish King, Gustavus Adolphus, saw bringing the enemy to battle as the objective of the whole campaign.

The perspective of the Dutch commander, Prince Maurice, can be judged from his own words – spoken as he saw the completion of his greatest battlefield success at the battle of Nieuwpoort (2 July 1600) and recorded by the English officer Sir Edward Cecil:

> This caused the late Prince of Orange (in my hearing) when hee had fought the Battel of Nieuport: to this purpose, to direct speech unto some

Hottspurrs of the French nation, that had often pressed him to give
Battell. Messirs (saith hee) now you have had your desires & now you
have fought a Battell, nay more, you have gained [i.e. won] a Battelll. But
lett mee tell you herewithall that the State hath not gotten so much as a
Quart d'escu by it; and had wee lost the Day, wee had lost all by it: Even
all that my self and my Ancestors have been these three scoore and ten
yeares a geting and preserving. And therefore Messirs, trouble mee no
more hereafter, with talking to mee of Battells.[1]

The Dutch army, in which most English officers with professional experience
had served, was trained to fight battles in the open field but actually fought few
battles. At first sight this appears contradictory as, amongst contemporary
soldiers, the most widely debated elements of the military reforms introduced
by Prince Maurice were infantry training and the tactical battlefield
deployment of his army in smaller units and mutually supporting battle lines.
The underlying reason for this extensive training in battlefield deployment was
credibility, the necessity in siege warfare for each side to have a field army
which could fight in the open field. This was necessary because a key part of
all siege warfare was the morale of the garrison and citizens of a besieged city
or town. The army which marched to relieve a siege must represent a credible
threat to the besiegers, or the latter would have no reason to raise the siege and
the garrison would have no hope of relief. A cautious commander of a relief
force might not actually commit his army to battle and might prefer to threaten
action though manoeuvre rather than risk a battle, but without a credible
battlefield army he was impotent. The same is true for a besieging army as, if
it cannot contest the relief force in battle, it has no option but to raise the siege
and march away.

The English professional soldier John Bingham, who had served in the
Dutch army, summarized this in his book *The Art of Embattailing an Army, or,
The Second Part of Aelians Tactics*, which was printed in 1629 with the
comment:

For the profit of the Treatise [Bingham's book], I say no more than this,
it containeth the practice of the best Generals of all antiquity concerning
the formes of Batailes. And whereas many hold opinion, that it sorteth
not with the use of or times, they must give me leave to be of another
mind: Indeed our actions in Warre are only now a dayes and [in] sieges
oppugnations of Cities, Battailes wee heare not of, save only of a few in
France, and that of Newport in the Low-Countries. But this manner will
not last always, nor is there any conquest to be made without Battailes. He
that is Master of the field, may dispose of his affaires as he listeth, hee
may spoyle the Enemies Countrey at his pleasure, he may march where
he thinketh best, he may lay siege to what Towne he is disposed, he may
raise any siege that the Enemy hath layed against him. Neither can any
man be Master of the field without Battaile.[2]

The net effect of this was that although officers trained in the Dutch school of warfare served in an army whose strategy was based on siege warfare, they were well trained and practised in battlefield deployments.

If John Bingham had written his treatise a few years later, he would have seen the realization of his theory, as the Swedish army under King Gustavus Adolphus followed a far more aggressive strategy with the objective of actively seeking battle. The Swedish were not limited to this battlefield strategy and were quite capable of using manoeuvre and siege warfare in the Dutch style where it suited them, but they were much more willing to risk battle, particularly after their initial success at the battle of Breitenfeld (17 September 1631). Apart from the personal preference of their commander, the environment they fought in lent itself to this form of strategy. The Swedish army fought over a far larger geographical area, and the Germany it fought over was not a unified country but was formed of a large number of separate states where each ruler had his own individual ambitions for advancement or simple survival. Victory in battle brought a huge boost to the victorious commander, as it would encourage wavering allies and lead other states to abandon their previous allegiance and join the winning side. From these allies, old and new, the victorious commander would gain access to the supplies of men, money and military equipment that he needed to continue his campaigns. One other factor was that although the Swedish King genuinely saw his war as necessary to support German Protestants in the face of the power of the Catholic Emperor, as well as a political opportunity to expand Swedish control over the southern Baltic coast, he was not fighting on Swedish soil. If his campaign failed, Gustavus Adolphus could retreat back across the Baltic Sea to Sweden, and his Imperialist opponents would not be able to pursue him immediately, as they did not have an effective navy in the Baltic.

The consequences of Gustavus Adolphus's victories had a profound effect on the officers of the day, particularly younger officers, and many saw his success not only as a significant strategic result but as one which would provide an immediate boost to the personal reputation of a successful general. The consequences of defeat were severe but the rewards of battlefield victory were far greater than the slow progress of siege warfare. The decision by the young Louis de Bourbon, Duc d' Enghien (and later the Prince de Condé), to fight a battle at Rocroi (19 May 1643) against the Spanish army of Flanders provided a clear example of this. The French commander, then aged only twenty-two, could have followed the advice of his subordinate general, Marshal Francois L'Hopital, Comte de Rosnay, and forced the Spanish army to retreat by manoeuvre but he chose to risk battle.

The Earl of Orrery, who had fought in Ireland during the Civil Wars, summarized this perspective in his book *A Treatise of the Art of War*, printed in 1677:

All who have commanded Armies, or written of the Military Art have universally agreed, that no one act of War, is so great in it self, or in the

Consequences of it, as Fighting a Battel; since the winning of one, has not only been the cause of taking of the place besieged, (if in the Field the Army is defeated which comes to relieve it) but also by the gaining of the Victory, a Province, nay, a Kingdom has often been the Reward of the Victorious.

But as the Advantages are eminent to him who wins it, so the Prejudices are no less to him who loses it; and therefore nothing ought to be more exactly consider'd and weigh'd in War, than whether a decisive Battel shall be given, before the resolution to fight it, is taken.[3]

In England during the First Civil War there were commanders who took a cautious approach and others who followed the Swedish model, seeing battle as the focus of their campaigns; there were others, of course, whose strategy was a combination of the two. The environment in which English commanders fought during the Civil Wars was closer to Germany than the Low Countries in the sense that there were few places which were fortified in the modern fashion. An example of a commander strongly influenced by the Swedish strategic style was the King's nephew, Prince Rupert. He was a young man, aged only twenty-three when the Civil War began, and the younger son of a German ruler, the Elector Palatine, who had been driven from his territory during the opening stages of the Thirty Years War. Although loyal to his uncle's cause, Prince Rupert had no ties to England itself and had a burning ambition to make a reputation as a successful general. He was a highly competent commander, his confidence in his military ability leading him to seek battle where another more cautious commander would not.

Prince Rupert's decision to risk battle at Marston Moor (2 July 1644), after he had already successfully raised the siege of York, underlines the downside of risking battle, as the Royalists' defeat lost them the north of England. Parliamentary commanders who followed Gustavus Adolphus's aggressive model, but with better success than Prince Rupert on the day, included Oliver Cromwell and the Parliament's commander in Ireland, Michael Jones. All three of these officers, Prince Rupert, Oliver Cromwell and Michael Jones, had been cavalry commanders before they led an army, and the contemporary viewpoint was that an officer with this background was more likely to favour aggressive tactics. Edward Cecil, Lord Wimbledon, provided an example of this perspective with his comment that 'the present Prince of Orange [Prince Henry] the right worthy successor of his famous brother, who having bin Generall of the Horse about twenty yeares together, is thereby become more daring than his Brother'.[4]

By way of comparison, the Earl of Manchester, commander of the Parliamentary Army of the Eastern Association, was a general whose caution mirrored that of Prince Maurice of Nassau. The most famous example of Manchester's perspective was at a council of war on 10 November 1644, where the Parliamentary generals met to consider whether they would challenge King Charles's march to recover field artillery he had left at Donnington Castle.

Manchester advised caution on the grounds that 'if we beat the King ninety and nine times, yet he is king still, and so will his posterity be after him, but if the King beat us once we shall all be hanged and our posterity made slaves'.[5] Manchester's cavalry commander, Oliver Cromwell, contemptuously responded: 'My Lord, if this be so, why did we take up arms at first? This is against fighting ever hereafter. If so, let us make peace, be it never so base.'

The creation of the New Model Army should be seen against this background. Its structure shows that it was originally designed as a battlefield army, an army whose objective was to win the war through battlefield success. The indications for this are simple. The New Model Army consisted of twelve regiments of infantry, eleven of cavalry and one of dragoons. In 1645 the infantry regiments of the New Model Army consisted of 1,200 men plus officers, and the cavalry regiments of 600 men plus officers. A contemporary army whose main objective was siege warfare would, by contemporary practice, have a ratio of three infantrymen to one cavalryman, but one whose service was to fight in the open field would have a ratio of two infantrymen to one cavalryman. George Monk referred to this in his book *Observations upon Military & Political Affairs*, written *c*.1645/1647, with the comment:

> Where your Service lieth in Campania [i.e. open country], the proportion of your Army ought to be two Footmen to one Horseman, besides your Dragooners. But where the Service of your Army shall be most in Sieges, there you ought to have three Footmen unto one Horseman; and sometimes four Footmen to one Horsemen, besides your Dragoons; provided your Enemy be not able to over master you in Horse.[6]

This was an army designed according to the military theory of the day with one aim in mind, the defeat of the best of the surviving Royalist armies, the King's Oxford Army.

The success of the New Model Army at its first great battle at Naseby (14 June 1645) set the tone for this new army and confirmed it as a force in which both officers and soldiers confidently saw themselves as a successful fighting army. In the army propaganda printed for distribution in London during the army mutiny of 1647, the proud boast of the New Model was that it had succeeded in breaking the Royalist opposition in one great campaign where other armies had previously been mired in stalemate – where 'Noe other Army could doe the Business'. Oliver Cromwell's comment on the campaign which ended in the battle of Preston (17 August 1648) continues this aggressive and confident tone: 'It was thought that to engage the enemy to fight was our business; and the reason aforesaid giving us hopes that our marching on the north side of Ribble would effect it, it was resolved that we should march over the bridge; which accordingly we did.'[7] To put this in context, Cromwell's army was outnumbered by its Scottish opponents on this campaign but, with a bold move, he attacked and defeated them before they could concentrate their forces. It was this confidence in its fighting ability and its commanders that enabled an army described by one of its officers in 1650 as a 'poor, shattered,

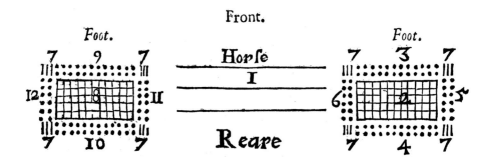

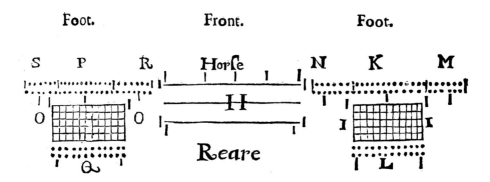

Cavalry and infantry deployed together, from George Monk's Observations upon Political & Military Affairs. Infantry support for cavalry wings usually consisted only of musketeers, but these plans show battalions of pikemen and musketeers (the musketeers being the dots and the pikemen the squares). This may represent the practice of English forces fighting in Ireland or it may simply be Monk's personal preference.

Foot.

Front.

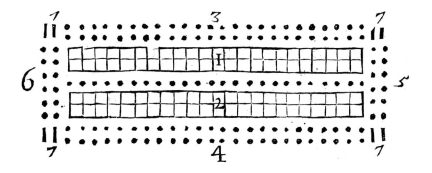

Reer.

Infantry in square. An infantry formation was composed of both musketeers and pikemen, and, as the bayonet had not yet been introduced, the whole formation depended upon its pikemen as defence against cavalry. Most manuals include a square or oblong formation of this type as defence against cavalry. This example is from Monk's Observations upon Political & Military Affairs.

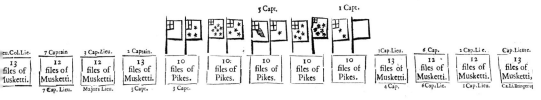

New Model infantry. This is the deployment of Colonel Thomas Rainsborough's regiment for its march through the City of London on 7 August 1647. This is a battle formation as the new Model Army, as this march was a demonstration of strength. Note that this example demonstrates that in 1647 the New Model Army used a ratio of two musketeers to each pikeman.

hungry, discouraged' English army to make one last great effort and, although outnumbered, to win Cromwell's greatest victory over the Scots at Dunbar (3 September 1650).

Battlefield Deployment

The tactics used by Civil War armies were influenced by three different tactical styles, the Dutch style designed by Prince Maurice of Nassau and his associates, the Swedish style designed by King Gustavus Adolphus and the German style which evolved during the Thirty Years War and which was, essentially, a composite of the other two. Whichever style, or styles, influenced him, a commander would commence his campaign with a clear idea of the tactical deployments that he intended to use, and if he was to have any hope of success, he would have carried out a series of practice deployments so as to ensure that his army could carry out his orders without confusion. As the Scottish professional soldier Sir James Turner commented:

> In the marshalling of Regiments, Brigades, Companies, and Troops either of Horse or Foot, Commanders, must be very cautious when they have to do with an enemy, not to change the ordinary forms, for if at that time you offer to introduce any new form wherewith your men are not acquainted, you shall not fail to put them in some confusion, than which an enemy cannot desire a greater advantage. If you have a new figure of Battel in your head, be sure to accustom your Companies and Regiment very often by exercise to the practice of it, before you make use of it in earnest.[8]

Both Prince Maurice of Nassau and King Gustavus Adolphus were noted for carrying out these practice deployments, and Prince Maurice's army is recorded doing so on campaign. A commander may formulate his plans in conjunction with his senior officers or particularly trusted colleagues, or he may simply impose them as his personal preference. Once the decision had been made, the chosen plan would be drawn out on paper by the general. The Sieur du Praissac, whose book *Discours militaires* followed the Dutch practice, described this process in detail. The extract below is taken from the English edition translated by John Cruso and published in 1639:

> The Sergeant major Generall receiveth from the Generall a plat [plan] of the forms which he will give to his Armie, the disposition and placing of the members of it, Cavallrie, Infanterie, Artillerie; the order which they should observe in fight, with commission signed by the Generall to dispose it in that manner.
>
>   To this commission the whole Armie must yield obedience, and the Sergeant major Generall with Marshals of the field shall dispose thereof, according to the form and place which the Generall shall have prescribed.[9]

Several copies of the plan would be made, and officers down to the level of brigade commanders (of infantry or cavalry) would receive a copy at the general's council of war, if they attended it, or from the sergeant major general. The plan had to be distributed down to brigade level because an army deployed from line of march into its fighting formation brigade by brigade, and so the brigade commander had to know his brigade's place in the deployment. When in enemy territory the army would also march out of camp brigade by brigade, in the same sequence it would use to deploy into battle formation, with the right-hand cavalry brigade of the chosen deployment marching out first, then the right infantry brigade and so on.

A commander's choice of battle plan would be based upon the range of deployment currently in use and, by the late 1630s, this would be based on one of four models. Two of these were Dutch, one was Swedish and the fourth was the composite 'German' style. These were all broad models, and there were variations in practice because of the actual number of infantry or cavalry available, or the commander's preference to have one cavalry wing stronger than the other on the day, but the basic model would be drawn from one of these four. All were based on the concept of a centre of infantry with cavalry on each wing and, if the commander chose to do so, additional cavalry troops deployed immediately behind the first infantry line.[10] Artillery pieces were usually placed in pairs or fours across the battle line but there was no absolute rule, and larger batteries were formed on occasion.

Of the two main Dutch deployment styles, the first deployed the central infantry in a wedge shape and the second deployed each of three brigades alongside one another in order to deploy the infantry in three separate battle lines, one behind the other. Both Dutch deployment styles were used by Protestant German and Danish armies during the early stages of the Thirty Years War, with the second being more popular. The English army practised this deployment style during the Bishops' Wars – as a contemporary engraving by Wenceslaus Hollar demonstrates – but neither of the Dutch styles was used

Deployment of the English army during the Bishops' Wars. An engraving by Wenceslaus Hollar showing the English army drawn up in a Dutch formation, three parallel brigades in a diamond pattern.

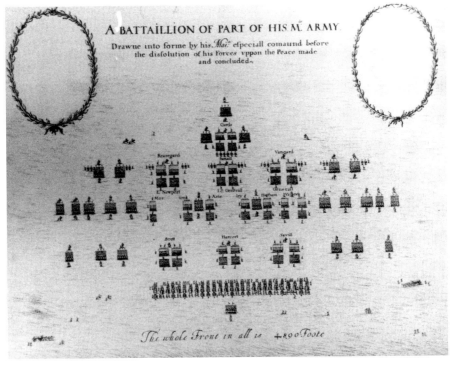

during the Civil War itself. Although there were fewer cavalry in Dutch armies than those fighting in Germany, some of Prince Maurice's deployments used supporting cavalry troops drawn up behind the first infantry line. There were real advantages in this deployment as it could serve to protect its own infantry if they were forced back or to support a successful infantry attack. The Imperialist commander Raimondo Montecuccoli summarized this advantage in his manual *Sulle battaglie*, written around 1642, with the comment 'a small squadron of cavalry, acting promptly can wreak great havoc amongst large infantry battle lines'.[11] As well as using heavy field artillery, Prince Maurice also introduced lighter, more mobile artillery to support his infantry, a tactic recorded in 1622 when 'his Exc[ellency] drewe out in Battalia' for a practice deployment at Rozendale near Bergen-op-Zoom, and 'to every Manipall or Battalion there was allowed two of his Exc newe devised peeces called Drakes'.[12]

The second formation, in particular, influenced the later composite German style which evolved during the Thirty Years War. It was based on the three-line or *triplex acies* formation of the late Roman Republic, while the battalion size of *c*.500 men was based on the cohort of the classical Roman Empire rather than the smaller Republican maniples. As with all the Dutch military reforms, the Dutch battle order was based on classical ideas but was not simply a copy of them. The objective of this three-line deployment was that the second line could be used to support or relieve the first, but the last line was the final reserve and was only to be used as a last resort either as the last push to secure victory or as a fighting rearguard if the day went badly. Committing the rearguard to the battle was always a critical decision for the commander. If he could hold off a victorious enemy long enough, then the main part of his army could retreat and survive to fight another day. With a surviving core of experienced soldiers, a beaten commander could rebuild his army with recruits and continue the war, but if his veteran army was completely destroyed then any new forces he raised would be so severely outclassed by his opponents that he could no longer compete on the battlefield. The veteran Spanish Army of Flanders found itself in this position after its defeat by the French at the battle of Rocroi, and the Royalists had the same experience after their defeat by the New Model Army at the battle of Naseby (14 June 1645).

The three lines of a Dutch infantry deployment were positioned with the distance between the first two being approximately the width of an infantry unit – the objective being to allow units in the second line to manoeuvre by wheeling if necessary – but the distance between the second and third lines would be twice that distance. The reason for this was that if the first line was disordered its units would fall back and rally behind the second line, but the reserves in the third line would only be committed as a last resort. On a unit level, the Dutch also intended their small, manoeuvrable units to be able to support one another on the battlefield. Although in theory this could work by using individual units from the second line to support the first, there was in practice some concern that this would break the cohesion of the battle lines,

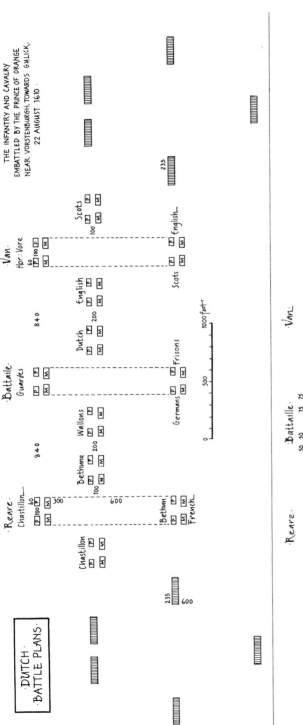
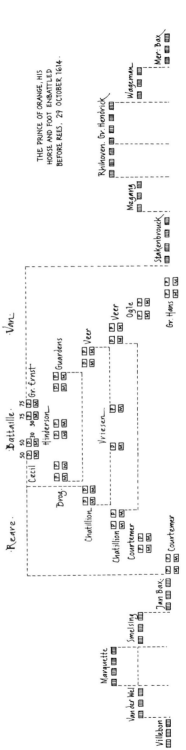

Dutch Deployments. The two types of deployment most used by Prince Maurice of Orange were three parallel brigades in diamond patterns or variations of a wedge shape.

THE DEPLOYMENT OF INFANTRY BRIGADES ACCORDING TO THE DUTCH MODEL

The tactical structure developed for the Dutch army by Prince Maurice of Nassau was influenced by the example of the classical past to use a large number of small infantry units - termed battalions. To get the most use out of the flexibility offered by the Dutch system, Prince Maurice needed a simple practical process to deploy his army from its marching formation to its fighting formation. The key to this process was to combine battalions in brigades and then deploy first the brigades themselves, and then the battalions within the brigades.

This plate shows contemporary manuscripts setting out how this process worked. The first of these, marked 'A' below, is from a manuscript drawn by Prince Maurice's cousin, Johann of Nassau, which records one of several practice deployments carried out by Prince Maurice's army during his campaign to take the city of Julich in 1610. This shows the second and third stages.

The second example, marked 'B' below, shows all three stages. This example was used in 1625 by the Danish Army of Christian IV, which copied the Dutch model. There are a smaller number of battalions in this example but the principle of using brigades remains the same. The third stage at the top shows where the two central battalions move from their original position (shown in white) to their final position (shown in black).

The deployment of infantry brigades according to the Dutch model.

and a commander was more likely to retire one line or part of it and replace it with the second. The Dutch usually deployed their battalions in pairs, one beside the other, and this gave the battalions the opportunity to operate flexibly in support of one another.

Although these deployments were intended for fighting in the open field, the large number of small units and concentration on the use of infantry firepower also made this a flexible design for battle on more broken ground, as Prince Maurice's victory amongst the sand dunes at Nieuwpoort demonstrated. The main strength of the Dutch army lay in its infantry, a reflection of the nature of the war of sieges in which the Dutch and their Spanish opponents were fighting. This was a position it could afford to take as its Spanish opponents organized their forces on similar lines and for the same reason; some cavalry were necessary but a large force of heavy battle cavalry were an unnecessary expense for siege warfare unless your opponent started recruiting them. The Dutch battle formations, as a whole, could be used both offensively and defensively, but the Dutch use of cavalry was defensive and based on the use of pistols, not swords, as the primary weapon. This use of cavalry kept them in close support of their infantry as a means of freezing opposing infantry formations and leaving them open to Dutch infantry firepower – as at the battle of Turnhout in 1597 – and as a balance against opposing cavalry where the Dutch objective was to keep a solid formation, break up attacking cavalry opponents through close-range firepower and then counter-attack. This preference for the use of pistols as the primary weapon for heavy cavalry – cuirassiers – was common to west European cavalry at the beginning of the seventeenth century, but was beginning to change in Germany by the 1620s. In the Dutch army lighter armed cavalry, arquebusiers armed with an arquebus or carbine, were used as supporting troops on the battlefield and for patrolling and scouting during the campaign.

The third option for deployment was Gustavus Adolphus's distinctive Swedish style. The Swedish developments did not exist in isolation and aspects such as the reduction in the depth of both infantry and cavalry units have to be seen in the context of developing military theory in the Netherlands and northern Germany. This said, Swedish tactics were also influenced by Gustavus Adolphus's campaigns in Poland against an opponent who had superior cavalry. This experience influenced the development of tactics marked by a unique infantry brigade formation – the 'Swedish Brigade', the concentration of volley firepower both in the main infantry formations and in direct support of the cavalry, and the use of aggressive cavalry tactics. The Swedish army was noted for its use of volley firing, concentrating its infantry fire with three ranks of musketeers firing together in one volley at close range – known as the 'Swedish salvee' – instead of firing rank by rank, and the use of light, mobile artillery in close support of the infantry and, by 1632, of the cavalry wings as well. For battle, musketeers formed in 'plottons' of fifty men were detached from the infantry regiments and deployed amongst the cavalry squadrons to provide firepower support. The Scottish professional soldier

Robert Munro, who served in the Swedish army, described the use of these detached musketeers at the battle of Breitenfeld

> by halfe three, our Cannon a little ceasing, the Horsemen on both wings charged furiously one another, our Horsemen with a resolution, abiding unloosing a Pistoll till the enemy had discharged first, and then at a neere distance our Musketiers meeting them with a Salve; then our horsemen discharged their Pistolls, and then charged through them with swords; and at their returne the Musketetiers were ready againe to give their second Salve of Musket amongst them; the enemy thus valiantly resisted by our Horsemen, and cruelly plagued by our Plottons of Musketiers, you may imagine how soone he would be discouraged after charging twice in this manner and repulsed.[13]

One disadvantage of this tactic, from the perspective of the musketeers, was that if the cavalry wing was broken then the cavalry would ride away, leaving the musketeers – without the pikemen necessary for infantry to resist cavalry – to be slaughtered, as in these circumstances 'these small Battalions are too much exposed to Ruine: for Shot onely, will not resist Horse in an open field, specially when those Shot also, are disanimated by the Flight or Routing of the Horse that had fought on their side'.[14] An exception to this general rule was provided by the Cornish musketeers of Sir Ralph Hopton's army, deployed in this way for an action on 5 July 1643, 'who, (poore men) though the horse were rowted between them kept their ground and preserv'd themselves till the E. of Carnarvon's Regiment of horse was drawn up to them', but this was unusual and the Cornish were notoriously tough infantry.[15]

Swedish cavalry were noted for their aggressive tactics and their use of lighter armed cavalry as battle cavalry instead of the heavy cuirassiers. The Swedes had little choice in this use of their cavalry, which would be classified as arquebusiers in other European armies, as they had neither the armour for cuirassiers nor native Swedish horses strong enough to bear the weight. Contemporary cavalry theory was moving away from the use of pistols as a primary weapon during the 1620s, but the caracole – a method of firing rank by rank at an opponent and then retiring – was still in use by many German mercenary cavalry regiments. The instructions for Swedish cavalrymen were 'only the first or at most the first two ranks, when near enough to see the whites of the enemy's eyes were to give fire, then to reach for their swords; the last rank however was to attack without shooting but with swords drawn, and to keep both pistols (or in the front ranks, one) in reserve for the melee'.[16] These instructions were closely observed in practice: Robert Munro recorded that at Breitenfeld 'the resolution of our horsemen on this service was praiseworthy, seeing they never loosed [fired] a pistol at the enemy till first they had discharged theirs'. Count Tilly, the commander of the combined Catholic League and Imperial troops at Breitenfeld, had been recorded as saying that 'he never had seriously considered using arquebusiers in a military engagement',

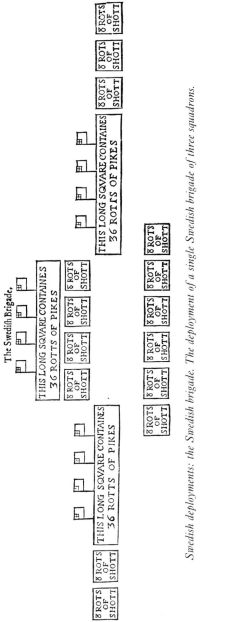

Swedish deployments: the Swedish brigade. The deployment of a single Swedish brigade of three squadrons.

so Gustavus Adolphus's Swedish troopers must have come as an unpleasant surprise.[17]

The distinctive Swedish infantry formation evolved during Gustavus Adolphus's campaigns, with the three-squadron arrowhead formation being used from around 1627. This was expanded by the addition of a fourth squadron to form a diamond formation around 1628, and this was used when the Swedish army first landed in Germany in 1630. By the time of the battle of Breitenfeld in 1631, the Swedish army had returned to the three-squadron arrowhead formation. The most significant difference between the Dutch and Swedish deployment patterns was that in the Dutch army, the diamond pattern brigades were used as a mechanism to form a three-line deployment with units from the same brigade in all three lines, but the Swedish brigade was a complete operational unit in itself and each of the two infantry lines of a deployment of Swedish brigades had complete brigades serving alongside one another. For example, at Breitenfeld there were four complete brigades in the first line and three complete brigades in the second. Sir Robert Munro described the deployment of the Swedish army at Breitenfeld:

> his Majestie then led up foure Briggads of foote, which were appointed to be the Battaile of the Armie, with a distance between every Briggad, that a regiment of horse might march out in grosse betwixt the Briggads, all foure being in one front, having their Ordnance planted before every Briggad ... Behinde these foure Briggads were drawne up the three Briggads of Reserve, with their Artillery before them.

Munro described the cavalry deployment at this battle: 'the Briggads of Horse which had Plottons of Musketiers to attend them were placed on the right and left wings of the foote, and some were placed betwixt the Battaile of foote and the Reserve, to second the foote as neede were'.[18] The Swedish infantry brigade could operate as a separate tactical unit. This offered advantages in opposing either infantry or cavalry – and the flexibility it offered was one reason why Gustavus Adolphus was able to move his reserve infantry brigades to fill the gap left by his fleeing Saxon allies at Breitenfeld – but it also required veteran officers and men for it to work effectively. It was probably last used by the Swedish army at the battle of Nordlingen in 1634 and was abandoned thereafter.

The fourth option was the composite German style. Gustavus Adolphus's outstanding battlefield successes had proved the advantage of the smaller battlefield units, called a battalion by the Dutch and a squadron by the Swedes, over larger formations, and the value of aggressive cavalry tactics over the caracole. The illustration opposite shows the last battle plan issued by the Imperialist general, Albrecht von Wallenstein, for his campaign of 1632; he used a slightly different deployment at the battle of Lützen (16 November 1632). The Imperialist officer Raimondo Montecuccoli, writing *c.*1642, showed that the Imperialists had accepted this change, commenting that while large units were useful in a retreat since 'they are immobile and of little offensive

HEADQUARTERS PLANS

GENERAL ALBRECHT VON WALLENSTEIN : IMPERIALIST BATTLE PLAN   1632

PRINCE RUPERT : ENGLISH ROYALIST BATTLE PLAN , RELIEF OF DONNINGTON CASTLE, 9 NOVEMBER 1644

PRINCE RUPERT : ENGLISH ROYALIST BATTLE PLAN, BATTLE OF NASEBY , 14 JUNE 1645

KEY

INFANTRY

CAVALRY

·105·B·

The latest deployment. The top plan shows the battle formation which the Imperialist generalissimo Albrecht von Wallenstein intended to use for his last campaign in 1632. He used one based on this at the battle of Lützen in 1632. Prince Rupert's battle plans for the relief of Donnington Castle, where no battle was fought, and the battle of Naseby show the influence of this latest European model in the infantry formations and the cavalry troops placed in support of the centre.

value, yet are difficult to break, they do serve a purpose when one wishes only to defend one's self. Nevertheless, their utility is limited and small units remain preferable. The latter can be led in any direction, are able to keep good order in all kinds of terrain and can fight repeatedly'.[19] On the use of the caracole Montecuccoli recorded that, at the battle of Nordlingen in September 1634, 'Although the Spanish cavalry, wont to fight after the manner of caracoles, was led by Gambacorta, a soldier of repute, it was nevertheless derided rather than praised because it was unable to hurt the enemy at all.'[20] By 1642 most European armies had trained their infantry to use the 'Swedish salvee' as well as other forms of infantry firing, and to use the tactic of attaching musketeers to their cavalry wings, although not all commanders made use of the latter.

By the later 1630s most armies fighting in Germany, Protestant and Catholic, had adopted a pattern of deployment using battalions of infantry, although the Imperialists retained a preference for larger battalions. After the defeat of Johannes Tserklaes, Count Tilly, at Breitenfeld, all commanders were very conscious of the importance of keeping a reserve in hand. Montecuccoli commented:

> Nowadays all captains are accustomed to arraying their troops in more than one line, a tactic which the Germans call treyfach. This is what the Imperials did at Lutzen, Soulz, Nordlingen, Wittstock, Freyburg and everywhere else except for Tilly in the battle of Breitenfeld-Leipzig. The latter placed his whole army along a single front and found himself in a bad way as a result.[21]

The importance of a reserve was by no means a new idea; the point was simply that Count Tilly's overconfidence at Breitenfeld had caused him to make a disastrous error, and this was seen as an object lesson in what not to do. The Earl of Orrery's comment on the importance of reserves illustrates the contemporary view: 'It is also observable that in a Battel, whoever keeps in Reserve a Body of Men that are not led to fight until the Enemies Squadrons have fought, rarely misses to carry away the Victory; and whoever has the last Reserves is very likely at last, to be the Victorious.'[22]

There was some difference of opinion as to how many lines of infantry should be deployed. The Earl of Orrery expressed the view that

> A General must never bring all his troops to fight at once; and therefore is still to draw up his Army, at least in two Lines, or orders of Battel, and in three in case the Ground, and the number of his Forces allow it: For those Lines are in effect so many Armies; and the second Line being intire, though the first should be broken, often recovers the day.[23]

An officer trained in the cautious Dutch school would still deploy his infantry in three lines with the third as his reserve, but this was by no means restricted to the Dutch, and the plans of the Imperialist General Albrecht von Wallenstein for his campaign in 1632 were also for a three-line deployment. An

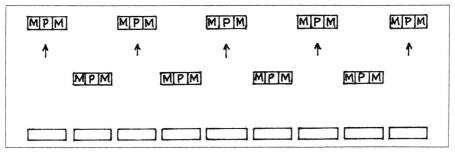

Deployment of the first two infantry lines in a battle formation: M = musketeers; P = pikemen. Although there was some debate amongst contemporary officers, most considered that it was necessary to leave enough space between battalions in the front line to enable those in the second line to support them. Most considered that the distance should equal the frontage of the second-line battalions. The simple way in which this was achieved was to form the battalions of the first two lines in one continuous line, then move forward alternate battalions. This would automatically provide the correct spacing.

alternative formation was to deploy in only two lines with a strong front line and weaker second line, the second line being referred to as the reserve. There are examples of this from officers serving on both sides in the Thirty Years War: the Imperialist Montecuccoli's *Sulle battaglie* and Sir James Turner's *Pallas Armata* both describe a line deployment with complete brigades in each line, a variation of the Swedish practice in deployment of battle lines – which also placed complete brigades in each line – but without the complex Swedish brigade itself.

This differed from the Dutch model which, in the late 1630s, continued to deploy units from the same brigade in both the first and second lines, and then have a separate third line in reserve. It is worth noting here that the Dutch would typically have three infantry brigades in a field army – called a 'marching army' – and used the structure as an easy means to manage their deployment, but it had evidently become normal practice in both Swedish and at least some of the later German armies to have a larger number of brigades and to use them as complete brigades in each separate line. During the English Civil War the deployment of the combined English Parliamentary and Scottish armies at the battle of Marston Moor used a deployment system of complete brigades in each battle line.

This section has given an impression of the theory and practice of army deployments in the late 1630s, at the time of the Bishops' Wars between England and Scotland. In the following section we will cover the extent to which they can be seen in the tactical preferences of different generals and their armies during the English Civil Wars. But before doing so there are three key points to consider.

The first point concerns the composition of the tactical units – brigades, battalions and squadrons – in the deployments. Ideally, the soldiers in each battalion or squadron would be drawn from the same regiment, but this would only be possible at the beginning of the year's campaign if each regiment in the army had been recruited to the same strength. In practice, both in Europe and in England during the Civil Wars, some colonels were more successful in recruiting their regiments and keeping them up to strength than others, and the harsh conditions of campaigning soon reduced the numbers of any regiment. This did not impact on battlefield deployment as the commander's main objective was to field operational fighting units, and he usually had a clear idea of what size he wanted them to be. If his regiments were at full strength he might divide his infantry into two or even three battalions, but if they were weak then a single regiment might provide only enough men for a single battalion, or the commander might have to combine soldiers from several weak regiments into a single battalion. As long as his infantry, both officers and men, were all trained to fight in the same way, this did not present any problems. The size of the units varied from army to army, but in general the Dutch would aim to have battalions of 500 men each, usually deployed in pairs; the Swedish deployed squadrons of around 500 men with three or four squadrons to the brigade. Imperial troops tended to use larger battalions, sometimes comprising complete brigades of around 1,000 men or more.

Cavalry squadron tactics. These two illustrations are from George Monk's Observations upon Political & Military Affairs. The first example shows the deployment of a cavalry squadron of 90 troopers in three subdivisions each of 30 men, deployed three deep with a frontage of 10 troopers. Monk advises that divisions A and C charge their opponents 'upon an easie trot', while the third division, B, acts as a reserve. The second example shows a deployment where the divisions are stronger. In this case, where each division is 300 strong, Monk advises dividing it into five subdivisions, each of 60 troopers drawn up three deep with a frontage of 20. Monk considered this more versatile, as well-trained cavalry could then use a range of tactical options, including charging with the central three subdivisions while attacking the enemy's flanks with the other two.

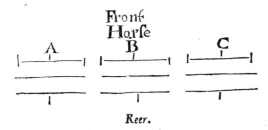

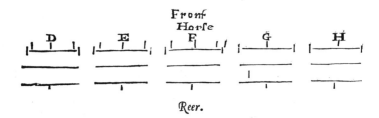

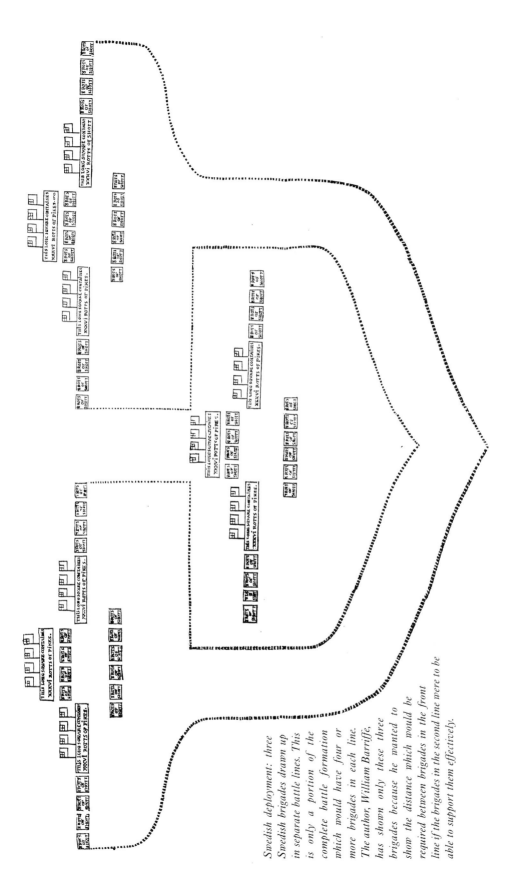

Swedish deployment: three Swedish brigades drawn up in separate battle lines. This is only a portion of the complete battle formation which would have four or more brigades in each line. The author, William Barriffe, has shown only these three brigades because he wanted to show the distance which would be required between brigades in the front line if the brigades in the second line were to be able to support them effectively.

The same principle applied when forming cavalry squadrons, but there was some debate at the time as to whether it was preferable to deploy a larger number of small squadrons of around 100 cavalrymen, or a smaller number of stronger squadrons of around 200 to 300 cavalrymen. Once the commander had decided which of these broad options he preferred, the key consideration was the number of cavalry troopers he wanted to have in his battlefield unit – the cavalry squadron – and he could either find them from the same regiment or from several regiments. An example of the composition of Swedish brigades is quoted by the English Militia officer and military writer William Barriffe, who noted 'one regiment and a half, of whole and complete companies, would perfect a brigade; or two regiments of torn and broken Companies, the overplus being alwayes added to the Reserve. Notwithstanding it so happened at the Battell of Lutzen, that Mizlaff, Gerstorfs, and Rosses, 3 crazed [broken] Regiments made up but one Brigade'.[24]

The second point is that the various battle deployments described above were intended for use in open country, and for a set-piece battle of this type both sides had to be willing to fight or be placed in a position where circumstances had left one side or the other with little choice. These tactical deployments were designed to get the most use out of the weapons of the day, but any commander would also give very careful thought to the advantages that the ground could offer him, or how it could inconvenience his opponent. A commander was expected, if at all possible, to view in person the ground on which he was to fight as he would not be able to change his dispositions once the battle commenced. The Earl of Orrery commented on the importance of viewing 'with great diligence ... so well the Field you will fight in, as when you have drawn up your Army on it, you may not afterwards alter the Order of it or change your Ground; for all such Mutations in the face of your Enemy are very dangerous, and gives him also the greater Confidence, and your own Men the less'.[25] Oliver Cromwell was deep in concentration as he viewed the battlefield at Dunbar on the night before the battle, as he 'rid all the night before through the several regiments by torchlight, upon a little Scots nag, biting his lip till the blood ran down his chin without his perceiving it, his thoughts being busily employed to be ready for the action now at hand'.[26]

A commander was expected to find, if he could, a

> Ground answerable to the Number of your Army, but also to the quality of those forces which compose it; and to those of your Enemies with whom you must have to do. As if my Enemy were stronger than I, in Cavalry, I would avoid all I might fighting him in a Plain; or if I were the stronger in Horse, I would use my utmost industry to engage him in open Countrey. And on the contrary, if I were stronger in Infantry, I would shun the Combat, unless it were in an inclosed Countrey, or incumbered by Woods, Brooks, Coppices, Rocks, or moorish Grounds; so if he were stronger in Foot, I would avoid fighting in a place where he who has the most Infantry, may therefore have the most hopes of Victory.[27]

The Parliament general, Sir William Waller, was considered to be a master in his choice of ground for battle, as one of his Royalist opponents ruefully commented, 'Indeede that Generall of the Rebells was the best shifter and chooser of ground when hee was not Master of the field that I ever saw, wch are great abilityes in a Souldier.'[28]

The third point is that the ground may prevent use of the full field deployment that the army practised, and it is here that the advantages of small battalions is felt, as this leaves the commander with the option of using the flexibility of trained bodies of infantry in less formal battle formations. These units, battalions of infantry and squadrons of cavalry, still used the basic tactics of the day in which they had been trained, but if the ground was broken then different groups might be deployed in different sectors of the battlefield rather than one single battlefield formation. Both Dutch and Imperialist officers stressed the value of the versatility and flexibility which small battalions offered in broken ground. George Monk summarized this point with the comment that 'small Divisions of Horse and Foot are much readier for Service, where you cannot imbattel them according to the rules of Art, by the nature of the place, or within inclosures, or where the brevity of the time will not give you leave.'[29]

Battle Formations during the English Civil War

The English armies which fought in the Bishops' Wars of 1639 and 1640 were trained for deployment in the Dutch style as most English officers with any professional experience had served in the Dutch army. This was also the style in which officers and men from the Trained Bands – many of whom served in these armies – had been taught, some of them by English sergeants seconded from the Dutch army. Direct evidence of the deployment style practised by the English army in the Bishops' Wars can be seen in contemporary engravings by Wenceslaus Hollar (see p. 145).

However, neither of the two Dutch deployment styles described was used in its perfect form during the Civil War itself. Both armies, Royalist and Parliament, had initially trained their men according to the Dutch style familiar to both officers and men. Lieutenant General Robert Bertie, Earl of Lindsey, the first field commander of the Royalist army, 'preferred the order he had learnt under prince Morrice and prince Harry, with whom he had served at the same time when the earl of Essex and he both had regiments [of Englishmen serving in the Dutch army]'. However, the Earl of Lindsey's preference was overruled by the King's nephew Prince Rupert, who successfully persuaded Charles to follow the Swedish deployment style of Gustavus Adolphus instead. As the Royalist historian the Earl of Clarendon recorded, 'the king was so indulgent to him [Prince Rupert] that he took his advice in all things relating to the army; and so upon consideration of their march, and the figure of the battle they resolved to fight in with the enemy, he concurred with prince Rupert's advice, and rejected the opinion of the General.'[30]

This caused changes to the depth in which the infantry and cavalry would fight – for the infantry from the Dutch ten deep to six deep, and for the cavalry from six deep to three. These changes were reasonable and followed the current practice of most armies fighting in Germany at the time. The change to more aggressive cavalry tactics also fitted current military thinking – the Dutch now being seen as out of date in their tactical use of cavalry. However, the deployment of the Royalist infantry in 1642 using Gustavus Adolphus's Swedish brigades was a much riskier decision, as the Swedish army had abandoned this eight years earlier, by 1634. The Swedish brigade had certainly served Gustavus Adolphus well, but it required veteran officers, non-commissioned officers and a core of veteran soldiers for it to work effectively. The Royalist army had received basic training and was certainly able to march, deploy for battle and fight, but it was inexperienced and, above all, the successful operation of a Swedish brigade required veteran soldiers.

Although this change of emphasis in training did not occur immediately before the battle of Edgehill, it will inevitably have caused a degree of confusion. This broke one of the key maxims of contemporary soldiers – not to use a battle formation without extensive practice – but the Royalist army also broke a much more serious one that day. The Royalist infantry had initially been drawn up in two lines with complete brigades in each line, but as they advanced their Parliamentary opponents recorded that the Royalist infantry 'came up all in Front' – i.e. they deployed from two lines, the second being the reserve, into one continuous line or 'Front' of brigades with no reserve. This essentially repeated the error of the Imperialist general Count Tilly at the battle of Breitenfeld. The Royalist cavalry also followed Swedish tactics, as before the battle Prince Rupert 'passed from one Wing to the other, giving positive Orders to the Horse, to march as close as was possible, keeping their Ranks with Sword in Hand, to receive the Enemy's Shot, without firing either Carbin or Pistol, till we broke in amongst the Enemy, and then to make use of our Fire-Arms as need should require, which Order was punctually observed',[31] an order clearly influenced by Gustavus Adolphus's instructions to his cavalry at the battle of Breitenfeld.

The deployment of the Earl of Essex at Edgehill used a combination of the Dutch and German styles and, on balance, was technically more modern than Prince Rupert's. The infantry were organized in three brigades, after the Dutch model, but were deployed in only two battle lines, not three. Only the cavalry deployment on the left wing is known for certain, as Sir James Ramsey, the commander of that wing, had to explain it in detail at his court martial. This was an advanced deployment on the latest Swedish/German style, with 'plottons' of detached musketeers deployed in support of the cavalry. Essex's use of selected troops of cavalry positioned behind the first infantry line was a tactic found in Dutch, Swedish and German deployments. There is no surviving plan for the Earl of Essex's deployment at Edgehill and this description is drawn from contemporary accounts.

In the opening phases of the English Civil War both sides had concentrated their attention on raising one main field army, but by the following year each side had several different armies operating in different parts of the country, sometimes separately and sometimes combined for a major expedition. Any field army whose officers drew their experience from, or were influenced by, the Dutch army retained a preference for an organization based on the use of three infantry brigades, but the concentration of several armies for a particular objective meant that it was increasingly common for there to be more than three infantry brigades in one army. Prince Rupert's deployment of the Royalist army at Edgehill was, of course, in the Swedish style, which used infantry brigades differently. Most of the surviving battle plans are for deployments of the Royalist army, and these are copies of the original plans – which would have been rough sketches – which were drawn more neatly by Sir Bernard de Gomme, an officer on Prince Rupert's staff. These show Prince Rupert's deployments for the battles of Edgehill, Marston Moor and Naseby, and for the deployment used by the Royalist army when it returned to Newbury after the second battle of Newbury in order to recover its artillery. This last deployment was referred to by one Royalist officer, John Gwyn, as the third battle of Newbury as the Royalist army drew up to offer battle although the Parliament generals declined to challenge it.

The most complete examples of the battle plans and deployments for both sides of an English Civil War battle are for Naseby. For this battle, there are two surviving contemporary plans: one is a pictorial representation engraved by

Detail of infantry battalions. From Robert Streeter's plan of Naseby published with Joshua Sprigge's Anglia Rediviva. In this example the infantry regiments shown are drawn up in single large battalions with artillery pieces placed in pairs between battalions. The distance between units is less than it would have been on the battlefield as it was an artist's convention at the time to show battalions closer together than they were, as it made for a better picture.

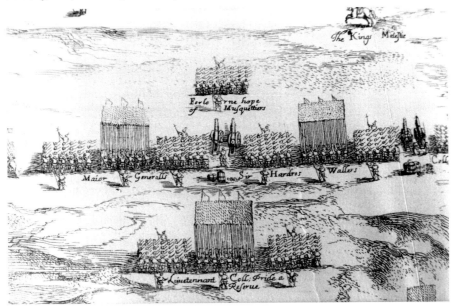

Robert Streeter and bound with Joshua Sprigge's *Anglia Rediviva*, which was published in 1647, and the other is one of the coloured plans drawn some years after the battle by Sir Bernard de Gomme. As a chaplain serving Sir Thomas Fairfax, Joshua Sprigge was well placed to have access to the New Model Army commander's plan as this would have been drawn up for circulation to his officers down to, at least, the level of brigade commander. The same plan was reproduced in John Rushworth's *Historical Collections* (see pp. 210–11 below), where he recorded the origin of the information used:

> The Exact Form of the Battel is represented in the following Figure: That of the King's Army being drawn up soon after by the Lord Ashley [Jacob, Lord Astley], who in an engagement near Stow in the Wold [21 March 1646] was taken prisoner; and whose Papers on Naseby Battel under his own hand I have by me, and that of the Parliament's Army given in, approved by several of the Commanders in Chief therein Concerned.[32]

Sir Bernard de Gomme was a Walloon officer who served on Prince Rupert's staff and would have had access to the original, roughly drawn, plans used for circulation amongst senior Royalist officers on the day, and later copied them more neatly. De Gomme gives a more detailed breakdown of the Royalist regiments at Naseby and some differences in their deployment. He would probably have taken details of the Parliamentary army's deployment from Robert Streeter's engraving.

One significant difference between the two surviving plans is in the space left between the units in each battle line, and this is a useful illustration of the purpose for which these surviving examples were produced. In de Gomme's plan, the battalions are drawn showing spaces between those in the front line equal to the frontage of the units in the second line. This was considered to be the optimum practice of the day. There was some debate about setting these distances amongst professional officers as the gaps created some danger to the flanks of the front-line battalions, as the 'enemy may easily get into these void places', but most officers considered that this was a risk that they would have to take as

> a Reserve [the second line of infantry battalions] is appointed to advance against an enemy, at one of these three occasions, which are when the battel [by which was meant in this case the first or front line] is weary, when it is in danger and when it is beaten. Now in none of these three can the Reserve be steedable if there be not ground for it to advance, to draw up, and to fight, but who can imagin that a Brigade with three hundred men in front, in the reserve, can advance, draw up, and fight on a spot of ground twenty four foot broad, or yet on a spot three hundred foot broad, for there they should only have ground to stand on, but no room to handle their arms, especially the Musquets. But it will be yet worse if the Brigades of the Battel [front line] be flying, and these of the Reserve

advancing, for they shall be in that case such a medley, an Embarras, that they shall ruin one another without the help of an enemy.[33]

De Gomme would, in any event, have been aware of Prince Rupert's intentions as he served on Rupert's staff. However, the key to this is that the plan showed the commander's intentions as it was the operational plan for Prince Rupert's army and had been drawn up as the preferred option for use on this campaign, and not specifically for the terrain of the battlefield over which it was fought. It is essentially similar to Prince Rupert's battle plan for Third Newbury, where no battle was fought, and represented the latest version of Rupert's plans for battle. The qualifying point is that deploying the battalions with the distances set out between battalions in this way would be Prince Rupert's preferred option, provided that the ground permitted him to do so. If there was insufficient ground to be able to deploy in this way then the army commander might have to make concessions and reduce the distances, but he would do so in the knowledge that this would compromise the ability of his second-line battalions to support his first line.

Robert Streeter's plan bound with the *Anglia Rediviva* was subject to different influences as it is an engraving illustrating the battle. There was an accepted artistic convention in the style used in European engravings of the period that the distances that would actually have been used on the field would be reduced in an engraving in order to make a better picture. Direct evidence can be seen in the comment in the *Swedish Intelligencer*, a series of contemporary newsbooks on the Swedish involvement in the Thirty Years War. An edition published in 1633 included an engraving of the battle of Lützen with the explanatory comment that 'We know, that betwixt every Brigade of Foote, there should be so much roome left, as that another Brigade might advance up betweene: the distance betweene them, being the breadth of one of them. But our Cutter [engraver] (plainely) to make his figures fairer hath straightened [reduced] the distances. And this (I hope) is mended by telling you of it.'[34] The figures engraved in Streeter's plan show his was influenced by European examples, and for this reason it is likely that, for an engraving, he would reduce the distances between battalions. The answer to this question lies ultimately in the constraints of the ground and, as Glenn Foard's pioneering work on this battle shows,[35] there would not be enough space for the optimum distances. This said, they would, even if reduced, have be wider than Robert Streeter shows in his engraving as otherwise the deployment would have seriously compromised the ability of either side to use its reserve second line of battalions.

During the English Civil war the major battles of Edgehill, Marston Moor and Naseby are examples of set-piece battles fought using these formal battlefield deployments. But others, such as the first battle of Newbury, were fought over terrain which made this form of complete deployment impossible. At Newbury the Earl of Essex had no option but to fight as the Royalists were now between him and his base. Although the southern sector of the battlefield was open enough to allow the deployment of infantry and cavalry in the usual way, the centre and northern sectors were broken up with hedgerows, and the Parliamentary colonels who wrote an account of the battle commented that in the northern sector cavalry 'could not be engaged but in small parties by reason of the hedges'.[36] Smaller engagements were also fought by commanders drawing up their armies in formal battle formations – in battalia – where the ground permitted, but with smaller numbers of soldiers and a smaller battlefield the influence of the local terrain was even more influential.

Beating up Quarters

Small actions were more common than major engagements, and an active commander would mount raids on the quarters of his opponents, an action called 'Beating up Quarters'.[37] These would be carried out at night or in the very early hours of the morning, and the scale could vary considerably. An attack on an outlying brigade could have a major impact on the campaign as, if successful, it could destroy a considerable portion of an opponent's army. The Parliamentary commander Sir William Waller was the best known exponent of these large-scale attacks, and the Royalist historian the Earl of Clarendon wrote that 'beating up of quarters was his master-piece',[38] after his attack on the winter quarters of a Royalist brigade at Alton on 13 December 1643. However, if the defenders managed to rally successfully, the attacking force could find itself too deeply committed to an attack to retreat. At Hamilton, on the night of 30 November 1650, a Scottish force of cavalry and dragoons made a night attack on the quarters of an English cavalry brigade under John Lambert. Initial success led the Scottish commander to commit his whole force, and when the English cavalry rallied and counter-attacked, the Scottish force was defeated and scattered, and its commander captured.

However, such large-scale attacks were exceptional, and the usual action of beating up quarters was a smaller raid of a few troops of horse and dragoons on outlying static garrisons or the outlying cavalry quarters of an opposing army. George Monk considered 'It is very fit a General should often command his Horse and Dragoons to fall upon his Enemies outermost Horse-Quarters. The which is one of the readiest, easiest, and securest ways that I know of to break an Enemies Army.'[39] An attack on a static garrison was so much a part of everyday military activity for cavalry that the optimum way of carrying out this type of raid was included in cavalry training manuals. Essentially, the attacking force relied on surprise to overwhelm the sentries and their supports, the 'corps de gard', and then take control of the main points in the town where their opponents could rally to put up a defence. By sending a troop of cavalry riding down the streets, the attackers could keep their opponents in small groups and kill or capture them in detail. Once the defenders gave up hope of resistance, they would try to escape and the troops outside the town were placed to capture them as they ran. The defending force understood this position equally well, and their main response was to slow down the attack as much as possible, sometimes by sending out as many men as they could get mounted quickly, and give the remainder of their troops –

who might well outnumber their attackers – time to rally. The key to success was always surprise and speed.

Siege Warfare

Commanders fighting in England during the Civil Wars faced a situation more like Germany than the Low Countries, because a prolonged period of peace meant that only a few coastal cities were fortified in anything approaching the modern style. Not unreasonably, as the English Channel stood between foreign armies and their siege artillery trains, there was little enthusiasm for the cost of the latest Italian style of fortifications. The latest design was based around the optimum use of artillery firepower, both in establishing batteries to attack a fortification and elaborate outworks designed to keep attacking artillery as far away as possible from the main defences, and to provide crossfire to devastate enemy storming parties. These modern fortifications were expensive if built in stone and took a long time to complete, but Dutch engineers demonstrated during the wars in the Low Countries that the same principles of fortification could be achieved by using thick earthworks. These were cheaper and quicker to build than stone fortifications and well able to absorb cannon shot. The Dutch also had the advantage that the high water table in the Low Countries enabled them to use wet ditches – water-filled ditches – as a defence in many areas, and their besiegers' trenches were also likely to be flooded. The disadvantage of earthworks was that rainfall would soon wear them away if they were not maintained, but that was a longer term problem. The new style was referred to as *alla moderna* – the modern style – in Italy, and came to be known as the *trace italienne* outside it. Sir James Turner, who had served extensively in Europe as well as the Civil Wars, also referred to this as the modern style – *a la Modern* – to distinguish it from the style *a l'antique*, the ancient or antique style.

Most Englishmen with professional experience had served in the infantry, and at the beginning of the Civil Wars there were few English engineers. English officers had practical experience in the siege warfare that characterized campaigns in the Low Countries but although they had carried out the work – and the aggressive nature of English mercenary soldiers meant they were highly regarded as good men to storm a breach or to defend one – they had not been involved in the design of either defences or the attacker's siege-works. Both the design of fortifications and the best ways to overcome them had become ever more sophisticated since the sixteenth century, in response to increasingly powerful artillery and increasingly sophisticated tactics to make use of it for both offence and defence. Anyone who had seen it done could supervise the digging of siege-trenches or the construction of an artillery battery, but the key requirement was to put them in the right place for the particular fortress or strong point which was to be taken. For this an experienced engineer was necessary, together with a good train of heavy siege guns. During the Civil Wars both sides employed foreign engineers, mostly Dutch or German, but there were never many of these.[40]

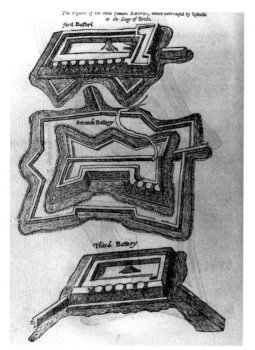

Artillery batteries. The Spanish batteries at the siege of Breda in 1625, from Robert Ward's Anima'dversions of Warre.

Although the technicalities were important and there were real advantages to well-designed fortifications or siege lines and the assistance of a competent engineer, the most important factors in siege warfare were the skill and determination of the governor of the place and his ability to inspire the soldiers of the garrison and the inhabitants of the town. George Monk made this point when he wrote that 'Every Commander knoweth that mans flesh is the best fortification that belongs to a Town; and where a Town is well manned, the best way of taking it is by Starving; and when a Town is weakly manned, the best way of taking it is by Battery and Assaults, or by Approaches, Mining, Battery and Assaults.'[41]

Sir James Turner made the useful point that before a commander 'form or lay down his Siege he ought to weigh and consider well all the advantages and disadvantages that may accrue to him: as to whether the gaining of the Town or Castle he Besiegeth will counterpoise the loss of men'.[42] Above all, the most important consideration was confidence that the siege would be successful. George Monk commented: 'If a General besiegeth any Town in which his intelligence, or his opinion hath deceived him so much, that he hath little hope of taking it, the speedy leaving off any such Enterprise doth excuse the rashnesse which might be imputed to the beginning'.[43] In other words, the cost of a siege, regardless of whether a commander sought to take a town by battery and assault or the more prolonged process of blocking it up and starving it into surrender, would be heavy losses amongst the besieging army. An assault would cost the commander heavily in direct casualties, and was 'certain to have his best men killed or spoiled upon such designs, and the rest so much discouraged that it would prove dangerous unto an Army if they should suddenly after it fight'.[44] A long-drawn-out siege often led to contagious disease – usually typhus, called *morbus campestris* or camp fever – breaking out in the camp of the besieging army, and it could cause at least as many losses as an assault. In these circumstances the strategic advantages of taking a city had to be worth the potential losses in the besieging army.

A Table of the Heights and Proportions of every particular Limbe of a Fort, belonging to a Fort.

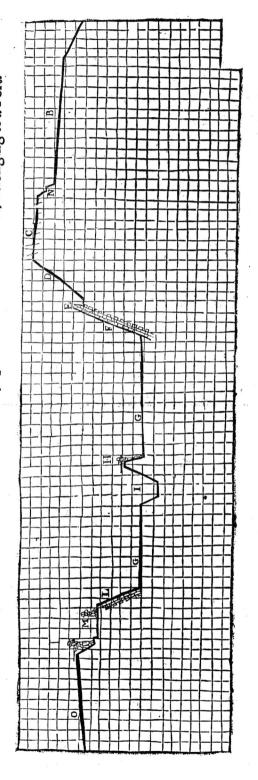

A The Mount of the Rampart within.
B The Rampart.
C The Parrapets.
D The sloping of the Parrapets.
E The way for the Rounds.

F The Walles.
G The Ditch or Mote.
H The Defence in the Mote called Cuve.
I The little Ditch in the middest of the Mote.

L The Counterscarpe and the Breastworke.
M The Curider.
N The Fote-banke to step on, to discharge over.
O The plaine Field lying steeving.

Cross-section of a fort's defences, from Robert Ward's Anima'dversions of Warre.

The potential damage that a siege represented to his army was the basis of the conventions of war under which a commander might offer terms to the besieged and under which they would consider his offer. No garrison commander would surrender at the first summons: he would be court-martialled for contravention of the army's *Lawes and Ordinances of Warre* – and most probably shot – if he did. The commander of the besieging army would send a series of further summons during the siege offering generous terms, on the one hand, and threatening to start offering much less generous terms if his offer wasn't accepted in the near future. This could be enough – if supplies were running short and there was no hope of relief – to persuade the garrison commander to surrender, but a resolute commander might well continue to hold out for as long as the city's walls remained defensible.

But there would come a point at which it was clear that enough damage had been done to a city's defences that an assault by the besieging army would be successful. This would have serious implications for both the besieging force and the besieged. The besieging army would still suffer terrible losses as their assaulting columns attacked a breach or breaches in the city's defences, and, when they did break through the defences, they would be beyond the control of their surviving officers. Soldiers of the besieging army would then sack the city and seek to kill any of the defending garrison of regular soldiers and city militia that they could find – as these would have been the men who shot down their friends by the score or the hundred as they fought their way up to and through the breach. As militia did not wear uniforms this could mean the death of every man of military age in the city. The commander of the besieging army would probably not be able to restrain his plundering soldiers for a couple of days; nor would he make the attempt until he felt reasonably sure his commands would be obeyed. From the perspective of the garrison commander, he would now be under pressure from the citizens to make terms in order to protect their families and their own lives and property. He would also be under pressure from the regular soldiers in his garrison who would begin to question whether they wished to die in a hopeless defence. At this point there would be advantages to all parties concerned in the surrender of the city on terms; the commander of the besieging army would get the city without losing men in an assault, the defending garrison would get to survive and march out with honour intact under a safe conduct to go to friendly territory, and the citizens would avoid the plunder of their town. Typically the citizens would also have to provide a ransom for the town to be paid to the soldiers of the besieging army as compensation for the plunder they might otherwise have made, but this would be a much better option than enduring the horrors of the city being sacked.

An important factor here is, of course, the necessity for the besieging commander to have a reputation as a man of his word. There was no point in surrendering on terms if the conditions were not kept, and this would not be the only siege of the war. A commander who broke his word might find that the next city he attacked would fight to the bitter end. It was accepted that the besieging commander might set very harsh terms if the defenders had little hope left when they finally agreed to discuss terms, and he might require the survivors of the garrison to march out without their weapons or flags, or he might offer them only their lives, not their liberty to march away.

It was also accepted that if the garrison and citizens chose to fight on once it was evident that an assault would inevitably lead to the taking of the city, then the consequences – slaughter and plunder – were on their heads and would particularly be the responsibility of the garrison commander. Underlying this convention was the simple – and broadly recognized – fact that the besieging commander would be genuinely unable to restrain his men from sacking a city if they had to fight their way into it. The siege of Chester provides a good example, as the Royalist governor, John, Lord Byron, was obliged to sue for terms in January 1646: he noted in his own account of the siege that 'both citizens and soldiers now began to be very impatient and mutinous, and multitudes of women (who are ever first employed in seditious actions upon the privilege of their sex) daily flocked about my house with great clamours asking whether I intended they should eat their children since they had nothing else left to sustain themselves withal.'[45]

Lord Byron sought better terms than he was first offered, claiming:

> Those demands of mine, which you term unparalleled, have been heretofore granted by far greater commanders than yourself, no disparagement to you, to places in a far worse condition, than God be thanked, this is yet. Witness the Bosse, Breda and Maestricht, and as many other towns have been beleaguered either by Spaniards or the Hollanders; or to come near, York and Carlisle, or nearest of all, Beeston Castle.[46]

Lord Byron, who had served as a professional soldier in the European Wars, was seeking to make capital out of his military past as his opponent, the Parliamentary commander Sir William Brereton, probably had no military experience before the English Civil War. However, the Royalists were in no position to bargain, and Sir William, annoyed at being patronized, sent back the following sharp answer:

> My Lord,
>
> I cannot believe that you conceive the war betwixt the Hollanders and the Spaniards to be made a precedent for us; neither can I believe that such conditions as you demand were granted to the Bosse, Breda or Maestricht. Sure I am, none such were given to York, Carlisle or Beeston, though some were maintained by as great commanders as yourself, and no disparagement to you. I shall therefore offer to your consideration the example of Liverpool, Basing and Lathom, who by their refusal of honourable terms when they were propounded, were not long after subjected to captivity and the sword. You may therefore, in pity to all those innocents under your command, tender their safety and the

preservation of the city, for which end I have sent you fair and honourable conditions, such as are the sense of all the officers and soldiers with me, which being rejected, you may expect worse from your servant,

Wm Brereton[47]

Lord Byron surrendered the city shortly afterwards. There were advantages for the besieging commander in adopting a carrot and stick approach, particularly if he was faced with having to take a number of separate fortified places – cities, towns or fortified country houses. An example of the stick can be seen in the taking of the house belonging to the Royalist Sir John Strangeways – Abbotsbury House – by Sir Anthony Ashley Cooper on 5 November 1644. Cooper recorded that the garrison refused two summons to surrender as 'they were so gallant that they would admit of no treaty, so that we prepared ourselves for to force it, and accordingly fell on'. After a fierce fight lasting some six hours and with

> the whole house in a flaming fire, so that it was not possible for it to be quenched, and then they cried for quarter; but we having lost divers men before it, and considering how many garrisons of the same nature we were to deal with, I gave command that there should be none given, but they should be kept in the house, that they and their garrison might fall together.[48]

Sir Thomas Fairfax's New Model infantry were more merciful in August 1645 at the siege of Sherborne Castle, but here the circumstances were different. The Parliament 'Great Guns began to play about eleven of the clock, and before six had made a breach in the middle of the Wall, that ten a breast might enter'. The Royalist governor, Colonel Lewis Dyves, rejected a third summons to surrender and threatened to hang the drummer who brought it, but on the following day, having 'cooled his brain after a little sleep (without any other provocation) sent out a Drummer with a message that he was willing to surrender upon honourable terms'. The besiegers were out of patience with him and 'the answer was returned, no terms but Quarter, seeing he had slipt and slighted the opportunity, and he was not to expect that unless he surrendered speedily'. The governor was still considering this when the New Model infantry commenced their assault, and the Royalist soldiers hung out a white flag. This was too late to stop the assault, but because the garrison soldiers offered no resistance and had 'thrown down their Arms and cryed for Quarter to our souldiers, which our souldiers (inclining rather to booty than revenge) gave them'.[49] On this occasion the attacking infantry had not taken casualties in the final assault and they would not kill fellow Englishmen in cold blood. They still sacked the castle, though, where 'The souldiers spoil lasted all that day, and most part of the night.'

In the early years of the Civil War the commanders of the New Model Army learnt from experience in terms of siege warfare as well as battlefield practice, took care to have a strong train of siege artillery available for all their campaigns and made use of expert engineers and 'firemasters' in its deployment. Apart from heavy siege cannon, the New Model Army made particular use of mortars for both their directly destructive effect and the impact that 'granadoes' falling from above had on the morale of the defending garrison. A good example is the siege of Devizes in September 1645, when the castle was 'a place of great strength, having been an old fortification, raised on a huge Mount of earth; the Governour Sir Charles Lloyd: a good Ingineer had added to the strength of its natural situation'. However, once the mortars were fired 'some of the Granadoes breaking in the midst of the castle (being open above) kill'd severall of their men, and much endangered the blowing up of the Magazine, which so startled the Enemy, that on the Monday about eight o'clock in the morning, the Governor sent forth for a Parley.'[50]

Although the New Model Army became increasingly proficient in siege warfare, its commanders' approach remained aggressive. In this, as in so much else, the New Model Army consciously sought inspiration from the practice of the Swedish commander King Gustavus Adolphus, and what had been read of him in newsbook reports. A useful illustration can be seen in the parallel between laudatory comments on Gustavus Adolphus published in the *Swedish Intelligencer*, describing the Swedish campaigns in Germany, and a similar comment in Joshua Sprigge's account of the campaigns of the New Model Army, *Anglia Rediviva*. The *Swedish Intelligencer* described Gustavus Adolphus's strategy:

> This was his order (mostly) in taking of a towne: he would not stand entrenching and building Redoubts, at a miles distance: but clapdowne with his Army presently, about Cannon shot from it. There he would begin his Approaches, get to their walls, Batter and Storme, presently; and if he saw the place were not by a running pull to be taken: he would not lose above 4. or 6. dayes before it, but rise and to another. And thus did hee at Ingolstadt.[51]

Joshua Sprigge's laudatory comment on Sir Thomas Fairfax was:

> He was still for action in Field or Fortification, esteeming nothing unfeasible for God, and for man to doe in God's strength, if they would be up and doing; and thus his successe hath run through a line crosse to that of old Souldiery, of long sieges and slow approaches; and he hath done all so soon, because he was ever doing.[52]

Chapter Eight

Professionalism: Honour, Self-Respect and Symbolism

Many Englishmen served as mercenaries in foreign, usually Protestant, armies in the years before the English Civil War. From their perspective, and that of most of their countrymen, a career as a professional soldier was a perfectly acceptable occupation. The concept of honourable military service in a foreign army was easier to understand in the context of the Dutch revolt against Spain, and many Englishmen served in English regiments in the Protestant Dutch army. But here the sides were clearly drawn and the distinctions were clear-cut. The perspective was different during the later stages of the Thirty Years War as, after the death of the great Protestant champion Gustavus Adolphus, the war became more political than religious, and the German princes changed their allegiance to suit the circumstances of the day. In this environment many mercenary soldiers adopted the pragmatic view expressed by Sir James Turner:

'I had swallowed without chewing, in Germanie, a very dangerous maxime, which militarie men there too much follow; which was, that so we serve our master honestlie, it is no matter what master we serve'.[1]

At the outbreak of the English Civil War, both Royalists and the Parliament needed the specialist assistance of professional officers and sergeants to train their inexperienced recruits. But the habits mercenary officers developed in Germany did not endear them to the volunteers who enlisted in the army of the Parliament. Many complained that such men were 'debosht' – debauched –

Ensign. An ensign of the Trained Bands, c.1635. Note the short staff to the flag.

and the Londoner Sergeant Nehemiah Wharton, writing home in August 1642, wrote that 'our soldiers generally manifested their dislike of our Lieutenant Colonell, who is a Godamme blade, and doubtlesse hatche in hell, and we all desire that either the Parliament would depose him, or God convert him, or the Devill fetch him away quick'.[2] Professional soldiers may have found more congenial company in the Royalist army, although the behaviour of the Croatian Captain Carlo Fantom – who once boasted 'I care not for your Cause: I come to fight for your halfe-crowne, and your handsome women: my father was a R. Catholiqu; and so was my grandfather. I have fought for the Christians against the Turkes; and for the Turkes against the Christians'[3] – was too much even for the more relaxed environment of that army, and he was hanged at Oxford for rape.

Captain Fantom was employed, first by the Parliament and then in the King's army, because he was 'an admirable Horse-officer'[4] – a technically competent and experienced cavalry officer – whose expertise was needed by both sides. But, from the beginning of the Civil War, there was always a sense amongst some of the officers and men in the Parliament armies that they were fighting for a just cause and one they passionately believed in. As the Agitator (soldiers' delegate or 'Representour') Edward Sexby said during the army debates after its mutiny, they did not see themselves as 'meere mercinarie souldiers'.[5] The Leveller pamphlet *The Hunting of the Foxes*, referring to an army declaration of 14 June 1647, used the same term when expressing the view that 'we were not a mere mercenary Army, hired to serve any Arbitrary power of a state, but called forth and conjured by the several Declarations of Parliament to the defence of our own, & the people's just Rights and Liberties'.[6]

Richard Baxter,[7] a preacher who served as an army chaplain, wrote of Oliver Cromwell that:

> At his first entrance into the wars, being but a captain of horse, he had a special care to get religious men into his troop; these men were of greater understanding than common soldiers, and therefore were more apprehensive of the importance and consequence of the war; and making not money, but that which they took for the publick felicity to be their end, they were the more engaged to be valiant; for he that maketh money his end, doth esteem his life above his pay, and therefore is like enough to save it by flight when danger comes, if possibly he can: but he that maketh the felicity of Church and State his end, esteemeth it above his life, and therefore will the sooner lay down his life for it.[8]

This had practical advantages from a purely military sense as, although Cromwell's first choice of men for his troop may have been principally affected by 'the very esteem and love of religious men', this led to the 'avoiding of those disorders, mutinies, plunderings, and grievances of the country, which deboist men in armies are commonly guilty of: By this means he indeed sped better than expected. Aires, Desborough, Berry, Evanson, and the rest of that troop, did prove so valiant, that as far as I could learn, they never once ran away before an enemy.'[9]

Richard Baxter's comments were written some years after the event, but they are similar to Joshua Sprigge's description of New Model Army officers in his book *Anglia Rediviva*, printed in 1647. Sprigge wrote:

> The Officers of this Army, as you may read, are such as knew little of War, then our owne unhappy Warres had taught them, except some few, so as men could not contribute much to this work: indeed I may say this, they were better Christians then souldiers, and wiser in faith than in fighting, and could beleeve a Victory sooner than contrive it; and yet I think they were as wise in the way of Souldiery as the little time and experience they had could make them.[10]

Sprigge was seeking to make a specific comparison here between the Royalists who had more experienced officers and the New Model Army which was led by better men.

Although many officers and soldiers in the New Model Army certainly saw themselves as an army of saints – one writing in 1647 that they were the 'army of the Living God' – they were also proud of what they had achieved as a victorious hard fighting army. They said themselves that they were not 'meere mercinarie souldiers' – not simply mercenaries who fought for a paymaster rather than a cause – but they did see themselves as soldiers, and they were proud of what they had achieved as soldiers. They respected and took care to live by the international military customs of the day. These were the customs and practices of a separate military world, with its own forms of accepted protocol through which soldiers or their regiments dealt with one another. The protocols of the seventeenth-century military world were internal: they related to and were followed by officers and soldiers within its own boundaries; these were not set by external civilian opinion. Respect for military customs was, effectively, respect for themselves as soldiers living in that military world. This can be seen in the way officers and soldiers approached the everyday activity of military life and how they would accept as fair solutions which were expressed according to or based on that military protocol.

A useful indication of military conventions and the way they operate can be seen in an example given by Joshua Sprigge as a 'passage of great wisdome and condescension in the General, very remarkable'. As the New Model Army marched on campaign, the regiment of the general, Sir Thomas Fairfax, 'claiming a priviledge to march always in the Van', was at the head of the infantry. This was certainly its right within the practice of the day and, apart from the honour of its place, this had real practical advantages for the regiment, as it would be the first into camp at night, while other regiments might not get to camp for hours later and would be marching in the dust cast up by the soldiers in front. There was no debate that the general's regiment had the right to this privilege, but it did cause some ill feeling in the army, as some thought it 'was convenient now to be waived for the relief of the rest; but they being unwilling thereunto'. Sir Thomas Fairfax's solution was to dismount from his horse, and he then 'marched on foot at the head of his Regiment, about two miles, and so brought up the Rear: and to this day, his own Regiment takes the turn upon all duties; A thing, if rightly considered, nothing to their dishonour (if it were to outvie others to do service) and redounding much to the good, and good successe of an Army'.[11] There was no disagreement that Sir Thomas Fairfax's regiment had the right to insist on its position, as Joshua Sprigge refers to the regiment being asked to waive the privilege, but doesn't dispute that it existed.

Fairfax's solution fitted in with the protocol of the day, as his own regiment could only be honoured if the man who was both its colonel and its general chose to march on foot at its head at whichever point in the column he preferred. With the general providing the example, the regiment's only real option was to make a virtue of necessity and make it a point of honour to take its turn in the march. The other regiments accepted that Sir Thomas Fairfax's regiment was waiving its rights in the interests of fairness – which removed any lingering sense of ill feeling – and, since the general had started the process by marching on foot at its head, the regiment itself was not being slighted in any way and was showing itself to be magnanimous and fair minded. This was a clever solution and one which worked because all parties involved were acting within a common military culture and perfectly understood the others' position within it. Fairfax was not unique in this approach, and European commanders often varied the order of march of their infantry brigades for much the same reason, but his decision – and the way he went about it – was evidently widely discussed within the English military community. The Earl of Orrery's manual has several references to his conversations with New Model Army officers, and he was clearly influenced by this incident when he gave the advice that

> All the Regiments should in course take their turns, to be in the Van, Rear, and other parts of the Body of the Army; For when there is equality of Duty, there must also be universal satisfaction therein; the General's Regiment the first day are still to have the Van of all, so daily every Regiment to have its turn according to its Priority, being a General Officers; or Antiquity, being a Colonels.[12]

This was probably the solution adopted within the New Model Army, and it is one which set the precedence of each regiment in a manner each could accept according to the custom of the day and without argument, but which also provided each with its turn at the head of the column.

For an individual example, the practice of releasing officers on parole is an indication that New Model Army officers closely followed the army custom and practice of the day. An officer giving his parole 'is set a liberty conditionally, as, if you do such a thing, enjoy your liberty; if not return to prison'.[13] Parole (or parol) was usually given for either of two reasons. A wounded officer might be left to recover from his wounds on the condition he would surrender himself once he was well, or he might 'ingage to get such a person of the adverse party set at liberty, and on that condition is set free himself' and would, if unable to make the exchange, return to prison. This most commonly applied to officers but could be extended to others. For example, it was recorded in 1651: 'Fifty prisoners of war of the enemy [Royalists], now in the several gaols of London, Winchester, Yarmouth &c to be released, on parole to go to Jersey, to procure the exchange of so many [i.e. the same number] of our men now prisoners there.'[14]

That was the accepted practice of parole, but an example which shows how officers themselves followed it is recorded by the Jersey diarist Jean Chevalier. Captain Samuel Clark, an officer in Colonel Alban Coxe's New Model infantry regiment, was wounded and captured in the failed assault on Castle Cornet in Guernsey in March 1651. Captain Clark

> was given leave by Colonel Burgess[15] to visit Guernsey Town [St Peter Port] on parole to recuperate, on condition that when he felt better he was to return to the Castle and give himself up. On reaching the town he divested himself of his buff coat and the clothes he had worn at the assault and sent them to the soldiers in the Castle, saying that they were their booty and belonged to them. After a good rest of six or seven days in Guernsey, he returned to the Castle, clad in a silver laced coat, and gave himself up.[16]

In doing this Captain Clark was sticking absolutely to the letter of accepted military practice: for him it was clearly a matter of personal self-respect to do so, to live and behave according to the accepted military code.

There is another element to consider about the everyday life of a professional soldier, plunder. An indication of a professional army and of professional soldiers in this period is the distance of their separate military world from that of civilian life. Soldiers who became expert plunderers were no longer as closely linked to, or sympathetic to, civilian life as they were when they joined the army. The Jersey diarist Jean Chevalier recorded the astonishment of the Jersey islanders commenting that it 'was marvelous how they [the soldiers] discovered things which had been buried in the ground. They even went straight to places where things had been hidden in the walls'. Chevalier was a keen observer and he also made some perceptive comments on the soldiers themselves, noting they were

> not all of the same creeds and were mostly young men and boys drawn from many counties in England. For the most part they had been in the service of the Parliament all this time past and had left their trades to follow war and had become accustomed to lead a life of debauchery and pillage, which they will find it hard to quit.

Chevalier's reference to creeds was to the religious or political adherence of the soldiers: 'the greater part of the troops were Independents who abhorred Royalty. The others were a kind of Brownists who, one and all, desired neither sermons nor prayers except as the spirit moved them, and of this they were filled like a cow with colic'.[17]

Colours: Ensigns, Cornets and Guidons

The visible symbol of the regiment and the company to which the soldiers, infantry, cavalry or dragoons belonged was their flag. This was seen in a very real sense to embody and symbolize the regiment and the military community to which the soldier belonged. During the seventeenth century, each company in a regiment of infantry or dragoons and each troop in a regiment of cavalry carried its own individual flag. The flags of an infantry regiment were designed as a complete set but with variations under a system to identify one company from another. Where dragoons were raised as complete regiments, the same system as was used for the infantry would be followed on the smaller dragoon flags. In the cavalry the influence of the individual troop commanders was stronger, a reflection of the fact that the general European practice of combining cavalry troops into regiments was more recent. The design of cavalry flags was also more elaborate, with a painted image which could be political or religious, such as the Parliament flag of Captain Langrish, which showed a skull and a mitre with the motto 'Mori potui quam papatus' ('I would die rather than be a papist'), or purely military such as Captain Richard Brown's, which showed a skull and a laurel wreath and the motto 'One of These'. Where all the troops were raised at one time all the flags would have a common background colour but with different painted designs for each captain, but where the troops were originally raised separately they may have kept their original flags. An infantry flag was called an 'ensign', a cavalry flag was called a 'cornet' and a dragoon flag was called a 'guidon'. The term 'colours' was generally used to describe any military flag.

Army regiments were not the only group to carry flags or banners; in London in 1643 the city guilds marched out under their own flags to work on the city's fortifications.[18] Other groups of citizens also marched out under banners, for example 'a thousand Oyster wives' who 'advanced from Billingsgate through Cheapside to Crabtree field, all alone, with drummes and flying collours, and in a civill manner, their goddess Bellona leading them in a martiall way'. The clubmen associations formed at the end of the First Civil War to defend themselves from plundering by any army, Royalist or Parliamentary, also carried their own flags, one of which was recorded by Joshua Sprigge as carrying the motto 'If you offer to plunder or take our cattel, Be assured we will bid you battel'.[19] Sprigge recorded that 'in others [other flags] they [the clubmen] had sentences of Scripture, profanely applied by their Malignant Priests, who were the principal stirrers up of the people to these tumultuous assembles'.

The original objective of the army's flags was to provide a recognizable point at which soldiers could muster when the companies formed up prior to marching or, in battle, where 'Troopers, if they are disordered in the Charge, may see under what they are to Rally; and it being a high disgrace to lose their

Colours, it makes Men fight the heartilier'.[20] Flags became the symbol of the regiment itself, and the subject of increasingly elaborate ceremonial, and the soldiers' pride in their regiment became focused on these visible symbols. Edward Davies in his book *The Art of War and England's Traynings* recommended that there should be

> certaine ceremonies used in delivery of the Enseigne [to the officer who is to carry it], receiving it by oath in the presence of his band [company], at which time he must make vow, and professe the same rather to be his winding sheet, and therein to lose his life, then through his default to lose the same, whereunto every private soldier should likewise be sworne.[21]

Because it was so important to the soldiers of the regiment, the capture of enemy flags was seen as one of the ways in which the extent of a victory could be measured, since its capture meant that the unit carrying it had been broken in pieces. This perspective is consistent in the military books of the day and in recorded practice. The principle was summarized by the Earl of Orrery with the comment that 'it is a disgrace to have had for any time, any of your Colours in your Enemies possession'.[22] The practice can be seen in the care with which any captured colours are mentioned in any account of a successful battle or skirmish, and the way in which captured flags were paraded through the capital: Royalist flags captured by Parliamentary forces were usually hung up for display in Westminster Hall,[23] Parliamentary flags captured by the Royalists were usually sent to the Royalist capital, Oxford,[24] and the flags captured by the Irish Confederacy at the battle of Benburb were taken to Limerick, where they were paraded through the streets and then hung up as trophies in the cathedral.[25]

The Militia officer Robert Ward described the objective of a common colour or recognizable design, stating that the colonel of a regiment of infantry

> ought to have all the Colours of his Regiment to be alike, both in colour and fashion to avoide confusion so that the souldiers may discerne their owne Regiment from other Troopes; likewise, every particular Captaine of his Regiment may have some small distinction in their Colours; as their Armes, or some Embleme, or the like, so that one Company may be discerned from another.[26]

There were different systems of this model, but the most common in use during the Civil War was described as follows by Thomas Venn:

> The Colonels Colours in the first place is of a pure and clean colour, without any mixture. The Lieutenant Colonels with only a Saint Georges Armes in the upper canton near the staff; the Majors the same but in the lower and outermost corner with a little stream blazant, And every Captain with Saint Georges Armes alone, but with so many spots or several Devices as pertain to the dignity of their respective places.[27]

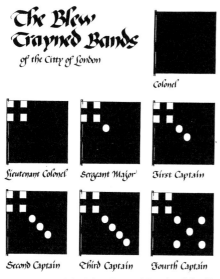

The Blew Trayned Bands *of the Citty of London*

Colonel'

Lieutenant Colonel'   Sergeant Major'   First Captain

Second Captain   Third Captain   Fourth Captain

The ensigns of the Blew Trained Bands of the City of London.

The most complete illustration of a series of infantry regiments using this type of system can be seen in contemporary painted records of the flags of London Trained Band regiments. These include regiments which followed exactly the system described by Thomas Venn or a very close alternative, where the sergeant major's colour had one of the regimental symbols rather than a 'stream blazant'. Examples of both variations are shown here and overleaf. These were not the only systems of flags flown by English infantry, Royalist or Parliamentarian, but these two were the most common. A letter dated 21 May 1649 from Colonel Charles Fairfax to Captain Adam Baynes in London sets out the design of the ensigns he required for his regiment, and provides confirmation that the system described by Thomas Venn was used by New Model Army infantry:

> I am now to provide colours for my regiments. My dear Lord [Charles Fairfax was the uncle of Sir Thomas Fairfax] is pleased I should have those I had before (being his own colours, blue and white), and may well accept his offer now, being deservedly his more cordial servant. I would have the best taffety of the deepest blue that can be gotten for ten colours, viz. five yards and a quarter for every two colours, and if more be used by others then take more. My own must have (within a well wrought round) these two words (one under the other) 'Fideliter Faeciliciter' and a handsome compartment round the word. I would have it painted by my old friend Mr Knight, a herault that dwells in Shoe Lane towards Fleet Street Conduit, and would have my own at least two yards square. The Lieutenant Colonel's is blue likewise, with the arms of England (viz. a cross gules) in the canton part. The major blue with the red cross and an white streaks. The eldest captain, and so every other captain in his seniority, to be distinguished by white mullets, in a blue field, as you will know how to direct. The taffety may be had at Mr Currer's or where it may best be had. I beseech you to hasten it.[28]

An example of the cost of an infantry flag can be found in the account book of the Committee of Kent, which paid £3 18s in total in June 1647 to 'Margaret Hollingsworth of London' for 'an enseigne's staffe with a silvered head, hatchd 8s., for a silke ensigne, white and blewe with a coat of armes in it £3. 5s., and for a leather case to keepe it in 5.s' for the Trained Band company of Captain William Skinner.[29]

An infantry regiment flying blue flags would be referred to by contemporaries as a blue regiment. This had nothing to do with the colour of the soldiers' coats, but related only to the colour of its flags. Where a regiment was distinctive because of the colour of its coats then any contemporary reference would refer specifically to the coat colour as, for example, 'The London Greycoats' or the 'Greene-coats (which Greene-coats are the four Companies of Farnham Castle)'.[30] Sir Thomas Morgan, who commanded the New Model infantry at the battle of the Dunes (14 June 1658) refers in his account of the campaign in France and Flanders to his men being redcoats after their uniform coats, but also referred to a blue regiment and white regiment, an indication of the colour of the flags carried by two of his infantry regiments.[31] There are few contemporary references to the flags carried by New Model infantry but those that exist suggest that the simple pattern described by Thomas Venn was followed. During negotiations to surrender the island of Jamaica to the English in May 1655, the Spanish ambassador described the English infantry as 'nine tercios of infantry with sixty-six flags, rather more than less, those of each tercio differing from those of others in colour, and that of each company being distinctive in design'.[32]

The material referred to as 'taffety' or 'taffeta' – or elsewhere as 'sarsanett' or 'damask' – was silk. The canton showing the cross of St George – a red cross on a white field – would also be made of silk and sewn on both sides of the flag, but the motto on the colonel's colour, the 'stream blazant' on the sergeant major's and the mullets on the captain's would usually be painted on. A surviving infantry ensign of Colonel Sir John Gell's regiment is 6 feet high by 6 feet 6 inches wide, and is made of two separate pieces of yellow cloth. The St George's cross in the canton at the upper left of the flag is 2 feet square, and there is a separate canton sewn on each side of the flag. The symbols on the flag – five dark blue mullets – have been painted on. An ensign was carried on a light pole about 7 to 8 feet long with a finial or spear point at the top and a pair of decorative cords attached beneath the finial. It was carried in one hand by the officer responsible for it and would be 'displayed' on ceremonial occasions and in battle. Thomas Venn described the way it should be carried: 'if he shall enter into any City or great town; then he shall unfold or open his Colours, and let them fly at full length, and carry them in his right hand close under the hose, with a lofty hand and extended arm'. Venn went on to specify that if 'the wind blow stiff, or there is a weakness or wearisomness in the Ensign-bearer, then he may set the butt end against his waste and not otherwise, and is to have but one hand upon his staff in any march whatever'.[33]

Scottish infantry flags followed a different pattern. The colonel's flag was usually white, with the other company flags showing the St Andrew's cross over the whole of the flag. Some of these carried the St Andrew's cross in the Scottish national colours – a white X or saltire over a blue field – but others used the same design but with different colours. For example, the Marquess of

Sergeant Majors' Colours
Trained Band Regiments

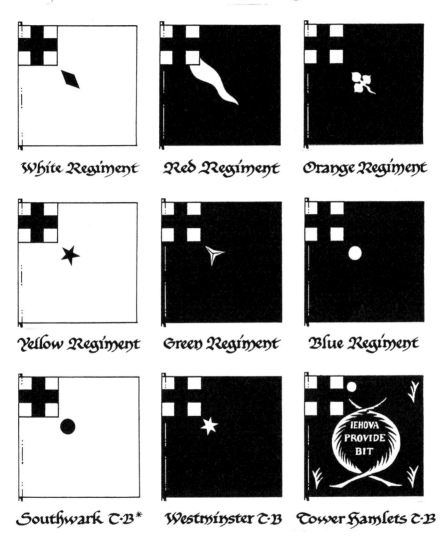

White Regiment | Red Regiment | Orange Regiment

Yellow Regiment | Green Regiment | Blue Regiment

Southwark T·B* | Westminster T·B | Tower Hamlets T·B

IEHOVA PROVIDE BIT

* First Captain's Colour

Sergeant majors' colours. The most complete set of infantry flags which survive from the English Civil War are those of the London Trained Bands and Auxiliaries, the surviving record being the illustrated report of a Royalist spy, William Levett. Each company in the regiment carried its own colour. This illustration shows the sergeant majors' colours of each of the nine Trained Band regiments – six from the City of London, and one each from the suburbs of Westminster and Tower Hamlets, and the borough of Southwark. Artwork by Dr Les Prince.

Argyle's regiment used a yellow saltire over a black field for the flags carried at the battle of Preston, and the regiment of Sir David Home of Wedderburn carried flags with a white saltire on a green field at the battle of Dunbar.[34] Unlike English flags it was usual for Scottish flags to carry a motto split into the four segments created by the St Andrew's cross.

Cavalry flags or 'cornets' were also made of silk but made smaller – about 2 feet square – and carried on a cavalry lance. Two surviving cornets measure 21 inches by 18 inches and 21 inches by 30 inches.[35] Cavalry flags were much more individual than those carried by the infantry and carried a painted image and motto favoured by the captain commanding the troop. Gervase Markham gave the most complete description in his book *The Souldiers Accidence*, where he stated that:

> The substance of the Cornet shall be Damaske, and the forme must be almost square (onely a little longer from the staffe then on the staffe) and fringed about suitablie. The staffe shall be small like a foote Ensigne, and not so long as an ordinarie Launce; it must be headed with Steele, and either guilt or silverd, with faire Tassels suitable to the Cornet. If the Cornet belong to a greater Officer it shall be of one entire Colour, of lesse quantitie and full square; and in this Cornet, the Captaine may carrie devise and word, or els none, at his owne pleasure.[36]

The design and motto on the flag – the 'devise and word' referred to by Gervase Markham – could be purely military, or it could be satirical, religious or political. The encouraging military image of skull and laurel wreath with the motto 'One of these' which 'signifieth Death or Victory' was used by at least three officers, Colonel Lord Brougham, Captain Richard Brown and Captain Richard Stevens. Royalist cornets provide the most vicious examples of satirical comment, sometimes referring to the marital difficulties of the Parliament general, the Earl of Essex – for example the motto 'Cuckolds We Come' on one Royalist cavalry flag. The flags of Parliamentary cavalry officers were often more directly political, but both sides used political or religious mottoes and designs.

Dragoons were mounted infantry, and the design of dragoon flags or guidons was part-way between that of an infantry and a cavalry flag. Colonel Wardlaw's regiment demonstrated this mixture of infantry and cavalry styles of flags as his regiment's blue guidons had a St George's cross in the upper canton, but each flag, except the Colonel's own, carried a motto in gold letter. However, there does not appear to have been any common practice, and five guidons of Sir William Waller's dragons mustered in September 1643 were all yellow, with each company being distinguished by a black ball,[37] one for the first, two for the second and so on. The guidons themselves were about the same size as a cavalry flag but had a swallowtail shape on the edge away from the standard pole; some were fringed in the same way as cavalry standards but others were not. They were carried on a standard pole rather than a cavalry lance.

Chapter Nine

Military Life in Camp and Garrison

Introduction

During the early stages of the Civil War, political and religious enthusiasm encouraged a wider spectrum of society to join the army than would normally be found in the seventeenth century. By 1643 both sides had turned to conscription to fill the ranks of their infantry regiments, but the early volunteers and those men who continued to volunteer through belief in the cause still meant that the army consisted of Englishmen with a broad range of backgrounds and connections to civilian life. Politics and religion could draw both soldier and civilian together, but it could also create further divisions. In the political sense, many soldiers sympathized with the Leveller movement led by Lieutenant Colonel John Lilburne and the civilian pamphleteers William Walwyn and Richard Overton. Many others supported religious groups with strong political connections in Parliament, Presbyterians or Independents, while some were members of smaller sects – Brownists, Anabaptists or Quakers. This said, military life did create a barrier between soldiers and civilians. On the one hand, the practice of quartering or billeting soldiers in civilian homes created serious tensions between soldier and civilian, and on the other shared hardship and a sense of military honour or mutual obligation meant the soldier soon thought of himself as part of the military family of his regiment or the particular army to which he belonged.

A Military Community

One distinguishing factor in all relationships between soldier and civilian was that the soldier was armed and was part of a larger armed group. An indication of the general experience can be seen in the account, recorded as a complaint by a Scottish householder, where four soldiers came to his house with orders to quarter there, beat his servants for trying to keep them out and 'all of them having att supper five pintes of ale and a pint they had before. The deponent said, they should have noe more, whereuppon they broke open the chamber door and being going to draw the drinke, his wife resisting them, one of them struck her with a pistol, that they sat uppe and sange, drinking until about midnight.'[1] An unhappy English householder complained in 1647 that 'My house is, and hath been full of soldiers this fortnight, such uncivil drinkers and thirsty souls that a barrel of good beer trembles at the sight of them, and the whole house is nothing but a rendezvous of tobacco and spitting.'[2] A fondness for beer seems to have been a consistent feature in the New Model Army, as Sir Samuel Luke wrote in a dispatch on 10 June 1645: 'I think these New Modellers knead all their dough with ale, for I never saw so many drunk in my life in so short a time.'[3]

From the soldiers' perspective, they became part of a military community, and this can be seen in the expressions of unity by both the New Model Army and the Army of the Northern Association during the army mutinies of 1647. A more personal example of this sense of being part of a close-knit group can be seen following an incident which occurred in March 1651 and was described by the contemporary Jersey diarist Jean Chevalier. This is a particularly relevant example because the soldiers involved were members of Colonel Alban Coxe's regiment, veterans from one of the original twelve infantry regiments of the New Model Army. Some of these men had been serving together in Parliamentary armies since 1642. This New Model Army regiment had been formed from Sergeant Major Philip Skippon's regiment in the Earl of Essex's army (which had served in all of Essex's campaigns during 1643 and 1644, including the first and second battles of Newbury) and from Sir Miles Hobart's and Sir Thomas Hogan's regiments in the Army of the Eastern Association (Sir Miles Hobart's had fought at the battle of Marston Moor). Its first colonel in the New Model Army had been Philip Skippon, and it had shared in that army's victorious campaign of 1645 and 1646, fighting at the battle of Naseby and the series of sieges which followed.

This regiment was in garrison on the island of Guernsey and took part in an assault on the Royalist-held Castle Cornet, a fortress built on a small island offshore. The assault failed and about 130 officers and soldiers were left stranded on the small island, when their boats, crewed by local seamen, fled back to Guernsey. The most seriously wounded, twenty-six men in all, were returned to Guernsey under parole, and the remainder were taken as prisoners to Jersey. The diarist Jean Chevalier described these men, the way they lived as prisoners and the ways in which their comrades and their officers back in Guernsey sought to assist them. Major James Harrison, the commander in Guernsey in the absence of Colonel Alban Coxe, was devastated by the loss of so many of his men, as Jean Bisson, the Jersey islander he released to carry a message to Jersey, related: 'since the assault the Guernsey Major had not left his room, being overcome with grief at the discomfortshire of his soldiers. He was still in it when Bisson sailed, for he said that in the loss of his troops he had lost, as it were, a fortune.' However, although affected by the loss of his men, altogether probably 200 killed, wounded and captured out of an attacking force of 300, Harrison swiftly took practical measures. Jean Bisson's message to the Royalist governor of Jersey, Sir George Carteret, included the request that he grant 'the prisoners who were in his charge certain extra sums over and above their ordinary prison allowances' and promised to send money to cover this. Harrison then maintained contact with his men, regularly sending a drummer – the accepted messenger for communication between officers on opposing sides – to Jersey.

The diarist Jean Chevalier described one occasion where 'the messenger who came from Guernsey brought an English half crown, worth twenty-seven sous for each of the prisoners, some of whom also received shirts and stockings. Others who had friends in Guernsey received from them a half pound of tobacco each, sewn up in linen packets on which their names were written, also spices, such as cloves and cinnamon'. Chevalier described these soldiers as 'all young, bold and active men. When they first arrived they used to sing, but in the end they sang no more.' But neither their spirit nor their sense of community was broken and Chevalier recorded, when some of the prisoners were exchanged for Royalist prisoners, of the New Model prisoners: 'These men all had such affection for each other that those who were going and had good clothes on their backs or shoes on their feet, gave them to their less fortunate comrades who were left behind and took their worn and shabby raiment in exchange. There was much sorrow in their leave taking.'[4] The image which emerges from Jean Chevalier's first-hand description is one of a group of men with an extremely strong sense of comradeship and community, where their commander was personally shattered by their loss but made immediate efforts to assist them, very probably from money he raised himself, as Parliament was always slow to vote funds, and kept in regular touch with them, where their fellow soldiers in Guernsey sent them packages of tobacco and other comforts, and where they themselves retained their sense of community while they were prisoners.

The Military Camp

The soldier's home – in the purely physical sense – was the camp, garrison or billet in which he, and any family who accompanied him, lived. In terms of the military camp, the Earl of Orrery defined 'three sorts of Camps, the Temporary Camp which is for a Night, or some short space. The Standing Camp, whereby Countries are kept in subjection, which have been Conquer'd, or in which Armies are lodged for some time, either to avoid being necessitated to Fight, till they saw a fitting time, or for some other great design. And the Besieging Camp.'[5]

The first of these, the temporary camp, was little used in England during the Civil Wars, as it was usually easier for an army on the march to billet soldiers in the towns and surrounding villages or country houses on their route of march. This practice meant that, in England, an army did not carry tents in its baggage train. This could lead to very cramped quarters, and the London Trained Bands sergeant Henry Foster recorded that on one occasion during the march to relieve the city of Gloucester 'our whole regiment was quartered at one Mr Cheyney's house, an esquire, where we were well accommodated for beere, having great plenty, two or three hundred of us this night lay in one

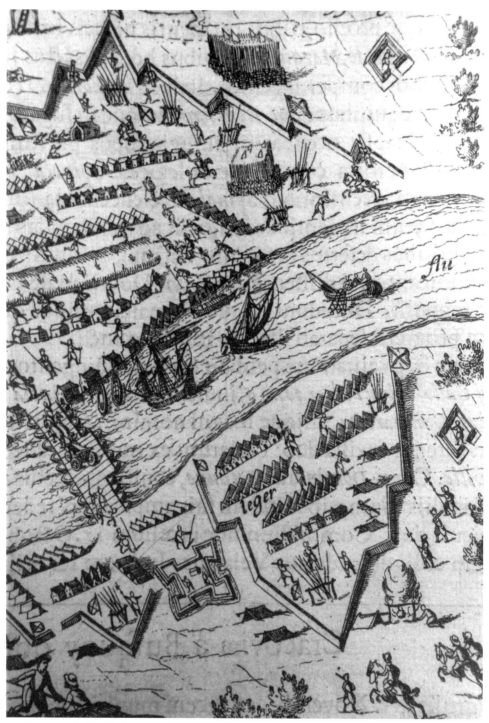

Encampment. Detail of a sixteenth-century military camp. Note the tent lines and the raised bars used to stack pikes.

barne'.[6] Where circumstances or sheer numbers made it impossible to quarter troops in buildings overnight, the soldiers would have to sleep in the open. This form of exposure overnight was deadly in poor weather, as one Parliament officer, writing in October 1642, recorded: 'Winter is already come and our lying in the field hath lost us more than have been taken away either by the sword or the bullet.'[7]

The New Model Army followed the same practice when campaigning in England, and a contemporary pamphlet recorded in July 1645 that 'for the most part we took barns and hedges for our night's repose, after our hard and hot days marches'.[8] But, when faced with more difficult conditions in sparsely populated or previously devastated territory, it was accepted that tents would be necessary, and they were issued to the army which Oliver Cromwell led to Ireland in 1649. Tents were also issued to the army which invaded Scotland in 1650, but not until 12 August when a London pamphlet reported that 'there is for every File [six men] a Tent, for their better quartering in the field, which they received this morning'.[9] General George Monk also used tents for his campaign in the highlands of Scotland in 1654. George Monk's request for the retention of several specialist officers in 1657 notes particularly that he 'desired that a tent-maker may bee continued, for there are noe men in this country that have any skill in making or mending of tents', on the basis that 'when our horse goe to grasse in the summer wee are faine to give orders for the horse-men to have tents to lye by their horses for a guard for them', and 'besides when wee have occasion to send those companies that goe to Loughaber through the hills, who make use of tents in their march, soe these tents are every yeare to bee repaired and unless this man bee continued your tents here will be destroyed'.[10] At least some of the tents used in Scotland appear to have been issued in pieces, with each soldier carrying one part of the tent, as an account of the tents held in store at various garrisons in Scotland includes an entry for 'eighteen pieces of tents'.[11]

The second type of camp, the standing camp, was used in the Civil Wars but not to the same extent as it was in European wars. For this sort of longer-term encampment, a well-organized camp became a military town and should be set out in an orderly manner according to a series of set principles. This had separate, specific locations for the quarters of the general and his staff, the provost, quartermaster, minister, chirurgeon (surgeon), artillery and wagon train, and a series of sectors for each regiment of infantry or cavalry. Each of these regiments would be camped in a series of lines of huts or tents. Each company of infantry in the regiment would have two lines of huts or tents separated by a lane between, with the opening facing towards the lane. Sergeants and officers had separate accommodation, larger for more senior officers, and the sutlers serving a particular regiment had a separate line of huts or tents close to the regimental lines. The arrangement was similar for a troop of cavalry with two lines of huts or tents for each troop facing inwards, but including stables for the horses immediately in front of the troopers' huts, on the basis that otherwise the horses 'by standing three or four nights in rain

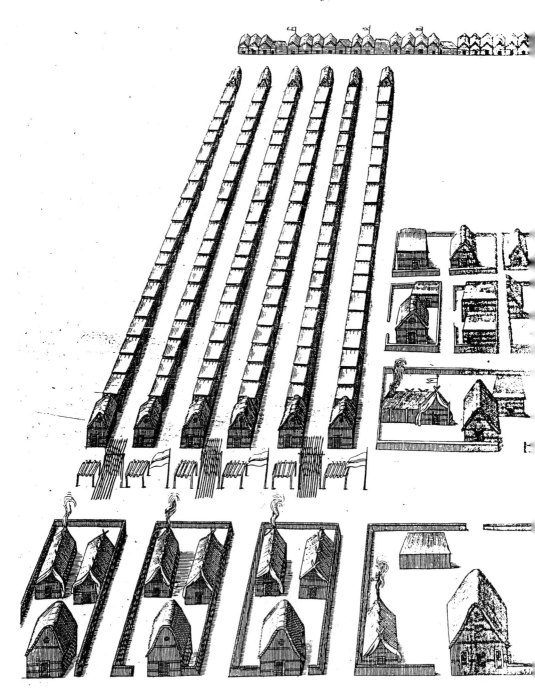

Infantry lines. A detailed view of the huts of three infantry companies. Note the pike-racks at the end of the rows.

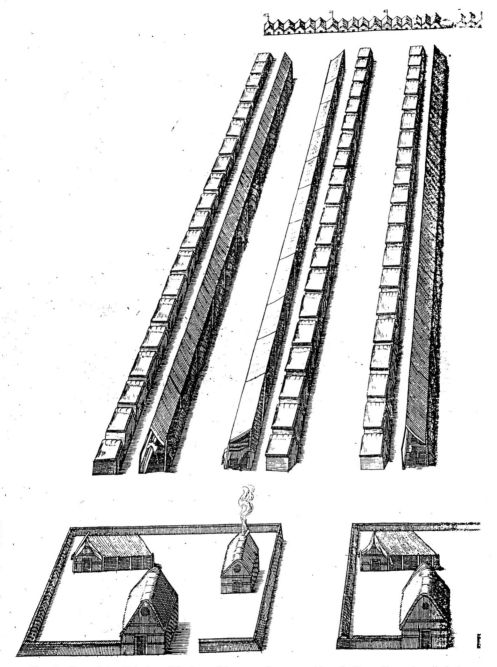

Cavalry lines. A detailed view of the huts of three cavalry troops. Note the lines of horses' stalls facing the troopers' huts.

and cold, would be in danger, to be spoiled and made unserviceable'.[12] The whole camp would be surrounded by some form of defensive outer earthwork and would be guarded by sentries and patrols on the inside and on the outside of the earthworks.

The accompanying contemporary plans (pp. 188–9) illustrate the layouts for both infantry and cavalry. The design used in England, and detailed in contemporary manuals, was based on the practice used in the well-trained and experienced Dutch army. From a contemporary engraving by Wenceslaus Hollar there is evidence that this form of camp was used during the Bishops' Wars, and there are references during the First Civil War to the use of huts in Royalist encampments, one example being the Royalist camp at Culham, near Abingdon, where the Royalist newsbook *Mercurius Aulicus* reported in May 1643 that 'severall Regiments of his Majesties Army, to the number of thirteene or thereabouts, marched out of Oxford to an appointed place beyond Abingdon, to be intrenched and settled into a leaguer'.[13] These large military camps or leaguers were common in Europe but not in England.

However, essentially the same principles were used in the third category, the besieging camp. Here there is both documentary and pictorial evidence of the use of this system in the camps of armies besieging cities or towns during the Civil Wars. This type of camp was usually composed of soldier's huts. For example, when the Parliament and Scottish armies abandoned their positions outside York on the approach of Prince Rupert's relief force, the Royalist

English army during the Bishops' Wars. An example of the encampment of an English regiment according to the model theory of the day, with separate lines for each company.

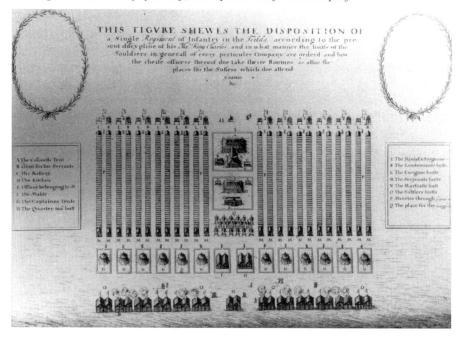

garrison sent out patrols which are recorded as having found the besiegers' 'Hutts empty'. Another example was the Royalist encampment at Borough Hill, where the Royalist army camped between 7 and 12 June, shortly before the battle of Naseby. Joshua Sprigge commented that Sir Thomas Fairfax, when checking his outposts in the early morning of 13 June, observed 'fires in abundance, as if they were firing their Huts; which gave some cause to believe they were about to march, as indeed it proved afterwards'.[14]

These examples suggest formal camps, with the huts being made by the soldiers out of anything that came to hand – turf, wooden boards, brushwood or straw. Captain Thomas Rudd's recommendations on this subject were that 'Officers must see the Souldiers build formally, and that they make their Beds a foot and a half or two foot long from the ground, to prevent sickness which they will be subject to fall into by lying on the ground.'[15] The Earl of Orrery, who gives the most detailed contemporary description, set out that, for infantry, the length of 'every Hutt is to be at most 7 Foot and 3 [infantrymen] are to be in one Hutt', while that for the cavalry troopers would be 10 feet: 'the Troopers accommodation is larger, because of his Armour and Furniture [horse furniture – saddle etc.]'. Cavalry lines would include 'Horses Hutts or Stalls' which 'are to be left open behind and before, and only shut up on the two sides, but covered over head to defend them from the rain, great cold and great heat'. Orrery also commented that when using tents in the field he 'allowed every six soldiers but one Trench-Tent, and every three Troopers but one Trench-Tent (because of their Saddles and Furniture)'.[16]

As with most contemporary military theory, these structured camps could be laid out by a straightforward method. They had to be if the system was to be workable in practice, and examples of contemporary evidence show that it was used. The successful use of this formal method of encampment relied upon the technical ability of the quartermaster general and the regimental quartermasters. The quartermaster general, 'knowing the place where the Quarters are to be',[17] would:

> consult with his List which he is to quarter; name'ly, how many Regiments of Horse, how many of Foot, what Waggons, what Artillery, and whatsoever else, as Sutlers, &c. he is to quarter; also how many Companies there is in each Regiment, and how many men in each Company. He having collected them all together in a Note, let him take some pieces of fine past-board, and cut them into pieces 300 foot (by some small scale) [i.e. a convenient scale to represent 300 feet] deep, and so broad as to contain the number of men of such a Regiment, either Horse or Foot, he is to quarter; allowing true distance of Ground both for Hut, Passage, Stable, &c, and at that length let him cut off his past-board square, and write upon the past-board the Colonel's name, and number of men; and this must he do for every Regiment both of Horse and Foot. In the like manner for the General's Quarters and his Retinue, for the Provost, Quarter-master, Minister, Chirurgeon, and all others that

The Paſt-boards laid together.

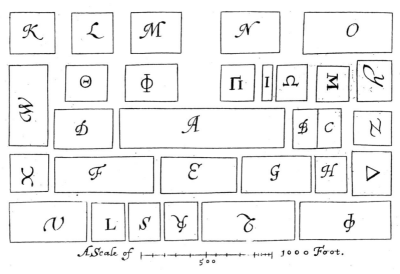

Design of quarters. To lay out a camp without confusion required some careful planning in advance. A competent quartermaster first cut out pieces of pasteboard using a common scale of measurement and the size of each unit from its last muster returns. Then he 'moved them this way and that' to see how they could fit together, much as we would now use a computer program to design the layout of a factory or an office.

require single Quarters; and likewise the Waggons and Sutlers. All these must he lay out according as he finds their Number greater or lesser in his List, and cut his past-boards accordingly, writing on them as before.

His past-boards being thus prepared, let him upon a Table, or rather upon a sheet of Imperial or Royal paper, draw divers occult parallel lines at 50 foot distance for Streets, and spaces of 300 foot for his several Regiments. By help of these parallel lines he may lay his past-boards upon this paper, and move them this way and that way, till he have brought them into a Square or Parrallogram, or as regular a form as they will permit.

He having thus disposed to the best advantage in his judgment he may draw a Scheme or Plat thereof upon fair Paper or Parchment, writing the name of every Colonel and his number of men upon his particular Quarter, with the Generals Quarters, Market, Streets, Lanes, &c making thereof a perfect Map; and adding a Scale thereto, he may measure the distance of any part thereof at pleasure. This being done, he may repair to his General, and shew him his design; which if he approve of, he may proceed to the laying out of the Quarters in the Field.

Once the general had approved his design, the quartermaster general would go to the site and mark out the perimeter of the camp using a 'Surveying Instrument'. Each corner of the place where each regiment was to set up quarters was marked by placing 'four staves nine or ten foot high, painted in the Colour of the Regiment [the same colour as its regimental flags], with a Standard or Banner at the top thereof'. Once this outline was laid out for his regiment it was then the responsibility of the regimental quartermaster 'to subdivide his Quarter according to the number of his men, putting in a stick at each end of every row of Huts and Streets end. Then the Serjeants of every Company presently fall a dividing the Souldiers Huts, and set up four sticks at the corner of each Hut.' The soldiers who were to live in the hut then had to build it, while the 'Serjeants are to see that they build them regularly, and not incroach one upon another, but as their Ground is allotted to them'[18] – an indication that soldiers commonly moved the perimeter sticks to have a larger area of ground for their hut if they were not watched closely.

However, it would take an experienced specialist officer to do this on a large scale, and many of those who served in the early stages of the Civil Wars did not have that experience. This consideration lies behind the Earl of Orrery's comment that

> I have the longer and more particularly insisted on this part of the Art of War [in his manual] of intrench'd incampings, because it is what in England we have not been much accustomed unto and therefore are generally the less knowing in it; for I have seen eminent Commanders there, when they came with Armies for the War of Ireland, so great strangers to the Rules of it [i.e. setting out encampments], as their camps appeared to me like Fairs; and some of them, not only have ingeniously acknowledged to me, they were to seek in that great part of War.[19]

From Orrery's remarks it is evident that the quality of organization within encampments must have varied widely during the early years of the war, with some being well laid out and others being chaotic. As the armies gained more experience the standard would have improved. There were strong practical advantages to a well laid out camp in terms of security, as well as greater efficiency and basic hygiene.

Contemporary commanders were well aware – simply from experiencing it – of the dangers of contagious disease in their camps, commonly typhus, often referred to as plague. The standing instructions of an army commander's *Articles of War* required 'all officers, whose charge it is, shall see the Quarters kept cleane and sweet, upon pain of severe punishment'. The Earl of Orrery expanded on this with advice that 'the Camp be kept exceeding clean, which is not only decent but healthy'. More specifically he stated that care should be taken that

> none of the Soldiers do their Easements within it [the camp], but in some convenient places, at least 100 Foot without it, as the Martials of every

regiment shall appoint, either in the River or Brook, or in some Pits to be digged by every Regiment for that end. That the Troopers every morning and evening be made carry out of the line, all the dung of their Horses. That the Butchers do the like as to all the filth in their Shambles, and be made kill their Beeves, Sheep &c out of the Camp, and that all dung and filth be buried; and that the Suttlers and Victuallers, keep their Cellars and Kitchins sweet.[20]

Disease could break out in a well-managed camp but would be more devastating in a chaotic one where basic cleanliness was not enforced.

When not in camps, a soldier would live in the garrison of a town or city, or he would be billeted in towns or villages. The operation of a major garrison was also organized in a structured way, with most of the soldiers billeted on the citizens of the town, usually with men from the same company in adjoining houses or streets. There would usually be some accommodation within the fortifications themselves, particularly if there was a castle within the city walls, and some soldiers may have been accommodated in huts built within the walls – the original word for soldiers' barracks being taken from the term *barracas* used in the Spanish Army of Flanders to refer to huts and later used more generally to describe more permanent soldiers' accommodation. The city or town was controlled by a formally appointed governor, with a 'town major' as the officer who managed the practical operation of the city and its garrison. The Earl of Orrery considered that 'A Town Major in a large Garison is very useful and necessary, for he is in effect the second eyes of the Governor', and his description of the duties of this officer provides a useful indication of everyday life in the garrison which the Town Major supervised. His duties included the responsibility to

mind the well quartering of the Soldiers when their Quarters are distributed by the Civil Magistrates; to see the Guards be duly furnish'd with Fire and Candle; and when any of the soldiers are sick or wounded, to have them carried to the Hospital or Pesthouse, for which end he must daily visit those places, and report to the Governor what he finde amiss; for the Officers of those Houses will be the more careful under such strict and frequent inspection. He is likewise to cause the Guard houses and Centry-houses to be kept clean, and in good Repair.[21]

Military Life

The Earl of Orrery recommended keeping soldiers occupied with labour, but he understood as well as anyone else that they needed some relaxation. One source of this was the sutlers' tents or huts, usually one for each company of infantry or troop of cavalry, shown at the top of the plans for his camps (see pages 188 and 189). The isolated forts built in Scotland in the 1650s also included a tavern, essentially a sutler's on site, where 'all manner of wines, viands [food], beer, ale and cider' were sold. The sutlers' tents or huts were the focal point of good

Relaxing in camp. While their commanders thought in terms of organized camps, guards, scouts and sentries, most soldiers saw any semi-permanent camp as a place where they could relax.

times in camp where soldiers could buy – or get credit to buy – additional food, drink beer or strong waters (i.e. spirits), smoke tobacco, gamble with cards or dice and sing the popular ballads of the day. Another contemporary source, the ballad 'The Gallant She-Souldier',[22] describes this form of recreation:

> Yet civill in her carriage and modest still was she,
> But with her fellow souldiers she oft would merry be;
> She would drink and take tobacco, and spend her money too,
> When as occasion served, that she had nothing else to do.

The sutler also commonly provided whores, one satirical pamphlet referring – in verse – to 'Sutlers wives with their faces tallow, who with their Trulls the Army follow'.[23] Not all the women accompanying an army made their living whoring, although many certainly did. Sir James Turner wrote that

> Women who follow an Army may be ordered (if they can be ordered) into
> three classes, one below another. The first shall be those who are Ladies,

and are the Wives of the General and other principal Commanders of the Army, who for the most part are carried in Coaches; but those Coaches must drive according to the quality of them to whom the Ladies belong, and as the Baggage of their Husbands is appointed to march by the Waggon-master General. The second class is of those who ride on Horseback, and these must ride in no other place than where the Baggage of the Regiment to whom they belong, marcheth, but they are very oft extravagant, gadding here and there.

Turner evidently considered that this second class was largely made up of ladies of negotiable virtue, as he commented that 'in some places they are put in Companies, and have one or more to command or over-see them, and these are called in Germany, Hureweibles, Rulers or Marshals of the Whores. I have seen them ride, kept Troop, rank and file very well, after that Captain of theirs who led them and a Banner with them, which one of the Women carried.' Although these women were certainly found accompanying both armies, Parliamentary armies – and particularly the New Model Army – made more of an effort to restrict their numbers. The Royalist cavalry retreating through Lancashire after their defeat at Marston Moor 'carried along with them many strumpets, which they termed Leaguer Ladies'. Contemporary accounts of the Royalist baggage captured after the battle of Naseby record 'wagons carrying the middle sort of Ammunition Whores, who were full of money and rich apparel'.

The third class described by Sir James Turner were 'those who walk on foot, and are the wives of inferior Officers and Souldiers; these must walk besides the Baggage of the several Regiments to whom they belong, and over them the several Regimental Marshals have inspection'.[24] Although he was concerned to reduce the amount of baggage wagons and camp followers in an army, simply on the grounds that a large train was a hindrance to quick marches, Turner saw real value in soldiers' wives accompanying the army, as

> women are great helpers in Armies to their husbands, especially those of the lower condition, neither should they be rashly banisht out of Armies, sent away they may be sometimes for weighty considerations; they provide, buy and dress their husbands meat when their husbands are on duty, or newly come from it, they bring in fewel for fire, and wash their linens, and in such manner of employments a Souldiers wife may be helpful to others, and gain money to her husband and her self; especially they are useful in Camps and Leaguers, being permitted (which should not be refused them) to go some miles from the Camp to buy Victuals and other Necessaries.

Turner went on to specify that 'among all these kinds of Women in well order'd Armies, there are none but those who are married. If there be any else, upon examination by the Minister, Priest, or Consistory, they are put away with ignominy.'[25] This form of enquiry was clearly more likely to happen in the

Parliament armies, and particularly the New Model, as they saw themselves to be the more Godly party. Although English wives and followers were accepted, specific army regulations were imposed restricting the marriage of English soldiers and Scottish women or Catholic Irish women. In neither case could the army actually prevent people getting married, but it could discharge soldiers from the army if they did so. In Scotland, the governor of Edinburgh issued an order that no one under his command should 'presume to be married to any woman in or of Scotland' without his consent or that of the deputy governor or the major of his regiment. Anyone disobeying this order was to be discharged from his regiment. In Scotland, where most of the women concerned would be Presbyterian Protestants, this was probably because the governor saw it as a security risk, since soldiers' wives lived in the garrison and would be in a position to spy or simply pass on information they overheard in conversation. In Ireland the army's objection was also based on religion, as many of the New Model officers had a visceral dislike of all things Catholic, and Irish Catholics in particular.

Life for the soldiers' wives or lovers, and their children, was hard, as a soldier's pay was often in arrears. But what they could not afford to buy could be obtained by theft or a loose interpretation of the concept of 'free quarter' when billeted on civilians. In camp they would live in the soldiers' huts, and in garrison they would live in the soldiers' quarters. If the New Model Army followed the practice of the professional long-service Spanish Army of Flanders – which is highly likely – then they would have made a greater allowance of space and consequently a larger number of huts according to the number of women, wives or otherwise, living with the soldiers.[26] The presence of army wives with the army in Scotland is indicated by the newsbook report that the execution of a soldier sentenced to death by a court martial at Leith in October 1652 was cancelled after 'all or most of the wives in this Garison had petitioned and prevailed with the Governour's clemency for his pardon'.[27]

Apart from what the sutlers' tents had to offer, there were other amusements in camp. The ballad 'The Gallant She-Souldier' describes some of them:

> For other manly practices she gain'd the love of all,
> For leaping and for running or wrestling for a fall,
> For cudgels or for cuffing, if that occasion were,
> There's hardly one of ten men that might with her compare.

Another popular pastime was shooting game – or anything else that could be found – for the pot. One of Sir Thomas Fairfax's army proclamations specified that:

> Daily complaints are made that some disorderly soldiers under my command, contrary to the laws of the nation and discipline of the army, have and still do commit very great outrages and riots, with their arms entering into parks, chases, and warrens, and thence stealing all sorts of

deer and conies [rabbits], menacing the death of the keepers and all such who anyways oppose them.

The soldiers were evidently using dogs to assist their hunting, and Fairfax's proclamation required his officers 'that forthwith they cause to be taken from their soldiers all such hounds, greyhounds, and other dogs which may any ways be hurtful to deer or conies'.[28]

A Woman Soldier

Report of Lieutenant-Colonel Roger Sawrey, Commander of the Garrison at Ayre, 6 April 1657.

I with my company got very well to Ayre upon Saturday, where I found all things in good order and friends in health, only a young person with Captain-Lieutenant Shockly, entertained the last muster, who is since discovered to be a woman. Her name she saith is Ann Dimack, daughter to one John Dimack of Keale, near Bullingbrooke Castle in Lincolnshire. She hath been with us but one muster, and saith her father and mother being dead she lived with her aunt, and fell in love with one John Evison, who had served his time in London, but was a Lincolnshire man. Her friends were against it, and would by no meanes yield to their marriage, nor had she any way of accomplishing her end left, but by putting herself into man's habit, which she did in May, 1655, and so went to London together, and finding him not to be in a capacity to live they both resolved to betake themselves to services, this maid still keeping in man's appreal, and went as two brothers. The young man lived at Islington and the maid at London with a coachman in Chick Lane, whose name was Taylor, where she served two years under the name of Stephen Evison, and after that coming away by sea the said John was cast away, and she, keeping still her man's habit, came to Carlisle, and there listed herself for a soldier under Major Tolhurst by the name of John Evison, and there she continued until she came to the garrison, and never was known to any, which she agrees very solemnly to be all the way of her progress in her disguise. And I can perceive nothing but modesty in her carriage since she hath been with us, and shall send to the other places where she hath been formerly to know the truth of her declaration. If you think it necessary you may acquaint my Lord General with it.

Source: Historical Manuscripts Commission, *Report on the Manuscripts of F. W. Leybourne-Popham* (Norwich, 1899).

Fairfax set out to create a strongly disciplined army which had the financial backing to pay for its provisions and sought to restrict his soldiers' plundering. In doing so he followed his own conscience and the example of the Swedish King Gustavus Adolphus – admired and emulated by most New Model Army officers – in seeking to behave fairly but firmly towards the civilian population, the objective being to ensure that even if they did not agree with his cause, civilians would see the New Model Army as less of a personal threat than the rapacious soldiers of an opposing army. But this was never easy and the practice of hunting game remained. All commanders had to strike some balance between public relations and the morale of their own men, and George Monk, when commanding in Scotland, did give specific permission for individual soldiers to 'carry a fowling-piece for the killing of fowls for his game, provided he kill no tame pigeons and rabbits'.[29] Since another order restricted a regiment in garrison to two greyhounds per company – a clear indication that there were a lot more – this evidently remained a popular pastime.

Chapter Ten

From Victory to Mutiny

Introduction
The strategic position facing the Parliament at the end of 1644 was that the intervention of the Scottish Covenanter army had tipped the balance of power in the north of England. The combination of the Scottish army and the two Parliamentary armies of the Northern Association and Eastern Association had proved too much for the two northern Royalist armies and had crushed them at the battle of Marston Moor. However, the Scots were unlikely to move their army too far from the north of England, and would not be the decisive factor in the war in southern England and the West Country.

Political Debate and the Appointment of New Generals
The Parliament now had a numerical advantage over the remaining Royalist armies in the south, but only by combining their independent armies, and the divided command structure that this created had proved unworkable. The Parliament generals' quarrels took place against a background of increasing war-weariness in the country as a whole, as the population saw no end to the personal cost in terms of the loss of life of family or friends, the damage to their homes and livelihood from soldiers of either side, high taxation and the general impact on their everyday lives. Victory in the north of England had provided a boost to Parliamentary support but this had been countered by the defeats suffered by the armies of the Earl of Essex and Sir William Waller, and the failure of its combined armies to defeat the Royalists at the second battle of Newbury, despite a clear advantage in numbers. This concept had been starkly portrayed by Oliver Cromwell in the opening passage of the first of his three speeches to the House of Commons on 9 December 1644:

> It is now a time to speak, or forever hold the tongue. The important occasion now is no less than to save a Nation out of a bleeding, nay almost dying condition, which the long continuance of this War hath already brought it into; so that without a more speedy, vigorous and effectual prosecution of the War, – casting off all lingering proceedings like [those

of] soldiers-of-fortune beyond sea, to spin out a war, – we shall make the kingdom weary of us and hate the name of a Parliament.[1]

Cromwell gave this speech during the debate in which it was proposed by the MP Zouch Tate 'that during the time of the war no member of either house shall have or execute any office or command, military or civil, granted or conferred by both or either of the Houses [Commons or Lords].'[2] In his second speech of the debate, summarized in the Royalist Earl of Clarendon's *History*, Cromwell concluded with an 'enlargement upon the vices and corruptions which were gotten into the army, the profaneness and impiety and absence of all religion, the drinking and gaming, and all manner of license and laziness; and said plainly that, till the whole army were new modelled and governed under a stricter discipline, they must not expect any notable success in anything they went about.'[3] As MP for Cambridge, Cromwell would be excluded himself, and in his third speech he sought to reassure the House of Commons with the comment that

> I am not of the mind that the calling of the Members [of both Commons and Lords] to sit in Parliament will break or scatter our armies. I can speak this for my own soldiers, that they look not upon me, but upon you; and for you they will fight and live and die in your cause; and if others be of that mind that they are of, you need not fear them. They do not idolize me, but look upon the cause they fight for.[4]

This would have been a hopeful assumption by Parliament as any army's loyalties – and particularly that of a veteran army where officers and men had shared both hardships and successes – were always strongly influenced by its generals and other officers. The MPs were perfectly well aware of this potential threat to their own authority, as many had sat in the Parliament which had refused to accept King Charles's right to appoint officers for the army to be raised to put down rebellion in Ireland in 1642. On that occasion the fear was that, once victorious, the army would follow its officers, and power would then lie with the faction which had appointed its own supporters as officers. However, the problem they faced was that the existing generals of their southern armies were discredited, the population was becoming increasingly war-weary and it was evident that they could bring their numerical superiority to bear only if they had a single united command in southern England. The House of Commons finally passed its Self-Denying Ordinance on 19 December 1644, after motions to exempt the Earl of Essex and the Lord Admiral, the Earl of Warwick, from the effect of the ordinance were defeated. After delays in the House of Lords, the House of Commons set about raising a new army without its approval, and resolved on 11 January 1645 that it would consist of ten regiments of cavalry, one of dragoons and twelve regiments of infantry, to be financed by a monthly assessment upon the seventeen Midlands, southern and eastern counties. This left the difficult question of appointing the generals and the officers of the new army.

The Regiments of the New Model Army in 1645

Regiment	Raised from
Cavalry	
Sir Thomas Fairfax's Lifeguard Troop	Army of the Earl of Essex
Sir Thomas Fairfax's Regiment	Army of the Eastern Association
Edward Whalley's Regiment	Army of the Eastern Association
Charles Fleetwood's Regiment	Army of the Eastern Association
Nathaniel Rich's Regiment	Army of the Eastern Association
Bartholomew Vermuyden's Regiment	Army of the Eastern Association
Richard Graves' Regiment	Army of the Earl of Essex
Sir Robert Pye's Regiment	Army of the Earl of Essex
Thomas Sheffield's Regiment	Army of the Earl of Essex
John Butler's Regiment	Army of Sir William Waller
Henry Ireton's Regiment	Provincial regiment (Kent)
Edward Rossiter's Regiment	Provincial regiment (Lincolnshire)
Dragoons	
John Okey's Regiment	Mixed
Infantry	
Sir Thomas Fairfax's Regiment	Army of the Eastern Association and the Earl of Essex's army
Robert Hammond's Regiment	Army of the Eastern Association
Edward Montagu's Regiment	Army of the Eastern Association
John Pickering's Regiment	Army of the Eastern Association
Thomas Rainsborough's Regiment	Army of the Eastern Association
Philip Skippon's Regiment	Army of the Earl of Essex
Richard Fortescue's Regiment	Army of the Earl of Essex
Edward Harley	Army of the Earl of Essex
Richard Ingoldsby's Regiment	Army of the Earl of Essex
Walter Lloyd's Regiment	Army of the Earl of Essex
Hardress Waller's Regiment	Army of Sir William Waller
Anthony Weldon's Regiment	Provincial (Kent)

The choice of a new commander was extensively debated as there was an obvious necessity to appoint a competent general, as well as one who would be able to draw together soldiers from the existing armies into one new united force. Sir Thomas Fairfax was certainly a good choice as army commander, the lord general. He had a good reputation as a cavalry commander in the Army of the Northern Association and as an officer who had proved himself capable of co-operating with other Parliamentary armies, and, as he had not served in any of them, he was not involved in the bitter disputes in the existing three southern Parliamentary armies. The appointment of Philip Skippon as sergeant major general was another sensible decision, as the officer who held this post had to be highly technically competent. Skippon was respected as an experienced and non-political veteran officer and, as he had held the same post in the Earl of Essex's army, the choice would have been popular amongst Essex's soldiers. The post of lieutenant general of the horse was left vacant for the time being. The appointment of the remaining officers was debated at length. After the final list was agreed, MPs were given forty days' grace before they were to give up their commissions. After this much trouble in the passage of the list, not all the officers named chose to serve. A number of Scottish professionals had served in the southern Parliamentary armies, but few had been included in the list of officers, and four named as colonels – Lieutenant General John Middleton, Sergeant Major General James Holborne, Sergeant Major General Lawrence Crawford and Colonel Harry Barclay – declined to take up commissions in the New Model Army. Oliver Cromwell remained active in the field during the period of grace provided by the Self-Denying Ordinance, and his commission was extended for a further forty days.

The catalyst for Oliver Cromwell's appointment as lieutenant general of the horse in the New Model Army was the Royalist storm and sack of the city of Leicester on 31 May 1645. The fears this raised in London, together with the likelihood that a major, and potentially decisive, battle was now imminent led the Parliament to give up its attempts to run the war from London and give broader authority to its field commander, Sir Thomas Fairfax. The same pressures finally made the Parliament accede to Fairfax's request, supported by the senior officers who made up his army's council of war, that Oliver Cromwell should be appointed to the vacant post of lieutenant general of the horse, 'there being like to be very speedily an engagement'.[5] After debating the proposal on 10 June, the House of Commons agreed to the appointment without seeking approval from the House of Lords.

On 11 June, Sir Thomas Fairfax wrote to Oliver Cromwell instructing him to join the New Model Army with whatever soldiers he could bring. On 13 June 'about six of the clock in the morning' Fairfax called a council of war 'to consider what attempt to make upon the Enemy. In the middest of the debate, came in Lieutenant General Cromwel, out of the [Eastern] Association, with 600 Horse and Dragoons, who was with the greatest joy received by the General and the whole army.'[6] The last of the three generals of the New Model Army had now been appointed and only just in time, as the decisive battle of Naseby was fought on the following day. As he had kept the post vacant for so long, even after he had commenced his campaign, Fairfax must always have intended to have Cromwell as his cavalry commander, and the most likely explanation is that he simply bided his time until circumstances made it possible to force the appointment. Fairfax had, in any case, been using Cromwell as a subordinate commander in charge of New Model regiments since April.

The original ordinance for the New Model Army had been set a strength of ten regiments of cavalry, twelve regiments of infantry and a regiment of dragoons. An eleventh cavalry regiment had been added when the final ordinance was passed on 11 February 1645. The three armies, the Earl of Essex's, the Army of the Eastern Association and Sir William Waller's, which were to provide the soldiers for the new army, had more than enough officers and enough cavalry troopers but only about half the infantrymen. The Earl of Essex's army could provide only 3,048 infantrymen, the Army of the Eastern Association 3,578 and Sir William Waller's only about 600, to give a total of about 7,226. The remaining infantry required to fill the ranks were raised through new levies.

The Campaign of 1645

Debates over the appointment of its officers and generals had delayed the formation of the New Model Army, leaving the initiative with the Royalists. However, the latter failed to make the best of their opportunity, perhaps disrupted by the actions of Oliver Cromwell, who led a small force of 1,500 cavalry and dragoons in a series of raids on outlying Royalist detachments. In May, Fairfax, acting on instructions from the Parliamentary Committee of Both Kingdoms,[7] divided his army, leaving part with Cromwell to besiege Oxford, and marched the main body into the west to relieve the siege of Taunton. The Committee, which had heard that the Royalist army had now taken the field, then countermanded its original instructions and ordered Fairfax to send a detachment to the relief of Taunton and return to the siege of Oxford with his main army. With the New Model Army divided, the Royalist commanders debated their options at a council of war on 8 May, with Prince Rupert favouring a march north to relieve Pontefract and restore some Royalist presence in the north of England, which had been 'the whole Design of this Winter past'. Others, principally George Digby and George Goring, considered that 'if the King's Army' marched to the west, 'it would either keep Fairfax from relieving Taunton, or fight him before those of his Party in the West and Cromwel were joined, and then in all probability would gain the Victory, and so make the King Master of all.'[8]

The decision taken, which some later Royalist writers put down to friction between Prince Rupert and George Goring, was to divide the Royalist army, with Goring leading some 3,000 cavalry to the west while the main army under Prince Rupert marched north to relieve Chester. The Royalists' logic was that if they re-enforced their remaining Western army with a strong body of cavalry, then it would be strong enough to keep Fairfax and his new army occupied while Prince Rupert reversed the effects of the battle of Marston Moor. This was not entirely unreasonable, as the Army of the Eastern Association, one of the three armies that had defeated the Royalists at Marston Moor, had now been incorporated in the New Model Army in the south. This significantly weakened the fighting ability of the Scottish and Parliamentary armies in the north of England, particularly in the Royalists' strongest arm, cavalry. Certainly, the main concern of the Committee of Both Kingdoms was centred on the fear of a new Royalist campaign in the north. This said, a better Royalist strategy would have been that suggested by Digby and Goring, to use their army in one body to fight Fairfax while his army, although it included veteran soldiers, was still newly formed and divided into two parts.

The Royalist march north was interrupted as they received news that Parliamentary forces had raised the siege of Chester but that Fairfax had 'sent a Party [i.e. a detachment] to relieve Taunton, and that himself with his Army was sate down before Oxford'. From the perspective of the Royalists this:

HISTORICAL DISCOURSES,

UPON

Several Occafions:

V I Z.

I. The happy Progrefs and Succefs of the Arms of K. *Charles* I. of ever bleffed Memory, from the 30ᵗʰ of *March*, to the 23ᵈ of *November*, 1644. Written by His MAJESTY's efpecial Command, and corrected, almoft in every Page, with His own Hand.

II. Memorials of His faid MAJESTY's unfortunate Succefs in the Year following.

III. A Journal of feveral Actions performed in the Kingdom of *Scotland*, after King *Charles* the Second's Arrival there in 1650.

IV. The Life and Actions of *Thomas Howard*, Earl of *Arundel* and *Surrey*, Earl-Marfhal of *England*.

V. A full Anfwer to a Book entituled, *Monarchy, or no Monarchy*; being a confufed Mixture of falfe, traiterous and contradictory Obfervations concerning King *Charles* I. Publifh'd by *William Lilly* in *July* 1651.

VI. Obfervations upon the Inconveniencies that have attended the frequent Promotions to Titles of Honour and Dignity, fince King *James* I. came to the Crown of *England*.

VII. Obfervations on the Annals of the Reign of King *Charles* the Firft, Publifh'd by *Hamond L'Eftrange*, Efq;

VIII. A fhort Review of the Life and Actions of King *Charles* I.

By Sir *E D W A R D   W A L K E R*, Knight, Garter, Principal King of Arms, Secretary of War to His MAJESTY King *Charles* I. and Clerk of the Council to King *Charles* II.

Together with

Perfect COPIES of all the VOTES, LETTERS, PROPOSALS, and ANSWERS relating unto, and that paffed in, the Treaty held at *Newport*, in the *Ifle of Wight*, in the Months of *September*, *October*, and *November*, 1648. Between His Majefty King CHARLES the Firft, and a Committee of the Lords and Commons of Parliament.

Entred by His MAJESTY's *efpecial Command.*

By the fame Sir EDWARD WALKER, who was the Chief Clerk employed by His MAJESTY during that Treaty.

L O N D O N :

Printed by *W. B.* for **Sam. Keble**, at the *Turk's Head* in *Fleetstreet*.   1705.

Frontispiece of Sir Edward Walker's Historical Discourses. Walker was secretary of war to Charles I, and his first-hand account is another valuable Royalist source.

staggered our Design, yet not so as instantly to return thither, or solely to abandon it; but only so retarded it, as to put the Army in a Capacity to come to the timely Relief of that place [Oxford] if there should be occasion; and also to act somewhat to divert Fairfax's Designs, by attempting the taking of Leicester, which was set on Foot as feasible.[9]

Leicester was stormed and sacked on 31 May.

Fairfax had already shown himself to be a field commander who believed, as did his second in command, Cromwell, in the Swedish strategic doctrine of seeking victory through decisive battle. The Royalist commander, Prince Rupert, followed the same model. As the two armies manoeuvred, Fairfax's scouts seem to have served him better, and his army was closer to the Royalist army by 13 June, when Cromwell joined him, than the Royalists had expected. On the evening of 13 June the Royalist council of war met at Market Harborough to consider their options, 'seeing the Enemy was so near, and (as 'twas plain) intended to Engage them'. The King's secretary of war, Sir Edward Walker,

The Illustrious & High-borne Prince Rupert, Count Palatine of y.e Rhine & Knight of the most noble Order of the Garter, & Generall of the Horse, to his Ma.tie King Charles. Æ 1643.

Prince Rupert (1619–1682). The third son of the Elector Palatine and King Charles's sister Elizabeth. He had served briefly with the Dutch army and in one of the campaigns of the Thirty Years War before joining his uncle as commander of the Royalist cavalry. Highly competent technically, he devised a battle plan for Edgehill that may have been more complex than his newly trained soldiers could manage. He was strongly influenced by the Swedish style of warfare which saw battle as the key to a successful campaign.

recorded in his 'Brief Memorials' that 'resolutions were taken to fight; and rather to march back and seek him [Fairfax] out, than to be fought or pursued, contrary (as 'tis said) to Prince Rupert's opinion'.[10] With an opposing army this close and willing to fight, it would now have been extremely difficult for the Royalist army to retreat successfully, and the Royalist council of war understood all too well that if they 'march on to Leicester, if the Rear were Engaged, the whole Army might be put in Hazard, and therefore there was no safety in marching with the Van unless they could bring the Rear clear off, which they foresaw would be very difficult to do'.[11] The professional soldier and military writer Sir James Turner made much the same general point on retreats with the comment that

if it [military information] be bad or uncertain, or that his Scouts and Parties disappoint him, nothing is more difficult; and in this place I refer you to my Discourse on Intelligence; when an Enemy is near, orders are given and obeyed with so great haste and confusion, that the March looks rather like a flight than a retreat and this hath ruined many Armies, and loaded their Generals with dishonour and disgrace.[12]

John Rushworth, Fairfax's secretary on this campaign, wrote in his extensive *Historical Collections* that the Royalists

resolv'd to put it to a Battel, taking themselves to be more strong in Horse, than Fairfax; to be better furnish'd with old Experience'd Commanders, and having no reason not to relye upon their Infantry; for indeed they were generally valiant stout men. And further they resolved, since Fairfax had been so forward in pressing upon him, they would not remain in that place where they were, expecting him, but forthwith advance to find him out and offer him an Engagement.[13]

Both sides drew out their armies formally 'in battalia', that is to say in their formal order of battle with their units deployed according to their general's plans. For the New Model Army, Philip Skippon had been 'desired to draw the Form of a Battel, and the Army was divided into several Brigades of Horse and Foot, in order to their being better disposed for an Engagement' on 11 June.[14] This plan would have been the basis of the infantry formation used at Naseby, as Fairfax's chaplain, Joshua Sprigge, recorded that 'the General, together with the Major-General [Skippon] put the severall Brigades of Foot into order', but Cromwell would certainly have made some changes to the plan for deploying the cavalry after his arrival on 13 June, as Sprigge also recorded that Fairfax 'committed the Ordering of the Horse to Lieutenant-General Cromwel'.[15] The Royalist army was deployed according to a plan set out by Prince Rupert and which represented the latest stage in the development of his ideas on tactical formations. He had used essentially the same formation for the army which he had drawn up to fight when he marched on Donnington Castle, some days after the second battle of Newbury, to recover the Royalist field artillery. On that occasion, the Parliament armies declined to fight, so this was his opportunity to see how well it would work. The deployment of the opposing armies is shown in the illustration overleaf.

Prince Rupert would have realized, if he had not done so previously, that he would be outnumbered, but he still chose the option of a fierce, fast-moving attack rather than taking up a defensive position. From his perspective, he evidently considered that the quality and experience of his officers and men, together with the technically advanced deployment of his army, would outweigh the numbers of his opponents – provided he made his advance with speed and elan and overwhelmed the New Model Army before those numbers could be made to count. This assumption is consistent with the view of contemporary professional officers that a smaller number of veteran soldiers could defeat a more numerous opposing army.

The Royalist attack was made with speed as they 'marched up in good order, a swift march, with a great deal of gallantry and resolution'.[16] The Royalist

THE ROYALIST AND PARLIAMENT ARMIES AT THE BATTLE OF NASEBY – 14ᵗʰ JUNE 1645.

· ROYALIST · ARMY ·

1 Prince Rupert's & Prince Maurice's Troops
2 Prince Rupert's Regiment
3 The Queen's & Prince Maurice's Regiments
4 The Earl of Northampton's Regiment
5 Sir William Vaughan's Regiment
SIR BERNARD ASTLEY'S TERSIA OF FOOT:
6 The Duke of York's Regiment
7 Colonel (Sir Edward) Hopton's Regiments
8 Colonel (Sir Richard) Page's Regiment
SIR HENRY BARD'S TERSIA OF FOOT:
9 Sir Henry Bard's & Colonel (Rhys) Thomas' Regiment
10 Sir John Owen's & Colonel (Radcliffe) Gerard's Regiments
SIR GEORGE LISLE'S TERSIA:
11 Sir George Lisle's & (Colonel William) St. George's Regiments
12 Shrewsbury Foot commanded by (Lieutenant Colonel (George) Smith
13,14,15   Three Divisions of Horse between the Foot commanded
    by Colonel (Sir Thomas) Howard.

LEFT WING OF HORSE COMMANDED BY SIR MARMADUKE LANGDALE,
BEING THE NORTHERN HORSE IN FIVE DIVISIONS & 200 MUSKETEERS
16,17,18 Three Divisions of Northern Horse
19 Colonel (Sir Horatio) Cary's Regiment
20 Northern Division of Horse
21,25 Two Divisions of Horse
22 His Majesty's Regiment of Foot
23 His Majesty's Life Guard of Horse with his own person
24 Prince Rupert's Regiment of Foot.

THE ARMY COMMANDED BY HIS HIGHNESS PRINCE RUPERT AS GENERAL
AND THAT DAY CHARGED IN THE RIGHT WING OF THE ARMY WITH PRINCE
MAURICE OF FIVE DIVISIONS OF HORSE AND 200 MUSKETEERS.

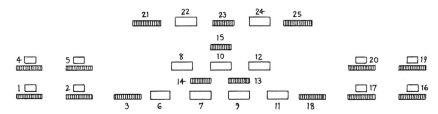

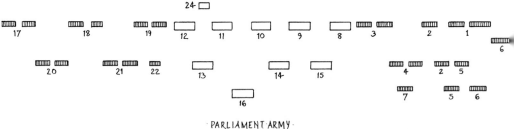

· PARLIAMENT · ARMY ·

1 General's Division of the Life Guards
2 Sir Robert Pye's Regiment
3 Colonel (Edward) Whalley's Regiment
4 Colonel (Thomas) Sheffield's Division
5 Colonel (John) Fienne's Regiment
6 Colonel (Edward) Rossiter's Regiment
7 The Associated Horse
8 The General's Regiment of Foot
9 Colonel (Edward) Montagu's Regiment
10 Colonel (John) Pickering's Regiment
11 Sir Hardress Waller's Regiment
12 Major General (Philip) Skippon's Regiment

13 Lieutenant Colonel Pride's Regiment
14 Colonel (Robert) Hammond's Regiment
15 Colonel (Thomas) Rainsborough's Regiment
16 (Lieutenant) Colonel Pride's Reserve
17 Colonel (John) Butler's Regiment
18 Colonel (Cornelius) Vermuyden's Regiment
19 Commissary General (Henry) Ireton's Regiment
20 Colonel (Nathaniel) Rich's Regiment
21 Colonel (Charles) Fleetwood's Regiment
22 The Troops of the Association
23 Train of Artillery guarded with firelocks
24 The Forlorn Hope of Commanded Musketeers

The Battle of Naseby. The battle formations of both sides.

right-wing cavalry led by Prince Rupert suffered casualties from the firing of the New Model dragoons from the hedges on their flank, but after a hard fight, they committed the reserves in their second line and defeated the New Model cavalry wing under Commissary General Henry Ireton. With both its first and second lines of cavalry involved in the fighting, and no formed reserve remaining, the Royalist cavalry then pursued the fleeing New Model cavalry off the field. In the infantry centre Joshua Sprigge recorded that 'the right hand of the Foot, being the General's Regiment stood, not being much pressed upon: Almost all the rest of the Main battail [the first line of New Model infantry] being overpressed, gave ground and went off in some disorder and fell in behind the Reserves [i.e. behind the second line of New Model infantry].' The New Model infantry in the second line, 'advancing, commanded by Col Rainsborough, Col Hammond and Lieut.col Pride, repelled the Enemy, forcing them into a disorderly retreat'.[17]

The retreating Royalist infantry were those of the Royalist first line, of three, and this was the opportunity for the Royalist second-line infantry to make a counter-attack. But this was lost because of the success of the cavalry under Oliver Cromwell on the right wing of the New Model Army. The Royalist cavalry were 'out front'd and overpour'd by their assailants, after they were close joyn'd, they stood a pretty while, and neither seemed to yield, till more came up to their flanks and put ym to rout'.[18] The New Model cavalry then rallied, and, as the Royalist Sir Edward Walker wrote, 'Four of the Rebels Bodies close and in good Order followed them [the Royalist cavalry], the rest charged our Foot',[19] taking the Royalist infantry in the flank. This flank attack prevented the Royalist infantry from exploiting the advantage that their three successive infantry lines would otherwise have had over the New Model infantry, and the small squadrons of cavalry deployed in close support of the infantry were not strong enough to stand against the larger cavalry formations Cromwell was able to bring against them.

The last defence of a defeated army was a final reserve which could be used as the last push towards victory or to cover an army's defeat. Prince Rupert's deployment included a third line of infantry and cavalry, including the King's 'Life Guarde of Horse', as his final reserve. Sir Edmund Walker recorded that

> the King's Horse Guards and the King at the Head of them were ready to charge those who followed ours, when a person of Quality, 'tis said the Earl of Cornwath, took the King's Horse by the Bridle, turned him about, swearing at Him and saying Will you go upon your Death? And at the same time the Word [was] given, March to the right Hand.

The reserve cavalry took this as 'a civil Command for everyone to shift for himself'[20] and fled. This was a problem often seen with reserve cavalry who were liable, if the day looked to be going badly, to turn any kind of motion into a rout. The remainder of the Royalist third line, the infantry, did its duty as best it could and managed a fighting retreat for about a mile before it was finally overwhelmed.[21] Prince Rupert, having rallied some of his troopers, attempted

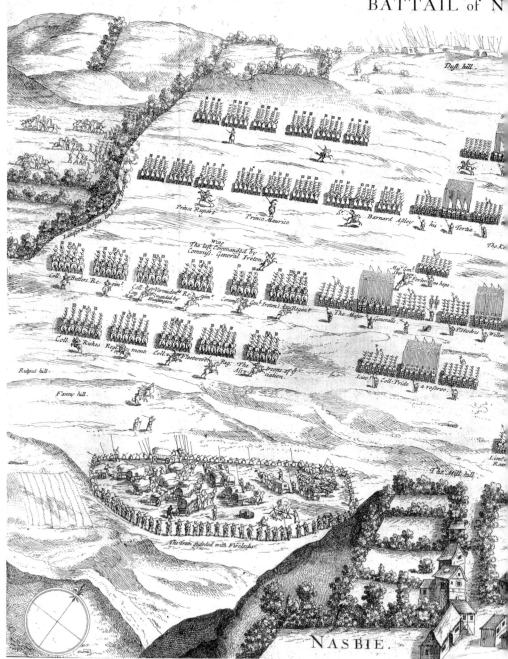

Engraving of the battle of Naseby. This is the copy of Robert Streeter's original plan that was printed with John Rushworth's Historical Collections in 1701. Rushworth recorded that the details of the Royalist battle plan had been found among the papers of Jacob, Lord Astley, when he was captured

Sᴿ THOMAS FAIREFAX: as they were drawn into several Bodies at the
e the 14ᵗʰ 1645·

*after the Royalist defeat at Stow-on-the-Wold in 1646 (p. 162 above). A more complete version of the
Royalist battle plan by Sir Bernard de Gomme is shown on p. 208.*

to capture the New Model artillery and baggage train as he rode back towards the battlefield, but it was 'well defended with the Fire-locks and a Rear-guard left for the purpose', and as he was now aware of Cromwell's success on the other flank he abandoned the attempt and rode on to join the King. The Royalist infantry, trapped with their final reserve broken and no cavalry support, surrendered and the Royalist artillery with their artillery and baggage trains (including the King's correspondence) were captured.

Fairfax and the New Model Army had taken the field with the objective of bringing the King's 'Oxford Army' to battle and defeating it, but they could not have expected to win so complete a victory as they did at Naseby. The King and his surviving cavalry retreated to Hereford to link up with Sir Charles Gerard, who had about '2,000 Horse and Foot', and to discuss what options remained. One option discussed was to draw out '3,000 Foot out of all his garrisons on those parts' and then 'fall on Fairfax's quarters' with these and the cavalry which had survived Naseby. This was a hopelessly optimistic plan which the King's secretary of war, Sir Edward Walker, described as 'a very plausible design in Paper', but one which he thought would have taken 'a longer time than we fancied to ourselves before we could have made all ends to meet'.[22] An alternative plan was the hope that negotiations with the Irish Confederation might lead to the dispatch of Catholic Irish soldiers to join with George Goring's Royalist army in the west to create a field army powerful enough to oppose the New Model Army. This option required Royalist control of the ports through where the Irish could land, principally Bristol or, for a new northern army, Chester.

While the King and council of war debated their options, Fairfax and his army moved west with the objective of defeating George Goring's army and taking the key Royalist base at Bristol. On 10 July 1645 George Goring's army was decisively defeated by the New Model Army at the battle of Langport. The solid control maintained over the New Model cavalry can be seen in Joshua Sprigge's account of the battle:

> The Forlorne under Major Bethell, and those under Major Desborough, were going in pursuit of the chase, but receiving orders to stay till more bodies of horse were come up, that the pursuit might be orderly, and with good reserves in case the enemy should face about, and charge again (which was not impossible) they obeyed their orders as good souldiers will, though it check their sweetest pleasure (as to pursue a flying enemy was no less).[23]

Prince Rupert, governor of the Royalist garrison at Bristol, lived up to his reputation as an active commander by making a series of sorties in strength, but his garrison was cut off, blockaded at sea by a naval squadron and by the New Model Army on land, and he did not have enough men to defend the extensive line of fortifications. Once the New Model soldiers broke through the outer fortifications, Prince Rupert called for a 'parley' or ceasefire to discuss terms of surrender and, having little choice, surrendered the city of Bristol with its magazine.

As the defeat of Goring's army and the loss of Bristol restricted the Royalists' options still further, King Charles and his advisers were encouraged by the victories of the Earl of Montrose in Scotland and determined to march north to link up with him, believing that Montrose was now 'Master of Scotland'. Blocked from their route north through Worcester by the Parliament Major General Sydenham Poyntz and forces drawn from the Army of the Northern Association, the Royalists took the decision to march through north Wales and take the opportunity to relieve the Royalist garrison besieged at Chester. The Royalists successfully relieved the siege but were then defeated at the battle of Rowton Heath on 24 September 1645 by a combination of the Army of the Northern Association under Sydenham Poyntz and the besieging Parliamentary forces under Colonel Michael Jones. The Earl of Montrose's string of victories in Scotland had already ended on 13 September at the battle of Philiphaugh.

The Royalist cause was now irrevocably lost; the last remnants of the Royalist army in the west, now commanded by Ralph, Lord Hopton, were defeated at the battle of Torrington on 16 February 1646, and the last Royalist army in the field was defeated at Stow-on-the-Wold on 21 February. King Charles left Oxford on 27 April and surrendered to the Scottish army at Southwell, near Newark, on 5 May 1646. The last Royalist garrisons surrendered: Newark on 6 May, Oxford on 24 June, Pendennis Castle on 16 August and the last, Harlech Castle, on 16 March 1647. By the time of this last surrender, relations between factions in the Parliament and between Parliament itself and the New Model Army had deteriorated, and in April 1647 the Army's mutiny began.

Chapter Eleven

Mutiny

Introduction

The New Model Army is famous today for the mutiny which ultimately brought the army and its leaders to power in England, but mutiny was not an unusual military activity in itself – it was as much a part of military life in the late sixteenth and early seventeenth centuries as training in the use of arms and unit tactics or plundering. The distinction in the eyes of New Model Army soldiers – expressed by their representatives during the army debates after the mutiny – was that they were not 'meere mercinarie souldiers'. Many of the New Model soldiers were levies not volunteers, and there were always those who served principally for pay. But as in any civil war, there were volunteers, in this case particularly amongst the officers and the cavalry, who had joined the army because they believed in the cause they were fighting for and expected to see that their victory would deliver a better world, a better England. The mixture of politics and religion associated with the mutiny is partly the expression of different factions – which included several of deep, if varied, religious conviction – and partly because political concepts were often expressed and debated through reference to Biblical examples. The Bible was the one common reference that all these men shared.

Mutiny

The main reasons for army mutinies were pay and conditions. The most influential example before the sixteenth century was the attitude of Swiss mercenaries of the fifteenth and early sixteenth centuries who took the essentially reasonable perspective that if they were going to risk their lives for pay, then they expected to receive it. Swiss mercenaries served under their own officers and were subject to their own discipline and, if not paid, would refuse to fight. The seventeenth-century playwright Jean Racine immortalized this attitude with the phrase 'Point d'argent, point de Suisse' ('no money, no Swiss'), and the Scottish soldier Sir James Turner said much the same when he wrote *c.*1670, 'It is said of the Switzers, that they will not fight, unless they be paid duly.'[1] This level of disobedience was exceptional and was possible because of the amount of independence that the Swiss enjoyed and the solidarity amongst all, both officers and soldiers, within their companies. However, the Swiss were mercenaries serving another country, usually France, not subjects of the ruler in whose army they fought.

The next significant stage was the mutinies of the Spanish Army of Flanders in the late sixteenth century which brought an entirely new perspective to army mutiny. As Sir James Turner commented,

> the effects of the bad payment of the Spaniards appeared, when their King stood most in need of their Service seventy years and a little upwards; and many times since; for that gave a rise to those terrible Mutinies, in which they possess'd themselves of Towns, and treated with their Generals and Superiours, as if they had been Free Estates. This incapacitated the Spanish Ministers to prosecute the War against the new Estates [Holland].[2]

Turner's succinct description, and he was a mercenary soldier himself, is an indication of the impression that the success of the Spanish mutinies made on all European soldiers of the time. The soldiers' grievances were reasonable and often extensive, covering lack of pay, food, clothing, shelter or mistreatment by their officers, but of all of these pay was the catalyst, as other commodities could be bought by a soldier with ready money for himself and his dependants.

The Spanish mutinies were successful because of the high degree of organization that the mutineers practised. Once a mutiny began, the local commander had a brief opportunity to restore order if he and his officers could use persuasion and the backing of loyal soldiers to isolate the ringleaders. However, in most cases, by the time mutiny broke out it was too late for this option to be successful. As soldiers, the mutineers were accustomed to acting together as an organized body and the usual practice of the Spanish mutineers was to expel all officers and soldiers who would not join the mutiny, choose an 'electo' as leader with a small council to work with him and find a defensible base. If a garrison mutinied then it already had a strong point, but mutineers in the field would have to seize one, often by persuading the garrison to join the mutiny. Once they were secure, the mutineers would negotiate with representatives of their general or their government over their demands for their arrears of pay, a full pardon for the mutiny itself and passes (permission to travel) for those, usually the ringleaders and their closest associates, who felt they would now need to leave the army and the country. This was also an opportunity to ask for resolution of specific grievances such as the provision of a hospital for their wounded. In the midst of its war in the Low Countries, the Spanish government desperately needed these soldiers and ultimately settled with them, typically agreeing an assessment of their outstanding pay and actually paying half of it with the balance being considered to have been made up by the plunder and provisions obtained during the mutiny. The Spanish Army of Flanders was by no means the only army to mutiny – and the campaigns of other armies fighting during the Thirty Years War in Germany could also be disrupted or stalled by mutinous soldiers – but it did provide the most influential and the most organized example.[3]

Brief mutinies were common during the First Civil War, sometimes over an unpopular officer such the MP John Venn, whose garrison at Windsor mutinied against him, but usually because of arrears of pay. The mutiny of the garrison at Henley-on-Thames in February 1645 provides an example of the catalyst for mutiny provided by arrears of pay and an indication of broader problems to come. The garrison commander, Lieutenant Colonel Gryme, recorded that 'All that I can do is little enough to appease and prevent combustion especially seeing that their pay is so little and private incendiaries many'. His overall assessment was prophetic as he saw that the potential for mutiny over pay had increased because of 'private incendiaries' stirring up trouble, and he went on to seek from his colonel the authority to manage the garrison through a council of war of his officers, as

> our distractions, by means of this mutiny, necessitate the taking of some exemplary course to prevent the like again, which how to do without a power to call a Council of War I know not. I desire your advice, whether any such power in your absence may be transferred upon us, and then we will take the best course we can, both to regain our authority and prevent the soldiers from drawing this their [ill] behaviour into a precedent for the future.[4]

The mutiny of the New Model Army arose initially over pay, the one unifying factor for all soldiers, and the demand for indemnities covering acts such as horse theft committed during the Civil War. Once begun, the existence of a mutinous army – and a victorious mutinous army that had just crushed all opposition to it – offered political opportunities to those who could take advantage of them. The First Civil War had ended in 1646 as the last Royalist field armies surrendered on terms or were defeated in battle and King Charles I surrendered to the Scots. The Scots exchanged the King in January 1647 in return for payment of their army's arrears – £100,000 paid on 30 January 1647 with a further £100,000 to follow in February – and handed him over to the Parliament on 30 January. By 11 February 1647 the last soldiers of the Scottish army in England had returned to Scotland. This seems remarkably callous at first sight, but the Scots were under pressure to withdraw their army from its quarters and garrisons in northern England, and their leaders were experiencing the difficulties common with all negotiations with Charles I. Unable to reach a political agreement with the King and unwilling to bring him back to Scotland where his presence would provide a focus for, at least, discontent and possibly rebellion, they made the best deal they could with the Parliament and left him in England.

This left the Parliament, then dominated by a Presbyterian faction of MPs, with two military problems to resolve. Firstly, the war in Ireland and, secondly, their suspicions that the New Model Army was dominated by officers of the 'Independent' faction. In fact, the army had officers with a wide range of political or religious sympathies, but of its three senior officers, Sir Thomas Fairfax, Oliver Cromwell and Philip Skippon, two were not political but the third, Oliver Cromwell, most certainly was, and he was a leading 'Independent'. The Parliament's solution was to form a new army of 3,000 cavalry, 1,200 dragoons and 8,400 infantry for service in Ireland from New Model regiments, retain some soldiers in garrisons and as a small field army in England under Presbyterian officers and disband the rest.[5] In itself, this was not an unreasonable plan, but it fell apart because the Presbyterian faction which pressed for it tried to do it cheaply by disbanding soldiers with only a portion of their arrears and promises of payment of the remainder in due course – which would effectively mean never. This was not an unusual course of action by the standards of the day, and Sir James Turner commented in his book *Pallas Armata* on the European practice of giving 'Officers a little satisfaction money (for so it was called) in lieu of their Arrears, when they disbanded them.'[6] But it was an unpopular practice with the soldiers for obvious reasons, and in this case it was combined with the soldiers' fear that they would not be indemnified by the Parliament for actions taken during the Civil War. A particular concern was horse theft: in an army which always needed replacement horses for its artillery and baggage trains as well as its cavalry, and often took them where it found them, this was a common crime, but also a hanging matter.

In this situation the Parliament still had the option of handling the soldiers' concerns with some tactful consideration. But its response to the series of petitions which first circulated amongst the soldiers, and were then summarized at a meeting of officers 'in the forme of a petition' to its commander Sir Thomas Fairfax, was to outlaw them and, on 30 March 1647, to threaten that anyone involved with them in future would be 'looked upon and proceeded against as enemies to the state and disturbers of the public peace'. The Presbyterian faction in Parliament felt able to make this confident move because it believed that it would be able to divide the army by offering pay to those who enlisted for service in Ireland and could, if necessary, oppose the New Model Army by a coalition of the other regiments still under arms in England, the London Militia and the army of its Scottish Presbyterian allies. However, this approach backfired spectacularly as it caused deep suspicion in the army, while simultaneously causing outrage by offending the soldiers' sense of professional pride with the accusation that men in an army which had fought so hard and experienced such hardship in the process were now being described by the Parliament they had fought for as 'enemies of the state'.

The mutiny began in April 1647 with an association of eight cavalry regiments. Each regiment elected two representatives and submitted requests for support to their commanders, Sir Thomas Fairfax, Oliver Cromwell and Philip Skippon. The infantry regiments followed their example in May. Having failed to divide the army between those retained for service in Ireland and those disbanded, the Presbyterian faction in Parliament next turned to the tactic of dividing officers from men by paying a more generous portion of their arrears

4. THE
DECLARATION
OF THE
ARMIE

U N D E R

His Excellency Sir THOMAS FAIRFAX,

As it was
Lately prefented at Saffron- Walden in Eſſex,unto

Major-Generall *Skippon*,   ⎞ ⎛Commiſſary-General *Ireton*,
Lievtenant-General *Cromwell*,⎟ ⎨And Colonell *Fleetwood*,

Members of the Houſe of Commons, and Commiſſioners there
for the Parliament , by
Colonell *Whaley*,   ⎞ ⎛ Colonell *Okey*,
Colonell *Rich*,   ⎟ ⎨ Colonell *Hewſon*,
Colonell *Hammond*,   ⎟ ⎬   And
Colonell *Lambert*,   ⎠ ⎝ Major *Diſborow*,
With the names of two hundred thirty and more
Commiſſion-Officers annexed.

Which Declaration is to manifeſt and ſet forth to them , they
being Members of Parliament, and of the Army, the Armies reall love
and diligent care to diſcharge that duty for which they were raiſed,
as will manifeſtly appeare in time to all that wiſh well
to Mercy, Peace, and Juſtice.

_____

The time is coming when God will execute juſtice and judgment on the earth.
_____

Printed by the appointment of the Officers, whoſe names are
hereunto ſubſcribed.   1 6 4 6.

The Declaration of the Armie. A summary of the early stages of the army's demands. Although the pamphlet has the date 1646, it was actually printed in May 1647.

to those soldiers who would disband. But by this time the army was suspicious of any approaches by the Parliament, and the soldiers' agents (now referred to as Agitators) were now, if they had not been previously, in contact with the radical political groups which drew their support, as one of their leaders wrote, from 'the middle sort of people' or 'the laborious and industrious people of England'.[7]

The leading group, and the one most influential amongst the soldiers, was the 'Levellers', a derisory nickname coined by opponents who claimed that the Levellers intended to level estates and create some form of equality. The association of soldiers' agents and radical civilians added another level of complexity to the power struggles between Presbyterians and Independents for control of the Parliament and of the government of the City of London. Leveller involvement with the soldiers' agents provided a challenge to the authority of the army's officers over their men. Different factions amongst the Levellers held differing views, but their leaders were articulate and they provided a source of direct information, with somewhat slanted commentary, on Parliamentary debates in London. One letter from London following news of a vote in Parliament on 18 May on disbanding the army read 'Believe itt, my deare fellows, wee must now be very active to send to all our several regiments of Horse and Foote and [let them] knowe that nothing but destruction is threatned,' and concluded with the comment 'Loving friends, be active, for all lies at the stake.'[8]

There was a strong sense that only unanimity would gain the soldiers their arrears and the security from prosecution which lay at the heart of their concerns. A circular letter from the regimental agents 'to the severall regiments' of 19 May read, 'Fellow Souldiers, the summe of all is this, if you doe but stand, and not accept of any thing, nor doe anything without the concent of the whole Army, you will doe good to your selves, your Officers, and the whole kingdome. Stand with your Officers, and one with another you need not feare. If you divide you destroy all.'[9] At about this time, the Agitators of the New Model cavalry regiments also sent representatives to the cavalry in the only other large English army still in service, the Parliamentary Army of the Northern Association. The Agitators' letter set out their actions to date, warned about the 'hard measure' they had received from Parliament, when 'wee [who] had not thought any thing too deare to part with for their sake, who have manifested ourselves not to be enemies but reall freinds and soe knowne to be in the dayes of their adversitie, and did little thinke that this should be our portion to be declared Enemies in the dayes of their prosperitie', and asked them to join forces with the compelling request 'Read and consider, and God direct you. Thinke wee are prosecuting just things in a just way, and if from such thoughts of us you have a desire to joyne with us, these Gentlemen that are the bearers hereof will direct you in the way of doing itt.'[10]

On 25 May the House of Commons formally ordered the disbandment of the army, with agreement from the Lords on the 27th. This was to be carried out by taking each regiment to a separate rendezvous and giving the soldiers the alternatives of service in Ireland or disbandment. As an additional precaution, the Parliament also ordered the removal of the army's artillery train from Oxford to London.[11] The train of artillery was not simply the army's artillery pieces but also consisted of all the operational equipment in terms of ammunition, replacement arms and the wide range of military tools and supplies that an army needed for an active campaign. These were bold but, given the degree of organization which the mutineers had demonstrated and the accuracy of the information they received from London, essentially stupid moves, as Henry Ireton wrote to Oliver Cromwell:

> I [do not] doubt the disobliging of so faithful an army will be repented of; provocation and exasperation makes men think of what they never intended. They [the soldiers] are possessed as far as I can discern with this opinion, that if they be thus scornfully dealt with for their faithful services whilst the sword is in their hands, what shall their usage be when they are dissolved?[12]

A council of war of Sir Thomas Fairfax and his officers on 29 May called for a general rendezvous of the army to be held near Newmarket on 4 June with a view to its officers being able to maintain better control over their men, a move which would also make it far harder to disband than if the army was scattered in individual regiments. The first indication that the Parliament's plan was unravelling was seen by its commissioners when they arrived at Chelmsford to supervise – as they thought – the disbanding of Sir Thomas Fairfax's own infantry regiment. The soldiers had refused to disband and were on the march to Newmarket. When their lieutenant colonel, Thomas Jackson, and other officers who were supporters of the Parliament caught up with Fairfax's soldiers at Braintree, they refused to listen and jeered 'There comes our enemies,' and when 'acquainted with the votes, declarations, and ordinances of Parlement, they asked the officers, what doe you bringing your two-penny pamphlets to us?'[13] The most significant comment here was that this regiment now regarded those of its own officers who sympathized with the Parliament as 'their enemies', and they and other regiments were now prepared to chase out those officers who would not stand with them.

At this point the initiative was taken by a group of 500 cavalry troopers drawn from several regiments under the command of Cornet George Joyce. On 1 June, Joyce and his troopers first took control of the artillery train in Oxford, where the soldiers in the city made common cause with him, and then marched on Holmby House to seize the King on 3 June. The garrison commander, Colonel Richard Graves, fled as he knew his men would not oppose the mutineers. Joyce claimed he had come 'with authority from the soldiers to seize Colonel Graves' as they feared a plot, and 'endeavouring to prevent a second war discovered by the design of some men privately to take away the King, to the end he might side with that intended army to be raised, which, if effected, would be to the utter undoing of the kingdom'.[14] On the evening of 3 June, Joyce expressed concern that a stronger opposing party might attempt to take control of the King and, under some pressure, Charles agreed to leave with Cornet Joyce and his troopers on the following morning. The next day King Charles once again questioned Joyce's authority, demanding 'what commission [i.e. as he was a junior officer what letter of authority and on whose authorization] have you to secure my person?' When pressed further by Charles, who asked 'I pray you, Mr. Joyce, deal ingenuously with me and tell me what commission you have,' Cornet Joyce pointed to the troopers drawn up behind him and replied 'Here is my commission.' In reply Charles said ruefully, 'It is as fair a commission and as well written as I have seen a commission written in my life: a company of handsome, proper gentlemen as I have seen in a great while.'[15]

It remains unclear whether Cornet Joyce was acting on the instructions of the soldiers' agents or of superior officers. A cornet was the third (of four) in seniority of the commissioned officers in a cavalry troop of 100 troopers and, in the current state of the army, only the soldiers' agents could draw together 500 cavalry troopers from several regiments and send them out under the command of so junior an officer. It is also probable, however, that the Independent faction of the officers was also involved, either directly or indirectly, as they would have seen the necessity of securing their artillery train and the advantages of replacing the guard over the King under the Presbyterian Colonel Graves with more politically reliable soldiers. The Presbyterian party in Parliament certainly claimed to see Oliver Cromwell's hand behind this, and they were probably correct to do so. Cornet Joyce brought the King under escort to Newmarket.

At the rendezvous at Newmarket, the officers and men of the New Model Army agreed to an arrangement published as the *Solemn Engagement of the Army*, a military echo of the Solemn League and Covenant between the Parliament and the Scots. This created a single governing body under the name of the 'General Council of the Army', which was to be 'a Council to consist of those general offices of the army (who have concurred with the army in the premises) with two commission officers and two soldiers to be chosen from each regiment, who have concurred and shall concur with us in the premises and in this agreement.'[16] The General Council was a unique arrangement. The

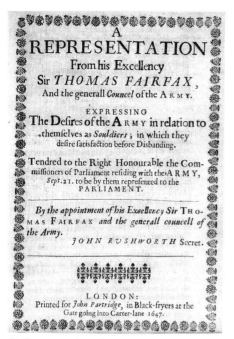

A Representation from His Excellency Sir Thomas Fairfax, and the Generall Councel of the Army. When this was drawn up, in September 1647, officers and soldiers were both represented at the General Council of the Amy.

concept of appointing soldiers' representatives to a governing council can be traced back to the well-known – and frequently successful – practice of the Spanish Army of Flanders, but a council which consisted of representatives of both officers and men with a view to negotiating with its former employers was a new departure. This was probably only possible because the Presbyterian-dominated Parliament appeared to be acting against the interest of both officers and men. It was common military practice to have a council of war composed of senior officers to discuss and advise their general, though the frequency with which this met tended to depend on the extent of the general's personal authority or the need he might feel for a show of unanimity. A council of war could also be held amongst the officers at regimental level, although here it tended to indicate some weakness or difficulty in relations between the colonel and his officers. Following the creation of the General Council of the Army, Sir Thomas Fairfax and his officers continued to meet as a council of war in the usual military sense, but all major policy decisions would now be made by the broader representation of the General Council of the Army.

Faced with outright and united mutiny, the Parliament sought to raise an army based in London from the disbanded soldiers of other Parliamentary armies, who had come to London to seek their arrears, and the London Militia. But this option fell apart as the New Model Army marched towards London, preceded by some very carefully expressed propaganda for circulation by its civilian supporters in London. This was masterfully phrased to show on the one hand that the New Model Army had no quarrel with – and represented no threat to –London and its citizens, and on the other that it was the army which had ended the stalemate of the Civil War, the army which had succeeded in ending the war on the battlefield when 'Noe other Army could doe the Business'.

The involvement of London sympathizers in the circulation of these papers made them believable to their fellow citizens, and one London correspondent reported back to the New Model Army:

upon the report of your being neere, all the Trayned Bands of London were commanded to rise on pain of death, and all the shopps to be shut up; and if this had taken, more pretty feates had been acted, the suspected party in London been secured, and they would have met your Army (after you had been declared enemies) and done strange things; but this design comes to nothing, for the trayned Bands would not budge, not 10 men of some companies appeared, and many companies none at all but the Officers; nay the very boyes in the streets jeered the drumms as they went about with their charge upon paine of death.[17]

Any hopes the Parliament may have had of the support of the only other large English army, the Army of the Northern Association, were ended when its soldiers elected their own agents as representatives, mutinied, seized their commander, Major General Sydenham Poyntz, and made common cause with the New Model Army. The soldiers' agents had been in contact with the Army of the Northern Association since May, and their commander, Poyntz, had lost control of his men by June, by which time his appeals to his officers and soldiers that the Parliament 'does value you much' were falling upon deaf, and probably incredulous in the circumstances, ears. Poyntz complained to Fairfax that agents' representatives from the New Model Army were active amongst his regiments, but Fairfax denied that it had been done by his orders, warning that 'if any such were come from his army and had endeavoured to satisfy any of the truths aforesaid, he and the forces under him would countenance and protect such good instruments'.[18]

On 8 July soldiers of the Army of the Northern Association seized Poyntz in his bed and sent him under escort to Sir Thomas Fairfax. The latter formally replied to appeals from the soldiers' agents of the Northern Association and gave them:

this assurance that I looke upon you as the same with the Army more immediately under my command, and shall in all things equally provide for you as God shall enable mee to provide for them, which I am the more engaged to doe because I cannot forget the former labours and hardshipps which you under my

Sydenham Poyntz. A professional soldier, he joined the Parliament in 1645 and was appointed commander of the Army of the Northern Association. He and his army were seen by the Parliament as a possible counter to the New Model Army, but his men mutinied in July 1647 and joined with the New Model Army.

Major Generall Poyntz

command have soe willingly undergone for the good and preservation of this Kingdome, and that upon as small and inconsiderable a satisfaction as any forces in this Kingdome.[19]

Fairfax, prior to his appointment to command the New Model Army, had been the popular and respected cavalry commander of the Army of the Northern Association. There had been some suspicion that Poyntz would act under Parliament orders to unite the Army of the Northern Association with the Scots against the New Model Army, but this was no longer an option.

With no remaining military opposition, the army leaders could afford the option of using their influence on Parliament without the necessity of taking the City by force. In the event mounting disorder in the City led to sympathetic MPs fleeing to the support of the army and, under the cover of returning them to Westminster, the Army entered London on 6 August, receiving a formal welcome from the lord mayor and aldermen. Just to make their position perfectly clear, the New Model Army then held a formal parade on 7 August with some 18,000 men marching through the City in good order. The Militia of London and its suburbs probably also consisted of at least 18,000 men if they all mustered, but the rank and file members of the Militia did not see the New Model Army as a threat to themselves, their families or their businesses unless they were provoked, and had no intention of provoking them. Simple military power left the New Model Army and its supporters as the most influential, but not the only, faction in Parliament and the City of London, and left open the question of what it would do next. As the army was still governed by the General Council of the Army, this meant proposals for the future had to be acceptable to both officer and soldier delegates. The army leaders had the option of dealing with a Parliament which was now more sympathetic to them, or the King who was in their custody, but they also had to consider the more radical political aspirations of the soldiers and the soldiers' civilian allies in the Leveller movement.

The New Model Army's proposals for the future had been set out in the 'Heads of Proposal of the Army' in July 1647, which was probably the work of Commissary General Henry Ireton, reviewed and revised by the General Council of the Army. These would have limited the powers of both Parliament and King, and neither would agree to them. In October 1647 Leveller influence encouraged five cavalry regiments to elect new agents to represent them on the grounds that the existing agents had become too closely associated with the officers. A Leveller document, *The Case of the Army Truly Stated*, purportedly in the name of the agents of the five regiments but probably written mostly by the Leveller John Wildman, was presented to Sir Thomas Fairfax on 18 October. A series of meetings of the General Council of the Army, since called the 'Putney Debates', were called to take place in St Mary's Church in Putney from 20 October to 11 November 1647 to debate this and a second Leveller document, *The Agreement of the People*. The escape of King Charles I on 11 November from detention at Hampton Court brought the Putney Debates to an end, with Oliver Cromwell and Henry Ireton having spoken against the Leveller proposals.

Having failed to reach agreement on the documents that the Levellers had brought to the Putney Debates, Sir Thomas Fairfax and his officers proposed to obtain acceptance of their own proposals drawn up as a *Remonstrance*. This denounced the newly appointed regimental agents as 'a few men, members of the army, who (without any authority, or just call thereunto, that we know of, assuming the name of agents for several regiments) have (for what ends we know not) taken upon them to act as a divided party from the said Council [the General Council of the Army] and Army,' and said that the 'said Agents and their associates have laboured to make parties and factions in the Army, to raise mutinies and disorders therein, to divide the soldiers from the officers, and both officers and soldiers amongst themselves'. The document also set out Fairfax's proposals for the soldiers, including pay and provision for 'maimed soldiers, and the widows and orphans of men slain in the service', and the army's relationship with the Parliament. For their part the officers and soldiers of each regiment would be asked to formally sign a brief declaration that they would 'acquiesce in what shall be agreed unto by the General Council of the Army', and would 'be observant of, and subject to, his Excellency, his Council of War, and every one of us to our superior officers in this Regiment and the Army, according to the Discipline of War'.[20]

Fairfax formally called several separate rendezvous for the regiments rather than a single general rendezvous, probably on the grounds that this would make it easier to control the outcome. The first of these was to be held at Corkbush Field near Ware in Hertfordshire on 15 November. Seven regiments, four of cavalry and three of infantry, were called to the rendezvous but two others, Colonel Robert Lilburne's mutinous infantry regiment and Colonel Thomas Harrison's cavalry regiment, also turned up without orders. The Leveller sympathizers in the army had called for, and failed to achieve, a general rendezvous of all the regiments in the south of England, but they and civilian Levellers still hoped to use the first rendezvous at Ware to raise support for their manifesto *The Agreement of the People* amongst the soldiers. Recently printed editions of this manifesto, 'with the Motto on the outside in capital Letters, "Englands Freedoms, Soldiers Rights"', had been circulated, and soldiers in both Lilburne's and Harrison's regiments arrived at Corkbush Field wearing these in their hatbands. However, Fairfax acted quickly to seize those officers who had been distributing the pamphlets and, together with Oliver Cromwell, overawed the soldiers so that the men of Colonel Harrison's regiment 'when they understood their error, tore them out of their Hats'.[21] Eleven mutineers were brought before a court martial and sentenced to death. Fairfax then reduced the sentence, requiring three of the mutineers to cast lots for their lives, with the loser, Richard Arnold, being shot by firing squad. The remainder appear to have been sentenced to 'ride the wooden horse',[22] and were then cashiered from the army. The final outcome was that the officers and men of the regiments at each rendezvous signed the declaration that Fairfax had asked from them. The failure of the mutiny at Ware severely weakened the influence of the Levellers with the army, and several regiments recalled their agents from the General Council of the Army. Over the winter of 1647 the General Council became exclusively composed of officers.

This did not end Leveller pamphleteering, and Levellers remained particularly influential in the City of London. However, it certainly became more personally focused in attacking both Cromwell and Ireton, and after the publication of the pamphlet *The Second Part of Englands New Chains Discovered*, which was printed on 22 March 1649 – and which contained direct incitement to the soldiers to mutiny – the Leveller leaders John Lilburne, Henry Overton, William Walwyn and Thomas Prince were arrested. The level of support which remained was demonstrated following the execution of another mutineer, Robert Lockyer, in April 1648. Lockyer's funeral on Sunday 29 April was turned into a massive rally for Levellers, where thousands of citizens marched with 'six trumpets dolefully sounding the soldiers knell, as in their cases usual, (though this more extraordinary) the trooper's horse advanced in the reer of this regiment [group of people, not an army regiment], clothed all over in mourning and led by a footman (a funeral honour, equal to a chief commander).' Many of 'this great number that thus attended the corps, had sea-green, and black ribbons in their hats'.[23]

Although this showed that it had considerable civilian support in the City of London, the Leveller movement attempted but failed to motivate widespread mutiny in the army in 1649. There were two recorded outbreaks which must have been co-ordinated at some level. In the first, William Thompson, formerly a corporal in Whalley's regiment, raised two or three hundred men at Banbury in Oxfordshire, but they were quickly dispersed on 10 May by loyal cavalry under Colonel Sir John Reynolds. A more serious mutiny broke out amongst the cavalry chosen by lot in April 1649 for service in Cromwell's campaign in Ireland. The army leaders were determined to stop this mutiny before it could spread further, and a force of cavalry and dragoons under Sir Thomas Fairfax and Oliver Cromwell made a night attack on the mutineers' quarters at Burford at about midnight on 14 May. The mutineers were scattered and four ringleaders, Cornet James Thompson (the brother of William Thompson, who had led the uprising at Banbury), Cornet Henry Den, Corporal Perkins and Corporal John Church, were brought before a court martial and sentenced to death by firing squad. Thompson, Perkins and Church remained defiant to the end and were shot in Burford churchyard. Cornet Henry Den expressed remorse 'with much relenting and acknowledgement of the just hand of God, the justice of the sentence, and his submission thereunto,'[24] a change of heart which caused the Levellers to call him 'Judas Den' but which won him a reprieve.

The mutiny crushed at Burford effectively ended the Leveller attempt to regain its influence in the New Model Army, and brought the period of army mutinies to an end.

Chapter Twelve

The Campaigns of the New Model Army, 1648–1653

Introduction

This is necessarily a brief account of the series of campaigns through which the New Model Army had, by 1651, defeated the field armies of all of its opponents in England, Scotland and Ireland. On 27 April 1653 the last remaining garrison held against it, Clough Oughter Castle in Ireland, surrendered.

These campaigns showed the commanders of the New Model Army followed a highly aggressive approach to both strategy and tactics. Its officers consciously modelled their approach on their perception of Gustavus Adolphus's campaigns during the Thirty Years War in Germany, and their commanders saw victory on the battlefield as the key to successful campaigning. The New Model Army had the initial advantage that it had been formed around cadres of veteran officers and soldiers from armies which had served in the early years of the English Civil War, and its early successes made it confident enough in itself and its commanders for its morale to survive occasional setbacks in a campaign.

Its tactical approach was not limited to exploiting its battlefield ability, and the New Model Army also made use of both propaganda and English naval supremacy. In terms of propaganda both Sir Thomas Fairfax and Oliver Cromwell issued pamphlets stating they would offer fair treatment to those who were not in arms against them, brought their own soldiers before courts martial for offences against civilians and very publicly carried out sentences. This did not necessarily win over the civilian population, English Royalist, Scottish or Irish, where they campaigned, but it was a stark contrast to the behaviour of other armies on either side, and led to an acceptance that ordinary life could continue under occupation and it was not necessary to fight to the last. In terms of naval power, English supremacy made it possible to transport provisions and, particularly, heavy siege artillery and mortars by sea.

By 1648, when this series of campaigns commenced, this was already a tough, professional army with high morale and a flexible and aggressive tactical style. By 1651 there was no longer any field army in England and Wales, Scotland or Ireland left to oppose it.

The Second Civil War, 1648

Although forced to deal with the New Model Army after his defeat in the First English Civil War, Charles I still had hopes that rising discontent in England and Wales, and an alliance or 'engagement' with the Scots, could restore his position. There was no longer any force in England strong enough to oppose the New Model Army, but a Scottish alliance could provide the King with an army which could. In addition, there were rumblings of discontent in the English navy, whose political sympathies were more Presbyterian than the Independent faction now dominant in the New Model Army. This combination of factors represented a serious threat to the latter and its supporters. Although it had proved to be a highly effective field army, the New Model Army was a relatively small force and would not be able to deal with uprisings all over England as well as concentrating enough men to oppose a Scottish invasion if all of these occurred at the same time.

A series of uprisings in England and Wales began with a mutiny on 22 February by Colonel John Poyer, governor of Pembroke Castle in south Wales. The underlying reason was that neither Colonel Poyer nor his men had received their arrears of pay, and they doubted they would if they were disbanded without it. The mutiny spread to other local soldiers under Major General Rowland Laugherne, and both Poyer and Laugherne declared support for King Charles. Neither had become Royalists by conviction but, once committed to opposition to the Parliament and the New Model Army, they had little option but to seek allies where they could find them. Concern over the extent of the uprising had caused Sir Thomas Fairfax to send Oliver Cromwell to take command in south Wales but, by the time he arrived, Colonel Horton had already defeated Poyer and Laugherne at St Fagan's near Cardiff.

There were Royalist uprisings and riots elsewhere in England, with the most significant being in the north, where small parties of Royalists took control of the key strategic cities of Berwick on 28 April and Carlisle on 29 April, and in the south-east, where there was an uprising in Kent on 21 May. On 27 May the squadron of the English fleet at anchor in the Downs mutinied, and Royalists took control of Walmer and Deal castles, whose artillery covered the anchorage. Sir Thomas Fairfax had already ordered Oliver Cromwell to south Wales and given command in the north of England to John Lambert. Fairfax was about to march north to re-enforce Lambert when he heard of the mutiny in Kent. He acted decisively to concentrate all available men[1] to put down the Kentish uprising before it could spread, even though this meant leaving London to be defended by the London Militia. The Royalists in Kent numbered about 10,000 to 11,000 men but they had little time to become organized before Fairfax's small force of about 6,000 men attacked the Royalist base at Maidstone. The New Model soldiers took the town after fierce street fighting as the Royalists had 'so lined the streets, in the several Houses, and

John Lambert (1619–1684). Another successful commander who had no professional military experience before the English Civil War but became one of the most capable of the New Model Army generals. He had served originally in the Army of the Northern Association, and later fought in the campaigns against the Scots in 1648 and 1650/1651. His greatest victory was at Inverkeithing in 1651.

placed so much case Shot in every Street, that the business became very disputable till almost twelve a Clock at Night and every Street in the Town was got by Inches'.[2] This broke the uprising in Kent as most scattered and returned home, while the hard core of some 3,000 marched under the Earl of Norwich towards London.

Fairfax kept the main body of his army in Kent, sending only 500 cavalry under Colonel Edward Whalley to pursue the Royalists. The approach of a defeated Royalist army aroused little support in London where the Militia was, once again, under the command of Philip Skippon, and the City's gates were barred against the Royalists, so that 'he [the Earl of Norwich] was necessitated to make use of boats or other means to transport his men over the river into the county of Essex'.[3] In Essex the Earl of Norwich and remains of his Kentish army joined forces with Essex Royalists under Sir Charles Lucas at Chelmsford. The danger this force represented was that, if not stopped, it could attract further recruits in southern England. As Colonel Whalley reported back to Fairfax, 'Our friends report the enemy to be 3,000 horses and foot and like a snowball increasing.' The combined Royalist force marched to Colchester with Fairfax now close behind them. The Royalist advance guard entered Colchester on 9 June, and Fairfax's army was at the outskirts of the town by the evening of 12 June. Fairfax assaulted the town on the next day, hoping to repeat his success at Maidstone, but was beaten out with heavy losses. But if Fairfax was unable to take the town, his army was now too close for the Royalists to risk being attacked as they marched out of it, and the Royalist army was now besieged – and trapped – in Colchester. The Parliament's response to the mutiny of the Fleet was to reappoint the popular Robert Rich, Earl of Warwick, as admiral. As a member of the House of Lords, Warwick had given up his command in compliance with the Self-Denying Ordinance. Although he was not accepted by the fleet in the Downs, Warwick was able to win over the squadron in Portsmouth, and this prevented the naval mutiny from spreading. The collapse of the uprising in Kent weakened the resolve of the mutinous ships which sailed for sanctuary at Helvoetsluys in Holland.

The Right Hon:ble Robert Earle of Warwick Lord Rich of Leeze & Lord High Admirall of the Seas

Robert Rich, Earl of Warwick (1587–1658). A supporter of the Parliament, he was commander of the English fleet between 1642 and 1645, retiring in accordance with the Self-Denying Ordinance. His return to command in 1648 prevented the naval mutiny of 1648 from spreading.

By the end of June the main problems in England and Wales had been resolved or neutralized. The Scottish army, under the Duke of Hamilton, did not cross the border into England until 8 July. This army consisted of two elements, the regiments 'new-modelled' after the First Civil War with the addition of regiments newly levied in 1648, and a veteran brigade drawn from the Scottish army in northern Ireland[4] under Major General George Munro. This army was joined by Royalists raised in northern England and commanded by Sir Marmaduke Langdale, Sir Philip Musgrave and Sir Thomas Tyldesley. The strength of the Scottish army was probably about 14,000 men under the Duke of Hamilton and 2,000 men under George Munro, with about 5,000 English Royalists.[5] The New Model Army regiments in the north under Major General John Lambert initially numbered around 3,000 men, and Sir Marmaduke Langdale certainly had the option of risking battle before the Scottish army arrived, but he chose not to take the risk. Lambert lacked the men to formally oppose the Scottish and Royalist advance, but he managed to slow it down in a series of small engagements while his small army was steadily re-enforced by additional New Model regiments from the south and local militia.

After Pembroke Castle surrendered on 11 July, Cromwell marched north, joining forces with John Lambert near Knaresborough on 12 August to form a combined army of around 10,000 men. A cautious general, or simply a prudent one, would have sought to delay the Scots' advance and await further re-

The Scottish advance into England, 1648.

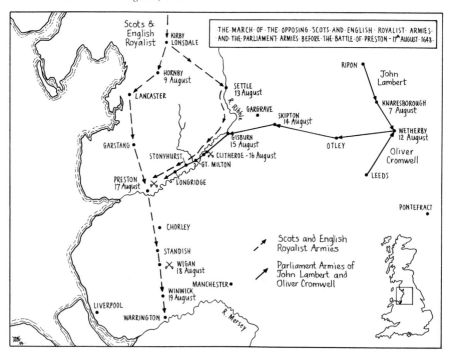

enforcements, but Cromwell decided on the bold option of attacking on the basis, as he wrote, that 'it was thought that to engage the enemy to fight was our business'. Cromwell was extremely fortunate that the Scottish and Royalist armies had no suspicion that they might be attacked in strength and were then strung out along the road to Preston. Langdale covered the advance to the east, while the Scottish cavalry rode ahead because of the 'scarcity of forage' and George Munro's brigade followed some distance behind the main body of the Scottish infantry.

Sir Marmaduke Langdale reported to the Duke of Hamilton on both 15 and 16 August that he was being pressed by opposing cavalry, but Hamilton did not take the reports seriously and took no action to concentrate his army as he simply could not believe that anyone would be foolish enough to chance the odds and attack him. On 17 August, Langdale's force was attacked in strength and retired slowly towards Preston. According to one contemporary account, the Scots had little sympathy for what they probably still regarded as a minor skirmish, and Hamilton was said to have remarked: 'Let them alone – the English dogs are but killing one another.'[6] After fierce fighting Langdale's regiments were routed, and the advancing New Model Army overwhelmed the few cavalry Hamilton had with his main force and caught the last two brigades of Hamilton's infantry as they were crossing the river south of Preston. The Scots attempted to hold the bridge but were beaten from it after a 'very hot' action. Overnight the Scots decided to retreat from their position as fast as possible, abandoning their guns, and their artillery and baggage trains. By the time the Scottish infantry reached Warrington, their comrades in the cavalry decided to make their own way back to Scotland. The remnants of the Scottish infantry surrendered at Warrington. The Scottish cavalry disintegrated during their retreat, and when they reached Uttoxeter they refused to go any further. Hamilton surrendered with what was left of his cavalry on 25 August. George Munro and his brigade of veteran Scottish soldiers from Ulster were well to the north when the Duke of Hamilton's army was defeated at Preston and retreated unopposed back to Scotland.

The defeat of the Scottish army at Preston made the position of the English Royalists at Colchester impossible. No army could come to their relief and they had no option but to make the best terms possible and surrender. Sir Thomas Fairfax was furiously angry at having to prosecute so severe a siege over fellow English men and women in Colchester in a Second Civil War, and over the losses his soldiers had suffered. On 24 August the besiegers 'sent a paper kite into the town' which carried the 'revelation of a great victory over the Scots and their general rout'. The terms offered were harsh 'free quarter' to the 'inferior officers and soldiers', but the officers would have to 'submit to mercy' – which meant no guarantee of their lives. This naturally split the allegiance of officers and men and, when the officers proposed a do-or-die breakout, the soldiers mutinied, fearing 'that the officers and the rest of the gentlemen were resolved to break through the leaguer and escape, leaving them all to shift for themselves'.[7]

Colchester surrendered on 27 August and Fairfax brought three of the leading officers, Sir Charles Lucas, Sir George Lisle and Sir Bernard Gascoigne, before a court martial. All three were sentenced to death by firing squad, but one, Sir Bernard Gascoigne, was reprieved at the last minute, as he was able to claim that he was an Italian and a subject of the Grand Duke of Tuscany. As for the remainder of the garrison:

> they [the New Model Army] marched them away on a day when it rained violently and conducted them from place to place in the country, lodging them in churches and such places, till many of them were starved and divers, who could not march by reason of their faintness, they pistolled them in the highways. Some they sold (as before they did the Scots) to be transported into foreign countries, from their wives and children, no matter to what part of the world.[8]

The Second Civil War created a major change in the thinking of the rank and file in the New Model Army. Previously there had

Firing squad at Colchester, 28 August 1648. A contemporary engraving of the execution after the siege of Colchester of Sir Charles Lucas, shown lying dead, and Sir George Lisle, standing before a firing squad of New Model Army musketeers.

The Execution of Charles I on 30 January 1649. Engraving of a contemporary painting c.1649. Charles is shown as he appeared at his trial (top left), and Sir Thomas Fairfax is shown with an executioner's axe in one hand and the King's head in another (top right). Fairfax had not in fact supported the trial and execution of Charles, although many of his officers and soldiers had sought it as revenge for what they saw as the unnecessary loss of comrades in the Second Civil War.

been discussion over reconciliation, but now hardline opinion prevailed and led directly to the trial and execution of Charles I.

Cromwell's Campaign in Ireland 1649/1650

Loyalties in Ireland were never straightforward as those outside saw opportunities for the extension of their broader wars, while those directly involved saw it far more personally in terms of an increasingly bitter and vicious war. The strongly Protestant, and increasingly anti-Catholic, English Parliament and later the New Model Army were sympathetic to fellow Protestant settlers, English or Scottish, under attack from Catholic Irish, and many also saw the rebellion as part of a broader Catholic conspiracy against Protestants generally. The Royalists in England saw Ireland as a potential source of soldiers, Protestant or Catholic, for service in the Royalist armies in England. The Scots saw north-eastern Ireland as a dangerous base from which attacks could be made, particularly where an extension of the clan rivalries between the Macdonalds and the Campbells could destabilize the highlands. In Ireland itself, Catholic leaders sought different solutions; all sought more influence in government but they differed, often violently, over exactly what that meant. In between all these conflicting strategies was the population, Protestant and Catholic, trying to survive in a war zone.

The Royalists had agreed a ceasefire or 'Cessation' with the Catholic Irish Confederation on 15 September 1643 with the objective of bringing back English regiments serving in Ireland as re-enforcements for Royalist armies. Their next objective was to negotiate the exchange of concessions in the political government of Ireland for regiments of Catholic soldiers to serve in England, but the negotiations dragged on interminably, as the Confederation required concessions that Charles I felt that he could not, at least publicly, offer. In the interim, the Royalist cause was defeated in England and the brief series of successes in Scotland by the Royalist commander James Graham, Marquess of Montrose, ended with his defeat at Philiphaugh on 13 September 1645. Despite negotiations the war had continued in Ireland, and the Confederation had one notable success on 5 June 1646 at the battle of Benburb, where the Ulster army of Owen Roe O'Neill inflicted a serious defeat over an army composed of Scottish regiments and English and Scottish settlers under the Scottish general Robert Munro. But the victory was not followed up and although it seriously damaged the prestige of the Scottish army in Ireland it was not enough in itself to change the course of the war.

It was increasingly evident, however, that with the end of the Civil War the Parliament would soon be able to spare resources of soldiers and military supplies for Ireland, and the Confederation made renewed efforts to take the remaining Protestant strongholds. In the face of this advance the Royalist commander in Ireland, James Butler, Earl of Ormonde, entered into negotiations with the Parliament to hand over Dublin on the basis that they could defend it and he no longer could. The Royalist court in exile attempted to delay the handover, but Ormonde's response in April 1647 was that 'he should give up those Places under his command rather to the English Rebels than the Irish Rebels'.[9]

The new commander appointed by Parliament, Colonel Michael Jones, was a sensible choice on both political and military grounds. He was a member of a prominent Protestant family in Ireland and had fought in Ireland during the early stages of the rebellion. He had refused to accept the 'Cessation' in 1643 and had crossed over to England, where he had fought as the cavalry commander in the Parliamentary army of Sir William Brereton. Re-enforcements were sent to bolster the garrison and Jones arrived at Dublin in June 1647. He lost little time in taking the offensive and on 8 August he defeated – and practically wiped out – Thomas Preston's Leinster army at the battle of Dungan's Hill. In the south the Protestant commander Murrough O'Brien, Earl of Inchiquin, also won a significant success with his decisive defeat of the Catholic Munster army at Knockanuss on 13 November 1647. But by then the political instability caused firstly by the army mutiny during 1647 and then the Second Civil War in 1648 had once again directed attention and resources away from Ireland. The Second Civil War changed alliances outside Ireland and affected those within it, as the Scots were now allied to English Royalists in opposition to a Parliament dominated by the New Model Army and its sympathizers.

The Earl of Ormonde returned to Ireland on 3 October with the objective of drawing together a broad alliance of the various factions whose common interest was opposition to the English Parliament. But, by the time he arrived, the best opportunity for success had been lost as the Scots and English Royalists had been decisively defeated by the New Model Army at the battle of Preston on 17 August 1648. Ormonde's alliance was consolidated after the execution of King Charles I as the majority of the English in Ireland were appalled by it, but Michael Jones remained loyal to the Parliament and kept control of Dublin. Apart from this, the only strong points held for the Parliament were Dundalk, where the former Royalist George Monk commanded the garrison, and Londonderry, under Sir Charles Coote. The only other force outside Ormonde's alliance was the Catholic Ulster army of Owen Roe O'Neill who chose to ally with the Parliamentary commanders George Monk and Sir Charles Coote rather than his former Confederation allies.

Ormonde's broad coalition remained an uneasy alliance of groups which had previously been fighting one another in a war characterized by increasingly brutal raids and counter-raids. But it did provide a large field army and, after George Monk was forced to surrender Dundalk, only Londonderry and Dublin – both of which could be supplied by sea – remained in Parliamentary hands. Now the Second Civil War was over, the Parliament could turn its attention to Ireland once again, and unless Ormonde could take it, Dublin could be used as a secure port for the landing of a new English army and its supplies. On 29 July 1649 Ormonde began to establish an artillery battery on the site of a ruined castle at Baggotrath with the objective of being able to fire upon supply ships en route to Dublin. The working party was covered by a detachment of some 1,500 infantry and 'some Horse' under Major General Sir Patrick Purcell. In response, Michael Jones sallied out of Dublin with a strong force of some 4,000 infantry and 1,200 cavalry, and overwhelmed the soldiers at Baggotrath 'not without strong dispute: Most of the enemy's foot there were slain and taken, their horse having deserted them after the first charge'.[10] Jones then seized this initial success offered and attacked Ormonde's camp at Rathmines before the Royalist officers could draw up and fully deploy their men. Ormonde's army broke up and fled, abandoning its artillery and baggage train, and suffering heavy losses.

Oliver Cromwell landed at Dublin on 15 August with the first elements of his army, and further transports followed on 23 August. This was a well-equipped army with a strong artillery train and the funds – £100,000 in ready money – to pay his soldiers and for local provisions, and to provide sweeteners to persuade Protestant officers in Ormonde's army to change sides. Cromwell had been in a strong enough position to insist upon this level of support before accepting the post of commander in Ireland as the Parliament needed a leader of his calibre for this expedition. His speech to the Council of State on 23 March 1649 demonstrates his perspective on the importance of this campaign:

> if we do not endeavour to make good our interest there [Ireland], and that timely, we shall not only have our interest rooted out there, but they will be able in very short time to land forces in England, and to put us to trouble here. I confess that I have had these thoughts with myself, that perhaps may be carnal and foolish. I had rather be overrun with a Cavalierish interest than a Scotch interest; I had rather be overrun by a Scotch interest, than an Irish interest.[11]

Service in Ireland was not popular, and the New Model Army and four cavalry and four infantry regiments, all veteran regiments, were chosen by casting lots. The four infantry regiments were John Hewson's, Isaac Ewers's, Richard Cooke's and Richard Deane's – the last becoming Oliver Cromwell's own regiment as Deane had been appointed to a naval command as a 'General-at-Sea'. The four cavalry regiments chosen for service were Henry Ireton's, Thomas Horton's, Adrian Scroope's and John Lambert's. However, the last of these could not be spared from service in the north of England and mutiny broke out amongst Adrian Scroope's and Henry Ireton's regiments. Their complaint was that although individual soldiers were not obliged to go to Ireland, they could not then join another regiment and their fears, encouraged by Leveller activists, that they would then be disbanded without 'a competent pay in hand of their arrears to carry them home, and inable them to follow their occupations' caused them to mutiny. When the mutineers moved from appeals for their arrears to demands that the former elected council of the army be reinstated, Sir Thomas Fairfax and Oliver Cromwell moved quickly to suppress the mutiny, surprising the mutineers at their quarters in Burford on 14 May. Scroope's regiment was disbanded but Ireton's was reformed around those soldiers who had remained loyal, and the regiment served in Ireland. In addition to the veteran regiments, new regiments were raised for the expedition, a 'double regiment' of twelve troops of cavalry with Oliver Cromwell for colonel, and another cavalry regiment under John Reynolds. Six additional infantry regiments were also raised under Robert Venables, Robert Tothill, Hercules Huncks, Henry Ireton, Peter Stubber and Robert Phayre.

After his army had disembarked in Dublin, Cromwell reorganized the regiments which had formed the army based in Dublin, disbanding several of them. He also followed the usual New Model Army practice of declaring his intentions to offer fair treatment to civilians and to keep his army under firm discipline. His proclamation specified:

> Whereas I am informed that, upon the marching out of the armies heretofore, or of parties from Garrisons, a liberty hath been taken by the soldiery to abuse, rob and pillage, and too often to execute cruelties upon the Country People: Being resolved, by the grace of God, diligently and strictly to restrain such wickedness for the future, I do hereby warn and require all Officers, Soldiers, and others under my command henceforth to forbear all such evil practices.[12]

Apart from offering some hope to civilians, this approach was also intended to encourage them to bring in provisions on the assurance that 'they shall not be troubled or molested in their persons or goods; but shall have the benefit of a free market, and receive ready money for goods and commodities they shall so bring and sell'.

Cromwell lost little time in commencing his campaign. His strategic preference was for a quick campaign won by bringing his opponents to battle, but Ormonde's army was already in disorder after its defeat at Rathmines and had neither the ability nor the inclination to 'put an issue upon a field-battle'.[13] On 30 August, Cromwell drew together 'eight regiments of foot and six of horse and some troops of dragoons' outside Dublin with the objective 'to endeavour the regaining of Tredagh [Drogheda]; or tempting the enemy upon his hazard of the loss of that place, to fight'.[14] The garrison of Drogheda consisted of both Protestant and Catholic regiments under the command of Sir Arthur Aston, an English Catholic who was a veteran of the Thirty Years War and had also fought in the Royalist army in England during the First Civil War. Both sides knew that the outcome of the siege of Drogheda would have a critical impact on the campaign. From the perspective of Ormonde and his fragile coalition, Cromwell was perfectly placed to capitalize on Michael Jones's victory at Rathmines. Ormonde's credibility amongst his allies had been seriously damaged and he needed time to reorganize his army and come to some agreement, if he could, with Owen Roe O'Neill and his Catholic Ulster army. Cromwell arrived with his reputation as a successful general enhanced by his victory at Preston the previous year, a fresh army with a core of veteran regiments and a strong siege train. From Cromwell's perspective he was determined to restore English control over Ireland and prevent its use as a base for any attack on England but he could not do that if he had to conduct sieges of every town or strong point in Ireland.

The governor of Drogheda, Sir Arthur Aston, had a strong garrison of around 3,000 men and was determined to defend to the last. His perspective towards the civilian population of a town which he defended can be seen in an earlier response when summoned to surrender the English town of Reading in 1643 during the First Civil War: 'he would not deliver the town until wheat was forty shillings a bushel, and as for the women and children they should dye with him'.[15] Comments like this explained why the Royalist Earl of Clarendon wrote of Aston that he 'had the fortune to be very much esteemed where he was not known, and very much detested where he was'.[16] On 9 September, Cromwell's siege artillery was in position and 'began to play' on the defences. On 10 September, Cromwell sent the following summons:

> To Sir Arthur Aston, Governor of Drogheda
>
> Sir,
>
> Having brought the army belonging to the Parliament of England before this place, to reduce it to obedience, to the end that the effusion of blood may be prevented, I thought fit to summon you to deliver the same into my hands to their use. If this be refused you will have no cause to blame me.
>
> I expect your answer and rest,
Your servant
O. Cromwell[17]

Cromwell's dispatch records only that he 'received no satisfactory answer'. Cromwell's artillery 'after some two or three hundred shot, beat down the corner tower, and opened two reasonable good breaches in the east and south wall'. By the practice of the day, with which Sir Arthur Aston was perfectly familiar, a garrison which chose not to make terms once a 'reasonable breach' had been made in their defences would receive no mercy. Aston's garrison received none and, after the first storming parties had been beaten out of the breach, a renewed attack took the town. Cromwell's dispatch recorded:

> The Governor, Sir Arthur Ashton, and divers considerable Officers, being there, our men getting up to them, were ordered by me to put them all to the sword. And indeed, being in the heat of the action, I forbade them to spare any that were in arms in the town, and, I think, that night they put to the sword about 2,000 men.[18]

Some of the garrison would have worn uniforms but others would not and in these circumstances it would have been impossible to distinguish between soldiers and civilians, so citizens of the town, men of military age, would have died alongside the garrison soldiers. After Drogheda, many other garrisons quickly surrendered or fled.

Having cleared the garrisons to the north of Dublin and linked up with Sir Charles Coote's forces, Cromwell moved south to the next town held against him, Wexford. The fort of Rosslare which commanded the harbour was abandoned by its garrison and Cromwell was then able to land the siege artillery he had shipped down the coast. When summoned, the governor, Colonel David Sinnott, tried to spin out negotiations in the hope that he would be relieved, but he managed only to exhaust the patience of the besiegers. While the final negotiations were ongoing, one of the garrison, Captain James Stafford, surrendered the castle at the south of the town defences and the besiegers stormed over the walls and sacked the town. About 1,500 of the garrison were killed in the sack of the town, and of the citizens 'most of them are run away, and many of them killed'.[19]

The next garrison that Cromwell summoned, New Ross, quickly surrendered after receiving a summons, and about 500 of the Protestant soldiers in garrison deserted and changed sides. This trend continued elsewhere in Ireland, and the prominent Munster landowner Roger Boyle acted as Cromwell's intermediary to persuade the Protestants in Munster to desert Ormonde. On 16 October the Protestant English part of the garrison of Cork joined with the Protestant citizens of the town to drive out the governor and his Catholic Irish soldiers, and declared for the Parliament. Other Munster towns soon followed, though Cromwell was unable to take Duncannon or Waterford before he finally put his army into winter quarters with his own headquarters at Youghal.

Although Ormonde still had more soldiers than Cromwell, and had been joined in October by Owen Roe O'Neill's Catholic Ulster army, his coalition was disintegrating through growing distrust between Protestant and Catholic factions. Ormonde had established his headquarters at Kilkenny and quartered his men where he could, including about 1,500 from the Ulster army under Major General Hugh O'Neill at Clonmel. Cromwell commenced his next campaign in late January 1650, very early by the standards of the day, as most commanders would have waited until spring. After successfully taking a series of small strongholds with little opposition, Cromwell summoned the garrison at Kilkenny on 22 March 1650. The garrison here put up a stronger resistance and Cromwell's storming parties were twice beaten out of the breach with heavy losses before another party under Colonel Ewer broke into the town at another point. The governor, Sir William Butler, held out for terms which allowed him and his men to leave under safe conduct on 28 March; Cromwell wrote:

> you desire some articles [of surrender] for honour's sake, which out of honesty I do deny: viz. that of marching in the equipage you mention. I tell you my business is to reduce you from arms, and the country to quietness and their due subjection; to put an end to War, and not to lengthen it; wishing (if it may stand with the will of God) this people may live as happily as they did before the bloody massacre and their troubles.[20]

An indication that Ormonde's men were losing heart can be seen in the action of the garrison of the nearby castle of Cantwell. After receiving orders from Butler that they should join his garrison at Kilkenny, the officers 'being English, Welsh and Scotch' sent two officers to Cromwell instead 'to offer me the place, and their service, that they might have passes to go beyond sea to serve foreign states, with some money to bear their charges'.[21] The English and Scottish Royalists were now ready to give up the war and make what terms they could, and began to surrender under terms which were restricted to 'such officers and soldiers, and gentlemen or clergymen (being English or Scottish and Protestants), as desire to come off from the Irish Popish party' – terms which clearly distinguished between the Protestant and Catholic groups in Ormonde's coalition and effectively ended it.

Cromwell's last siege in Ireland was at Clonmel. The garrison commander, Major-General Hugh O'Neill, was an experienced professional officer who had served in the Spanish army, and the defences he built behind the breach turned it into a death trap for Cromwell's storming parties. A series of assaults were beaten out with heavy losses on 17 May, but that was as much as O'Neill and his garrison could do, and they slipped out of the town that night, leaving the mayor to make what terms he could. The mayor negotiated terms 'on behalf of the town and garrison of Clonmel' as if the garrison was still present, and Cromwell was furious to discover that the garrison had already left the town. However, he kept to the terms he had agreed, being reminded by the mayor that 'his Excellency [Cromwell] had the reputation of keeping his promises'.[22] In this type of siege warfare, a commander's reputation for honesty in abiding by the terms he offered was crucial as it encouraged towns and their garrisons to surrender rather than fight to the end.

In England there was now increasing concern that negotiations between Charles II and the Scots would lead to another attempt to link a Scottish army and English Royalists in opposition to the Parliament and the New Model Army, and Cromwell was ordered to return home. Cromwell had achieved his objectives in restoring English rule in Ireland and left Henry Ireton in command there to deal with the remaining Catholic Irish forces.

The Third Civil War

The Scottish Parliament had been negotiating with Charles for his return to Scotland under conditions which would severely restrict his actual authority. He had sought to improve his bargaining position by applying pressure through a military expedition to the north of Scotland in September 1649. James Graham, Earl of Montrose, took command of this small army in March 1650, but he was unable to raise much support and it was defeated when he fell into an ambush at Carbisdale on 27 April 1650. Montrose escaped but was betrayed and captured shortly afterwards, and he was executed in Edinburgh on 21 May 1650.

From an English perspective any arrangement which brought back Charles II as King of Scotland could only lead to renewed warfare, sooner or later. The Council of State

having Intelligence of the King's resolution for Scotland, and of the Laws
there made, of Forces to assist him in his intended Invasion of England;
wherof they had more than ordinary assurance; They thought it therefore
not prudent to be behind hand with their Enemy, nor to be put to an other
Game, to stay till they [the Scots] should first invade England, but rather
to carry the War from their native Country into Scotland.[23]

Given the devastation that an invading army created this was certainly a
reasonable decision and one which would enable 'the Parliament to provide for
the Security of themselves and Countreymen'. However, the New Model
Army's commander, Sir Thomas Fairfax, disagreed, declaring himself
'unsatisfyed that there was a just ground for the Parliament of England to send
their Army to invade Scotland'.

Three of the leading army commanders, Oliver Cromwell, John Lambert
and Thomas Harrison, together with the MPs Oliver St John and Bulstrode
Whitelocke, were sent to attempt to change his mind but were unsuccessful.
Although he accepted the point made by Thomas Harrison – that 'there cannot
be greater assurance or humane probability of the intentions of any State, than
we have of theirs to invade our Countrey, else what means their present Levyes
of Men and Money, and their quartering Souldiers upon our Borders?' –
Fairfax would not break his point of principle, and replied that 'Humane
Probabilities are not sufficient grounds to make War upon a Neighbour Nation,
especially our Brethren of Scotland, to whom we are engaged in a Solemn
League and Covenant.'[24] From Bulstrode Whitelocke's account in his memoirs
all three army officers in the committee genuinely sought to persuade Sir
Thomas Fairfax to change his mind and appealed to him to continue to serve
in the interests of the cause they had fought for – that cause that Thomas
Harrison pleaded was 'the most glorious Cause that ever any of this nation
appeared in, and now when we hope that the Lord will give a gracious issue and
conclusion to it, for your Excellence then to give it over, will sadden the hearts
of many of God's People'.

Further attempts were made by the Parliament to persuade Sir Thomas
Fairfax to reconsider, but if his own officers could not persuade him, then the
only other who might have done was his wife, Anne. However, she was a
staunch Presbyterian who was strongly opposed to any invasion of Presbyterian
Scotland. There was always some suggestion that Sir Thomas Fairfax's
position was reached as a result of persuasion by his wife, to whom he was
devoted, and Bulstrode Whitelocke suggested as much in his memoirs, but this
was unfair. Numerous accounts of his actions as commander of the New Model
Army, in both major decisions and everyday, make it clear that he was a man
who followed his set of principles absolutely. With the imminent threat of
Scottish invasion in mind, circumstances were 'of so great consequence, and
which would admit no delay, it not being safe for the Army to be without a
Head, Cromwel, was presently (by contrivance) named to be General and
Commander in chief of all the Parliaments Forces'. Now the New Model
Army really was Cromwell's Army.

Charles landed in Scotland on 24 June, after signing the Solemn League and Covenant on board ship and agreeing to give his assent, as King of England, to the passage of Acts of the English Parliament enforcing its conditions in England. Once commissioned as captain general – or lord general as he and his predecessor, Fairfax, were usually called – Oliver Cromwell quickly went north to Berwick, which he had appointed as the rendezvous for the regiments chosen to invade Scotland. Once there he held a brief formal exercise at which the New Model Army regiments were 'all drawn into Battalia, and marched 2 or 300 paces, then were discharged and went to their quarters'. Apart from the morale effects of a formal parade in the presence of their commander, this form of exercise was also an indication of the regiments' state of readiness and their ability to deploy for battle.

Opposing Strategies

The English strategy was straightforward and made use of the dominance of English naval power, as well as their veteran army. The invasion plan was to use Berwick as the concentration point for the army, then march north to take ports on the Scottish east coast. These ports could then be used as bases to be stocked with provisions and military supplies transported by sea and protected by the English fleet. With its supply bases secured, the New Model Army could then march to take the Scottish capital, Edinburgh, with the expectation that this threat would lead the Scottish army to fight a decisive battle. Oliver Cromwell also followed the usual New Model Army campaign practice of seeking to enforce strict discipline in order to avoid raising the country against them, together with carefully targeted propaganda. For the first of these the General published a proclamation which promised that those Scots who 'by their Councils or otherwise have not confederated against the Peace of England, or laid a foundation of a second invasion of England' could 'stay in their own habitations and houses, where they in peace shall enjoy what they have without least offer of violence or injury by any of the army'.[25]

The Scottish strategy was to avoid battle on unequal terms and wait for the losses through sickness from harsh campaigning conditions or disease – which any army suffered on campaign – to weaken the New Model Army. Unequal terms, in this sense, was more than simply numbers, as in terms of quality the veteran English regiments were superior. Although the Scottish army certainly included veterans from previous campaigns, the majority of the Scottish regiments were newly raised and their officers needed time to train their men and establish a sense of regimental identity. The decisive advance of the English army, which crossed the border into Scotland on 22 July, had caught the Scots at a disadvantage, and the orders to raise further levies had only been given by the Scottish Parliament on 25 June, with an increase in numbers ordered on 3 July. Effective training of recruits took about two months and many of the Scottish regiments, once formed, would have a long march to reach their concentration point at Edinburgh. In these circumstances, the longer the Scots could avoid battle, the better their chances of winning it.

The Campaign of 1650

The New Model Army crossed the border on 22 July and took control of the port of Dunbar on 26 July. With its supply base secure, the New Model Army marched quickly on Edinburgh only to find that the Scottish commander, Alexander Leslie, first Earl of Leven, had prepared the ground and placed his army behind field fortifications stretching from Holyrood and Abbey Hill in Edinburgh to the coast at Leith. With one flank of the fortifications anchored on Edinburgh and the other by the sea at Leith, this was too strong a position for the English to attack, and Cromwell's attempts to lure the Scottish army out to fight in open ground proved unsuccessful. On 30 July, as the weather turned foul and his men were running short of supplies, Cromwell fell back on Musselburgh, a port on the Firth of Forth, with the intention 'there to refresh

The New Model Army's march into Scotland in 1650.

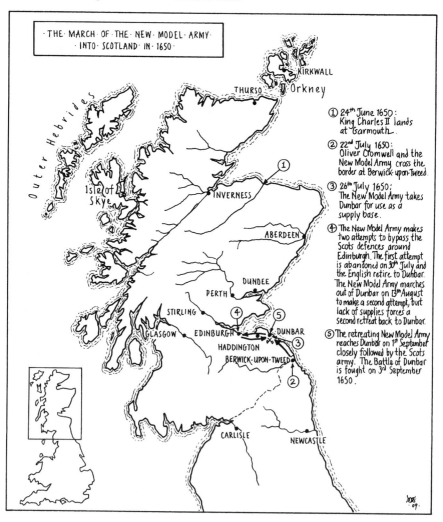

and revictual'. A retreat in the face of the enemy was always a difficult manoeuvre as a rear of a retreating army was vulnerable to attack and this proved no exception. The Scottish commander sent out two bodies of cavalry to harass the English retreat, one from Edinburgh and one from Leith. Those from Leith were quickly driven back, but the Scottish cavalry from Edinburgh gave the English a much harder time before they were driven off. This was a large-scale attack, with each side feeding in more troops of cavalry as the skirmish developed. The English cavalry were twice driven back and their commander, Major-General John Lambert, was briefly captured when his 'horse was shot in the neck and head; himself run through the arm with a lance, and run into another place of his body';[26] but the English finally had the victory, and Lambert was rescued by Lieutenant Empson, who 'pursued with five or six of our soldiers, and hewed him out'.[27]

The New Model Army reached Musselburgh on the evening of 30 July, and the Scottish cavalry mounted a raid on the English camp at around 3 or 4 o'clock the following morning, with a strong party of fifteen troops of horse, perhaps 800 cavalrymen, under Major General Robert Montgomerie and Colonel Archibald Strachan. The Scots' raid overran the outlying horse guards, but the guard commander, Captain George Watkinson, 'gave the foot the alarm, and we were all roused up, having little to do but to shake ourselves; and being drawn forth, and day approaching, the enemy falls pell-mell upon our horse guard; but the foot lying so near baffled them'. With the camp aroused and the infantry standing ready in formation, the Scottish cavalry were unable to make any serious impact and retreated, both sides claiming the other had suffered heavy losses while their own had suffered only a few. On 5 August the New Model Army retreated back to Dunbar; they had hoped to ship in supplies by sea, but bad weather prevented the English supply ships from landing their cargoes any nearer than Dunbar and the soldiers were then 'brought under great distress for want of provisions'.[28]

Having refreshed his army, Cromwell marched out of Dunbar on 13 August to make a second attempt on Edinburgh. This time, he sought to outflank Edinburgh to the south-west and this did draw out the Scots under Lieutenant General David Leslie, who took up a strong position at Gogur on 28 August. However, although 'both armies were entirely drawn up, ready for battle', the Scottish position was too strong to attack as 'it was discovered such a bog on both our wings of horse, that it was impossible to pass over'. The English army then 'drew back at night, to see if they [the Scots] would advance, but having no great stomachs, we drew back to Pentland Hills and they to Edinburgh and Leith'.[29] The English army was again short of supplies and fell back on Musselburgh. The harsh conditions of the campaign meant that many men were sick, and some 500 men were put on board ship for transport back to England while the main army marched out of Musselburgh on 31 August to retreat back through Haddington to Dunbar. Captain John Hodgeson recorded in his memoirs that on 1 September the English army marched from Haddington, having:

been at prayer in several regiments, sent away our waggons and carriages towards Dunbar, and not long afterwards marched, a poor, shattered, hungry, discouraged army; and the Scots pursued very close, that our rearguard had much ado to secure our poor weak foot that was not able to march up. We drew near to Dunbar towards night; and the Scots ready to fall upon our rear: Two guns [English cannon] played upon them, and so they drew off, and left us for that night, having got us into a pound as they reckoned.[30]

The Scots did indeed think they had Cromwell and his army in a trap at Dunbar as they had sent a brigade of infantry to Cockburnspath to block the land route south to Berwick.

The English army was now in a difficult but not impossible position, although it was one which its officers were already comparing to that of the Earl of Essex and his army at Lostwithiel in 1644. The land route south to England was blocked, but English naval power would keep the port open for receipt of provisions, ammunition and military supplies, and Cromwell and his army still had options open to them. However, if they chose to defend Dunbar and rely on supplies brought by sea, they would find it extremely difficult to ship in sufficient fodder for their horses, both cavalry mounts and those of the artillery and baggage train. The Scottish army was now confident of success: the Royalist Sir Edward Walker recorded[31] that they thought that

Cromwell had shipped most of Cannon and Colours [regimental flags], wanted Provisions, and only designed the next Day to have endeavoured to have broken through with his Horse, for he was then hemmed in on every side, and a Party sent to stop the Pass at Coberspath, between that and Barwick; but then the Committee would not give way to attempt on him [Cromwell], saying that it were a pity to destroy so many of their Brethren; but seeing the next Day they were like to fall into their Hands, it were better to get a dry Victory and send them back with Shame for their Breach of Covenant.

This is probably the reason that the Scots made the fatal decision to move their army from its strong position on the heights of Doon Hill to move closer to the English positions around Dunbar. The Scots thought their opponents were trapped and demoralized, and close pressure would make it more difficult for the English cavalry to break out or for the embarkation of their infantry onto ships. The Scots did not expect to fight; they thought the English army would capitulate if it could not escape, and surrender on terms which would allow it to march back to England, perhaps after the humiliation of surrendering its arms.

It rained heavily on the evening of 2 September and the Scottish army 'was exposed in the fields'. The Scots were so confident that:

Charles Fleetwood (1618–1692). A close associate of Oliver Cromwell, Fleetwood married Cromwell's daughter Bridget. A cavalry colonel in the Army of the Eastern Association and then the New Model Army, he was lieutenant general of the horse at the battle of Dunbar in 1650 and then commander in Ireland from 1651.

towards Morning [on 3 September] the Committee proposed they might take some rest, and 'tis said Holborne Major General gave order to put out all Matches [the smouldering match-cord used to fire matchlock muskets] but two in a Company. Thus in great Security (the Rain continuing) they made themselves shelter of the Corn new reaped and went to sleep. The Horse likewise went to Forage, and many unsadled their Horses.[32]

Many of the Scottish officers evidently sought more comfortable shelter: their commander, Leslie, wrote afterwards that 'I know I get my owen share of the falt for drawing them so neer the enemie ... though I tak God to witness we might have as easily beaten them as wee did James Graham [the Earl of Montrose] at Philiphauch, if the officers had stayed by theire troops and regiments.'[33]

The Scots had made a serious mistake, as they had thought the English army was demoralized and, with a little more pressure, they would force its commanders to surrender. Several armies had done exactly that during the First Civil War. But the Scots had miscalculated as this army was composed of veteran regiments which still trusted their commanders, Oliver Cromwell and John Lambert. Essentially the New Model Army retained is morale and its willingness to fight. Its commanders saw an opportunity when the Scots abandoned their commanding position on Doon Hill and deployed on ground where they could be attacked. Oliver Cromwell's dispatch after the battle recorded that

the Major General [John Lambert] and myself coming to the Earl of Roxburgh's House, and observing this posture [of the Scots army], I told him it did give us an opportunity and advantage to attempt upon the enemy, to which he immediately replied, that he had thought to have said the same thing to me. So that it pleased the Lord to set this apprehension upon both of our hearts, at the same instant. We called for Colonel Monk, and showed him the thing; and coming to our quarters at night, and demonstrating our apprehensions to some of the colonels, they also cheerfully concurred.[34]

It requires a confident general and officers and experienced soldiers to be able to respond to a quick decision to take advantage of an enemy's position and attack. Very few armies in this period could have succeeded but the English army, the New Model Army, was exceptional. It was already camped in its brigades, and the New Model regiments, veteran soldiers under experienced officers, could be relied upon to be flexible enough to carry out Cromwell's decision to attack. The army was intended to be ready for 'break of day, but through some delays it proved not to be so till six o'clock in the morning'. The Scots had camped in their battle lines and the delays gave them some time to get their regiments in order, although they would have been hampered by the absence of some of their officers. But this was not enough and, as Cromwell's dispatch recorded, 'the best of the enemy's horse and foot being broken through and through in less than an hour's dispute, their whole army being put into confusion, it became a total route'. It was a complete victory in which, as Cromwell's dispatch recorded, 'both your chief commanders and others in their several places, and soldiers also, were acted with as much courage as ever hath been seen in any action since this war. I know they look not to be named; and therefore I forbear particulars.'[35] The remnants of the Scottish army were now too weak to defend the fortified line around Edinburgh, and they retreated to Stirling, leaving a garrison in Edinburgh Castle.

The fragile alliance of factions amongst the Scots did not survive the defeat at Dunbar, and the more extreme Covenanters sought to raise a separate army in the west under colonels Archibald Strachan and Gilbert Kerr. At first Cromwell endeavoured to negotiate with the Covenanters, who probably disliked the Stuart monarchy almost as much as he did, but when this failed he turned to more direct means. On 27 November he led a strong force of eight cavalry regiments, about 3,000 cavalrymen, to campaign in the west. He had arranged to rendezvous with a further 2,500 cavalrymen under John Lambert at Hamilton on the south bank of the River Clyde, where his military intelligence advised him that the Scots' western army was quartered. However, as the Scots retreated before him, and John Lambert's troops had not appeared, Cromwell commenced a 'sad, cold and tedious march' back to Edinburgh at around 7 o'clock in the morning on 30 November since, as one of his soldiers wrote, 'the Major Generall not meeting us according to appointment, we were inforced to draw back to our severall Quarters'.[36] Cromwell thought John Lambert had been unable to reach Hamilton 'by reason of the waters' but, in fact, Lambert's troops arrived at Hamilton later the same day and quartered there for the night.

The Scottish commander Gilbert Kerr had about 3,000 cavalry and dragoons, and saw an opportunity here to inflict a major defeat on the English by attacking – beating up – the quarters of John Lambert's troops by night. At first the Scottish attack was successful, and this led Kerr to commit the rest of his force, but the English cavalry rallied and his force was defeated and scattered. This second defeat had a serious impact on the Scots' morale and this, together with the emplacement of siege artillery and mortars shipped up from London, finally persuaded the governor of Edinburgh Castle, Sir Walter Dundas, to surrender on terms. On 24 December 1650 the garrison marched out the honour of war – 'drums beating, and colours flying, matches lighted at both ends, and ball in their mouths' – and handed over Edinburgh Castle to the English.

The Campaign of 1651
Defeat at Dunbar and Hamilton had, at least, simplified the political infighting amongst the Scottish leaders as it forced the Scottish Parliament and the Royalists, both Scottish and English, to co-operate. Prince Charles was formally crowned King of Scotland at the traditional site of Scone on 1

January 1651. The strategic position of the Scots was still tenable as they were able, from their base at Stirling, to bar the English from the north of Scotland. However, this position would change if the English army could outflank the Scots either by controlling the fords to the west of Stirling or by establishing themselves on the northern shore of the Firth of Forth. Oliver Cromwell made an attempt to take control of the fords in February, but turned back as the weather was 'so tempestuous with wind, hail, snow and rain'. The one significant impact of this was that the exposure caused Cromwell to fall seriously ill and he did not recover until the end of May, one of his officers writing home on 27 May that 'the General is reasonable well recovered'. The English army was largely inactive while its General was ill, and the Scots were able to extend the area under their control. There were also widespread rumours in the English army that the Scots' 'great endeavours are for a great body of horse, intending (as reports go) to make an inroad into England'.[37] Similar reports were being printed in London, and Major General Thomas Harrison, who had been appointed to command the English forces, both regular soldiers and militia, in the north of England had been ordered to concentrate his regiments at Carlisle as a precaution.

Although this was an option, the Scots' field commander, David Leslie, preferred a strategy of keeping the Scottish army in Scotland and avoiding battle by using his fortified base around Stirling, in much the same way as he had used fortified lines outside Edinburgh the previous year. This position was too strong to attack directly, but it could be outflanked. On 17 July, while the manoeuvring of the main army occupied the attention of the Scottish army, Colonel Robert Overton crossed the Firth of Forth with around 1,600 infantry and four troops of cavalry. This force took up a position where 'almost three sides of sea incompasseth a rocky piece of ground', and this done, 'presently fell to intrenching of themselves'. A bridgehead having been established, reenforcements of two regiments of infantry and two of cavalry under John Lambert were ferried across on Saturday 19 July. Lambert worked hard throughout Saturday, finally bringing the last of his cavalry ashore early on Sunday morning to give him a force of about 5,000 men. The Scots' response was to send a force of some 4,500 men under major generals Sir James Holborne and Sir John Brown.

Both sides deployed for battle at Inverkeithing, where the Scots 'drew up in battalia, and we in the same manner', with the English having 'more in number in my judgement by at least 500 or 600, but on the other side the enemy had the advantage of the ground'. The two sides faced each other for about an hour and a half until, hearing that 'more forces were come from Stirling to their assistance', John Lambert resolved to attack the Scots before they could be re-enforced. The English made a swift attack uphill and 'through the Lord's strength by a very short dispute put them to an absolute rout'. John Lambert's dispatch reported that 'we killed upon the place (as most judge) 2000, and took 1,400 prisoners', including one of the Scottish commanders, Sir John Brown.[38]

With the English army divided on either side of the Firth of Forth, the Scots had the option of concentrating their whole army to fight either part, Lambert's to the north or Cromwell's to the south. But their field commander, Leslie, was concerned that if he did so, the other part would march to take the Scots army in the rear and destroy it. As the English had now outflanked Stirling and could cut it off from receiving supplies, the Scots now decided to take the desperate chance of marching their army into England in the hope of raising support and recruits from English Royalists. On 31 July the Scottish army marched out of Stirling; one of its officers, Sir James Turner, estimated its strength: 'the horse and dragoons might be about four thousand; and the foot, as I reckoned them that day we marched from Stirling Park, were upwards of nine thousand. A train of artillery of some field pieces and leather cannon we had, with suitable ammunition under the conduct of Sir James Wemis Generall of the Artillerie.'[39] The Scottish army, including some English Royalists, crossed the border into England on 6 August. The Scottish high command was not optimistic about the result, the Duke of Hamilton commenting to a friend that 'I cannot tell you whether our hopes or fears are greatest, but we have stout argument, despair.'[40]

In response, Cromwell sent John Lambert with about 4,000 cavalry to 'trouble the enemy from the rear', while Major General Thomas Harrison was to 'march with the horse and dragoons with you towards the enemy where you may best flank them, straighten their provisions, and do service as you see opportunities upon them'.[41] The English Parliament also gave orders for the mustering of the militia. In the north, Sir Thomas Fairfax organized the Yorkshire Militia, while militia regiments from the north-west were sent to assist Major General Harrison. In the south and Midlands militia regiments were concentrated in Northampton for the Midlands; Gloucester for Wales and the West Midlands; St Albans for East Anglia; and Barnet for the defence of London. The London Militia, Trained Bands and Auxiliaries mustered some 14,000 under their commander, Philip Skippon. Oliver Cromwell had left Major General George Monk to hold down Scotland with 5,000 men and marched out of Leith with his artillery, nine regiments of infantry and two of cavalry on 6 August.

The route taken by the Scots took them through territory they had marched across in 1648 when their plundering had alienated the population and, despite the assurances of English Royalist exiles, very few Englishmen rallied to King Charles. The Scottish army marched through Carlisle to Lancaster, with Lambert's cavalry close behind. On 11 August, Lambert wrote that 'we are this night with five of our best regiments of horse quartered at Settle in Craven … the enemy, as we hear, are quartered about Lancaster. They have not above 4,000 horse and dragoons and 8,000 foot, and they are very sickly and drop off daily.'[42] After this Lambert's cavalry marched on ahead to join forces with Thomas Harrison, concentrating at Haslemoor in Lancashire on 14 August, while the Scottish army marched on through Preston to Wigan. The combined forces of Lambert and Harrison managed to get ahead of the Scots and

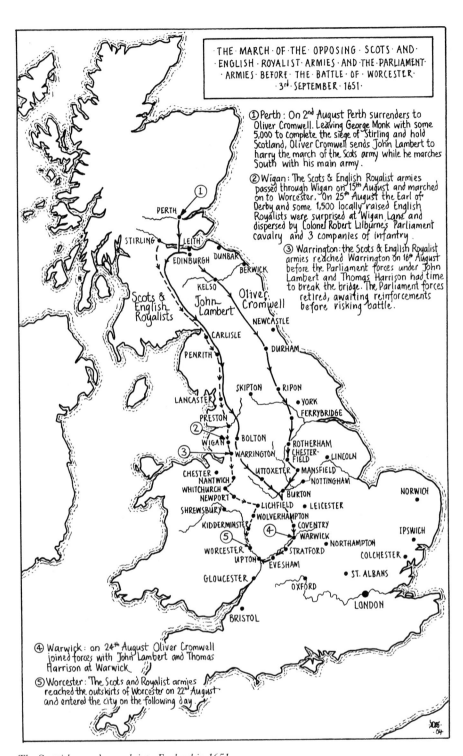

THE MARCH OF THE OPPOSING SCOTS AND
ENGLISH ROYALIST ARMIES AND THE PARLIAMENT
ARMIES BEFORE THE BATTLE OF WORCESTER
3rd SEPTEMBER 1651

① Perth: On 2nd August Perth surrenders to
Oliver Cromwell. Leaving George Monk with some
5,000 to complete the siege of Stirling and hold
Scotland, Oliver Cromwell sends John Lambert to
harry the march of the Scots army while he marches
South with his main army.

② Wigan: The Scots & English Royalist armies
passed through Wigan on 15th August and marched
on to Worcester. On 25th August the Earl of
Derby and some 1,500 locally raised English
Royalists were surprised at Wigan Lane and
dispersed by Colonel Robert Lilburne's Parliament
cavalry and 3 companies of infantry.

③ Warrington: the Scots & English Royalist
armies reached Warrington on 16th August
before the Parliament forces under John
Lambert and Thomas Harrison had time
to break the bridge. The Parliament forces
retired, awaiting reinforcements
before risking battle.

④ Warwick: on 24th August Oliver Cromwell
joined forces with John Lambert and Thomas
Harrison at Warwick

⑤ Worcester: The Scots and Royalist armies
reached the outskirts of Worcester on 22nd August
and entered the city on the following day

The Scottish army's march into England in 1651.

contested the crossing of the River Mersey at Warrington bridge. But the Scottish vanguard arrived at the bridge just ahead of them, and after some skirmishing Lambert and Harrison drew off. Although the English probably had about equal numbers to the Scots, many of their regiments were inexperienced militia, and Lambert followed his orders to wait for Cromwell and overwhelming force before committing to battle. The Scots had the opportunity to attack Lambert as he retired, but, fearing they would be led into a trap, 'it was not thought fit to pursue Lambert' as he was 'known to be a man of courage and conduct, and his troops to be of the best',[43] and continued their march, arriving at Worcester on 22 August. The few hundred Royalists that the Earl of Derby had managed to get together were caught at Wigan on 25 August by Colonel Robert Lilburne, broken and routed – a 'comfortable success', as Lilburne wrote in his dispatch to Cromwell. The Earl of Derby with the few Royalists who had escaped reached Worcester on 27 August to add to the general gloom. The Scottish army was now trapped at Worcester with no hope of relief, while English forces converged upon it from all directions.

Cromwell waited until he had overwhelming force of regular regiments and militia concentrated around Worcester, perhaps 30,000 men in all, to oppose a force of about 12,000 Scots and a few hundred English Royalists. Cromwell waited until 3 September, the anniversary of his great victory at Dunbar the previous year, before committing his army to battle. As he wrote in his formal account to the English parliament:

> This battle was fought with various success for some hours, but still hopeful on your part; and in the end became an absolute victory, and so full an one as proved a total defeat and ruin of the enemy's army; a possession of the town (our men entering at the enemy's heels, and fighting with them in the streets with very great courage); and took all their baggage and artillery.[44]

As the city fell David Leslie, with about 3,000 cavalry, fled together with King Charles. Leslie may have hoped that this cavalry force could form the nucleus of continued resistance in Scotland if he could get them back across the border, but he was closely pursued and the countryside was up in arms against him.

Sir James Turner recorded in his memoirs 'here [Worcester] was the gros of the royal army routed; some great officers escaped, and three thousand horse with them; which body might have no doubt made a second war in Scotland, but falling in pieces by bad conduct, they came every mother's son in the power of the enemy'.[45] Theirs was a terrible march as the account of one later taken prisoner recorded:

> our body consisted of 3,000; in the day we often faced the enemy, and beat their little parties but still those of us whose horses tired or were shot were lost, unless they could run as fast as we rode. In the night we kept close together, yet some fell asleep on their horses, and if the horses

tarried behind, we might hear by their cries what the bloody country people were doing with them.[46]

King Charles abandoned the Scottish cavalry on the first night of their retreat from Worcester: 'when the night covered them, he found means to withdraw himself with one or two of his servants [whom] he likewise discharged'. After extensive adventures King Charles finally managed to get across the English Channel to Normandy and then joined his mother, Queen Henrietta Maria, in Paris.

The End of the Civil Wars

Cromwell's victory at Worcester brought the Civil Wars to an end, a 'crowning mercy', as Cromwell wrote in his dispatch to the Parliament. He had left George Monk to control Scotland, and on 14 August, Stirling Castle had surrendered, unable to resist Monk's siege artillery and mortars. On 28 August a daring cavalry raid led by Colonel Matthew Alured captured most of the Scottish government where it had taken refuge at Alyth in Perthshire. Having taken the key military and political targets in Scotland, Monk completed the conquest of the country, taking Dundee by storm on 1 September.

In Ireland the last effective Catholic army, the Ulster army which had been led by Bishop Emer MacMahan after the death of Owen Roe O'Neill, was defeated by Sir Charles Coote at Scarrifhollis, near Letterkenny, in June 1650. All that remained for Cromwell's deputy in Ireland, Henry Ireton, was to complete the long process of taking the remaining Catholic strongholds by siege. Waterford surrendered on 10 August and Duncannon followed on 17 August. Having successfully divided the Protestants and Catholics in Ormonde's coalition, the same policy was then followed by negotiations with individual Catholic leaders. The first of these was Colonel John Fitzpatrick, who surrendered on generous terms at Streamstown in Westmeath on 7 March 1652. The terms included permission for his garrison to be recruited to serve as mercenaries abroad. In their own account of the reasoning behind the terms offered, the New Model Army officers put forward the perspective that 'Col Fitzpatrick's submission may be leading to the breaking of the Irish confederacy and to their insisting on national conditions, and may bring in others by submission to provide in time for their security, whereas our breaking off with him may discourage others and harden them in their rebellion.'[47]

Edmund Ludlow, the commander in Ireland after the death of Henry Ireton, and the New Model officers were convinced that most of the Catholic Irish saw no hope in continuing to fight and were now only looking to surrender on some form of reasonable terms while they still had some bargaining power. Ludlow was willing to grant terms, particularly if this meant that the remaining Catholic soldiers would be transported abroad as mercenary soldiers, mostly to Spain. The terms were pragmatic, usually including arrangements to quarter the garrisons pending their transportation overseas, on the basis that it would be 'impossible to keep their party together, to be transported beyond the seas, if not by such a way of subsistence'.[48] The last garrison, at Clough Oughter Castle, once part of the Ulster army, surrendered on 27 April 1653. This garrison and its commander, Philip Mac Hugh O'Reilly, together with other remnants the Catholic Ulster army immortalized by the Dominican poet Padraigin Haicead as the Fianna Fáil – soldiers of destiny – were transported as mercenary soldiers to Spain.

The remaining Royalist outposts were the privateering bases in the Scilly Isles, the Isle of Man and Jersey, and the American colonies. The Jersey privateers, in particular, had represented a real threat to Cromwell's supply ships during his Scottish campaign in 1650. Sir John Grenvile surrendered the Scilly Isles to the Parliament general at sea, Robert Blake, on 23 May 1651. On 31 October the Isle of Man surrendered to Colonel Robert Duckenfield. In the Channel Isles, the Royalists held the island of Jersey and on Guernsey they held Castle Cornet, which dominated the main harbour, St Peter Port, while the rest of the island was held for the Parliament. The Royalist governor, Sir George Carteret, hoped that his force of Royalists, mercenaries and island militia would be able to prevent any invasion force from landing by defending the beaches. But the Jersey militia had become mutinous, seeing no point in risking their lives now that the Royalist cause had been lost at Naseby, and melted away. Carteret fell back on his garrisons at Mont Orgueil Castle and Elizabeth Castle, but neither could withstand the heavy mortars landed by Colonel Heane. Mont Orgueil surrendered on 25 October, and Carteret surrendered Elizabeth Castle on 15 December 1651. Only the colonies remained and, as in the Channel Islands, there were divided loyalties, with New England sympathetic to the Parliament while the remainder, Virginia, Maryland, the Bermudas, Barbadoes, Antigua and St Kitts were held for the King. The governor of the main Royalist stronghold, Barbadoes, surrendered in January 1652 on generous terms once he heard of the Royalist defeat at Worcester. The other colonies in the West Indies and on the American mainland soon followed suit.

Chapter Thirteen

The Rise and Fall of a New World Power

Introduction

The victory of the New Model Army and the English Trained Bands at the battle of Worcester brought an end to the English Civil Wars as there was no longer any effective army to form a core around which any opposition could form. But Oliver Cromwell and his supporters in the New Model Army were never able to form a government which worked as they thought it should; his dissolution of the Long Parliament on 20 April 1653 showing his exasperation at political manoeuvrings which would have 'thrown away the liberties of the nation into the hands of those who had never fought for it',[1] and the way in which the MPs were expelled underlined that the key to power in England, Scotland and Ireland lay not with politicians intriguing in Parliament but with the New Model Army. Of several accounts of the event Major General Harrison's was the most evocative:

> The General stepped into the midst of the House (of Commons) where continuing his distracted language, he said 'Come, come, I will put an end to your prating'; then walking up and down the House like a mad-man, and kicking the ground with his feet, he cried out, 'You are no Parliament, I say you are no Parliament; I will put an end to your sitting; call them in, call them in': whereupon the serjeant attending the Parliament opened the doors, and Lieutenant-Colonel Wortley with two files of musquteers entred the House. [Then] looking upon one of the members, he said 'There sits a drunkard'; and giving much reviling language to others, he commanded the mace to be taken away, saying 'What shall we do with this bauble? Here, take it away.'[2]

Cromwell's ejection of the Members of Parliament was possible because he had brought a few musketeers – two files (twelve men) according to Harrison and 'five or six files of musqueteers' according to the MP Algernon Sidney[3] – into the House as a symbol of the army's strength. There was no longer any power in England that could oppose the New Model Army as long as it remained united. Cromwell's experiments with other forms of elected parliaments or the

Uytbeeldinge van de Hoogmoedige Republijk van

E N G E L A N D T ,

Mitsgaders een Prognosticatie van den wijtvermaerden D. Nostradamus, al over de 60. Iaren van hem voorseydt,
noopende den Oorlog tusschen Engelandt en Hollandt.

Ziet aan dit wonder zinnebelt,
Dat hier voor oogen wordt gestelt,
En letter op met goet verstant,
Het is 't verblinde *Engelandt*.
Aanschout doch wel den vreemden gast,
Die noch op Prins of Koning past;
Maar met de Bijl hy kopt en kapt,
De Staf en Kroon met voeten trapt.
Hy acht ook niet op eedel bloet,
Maar neemt hun af hun haaf en goet,
Speelt kip jou toug en houdt u mont,
Indien ghy dat niet doen en kunt,
En tegen hunnen Staet iet zeit,
Dan is 'er galg en strop bereit;
Want hunnen nieuwe Heerschappy
Bevestigt met der Tiranny,
Op God noch geen Gebuuren past,
Maar ieder een zijn goet aantast,
Den Koopman rooven Schip en goet,
Zoo zijnze op het gelt verwoet,
En haar verrijken met de schat,
Die Vogel Grijp schiet uit 'et gat,
Met eenen klauw houdt hy de Kroon,
In d'ander heft hy 't Swaert ten toon.

Dat is, hy houdt het met geweld,
En dempt wie zich hier tegenstelt,
Hy treet de Schotsman met de voet,
Dat die genade zingen moet;
Zoo niet, hy word om gelt verkocht,
En als een Slaaf op Zee gebrocht,
Voor Spanjaart, of Venetiaan,
Of Turk, of zwarte Moriaan:
Dit zijn al Broers van eene Kerk
Geweest, het is een Duivels werck,
Den Yrsman parst hy ook zoo hert,
Dat het hem aan de lenden smert,
Den Batavier die leit hy plat,
Hy heeft hem in den darm gevat,
En haalt hem uit zijn ingewant;
Het is een byster misverstant.
Den lichten Fransman spartelt vast,
Hy heeft hem in zijn zy getast.
Mocht hy begaan op zijn geloof,
Hy haalde voor de Hel een roof;
En mocht hy naar zijn zin begaan,
Hy badt wel zelfs den Duivel aan,
Die zich verheft in hoogen moedt,
En hem verrijkt met anders goet;
Want wat 'er met den Pijper quam,
Den Trommel-slager dikwils nam.

Fortuin betekent het geluk,
Dat keert wel zomtijds zijnen ruk,
En lichtelijk het wel gebeurt
Dat men wel haalt verand'ring speurt,
En hem de Leeuw geeft zulken slach,
Dat hy het wel beklagen mach,
En slaat de klaauwen in zijn Kroon,
En helpt den Koning op zijn Troon;
Dan tast den Schot, nu vechtens moe,
Eens teffens met den Yrsman toe.
En komt den Deen meê voor den dag,
Zoo krijgt de Staertman slag op slag;
Want wie zich elk tot vyant maakt,
Ten laatsten zelf te gronde raakt.

Leeft dit Dicht met goet opmerk,
Het is 't begin en eynd van 't werk.

Celuy qui par grand Cruaute
Maintiendra sa principaute,
On verra de grand Phalange
Par coup de feu tres dangereux
Car par accort il serra mieux,
Autrement boira le suc d'Orange.

Het Rijck dat met de Tyranny
Wil houden staan zijn Heerschappy,
Zal door 't veranderen zich bedroeven,
Door slagh van Vierwerk toebereyt,
't Was beit door Vreede by-geleyt,
Aars zal 't rap van Orangien proeven.

A Beteikent d'Engelsche Regeeringe.
B Den Schotsman.
C Den Yrsman.
D Den Hollander.
E Den Fransman.
F Den Grijfioen, of Roof-vogel.
G De onschuldige booding des Konings.
H Het verstooren der geroofde Goederen.
I Den Hollandtschen Leeuw balt / met hulp van den Schotsman / Fransman en Yrsman / den Engelsman op 't lijf.
K Beteikent / dat door Vlaanders de Engelsche Vloot sal vernielt worden.
L Is dat afgedwongen Gelt der Malignanten.

C. vande P A S.

Dutch engraving. A satirical engraving c.1652–1654 depicting Oliver Cromwell wearing a triple crown for England, Scotland and Ireland, and easily mastering four figures representing a Frenchman, a Dutchman, a Scot and an Irishman. British Library

A Dutch Medallion c.1654/1655. The coin shows Oliver Cromwell and the symbol of Britannia in the foreground, and French and Spanish ambassadors in the background quarrelling over who should be first to kiss Cromwell's arse. The French ambassador's words around the rim of the coin translate as 'Withdraw you, the honour belongs to the king, my master'. Museum of London

brief division of England and Wales into sectors controlled by major generals were never successful, but as he retained the support of the majority of his officers and men, there was nothing to remove him from power and he was king in all but name.

One consequence of military rule was that the veteran army which had fought in the English Civil Wars and the powerful English fleet remained in existence at a time when the two major European powers, France and Spain, were still locked in war against one another. Neither side could ignore the existence of the English army or afford to see it allied to the other side. English naval victories during their brief war with the Dutch served only to underline the nature of English power, a powerful, veteran army with an effective fleet to guard its transport into Europe and keep clear its lines of communication back to England. The combination of these factors made England a power to be reckoned with, a new world power in a way it had never been, or could ever be, under the Stuart dynasty.

The War with Spain
During 1654 Cromwell conducted negotiations with both France and Spain, but of the two a war with Spain remained the preferable option. The English still harboured resentful memories of attack by Philip II's Spanish Armada, and in purely strategic terms Spain was an easier and more rewarding target because its overseas possessions, and its annual treasure fleet from the Spanish colonies in America, were vulnerable to attack by the English fleet, while France was essentially a land power. A strong expedition was formed for an attack on the Spanish colonies in America under Admiral William Penn and Colonel Robert Venables,[4] and it set sail from Portsmouth in December 1654

with its precise target left to the discretion of Venables and his officers. On arrival in the West Indies, Venables chose Hispaniola (modern Haiti) as his target. The invasion of Hispaniola was a dismal failure and the expedition's commanders, unwilling to return to England with nothing to show for their efforts, sailed for the smaller island of Jamaica, arriving offshore on 9 May 1655. Forced out of the island's capital, Santiago de la Vega, the Spanish continued a guerrilla war, but finally abandoned Jamaica to the English in 1660.

An attack on the Spanish colonies in the West Indies need not necessarily have led to war in Europe as the Spanish were already overstretched in their war with France, and there was reason to suppose the Spanish response might be negotiation. The English fleet was also active in the Mediterranean during 1654 and 1655, causing widespread concern over exactly what instructions its general at sea, Robert Blake, had been given. One target was certainly to persuade the north African corsairs – the Barbary corsairs – from attacks on English shipping and, after unsuccessful negotiations, Blake attacked and destroyed a corsair fleet at Tunis as an object lesson. In October 1655 Cromwell agreed a commercial treaty with France, which included the provision that the court of Charles II should be expelled from France. The Spanish formally declared war on England in March 1656.

The main focus of the English naval campaign of 1656 was to capture the annual Spanish treasure fleet. This would at a stroke cripple finances for the Spanish war effort while providing Spanish gold and silver to pay English war expenses. An English fleet under Robert Blake and Edward Montagu returned to the Mediterranean and blockaded the Spanish fleet in Cadiz, and its blockading squadron intercepted seven Spanish treasure galleons outside Cadiz, capturing two and sinking two others. The following year Blake left a small squadron to maintain the blockade of Cadiz, as he had heard the Spanish fleet was not ready for sea, and sailed with the main part of his fleet to intercept the Spanish treasure fleet of 1657 in the Canary Islands. The Spanish treasure fleet of sixteen ships was at anchor at Santa Cruz de Tenerife, although the treasure itself had been unloaded and taken ashore. Blake made a successful attack, as he had done on the anchored corsair fleet at Tunis in 1655, and completely destroyed the Spanish fleet. The Spanish treasure was not captured, but while it remained at Santa Cruz it was of no value to the Spanish war effort. Robert Blake had been ill for some months and died at Plymouth Sound as the fleet returned home to England. He was buried with ceremony at Westminster Abbey and left as his legacy an English fleet whose victories over the Dutch and Spanish had made it feared throughout Europe.

The focus of the English war against Spain now changed to the Spanish Netherlands. On 23 March 1657 the Treaty of Paris was agreed as a military alliance between England and France. Under the terms of this treaty England would provide 6,000 men to serve with the French army against the Spanish Army in Flanders, and would receive the ports of Dunkirk and Mardyke once they were captured. The allied French and English army under the Maréchal de Turenne took the small port of Mardyke on 2 October 1657. The focus for

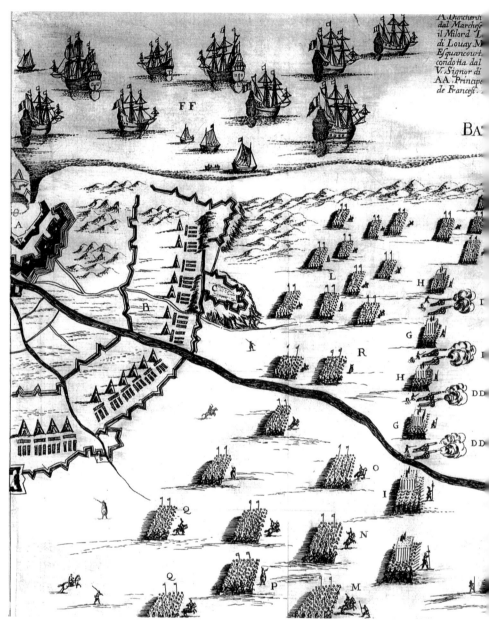

An Italian engraving of the battle of the Dunes, 14 June 1658. This was fought between the French and the Spanish, but each had English allies, the New Model Army fighting with the French and Charles II's Royalists with the Spanish. The battle was fought between major European land powers, with the New Model infantry having a significant role in the victory.

the campaign of 1658 was to take the port, and notorious privateering base, of Dunkirk. The siege of Dunkirk began on 25 May 1658 and the Spanish response was to march to its relief with an army which included the English

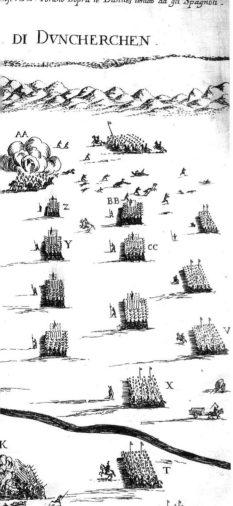

je.C.Fortino Sopra le Dunnes.D.Loreni.E.Cauallería condotta
ualleria del Sig.r di Gaſſion.G.H.Fanteria Franceſe.I.Ingleſe ſotto
anceſe Commandata dal Sig.r di Guadagne.L.Cauallería ſotto il Sig.
Turena.N.il Marcheſe de Criquy.O.Sig.r di Eſpance e Sig.r di
S.r de Bodeuis.Q.Roche paira e Marcheſe de Buſſy.R.Fanteria
eſons.S.Cauallería del Principe di Ligne.T.Marcheſe di Caraco
Gio: d Auſtria.Y.Don Stefano di Gammara.Z.Duca di Yorch.
nte Colignij CC.Don Gaſparo Bonifacio DD.Cannone
eſe.GG.Fortino Sopra le Dunnes tenuto da gli Spagnoli .

DI DVNCHERCHEN .

and Irish regiments of the King in exile, Charles II. On 14 June 1658 the Spanish army deployed in battalia in the dunes to the north of Dunkirk. The New Model infantry under Sir William Lockhart on the left wing of the allied French and English armies made a storming attack on the Spanish left, carrying all before it, and their success was a major factor in the decisive defeat of the Spanish army. Dunkirk, which now had no hope of relief, surrendered on 24 June 1658.

Oliver Cromwell died on 3 September 1658, the anniversary of his great victories at Dunbar in 1650 and Worcester in 1651. At the time of his death, his army had just proved itself to be at least as good as the best in Europe, and his navy had proved superior to the two leading naval powers, the Dutch and the Spanish. England under Oliver Cromwell was a major world power with a powerful army and a powerful navy, and its possession of Dunkirk gave it a bridgehead and base in Europe which its naval superiority could supply by sea. But Cromwell's successor, his son Richard, had no strong support within the New Model Army, and the administration of 'Tumbledown Dick' Cromwell lasted less than a year, until he resigned in May 1659.

John Lambert established himself as the leading army commander in England, while George Monk consolidated his control over the English garrison in Scotland through judicious purging of his officer corps. Without any sense of clear leadership, the New Model Army was divided amongst itself and its old commander Sir Thomas Fairfax raised forces in Yorkshire opposed to Lambert. Lambert's army in the north of England disintegrated in the face of Monk's advance from Scotland. George Monk brought his army to London and acted as power broker in the restoration of Charles II, becoming Duke of Albemarle in the process.

Disbandment

On the restoration of the monarchy, Charles II disbanded the New Model Army with full payment of its arrears. Small garrisons remained in Scotland and Ireland, and at Dunkirk and Mardyke, and King Charles retained a small lifeguard. The lifeguard included George Monk's old infantry regiment, now the Coldstream Guards, and his lifeguard of horse became the third troop of the King's lifeguard of horse, styled until his death as the Duke of Albemarle's troop. Dunkirk and Mardyke were sold to the French in 1662 by Charles II's government and the New Model soldiers transferred to a hell-hole of a garrison at Tangier in North Africa, part of the dowry of Charles II's wife, the Portuguese princess Catherine of Braganza. One of these regiments, Colonel Sir Robert Harley's, was amalgamated with the 'Old Tangier' regiment in 1668, and this became the Queen's Foot in 1684 when Tangier was abandoned.

THE PORTRAICTVRE OF HIS ROYAL MAJESTIE
KING CHARLES II

Thus when His Sullen Starrs were milder grown
Came our Great Charles to his Imperiall Throne
Farre Nobler though not finer than the rest
His Gallantry was all within his Breast

Charles II (1630–1685). The eldest son and successor to Charles I. He was crowned in Scotland in 1650, and his army was decisively defeated at Worcester the following year. He returned to England on the invitation of George Monk.

Several of the leading officers were excepted from the general amnesty – the Act of Oblivion – on the Restoration as having been closely implicated in the execution of King Charles I. Thomas Harrison, John Okey, Daniel Axtell, Hercules Huncks, Francis Hacker and John Barkstead were executed; others were imprisoned, some for life, while others such as Edmund Ludlow and Edward Whalley lived and died in exile. Of the soldiers themselves, many, perhaps most, were able to settle back into civilian life. Samuel Pepys, writing in 1663, suggested that 'of all the old Army now you cannot see a man begging about the street; but what? You shall have this captain turned haberdasher; the lieutenant a baker, this a brewer, this a haberdasher; this common soldier a porter; and every man in his apron and frock etc, as if they had never done anything else.'[5] Not all old soldiers can have had the transition quite so easy, and a common feature of Restoration ballads was the poor, ragged 'wandring soldier' in his 'red-coat rags'.

The Decline of a World Power
The Restoration of Charles II led directly to the disbanding of the New Model Army and the reduction in size of the English navy, and most European statesmen must have breathed sighs of relief. In 1667 a Dutch fleet sailed up the River Medway, burnt three Royal Navy warships at anchor and sailed away with the flagship *Royal Charles* as a prize, a singularly humiliating event. The diarist John Evelyn who visited the site soon afterwards recorded that it was 'as Dreadful spectacle as ever any Englishmen saw and a dishonour never to be wiped off'. Within a few years, there was a general feeling that whatever else Cromwell had been he could still be admired for briefly making England a powerful country, as Samuel Pepys wrote: 'What brave things he did and made all the neighbour princes fear him.' In 1672 Charles II complained to the French ambassador that the French were harbouring English rebels, commenting that this would never have been done in Cromwell's time. He received the reply, 'Ha, Sire, that was another matter: Cromwell was a great man and made himself feared by land and sea.'[6]

Beggar. After the New Model Army's disbandment many soldiers were able to return to civilian life, but the number of Restoration ballads which refer to former soldiers as beggars clad in 'red-coat rags' suggests many had a harder time.

Notes

1. Background to Civil War: 1637–1642

1. Verney, Frances, *Letters and Papers of the Verney Family*, ed. J. Bruce, Camden Society, 56 (London, 1853), p. 246.
2. Ryder, Ian, *An English Army for Ireland* (Leigh-on-Sea, 1987), p. 8, and Perceval-Maxwell, M., *The Outbreak of the Irish Rebellion of 1641* (Dublin, 1994), p. 241.
3. Razzell, Edward, and Razzell, Peter (eds), *The English Civil War: A Contemporary Account*, vol. 2, *1640–1642* (London, 1996), pp. 53 and 54. This series of five volumes consists of letters written between 1625 and 1675 from a succession of Venetian ambassadors in London.
4. Hyde, Edward, Earl of Clarendon, *The History of the Rebellion and Civil Wars in England*, ed. W.D. Macray (Oxford, 1888), vol. 2, p. 45.
5. Ibid., p. 46.
6. Ibid., p. 50.
7. Ibid., pp. 223 and 224.
8. Rushworth, John, *Historical Collections, the Third Part* (London, 1691), vol. 2, p. 16.
9. Clarendon, *History*, vol. 2, p. 293.
10. Ibid., p. 346.
11. Rushworth, *Historical Collections*, p. 19.
12. Clarendon, *History*, vol. 2, p. 361.
13. Roberts, Keith, and Tincey, John, *Edgehill, 1642: The First Battle of the English Civil War* (Oxford, 2001), p. 28.
14. Barker, T.M. (ed.), *The Military Intellectual and Battle: Raimondo Montecuccoli and the Thirty Years War* (New York, 1975).
15. Whitelocke, Bulstrode, *Memorials of the English Affairs* (London, 1682), p. 62.
16. Ibid., p. 62.
17. Ibid., p. 63.
18. Roberts, Keith, *First Newbury, 1643: The Turning Point* (Oxford, 2003), p. 12.
19. Clarendon, *History*, vol. 3, p. 134.
20. Ibid., pp. 261 and 262.
21. Chadwyck Healey, C.E. (ed.), *Sir Ralph Hopton's Narrative of his Campaign in the West, 1642–1644*, Somerset Record Society, 18 (Taunton, 1902), p. 61.
22. Clarendon, *History*, vol. 3, p. 338.
23. Ibid., p. 443.
24. Abbott, Wilbur Cortez (ed.), *The Writings and Speeches of Oliver Cromwell*, vol. 1, *1599–1649* (Oxford, 1937), p. 302.

2. The European Background: War, Politics and the Military Revolution

1. Zagorin, Perez, *Rebels and Rulers, 1500–1660*, vol. 2, *Provincial Rebellion, Revolutionary Civil Wars, 1560–1660* (Cambridge, 1982), p. 97.
2. Caldecott-Baird, Duncan, *The Expedition in Holland, 1572–1574* (London, 1976), p. 112.
3. Parker, Geoffrey, *The Dutch Revolt* (London, 1977), p. 160.
4. Bingham, John, *The Art of Embattailing an Army, or, The Second Part of Aelians Tacticks* (London, 1629). This comment is made in the 'Epistle Dedicatory'.
5. *Jacob de Gheyn: The Exercise of Armes. A Commentary by J. B. Kist* (New York, Toronto, London, 1971), p. 10.
6. Bingham, John, *The Tactiks of Aelian, or, Art of Embattailing an Army after ye Grecian Manner* (London, 1616).
7. Brzezinski, Richard, *Lützen, 1632: Climax of the Thirty Years War* (Oxford, 2001).
8. Turner, Sir James, *Memoirs of His Own Life and Times*, Bannatyne Club (Edinburgh, 1829), p. 14.
9. Roberts, Keith, 'Musters and May Games: The Effect of Changing Military Theory on the English Militia', *Cromwelliana* (1991), pp. 5–9.
10. Parker, Geoffrey, *The Military Revolution, Military Innovation and the rise of the West*, 2nd edn (Cambridge, 1996).
11. Markham, Francis, *Five Decades of Epistles of Warre* (London, 1622), pp. 25–28. The term 'voluntaries' was sometimes used in England to refer to soldiers who volunteered for service as opposed to being levied.
12. Dalton, Charles, *Life & Times of General Sir Edward Cecil, Viscount Wimbledon* (London, 1885), p. 131.
13. Sprigge, Joshua, *Anglia Rediviva: Englands Recovery, Being the History of the Motions, Actions and Successes of the Army under the Immediate Conduct of His Excellency, Sir Thomas Fairfax* (London, 1647), p. 41.
14. Roberts, 'Musters', p. 8.
15. Ward, Robert, *Anima'dversions of Warre* (London, 1639), p. 30.
16. Carasso-Kok, M., 'Der stede scut: De schutterijen in de Hollandse steden tot het einde der zestiende eeuw', in Carasso-Kok,

M., and Halm, J. Levy van, *Schutters in Holland: kracht en zenuwen van de stad* (Haarlem, 1988); 'Schutters' translates as 'shooters'.

17. The National Archives, PRO, PC 2/28, f. 489; PC 2/31, ff. 64 and 502; PC 2/32, f.671; PC 2/33, ff. 141, 211, 325 and 333; PC 2/36, f. 139; PC 2/39, ff. 446 and 569.

18. Raikes, G.A., *History of the Honourable Artillery Company* (London, 1878), vol. 1, pp. 324–363. The first captain, Robert Keayne had been a London merchant and a former member of the Society of the Artillery Garden.

19. Boynton, Lindsay, *The Elizabethan Militia, 1558–1638* (London, 1967), p. 284.

3. Recruitment, Uniform, Arms and Equipment

1. Gibson, Rev T. Ellison (ed.), *A Cavalier's Note Book, Being Notes, Anecdotes & Observations of William Blundell of Crosby, Lancashire, Esquire, Captain of Dragoons under Major-Gen Sir Thos Tildesley, Knt in the Royalist Army of 1642* (London, 1880). The commission of the Catholic Royalist William Blundell as a captain of a company of dragoons in Sir Thomas Tyldesley's regiment specifies that he was authorized 'to raise, impresse and retaine the said companie, raised or to bee raised by sound of Drumme or anie other waie'.

2. *Perfect Passages* (London, 1645): see the entry under 1 May.

3. Morgan, Thomas, *A True and Just Relation of Major-General Sir Thomas Morgan's Progress in France and Flanders with the Six Thousand English in the Years 1657 and 1658* (London, 1699).

4. Sells, A. Lytton (ed.), *The Memoirs of James II, His Campaigns as Duke of York, 1652–1660* (London, 1962), p. 259.

5. 'Commanded' men were literally soldiers commanded out of their companies for service away from their regiment. These contingents were usually musketeers and were detached to fight in squadrons of about 50 men alongside cavalry or to fight in broken or wooded ground, or amongst hedgerows.

6. *A True and Punctuall Relation of the Skirmishes betweene the Northamptonshire Forces and Party of the King's Horse and Foot under Prince Rupert and Col Urry* (London, 1643).

7. Boyle, Roger, Earl of Orrery, *A Treatise of the Art of War* (London, 1677), p. 183.

8. Ryder, Ian, *An English Army for Ireland* (Leigh-on-Sea, 1987), p. 29.

9. Peachey, Stuart, and Turton, Alan, *Old Robin's Foot* (Leigh-on-Sea, 1987), p. 20. For an example of a Monmouth cap see Buckland, Kirsty, 'The Monmouth Cap', *Costume*, 13 (1979).

10. Mungeam, Gerald M., 'Contracts for the Supply of Equipment to the New Model Army in 1645', *Journal of the Arms and Armour Society*, 6, no. 3 (1968). This provides a complete transcription of this account book.

11. Ibid., p. 69.

12. Ibid.

13. *Calendar of State Papers Domestic, 1649–1650*, p. 343.

14. Mungeam, 'Contracts', p. 89.

15. Peachey, Stuart, and Turton, Alan, *Common Soldiers Clothing of the Civil Wars, 1639–1646* (Bristol, 1995), p. 30.

16. Mungeam, 'Contracts', p. 100.

17. Turton, Alan, *The Chief Strength of the Army, Essex's Horse (1642–1645)* (Leigh-on-Sea, 1992).

18. *Journal de Jean Chevalier*, 9me fascicule et table des matières (Jersey, 1914), p. 954.

19. Ede-Borrett, Stephen (ed.), *The Letters of Nehemiah Wharton* (Wollaston, 1983), p. 18.

20. Historical Manuscripts Commission, *The Letter Books of Sir Samuel Luke, 1644–1645* (London, 1963), p. 244.

21. I am indebted to John Sutton for this information.

22. PRO, SP 28/8/15.

23. Roy, Ian (ed.), *The Royalist Ordnance Papers, 1642–1646*, part 2 (Oxford, 1975).

24. Verney, Frances, *The Memoirs of the Verney Family during the Civil War* (London, 1892), vol. 1, p. 304.

25. *Calendar of State Papers Domestic, 1638–39*, p. 108.

26. Clarendon, *History*, vol. 3, p. 104.

27. Turton, *Chief Strength*, p. 63.

28. J.B., *Some Brief Instructions for the Exercising of the Horse-Troopes* (London, 1661). This was bound with the sixth edition of William Barriffe's *Military Discipline, or, The Young Artilleryman* (London, 1661), and the identity of J.B. is not known. The word 'Artilleryman' refers to membership of the London voluntary association the Society of the Artillery Garden, and Barriffe's work relates to infantry training, not cannon.

29. Reid, Stuart, *Scots Armies* (1982), p. 24.

30. Turner, Sir James, *Pallas Armata* (London, 1683), p. 173.

31. *The Moderate*, 15–22 May 1649.

32. Orrery, *Treatise*, p. 32.

33. Blackmore, David, *Arms & Armour of the English Civil Wars* (London, 1990), p. 51.
34. Turton, *Chief Strength*, p. 26.
35. Firth, C.H. (ed.), *The Clarke Papers: William Clarke Secretary to the Council of the Army 1647–49 and to General Monck and the Commanders of the Army in Scotland*, vol. 1, Camden Society, new series, 49 (1891), pp. 235 and 236.
36. Tincey, John, *Ironsides: English Cavalry, 1588–1688* (Oxford, 2002).
37. Barker, T.M. (ed.), *The Military Intellectual and Battle: Raimondo Montecuccoli and the Thirty Years War* (Albany, New York, 1975).
38. Turner, Sir James, *Memoirs of His Own Life and Times*, Bannatyne Club (Edinburgh, 1829), pp. 5 and 6.
39. Abbott, Wilbur Cortez (ed.), *The Writings and Speeches of Oliver Cromwell*, vol. 2, *1649–1653* (Oxford, 1939), pp. 361 and 362.
40. Ibid., p. 362.
41. Whitelocke, Bulstrode, *Memorials of the English Affairs* (London, 1682), p. 363. Captain Augustin was probably Captain Augustine Hoffman, a German mercenary.
42. Elton, Richard, *The Compleat Body of the Art Military*, 2nd edn (London, 1659), p. 2.
43. Krenn, Peter, *Von Alten Handfeuerwaffen Entwicklung, Technik, Leistung* (Graz, 1989). This useful booklet describes a series of experiments using original contemporary firearms.
44. Turner, *Pallas Armata*, p. 168.
45. Monk, George, *Observations upon Military & Political Affairs* (London, 1671), p. 27.
46. Fassnidge, John, *English Civil War Documents*, unit 1, *Finance and Parliament's Army* (London, 1984), pp. 4 and 5.
47. Thurloe, John, *A Collection of the State Papers of John Thurloe, Esq; Secretary to the Council of State* (London, 1742), vol. 7, p. 215.
48. Blackmore, *Arms*, p. 63.
49. Orrery, *Treatise*, p. 28.
50. Monk, *Observations*, p. 28.
51. Ibid., pp. 26 and 27.
52. Mungeam, 'Contracts', p. 78.
53. *Directions For Musters: wherein is Shewed the Order of Drilling for the Musket and Pike* (Cambridge, 1638).
54. Kaufman, Helen A., *The Conscientious Cavalier* (London, 1962), pp. 153 and 154. This transcribed an order from the Royalist Colonel Thomas Bassett requiring 'every Soldier has always in garrison, 12 bullets att his bandeleers, fitted to the boare of his peece, and that hee never charge his peece when hee hath leasure without putting a Tampking after the powder and another after the bullet'.
55. *Calendar of State Papers Domestic, 1638–39*, p. 444.
56. Mungeam, 'Contracts', p. 90.
57. Elton, *Compleat Body*, p. 145.
58. Pennington, D.H., and Roots, Ivan, *The Committee at Stafford 1643–1645* (Manchester, 1957), pp. 230 and 296.
59. Turner, *Pallas Armata*, p. 230.
60. Hahlweg, W., *Die Heeresreform der Oranier, Das Kriegbuch des Grafen Johann von Nassau-Siegen* (Wiesbaden, 1973), pp. 314 and 317. The second reference specifically states 'tragons (dass ist musketirer zu pferdt)'.
61. Monk, *Observations*, p. 27. 'Swinefeathers' or 'Swedish' feathers were simply stakes used as defence against cavalry. Sir James Turner described them as 'a stake five or six feet long, and about four finger thick, with a piece of sharp Iron nail'd to every end of it' (*Pallas Armata*, p. 169).
62. Monk, *Observations*, p. 28.
63. Markham, Francis, *Five Decades of Epistles of Warre* (London, 1622), p. 119.
64. Monk, *Observations*, p. 34.
65. Roberts, Keith, *First Newbury, 1643: The Turning Point* (Oxford, 2003), pp. 56 and 57. See also Evans, D.S., 'The Bridge of Boats at Gloucester, 1642–1644', *Journal of the Society for Army Historical Research*, 71, no. 288 (1993), pp. 232–242.
66. Ward, Robert, *Anima'dversions of Warre* (London, 1639), p. 379.
67. Roy, *Royalist Ordnance Papers*, p. 428.
68. Ibid., p. 427.
69. Monk, Observations, p. 34.
70. Young, Peter (ed.), *Military Memoirs of the Civil War: The Vindication of Richard Atkyns*, (London, 1967), p. 20.
71. Markham, *Five Decades*, p. 94.
72. Mungeam, 'Contracts', p. 101.
73. Ibid., p. 114.

4. Training Methods and Training Manuals

1. Parker, Geoffrey, *The Army of Flanders and the Spanish Road* (Cambridge, 1972), p. 13.
2. Roberts, Keith, 'Citizen Soldiers: The Military Power of the City of London', in *London and the Civil War*, ed. Stephen Porter (London, 1996), p. 107.
3. Turner, Sir James, *Pallas Armata* (London, 1683), p. 209.
4. *Jacob de Gheyn: The Exercise of Armes. A Commentary by J. B. Kist* (New York, Toronto, London, 1971), p. 39.
5. Ward, Robert, *Anima'dversions of Warre* (London, 1639), p. 283.

6. Ibid., p. 292.
7. Ibid., p. 291.
8. Barriffe, William, *Military Discipline, or, The Young Artilleryman*, 6th edn (London, 1661), p. 4.
9. Ward, *Anima'dversions*, p. 298.
10. Turner, *Pallas Armata*, p. 302.
11. Barriffe, *Military Discipline*, p. 5.
12. Turner, *Pallas Armata*, p. 215.
13. Elton, Richard, *The Compleat Body of the Art Military*, 2nd edn (London, 1659). At the time the second edition was printed, with four additional pages, Elton was an officer in the New Model Army. This quotation is from the third of these four pages.
14. Barriffe, *Military Discipline*, p. 14.
15. Elton, *Compleat Body*, p. 13.
16. Vernon, John, *The Young Horse-man, or, The Honest Plain-dealing Cavalier* [London, 1644], ed. John Tincey (1993), p. 45.
17. Cruso, John, *Militarie Instructions for the Cavall'rie* (Cambridge, 1632), p. 45.
18. Vernon, *Young Horse-man*, pp. 45 and 46.
19. Brzezinski, Richard, *The Army of Gustavus Adolphus, 1: Infantry* (London, 1991), p. 15.
20. Elton, *Compleat Body*, pp. 164 and 165, together with the chart inserted between them.
21. Peachey, Stuart, *The Mechanics of Infantry Combat in the First English Civil War* (Bristol, 1992), pp. 16 and 17.
22. Barriffe, *Military Discipline*, p. 87.
23. Archer, Elias, *A True Relation of the Marchings of the Red Trained-Bonds of Westminster, the Greene Auxiliaries of London and the Yellow Auxiliaries of the Tower Hamlets; under the Command of Sir William Waller; from Munday the 16 of Octob. to Wednesday the 20 of December 1643* (London, 1643).
24. Brockington, William S., *Monro, His Expedition with the Worthy Scots Regiment Called Mac-Keyes* (Westport, Connecticut, 1999), p. 323.
25. Turner, *Pallas Armata*, p. 237.
26. Walker, Sir Edward, *Historical Discourses upon Several Occasions* (London, 1705), p. 130.
27. Monk, George, *Observations upon Military & Political Affairs* (London, 1671), p. 57.
28. Ibid., p. 70.
29. Elton, *Compleat Body*, on the fourth of four pages bound after p. 192.
30. Shea, William L., *The Virginia Militia in the Seventeenth Century* (Baton Rouge, 1983), p. 51. The English trained band system was copied in its colonies, and the libraries of officers of the Virginia Militia included copies of William Barriffe's and Robert Ward's manuals.
31. Elton, *Compleat Body*, on the third of four pages bound after p. 192.

5. Pay, Rations and Free Quarter

1. Turner, Sir James, *Pallas Armata* (London, 1683), p. 198.
2. Hyde, Edward, Earl of Clarendon, *The History of the Rebellion and Civil Wars in England*, ed. W.D. Macray (Oxford, 1888), vol. 2, p. 337.
3. Turner, *Pallas Armata*, p. 198.
4. Ibid., p. 201.
5. Ibid., p. 199.
6. J. B., *Some Brief Instructions for the Exercising of the Horse-Troopes* (London, 1661), p. 15, bound with Barriffe, William, *Military Discipline, or, The Young Artillery-man*, 6th edn (London, 1661).
7. Lee, Maurice (ed.), *Dudley Carleton to John Chamberlain, 1603–1624: Jacobean Letters* (New Brunswick, New Jersey, 1972), p. 290.
8. *A True Relation of the Late Expedition of His Excellency, Robert Earle of Essex, for the Relief of Gloucester* (London, 1643).
9. Historical Manuscripts Commission, *The Letter Books of Sir Samuel Luke, 1644–1645* (London, 1963), p. 261.
10. Turner, *Pallas Armata*, p. 200.
11. Ryder, Ian, *An English Army for Ireland* (Leigh-on-Sea, 1987), p. 25.
12. Markham, Francis, *Five Decades of Epistles of Warre* (London, 1622), p. 102.
13. Gentles, Ian, *The New Model Army* (Oxford, 1992), p. 47. See also Blackmore, David, 'Counting the New Model Army', *English Civil War Times*, no. 58 (2003), p. 3.
14. Spring, Laurence, *The Regiments of the Eastern Association* (Bristol, 1998), vol. 1, pp. 11–15; vol. 2, pp. 77–82. See also Holmes, Clive, *The Eastern Association in English Civil War* (Cambridge, 1974), p. 279.
15. Firth, C.H., *Cromwell's Army*, 2nd edn (London, 1912), p. 186.
16. J.B., *Some Brief Instructions*, p. 18.
17. Sprigge, Joshua, *Anglia Rediviva: Englands Recovery* (London, 1647), p. 82.
18. Ibid., p. 94.
19. *Journal de Jean Chevalier*, 9me fascicule et table des matières (Jersey, 1914), p. 954.
20. Laing, David (ed.), *A Diary of Public Transactions and Other Occurrences, Chiefly in Scotland, from January 1650 to June 1667, by John Nicoll*, Bannatyne Club (Edinburgh, 1836).
21. Carlyle, Thomas (ed.), *Oliver Cromwell's Letters and Speeches* (London, 1897), vol. 2, p. 149.

22. Abbott, Wilbur Cortez (ed.), *The Writings and Speeches of Oliver Cromwell* (Oxford, 1939), vol. 2, p. 229.

23. Turner, *Pallas Armata*, p. 201.

24. Markham, *Five Decades*, pp. 102 and 103.

25. Thurloe, John, *A Collection of the State Papers of John Thurloe, Esq; Secretary to the Council of State* (London, 1742), vol. 7, p. 216.

26. Firth, *Cromwell's Army*, p. 227.

27. Toynbee, Margaret (ed.), *The Papers of Captain Henry Stevens Waggon-Master General to King Charles I*, Oxfordshire Record Society (Oxford, 1962), p. 25.

28. Firth, C.H. (ed.), *The Memoirs of Edmund Ludlow, Lieutenant-General of the Horse in the Army of the Commonwealth of England, 1625–1672* (Oxford, 1894), pp. 44 and 45.

29. Turner, *Pallas Armata*, p. 201.

30. Boyle, Roger, Earl of Orrery, *A Treatise of the Art of War* (London, 1677), p. 29.

31. Sprigge, *Anglia Rediviva*, p. 132.

32. Lewis, J. (ed.), *The Siege of Chester: Nathaniel Lancaster's Narrative* (Leeds, 1987), p. 33.

33. Firth, *Cromwell's Army*, p. 181.

34. Lewis, *Siege of Chester*, p. 25.

35. Historical Manuscripts Commission, *Report on the Manuscripts of F.W. Leybourne-Popham, Esq of Littlecote, Co. Wilts.* (Norwich, 1899), pp. 21 and 22.

36. Davies, G., *The Early History of the Coldstream Guards* (Oxford, 1924), p. 63.

37. Turner, *Pallas Armata*, p. 201.

38. Lee, *Dudley Carleton*, pp. 290 and 291.

39. Turner, Sir James, *Memoirs of His Own Life and Times*, Bannatyne Club (Edinburgh, 1829), p. 7.

40. Rushworth, John, *Historical Collections* (London, 1701), vol. 7, p. 838.

6. Regiments, Roles and Responsibilities

1. Turner, Sir James, *Pallas Armata* (London, 1683), p. 247. The roles and responsibilities of the various officers and men within an army were a popular subject for military writers in the early seventeenth century, as they had been since the middle of the sixteenth. Most of the sources used for this section of the book are taken from books written by soldiers with strong practical knowledge and well as an interest in the military theory of the day. The leading works in this sense were Turner's *Pallas Armata*, George Monk's *Observations upon Military & Political Affairs* (London, 1671), and the *Treatise of the Art of War* by Roger Boyle, Earl of Orrery (London, 1677).

2. Hyde, Edward, Earl of Clarendon, *History of the Rebellion and Civil Wars in England*, ed.

W.D. Macray (Oxford, 1888), vol. 3, p. 77.

3. Turner, *Pallas Armata*, p. 251.

4. Ibid., p. 251.

5. Ibid., pp. 257 and 258.

6. The two generals who fled were Ferdinando, Lord Fairfax (commander of the Parliamentary Army of the Northern Association and also the father of Sir Thomas Fairfax) and Alexander Leslie, first Earl of Leven (commander of the Scottish army then allied to the Parliament).

7. Turner, Sir James, *Memoirs of His Own Life and Times*, Bannatyne Club (Edinburgh, 1829), p. 38.

8. Whitelocke, Bulstrode, *Memorials of the English Affairs* (London, 1682), p. 145.

9. Turner, *Pallas Armata*, p. 247.

10. Edgar, F.T.R, *Sir Ralph Hopton, the King's Man in the West, 1642–1652: A Study in Character and Command* (Oxford, 1968), p. 142. Sir Edward Walker in his *Historical Discourses upon Several Occasions* (London, 1705), p. 7, described Sir Ralph Hopton as 'Lord Hopton, Field Marshal General of the West and Southern Counties'. This was an extension of Sir Ralph Hopton's original commission and was granted on 27 October 1643.

11. Adair, John, *Roundhead General: A Military Biography of Sir William Waller* (London, 1969), p. 54.

12. Turner, *Pallas Armata*, p. 259.

13. J.B., *Some Brief Instructions for the Exercising of the Horse-Troopes* (London, 1661), bound with Barriffe, William, *Military Discipline, or, The Young Artillery-man*, 6th edn (London, 1661), p. 4. This work is clearly by an officer who had served in the Civil Wars and, by his reference to the 'late unhappy Civil Wars', must have been written in late 1660 or 1661.

14. Turner, *Pallas Armata*, p. 248.

15. Ibid.

16. Ibid., p. 249.

17. Ibid.

18. The concept that the right-hand position was considered more honourable dates from the classical past when a soldier was armed with a shield in his left hand and a spear in his right. The right-hand side, being unshielded, was more exposed, and so it was a position of greater risk and honour.

19. Turner, *Pallas Armata*, p. 249.

20. The Lord of Praissac, *A Short Method for the Easie Resolving of Any Military Question, Englished by I.C.* (Cambridge, 1639), p. O2. This was an English translation of du Praissac's work by John Cruso, the author of the famous cavalry manual. Cruso included a dedication to

Philip Skippon and commented upon Skippon's extensive military experience as a professional soldier.

21. Turner, *Pallas Armata*, pp. 194 and 195.
22. Ibid., 195.
23. Elton, Richard, *The Compleat Body of the Art Military*, 2nd edn (London, 1659), p. 175.
24. Turner, *Pallas Armata*, p. 232.
25. Ibid., p. 233.
26. Peacock, Edward, *Army Lists of the Roundheads and Cavaliers, Containing the Names of the Officers in the Royal and Parliamentary Armies of 1642* (London, 1863), pp. 19–54.
27. Turton, Alan, *The Chief Strength of the Army, Essex's Horse (1642–1645)* (Leigh-on-Sea, 1992), p. 27.
28. Firth, C.H., and Davies, Godfrey, *The Regimental History of Cromwell's Army* (Oxford, 1940), vol. 1, p. 2.
29. Carlisle, Thomas (ed.), *Oliver Cromwell's Letters and Speeches* (London, 1897), vol. 1, pp. 158–159. Also calendared in W.C. Abbott (ed.), *The Writings and Speeches of Oliver Cromwell* (Oxford, 1988), vol. 1, p. 248.
30. Turton, *Chief Strength*, p. 4.
31. Holmes, Clive, *The Eastern Association in the English Civil War* (Cambridge, 1974), p. 236.
32. J.B., *Some Brief Instructions*, p. 18.
33. Turner, *Pallas Armata*, p. 223.
34. Turton, *Chief Strength*, p. 8. From the pay list for the 'Officers of Army and Trayne', PRO, SP 28/140/p4.17.
35. Vernon, John, *The Young Horse-man, or, The Honest Plain-dealing Cavalier* [London, 1644], ed. John Tincey (1993), pp. 35–36. The reference to 'cavalier' simply means cavalryman, as the author was not a Royalist.
36. Elton, *Compleat Body*, p. 185.
37. Davies, Godfrey, 'The Army of the Eastern Association', *English Historical Review*, 46 (1931), pp. 89–90.
38. Vernon, *Young Horse-man*, pp. 36–37.
39. Turner, *Pallas Armata*, p. 223.
40. Monk, *Observations*, p. 93.
41. Turner, *Pallas Armata*, p. 223.
42. Firth, C.H., *Cromwell's Army: A History of the English Soldier during the Civil Wars, the Commonwealth and the Protectorate*, 2nd edn (London, 1912), p. 256.
43. Turner, *Pallas Armata*, p. 223.
44. Arni, Eric Gruber von, *Justice to the Maimed Soldier: Nursing, Medical Care and Welfare for Sick and Wounded Soldiers and their Families during the English Civil Wars and Interregnum, 1642–1660* (Aldershot, 2001), pp. 94–95.
45. Vernon, *Young Horse-man*, pp. 37–38.
46. Ibid., pp. 38–39.

47. J.B., *Some Brief Instructions*, p. 7.
48. Ibid., pp. 8–9.
49. Vernon, *Young Horse-man*, p. 40.
50. Ibid., p. 40.
51. J.B., *Some Brief Instructions*, p. 9.
52. Vernon, *Young Horse-man*, p. 41.
53. Ibid., p. 41.
54. Turton, *Chief Strength*, p. 4.
55. Turner, *Pallas Armata*, p. 236.
56. Markham, Francis, *Five Decades of Epistles of Warre* (London, 1622), p. 162. This book is divided into five parts, each of ten 'Epistles'. Each 'Epistle' is an essay on the role, duties and responsibilities of a particular officer.
57. Leslie, Alexander, Earl of Leven, *Generall Lessley's Direction and Order for the Exercising of Horse and Foot* (London, 1642), p. 7. Despite the title this short work covers only infantry training.
58. Stevenson, David, *Scottish Covenanters and Irish Confederates* (Belfast, 1981), p. 322.
59. Peacock, *Army Lists*, p. 44.
60. Peachey, Stuart, and Turton, Alan, *Old Robin's Foot: The Equipping and Campaigns of Essex's Infantry, 1642–1645* (Leigh-on-Sea, 1987), p. 11.
61. Chadwyck Healey, C.E. (ed.), *Sir Ralph Hopton's Narrative of his Campaign in the West, 1642–1644, and other papers*, Somerset Record Society, 18 (1902), p. 60.
62. *Calendar of State Papers Domestic, 1651*, p. 334.
63. Davies, Godfrey, *The Early History of the Coldstream Guards* (Oxford, 1924), pp. 117–118.
64. Ibid., p. 57.
65. Elton, *Compleat Body*, p. Cc2. This section is an appendix not found in the first edition and dates from the period during which Elton was a New Model Army officer, hence his reference to the current practice of the 'Army'. The main body of the book was written while Elton was a militia officer.
66. Davies, *Early History*, pp. 117–118.
67. A wagon-master can be found on the rolls of cavalry regiments, but this officer was not part of the usual cavalry establishment.
68. Elton, *Compleat Body*, p. 183.
69. Ibid., p. 183.
70. Ibid., p. 184.
71. Turner, *Pallas Armata*, p. 230.
72. Ibid., p. 276.
73. Ibid., p. 224.
74. Elton, *Compleat Body*, p. 178.
75. Firth, *Cromwell's Army*, p. 425.
76. Elton, *Compleat Body*, p. 181.
77. Ibid., pp. 178 and 179.
78. Ibid., p. 178.

79. Spring, Laurence, *The Regiments of the Eastern Association* (Bristol, 1998), vol. 1, pp. 12–15, and vol. 2, pp. 77–82. This officer was written as 'Lance Pasidore' in the Eastern Association muster rolls.

80. Turner, *Pallas Armata*, p. 220.

81. Elton, *Compleat Body*, p. 177.

82. Turner, *Pallas Armata*, p. 236.

83. J.B., *Some Brief Instructions*, p. 26.

84. Orrery, *Treatise*, p. 34.

85. Ibid., p. 35.

86. J.B., *Some Brief Instructions*, pp. 19–29.

7. Strategy, Tactics and Siege Warfare

1. Cecil, Edward, Lord Wimbledon, 'Demonstration of Divers Parts of War', British Library, Royal MS 18 CXXIII, ff. 9 and 10.

2. Bingham, John, *The Art of Embattailing an Army, or, The Second Part of Aelians Tacticks* (London, 1629), second page of the 'Epistle Dedicatory'.

3. Boyle, Roger, Earl of Orrery, *A Treatise of the Art of War* (London, 1677), p. 148.

4. Cecil, 'Demonstration', p. 16.

5. Gardiner, S.R., *History of the Great Civil War* (reprint, London, 1987), p. 59.

6. Monk, George, *Observations upon Military & Political Affairs* (London, 1671), pp. 21 and 23.

7. Bull, Stephen, and Seed, Mike, *Bloody Preston: The Battle of Preston, 1648* (Lancaster, 1998), p. 62.

8. Turner, Sir James, *Pallas Armata* (London, 1683), p. 238.

9. *The Arte of Warre or Military Discourses by the Lord of Praissac*, Englished by John Cruson (Cambridge, 1639), p. 139.

10. Roberts, Keith, 'Battle Plans: The Practical Use of Battlefield Plans in the English Civil War', *Cromwelliana* (1997).

11. Barker, Thomas M., *The Military Intellectual and Battle: Raimondo Montecuccoli and the Thirty Years War* (Albany, New York, 1975), p. 150.

12. Dalton, Sir Charles, *Life & Times of General Sir Edward Cecil, Viscount Wimbledon* (London, 1885), pp. 27 and 28.

13. Brockington, William S., *Monro, His Expedition with the Worthy Scots Regiment Called Mac-Keyes* (Westport, Connecticut, 1999), p. 193.

14. Orrery, *Treatise*, p. 188.

15. Chadwyck Healey, C.E. (ed.), *Sir Ralph Hopton's Narrative of his Campaign in the West, 1642–1644*, Somerset Record Society, XVIII (Taunton, 1902), p. 53.

16. Brzezinski, Richard, *The Army of Gustavus Adolphus, 2: Cavalry* (London, 1993), p. 23.

The quotation is from B.P Chemnitz, *Koniglichen Schwedischen in Teutschland gefuhrten Kriegs* (Alte Stettin, 1648), vol. 1.

17. Barker, *Military Intellectual*, p. 108.

18. Brockington, *Monro*, pp. 191 and 192.

19. Barker, *Military Intellectual*, pp. 90 and 91.

20. Ibid., p. 110. The officer was Gerardo Gambacorta.

21. Ibid., p. 95.

22. Orrery, *Treatise*, p. 157.

23. Ibid., p. 158.

24. Barriffe, William, *Military Discipline, or, The Young Artilleryman*, 6th edn (London, 1661), p. 173.

25. Orrery, *Treatise*, p. 153.

26. Reid, Stuart, *Dunbar, 1650: Cromwell's Most Famous Victory* (Oxford, 2004), p. 63.

27. Orrery, *Treatise*, pp. 151 and 152.

28. Chadwyck Healey, *Sir Ralph Hopton's Narrative*, p. 91. This is from one of the additional documents published with Hopton's narrative and is an account by Colonel Walter Slingsby.

29. Monk, *Observations*, p. 43.

30. Hyde, Edward, Earl of Clarendon, *The History of the Rebellion and Civil Wars in England*, ed. W.D. Macray (Oxford, 1888), vol. 2, p. 351.

31. Young, Peter, *Edgehill, 1642: The Campaign and the Battle* (Kineton, 1976), pp. 269 and 270. The quotation is from Sir Richard Bulstrode's account of the battle.

32. Rushworth, John, *Historical Collections* (London, 1701), vol. 6, p. 42.

33. Turner, *Pallas Armata*, p. 271.

34. *The Swedish Intelligencer, The Third Part* (London, 1633), p. 130.

35. Foard, Glenn, *Naseby: The Decisive Campaign* (Guildford, 1995).

36. *A True Relation of the Late Expedition of His Excellency, Robert Earle of Essex, for the Relief of Gloucester* (London, 1643).

37. Roberts, Keith, 'Beating up Quarters', *Cromwelliana* (1990), pp. 29–32.

38. Clarendon, *History*, vol. 3, p. 333.

39. Monk, *Observations*, p. 38.

40. Osborne, Mike, *Sieges and Fortifications of the Civil Wars in Britain* (Leigh-on-Sea, 2004). This includes a useful series of biographies of the engineers who served during the Civil Wars, pp. 26 to 28.

41. Monk, *Observations*, p. 121.

42. Turner, *Pallas Armata*, p. 314.

43. Monk, *Observations*, p. 119.

44. Ibid., p. 121.

45. Barratt, John, *The Great Siege of Chester* (Stroud, 2003), p. 154.

46. Ibid., p. 158. 'Bosse' was 's-Hertogenbosch, also referred to as Den Bosch or Bois-le-Duc.

47. Ibid., pp. 159 and 160.
48. Firth, C.H. *Cromwell's Army*, 2nd edn (London, 1912), pp. 166 and 167.
49. Monk, *Observations*, p. 86.
50. Sprigge, Joshua, *Anglia Rediviva: Englands Recovery* (London, 1647), pp. 123 and 124.
51. *The Swedish Intelligencer, The Third Part* (London, 1633), p. 188.
52. Sprigge, *Anglia Rediviva*, p. 322.

8. Professionalism: Honour, Self-Respect and Symbolism

1. Turner, Sir James, *Memoirs of His Own Life and Times*, Bannatyne Club (Edinburgh, 1829), p. 15.
2. Ede-Borrett, Stephen (ed.), *The Letters of Nehemiah Wharton* (Wollaston, 1983), p. 7.
3. Dick, Oliver Lawson (ed.), *Aubrey's Brief Lives* (London, 1987), p. 193. John Aubrey, who was a student at Oxford during the First Civil War, recorded that 'Captain Carlo Fantom, a Croation, spake 13 languages; was a Captain under the Earle of Essex. He was very quarrelsome and a great Ravisher.' Fantom joined the Parliamentary army as a lieutenant in Captain Richard Grenville's troop in Colonel Arthur Goodwin's Parliamentary cavalry regiment, and was wounded fighting for the Parliament at the battle of Edgehill. By August 1643 he was captain of his own troop in the same regiment, but then fled the Parliamentary army to join the Royalists, probably one step ahead of the provost.
4. Dick, *Aubrey's Brief Lives*, p. 194.
5. Firth, C.H. (ed.), *The Clarke Papers*, vol. 1, Camden Society, new series (1891). These are the personal papers of William Clarke who was, at the time of this reference, secretary to the General Council of the Army. Edward Sexby was an Agitator, one of two representatives or 'representours' of the private soldiers of each regiment, after the mutiny.
6. Anon, *The Hunting of the Foxes from New-Market and Triploe Heaths to Whitehall by Five Small Beagles (Late of the Armie), or, The Grandie-Deceivers Unmasked* [Thomason Tracts, E546 (7)] (London, 1647), p. 3. A Leveller pamphlet which purported to have been written by five former cavalry troopers cashiered for mutiny, but was probably written by one of the leading Leveller writers, either Richard Overton or John Lilburne.
7. Baxter, Richard (1615–1691). Author of *Reliquiae Baxterianae, or, Mr Richard Baxter's Narrative of the Most Memorable Passages of His Life and Times* (London, 1696). See Anne Lawrence, 'Parliamentary Army Chaplains, 1642–1651', *Royal Historical Society Studies in History*, 59 (1990), for a brief biography of his involvement with the army as a preacher.
8. Baxter, *Reliquiae Baxterianae*, p. 8.
9. Ibid., p. 98.
10. Sprigge, Joshua, *Anglia Rediviva: Englands Recovery* (London, 1647), p. 323. Sprigge was an army chaplain on Sir Thomas Fairfax's staff.
11. Ibid., pp. 19 and 29.
12. Boyle, Roger, Earl of Orrery, *A Treatise of the Art of War* (London, 1677), p. 59. The reference to 'Antiquity, being a Colonels' refers to the comparative date of an individual colonel's commission, as this established his seniority over other colonels.
13. Turner, Sir James, *Pallas Armata: Militarie Essayes of the Ancient Grecian, Roman and Modern Art of War* (London, 1683), p. 341.
14. *Calendar of State Papers Domestic, 1651*, p. 253.
15. Sir Roger Burgess, the Royalist Governor of Castle Cornet in Guernsey.
16. Chevalier, Jean, *Journal de Jean Chevalier*, 8me fascicule et table des matières (Jersey, 1913), p. 881. The reference is a translation as Jean Chevalier wrote in his native Jersey-French patois.
17. Ibid.
18. *A Perfect Diurnal of the Passages in Parliament* (London, 1643). Several editions of this weekly newsbook refer to the guilds marching out under their banners – see Thomason Tracts E249 (10), E249 (12), E249 (16) and E249 (17). See also Pearl, Valerie, *London and the Outbreak of the Puritan Revolution: City Government and National Politics, 1625–1643* (Oxford, 1961), pp. 264–5.
19. Sprigge, *Anglia Rediviva*, p. 80.
20. Orrery, *Treatise*, p. 200.
21. Davies, Edward, *The Art of War and England's Traynings* (London, 1619), p. 94.
22. Orrery, *Treatise*, p. 201.
23. Young, Alan R. (ed.), *The English Emblem Tradition, 3: Emblematic Flag Devices of the English Civil Wars, 1642–1660* (Toronto and London, 1995), p. xxvii.
24. Ibid., p. xxvii.
25. Meehan, C.P., *The Confederation of Kilkenny* (Dublin, 1846).
26. Ward Robert, *Anina'dversions of Warre, or, A Militarie Magazine of the Truest Rules, and Ablest Instructions, for the Managing of Warre* (London, 1639), p. 205.
27. Venn, Thomas, *Military & Maritime Discipline in Three Books: Book I, Military*

Observations or the Tacticks Put into Practice (London, 1672), p. 181.

28. Firth, C.H., and Davies, G., *Regimental History of Cromwell's Army* (Oxford, 1940), p. 501. The reference is from the *Proceedings of the Society of Antiquaries of London* (1853), vol. 2, p. 250.

29. *A Seventeenth Century Miscellany*, Kent Archaeological Society, 17 (Ashford, 1960), p. 145. The addition of a coat of arms to an infantry flag was unusual, but not unknown.

30. The 'London Greycoats' were Colonel Sir John Merrick's infantry regiment in the army of the Earl of Essex; it was raised in London. The Greencoats from Farham were Colonel Samuel Jones's regiment which formed the garrison of Farnham. The reference is from the account of the Londoner Elias Archer, *A True Relation of the Marchings of the Red Trained-Bonds of Westminster, the Greene Auxiliaries of London, and the Yellow Auxiliaries of the Tower Hamlets; under the command of Sir William Waller; from Munday the 16 of Octob. To Wednesday the 20 of December, 1643* (London, 1643). Archer was a lieutenant in the Yellow Auxiliaries. Elsewhere in his account he refers to 'the Greene-coats and part of the Musquetiers of the Red, and our Yellow Regiment entred while the rest of our Regiment marched into the Towne with Colours flying' in his description of the attack on the Royalist brigade in winter quarters at Alton. A contemporary reference to a 'red regiment' meant that it carried red flags, but did not necessarily mean that the soldiers wore red coats. If a regiment was distinguished by contemporaries by the colour of the men's coats then the reference would be to the coat colour, as in 'Greenecoats'.

31. Morgan, Sir Thomas, *A True and Just Relation of Major-General Sir Thomas Morgan's Progress in France and Flanders* (1831), reprinted in *English Civil War Notes and Queries*, no. 34, pp. 2–8, and no. 35, pp. 12–17.

32. Wright, I.A. (ed.), 'The English Conquest of Jamaica (1655–1656)', *Camden Miscellany*, 13 (1924).

33. Venn, Military & Maritime Discipline, p. 184.

34. Reid, Stuart, *Scots Colours* (1990), pp. 12 and 28.

35. Fraser, Edward 'Notes on Two Cavalry Standards of Cromwell's Time', *Journal of the Society for Army Historical Research*, no. 9 (1923), pp. 74–77.

36. Markham, Gervase, *The Soldier's Exercise in Three Bookes* (London 1639). This is a reprint of three of Gervase Markham's works. The reference is from the first book, *The Souldiers Accidence, or, An Introduction into Military Discipline*, p. 44.

37. Levett, William, 'The Enseignes of the Regiments in the Rebellious Citty of London both of Trayned Bands and Auxiliaries'. This was the illustrated report by a Royalist spy in London of a muster of the London Trained Bands and Auxiliary regiments on 26 September 1643. The manuscript is in the library of the National Army Museum.

9. Military Life in Camp and Garrison

1. Davies, G., *The Early History of the Coldstream Guards* (Oxford, 1924), p. 74.

2. Firth, C.H., *Cromwell's Army*, 2nd edn (London, 1912), p. 297.

3. Historical Manuscripts Commission, *The Letter Books of Sir Samuel Luke 1644–1645* (London, 1963), p. 311.

4. *Journal de Jean Chevalier*, 9me fascicule et table des matières (Jersey, 1914), p. 917.

5. Boyle, Roger, Earl of Orrery, *A Treatise of the Art of Warre* (London, 1677), p. 73.

6. Foster, Henry, *A True and Exact Relation of the Marchings of the Two Regiments of the Trained Bands of the City of London, Being the Red and Blew Regiments, as also of the Three Regiments of Auxiliary Forces, the Blew, Red and Orange* (London, 1643).

7. Carlton, Charles, *Going to the Wars: The Experience of the British Civil Wars, 1638–1651* (London, 1992), p. 209.

8. Firth, *Cromwell's Army*, p. 248.

9. Terry, Charles Sanford, *The Life and Campaigns of Alexander Leslie, First Earl of Leven* (London, 1899), p. 466.

10. Firth, *Cromwell's Army*, p. 426.

11. Davies, *Early History*, p. 67

12. Rudd, Thomas, *The Art of Designing, Measuring and Laying out of the Quarters for the Encamping of an Army in the Field* (London, 1668), p. 232. This was bound with the third edition of Richard Elton's *The Compleat Body of the Art Military*.

13. Rowland, A.J., *Military Encampments of the English Civil Wars, 1639 to 1659* (Bristol, 1997), p. 19.

14. Sprigge, Joshua, *Anglia Rediviva* (London, 1647), pp. 56 and 31.

15. Rudd, p. 231.

16. Orrery, *Treatise*, p. 84 and p. 92.

17. Rudd, pp. 227 and 228.

18. Ibid., p. 230.

19. Orrery, *Treatise*, p. 129.

20. Ibid., pp. 126 and 129.

21. Ibid., p. 54.

22. Firth, *Cromwell's Army*, p. 301.

23. *The Armies Letanie Imploring the Blessing of God on the Present Proceedings of the Armie*, [Thomason Tracts E 408 (20)] (London, 1647).

24. Turner, Sir James, *Pallas Armata* (London, 1683), pp. 276 and 277.

25. Ibid., p. 277.

26. Parker, Geofrey, *The Army of Flanders and the Spanish Road, 1567–1659* (Cambridge, 1972), p. 166.

27. Firth, *Cromwell's Army*, p. 288.

28. Ibid., p. 299.

29. Ibid., p. 300.

10. From Victory to Mutiny

1. Abbott, Wilbur Cortez (ed.), *The Writings and Speeches of Oliver Cromwell*, vol. 1, *1599–1649* (Oxford, 1937), p. 314.

2. Ibid., p. 315.

3. Hyde, Edward, Earl of Clarendon, *The History of the Rebellion and Civil Wars in England*, ed. W.D. Macray (Oxford, 1888), vol. 3, p. 459.

4. Abbott, *Writings*, p. 316.

5. Sprigge, Joshua, *Anglia Rediviva* (London, 1647), p. 29.

6. Ibid., pp. 31 and 32.

7. The Committee of Both Kingdoms was the Parliamentary Committee set up to manage the war in England. It was composed of four MPs from the House of Commons, seven peers and four Scottish commissioners.

8. Walker, Sir Edward, *Historical Discourses upon Several Occasions* (London, 1705), p. 126.

9. Ibid., p. 127.

10. Ibid., p. 129.

11. Rushworth, John, *Historical Collections* (London, 1701), vol. 6, p. 41.

12. Turner, Sir James, *Pallas Armata* (London, 1683), p. 309.

13. Rushworth, *Historical Collections*, vol. 6, pp. 41 and 42.

14. Ibid., p. 40.

15. Sprigge, *Anglia Rediviva*, p. 35.

16. Ibid., p. 35.

17. Ibid., pp. 36 and 37.

18. Foard, Glenn, *Naseby: The Decisive Campaign* (Guildford, 1995), p. 268.

19. Walker, *Historical Discourses*, p. 115. This is wrongly paginated in the 1701 edition and should be p. 131.

20. Ibid., p. 115. As above re pagination.

21. Foard, Naseby, p. 277.

22. Walker, *Historical Discourses*, p. 129. This is wrongly paginated in the 1701 edition and should be p. 137.

23. Sprigge, *Anglia Rediviva*, p. 65.

11. Mutiny

1. Turner, Sir James, *Pallas Armata* (London, 1683), p. 198.

2. Ibid.

3. Parker, Geoffrey, *The Army of Flanders and the Spanish Road, 1567–1659* (Cambridge, 1972), pp. 185–206.

4. *Calendar of State Papers Domestic, 1644–1645* (London, 1890), p. 315.

5. Firth, C.H., *The Clarke Papers*, Camden Society, new series, 49 (1891), vol. 1, p. x.

6. Turner, *Pallas Armata*, p. 200.

7. Brailsford, H.N., *The Levellers and the English Revolution* (Nottingham, 1976), p. 10.

8. Firth, *Clarke Papers*, pp. 85 and 86.

9. Ibid., p. 87.

10. Ibid., p. 91

11. Ibid., pp. 114 and 115.

12. Gardiner, S.R., *History of the Great Civil War*, vol. 3, *1645–47* (London, 1987), p. 261.

13. Firth, Sir Charles, and Davies, Godfrey, *The Regimental History of Cromwell's Army* (Oxford, 1940), vol. 1, p. 324.

14. Gardiner, *History*, pp. 269 and 270.

15. Ibid., pp. 271 and 272.

16. Firth, C.H., *Cromwell's Army*, 2nd edn (London, 1912), p. 353.

17. Firth, *Clarke Papers*, vol. 1, pp. 132 and 133.

18. Ibid., p. 146n.

19. Ibid., p. 146.

20. Thomson, Alan, *The Ware Mutiny, 1647: Order Restored or Revolution Defeated* (Ware, 1996), pp. 93–98.

21. Ibid., p. 87.

22. The punishment of 'riding the wooden horse' was carried out by placing a soldier on a wooden frame with two planks forming a ridge, often with a mock horse's head at the front. The soldier was placed astride it, which would have been painful in itself, and then had weights added by tying one or more muskets to his feet.

23. Firth and Davies, *Regimental History*, vol. 1, p. 220.

24. Ibid., p. 113.

12. The Campaigns of the New Model Army, 1648–1653

1. Whitelocke, Bulstrode, *Memorials of the English Affairs* (London, 1682), p. 305. Whitelocke recorded that Sir Thomas Fairfax mustered only four regiments of cavalry and three complete regiments of infantry, together with some companies from Colonel Richard Ingoldsby's regiment.

2. Ibid., p. 305.

3. Firth, C.H. (ed.), *The Memoirs of Edmund Ludlow* (Oxford, 1894), p. 194.

4. Stevenson, David, *Scottish Covenanters and Irish Confederates* (Belfast, 1981), pp. 258 and 259.
5. Bull, Stephen, and Seed, Mike, *Bloody Preston: The Battle of Preston, 1648* (Lancaster, 1998), pp. 104–109.
6. Ibid., p. 70.
7. Jones, Phil, *The Siege of Colchester, 1648* (Stroud, 2003), p. 127.
8. Ibid., p. 147.
9. Lenihan, Padraig, *Confederate Catholics at War, 1641–49* (Cork, 2001), p. 99.
10. Wheeler, James Scott, *Cromwell in Ireland* (Dublin, 1999), p. 78.
11. Abbott, Wilbur Cortez (ed.), *The Writings and Speeches of Oliver Cromwell* (Oxford, 1939), vol. 2, p. 38.
12. Ibid., p. 111.
13. Ibid., p. 124.
14. Ibid., p. 125.
15. Roberts, Keith, *First Newbury, 1643* (Oxford, 2003), p. 11.
16. Hyde, Edward, Earl of Clarendon, *The History of the Rebellion and Civil Wars in England*, ed. W.D. Macray (Oxford, 1888), vol. 3, p. 406.
17. Abbott, *Writings*, p. 118.
18. Ibid., p. 126.
19. Ibid., p. 143.
20. Ibid., p. 227.
21. Ibid., p. 233.
22. Ibid., p. 252.
23. Whitelocke, *Memorials*, p. 444.
24. Ibid., p. 445.
25. Abbott, *Writings*, p. 293.
26. Ibid., p. 300.
27. *Original Memoirs Written during the Great Civil War Being the Life of Sir Henry Slingsby and Memoirs of Capt Hodgson* (Edinburgh, 1806), p. 133. This extract is from the memoirs of Captain John Hodgson.
28. Ibid., p. 137.
29. Ibid., pp. 141 and 142.
30. Ibid., pp. 143 and 144.
31. Walker, *Historical Discourses*, p. 180.
32. Ibid., p. 180.
33. Abbott, *Writings*, p. 320.
34. Ibid., p. 323.
35. Ibid., p. 324.
36. Farr, David, *John Lambert, Parliamentary Soldier and Cromwellian Major-General, 1619–1684* (Woodbridge, 2003).
37. *Letters from Roundhead Officers Written from Scotland and Chiefly Addressed to Captain Adam Baynes*, Bannatyne Club (Edinburgh, 1856), p. 24.
38. Dawson, William Harbutt, *Cromwell's Understudy: The Life and Times of General John Lambert* (London, 1938), p. 125.
39. Sir James Turner, *Memoirs of His Own Life and Times*, Bannatyne Club (Edinburgh, 1829), p. 94.
40. Gentles, Ian, *The New Model Army* (Oxford, 1992), p. 404.
41. Dawson, *Cromwell's Understudy*, p. 135.
42. Ibid., pp. 136 and 137.
43. Hyde, *History of the Rebellion*, vol. 5, p. 180.
44. Abbott, *Writings*, p. 462.
45. Turner, *Memoirs*, p. 95.
46. Atkin, Malcolm, *Cromwell's Crowning Mercy: The Battle of Worcester, 1651* (Stroud, 1998), p. 115.
47. Dunlop, R., *Ireland under the Commonwealth* (Manchester, 1913), vol. 1, p. 155.
48. Ibid., p. 156.

13. The Rise and Fall of a New World Power

1. Abbott, Wilbur Cortez (ed.), *The Writings and Speeches of Oliver Cromwell*, vol. 3, *1653–1655* (Oxford, 1945), p. 641.
2. Ibid., vol. 2, *1649–1653* (Oxford, 1939), p. 643.
3. Ibid., p. 641.
4. Sutton, Paul, *Cromwell's Jamaica Campaign: The Attack on the West Indies, 1654–55* (Partizan Press, 1990), p. 16.
5. Childs, John, *The Army of Charles II* (London, 1976), p. 11.
6. Fraser, Antonia, *Cromwell, Our Chief of Men* (London, 1974), p. 551.

Index

The index is in three parts. The first covers the names of the leading commanders, and the second the major battles and sieges where they fought; the third provides a quick link to specific military subjects.

1. People

2. Battles and Sieges